SO-CFB-051

THE REAL ESTATE INVESTOR'S

TAX GUIDE

What Every Investor Needs To Know To Maximize Profits

3rd Edition

Vernon Hoven

Real Estate
Education Company®
a division of Dearborn Financial Publishing, Inc.

This publication is designed to provide accurate and authoritative information in regard to the subject matter covered. It is sold with the understanding that the publisher is not engaged in rendering legal, accounting or other professional service. If legal advice or other expert assistance is required, the services of a competent professional person should be sought.

Publisher: Carol L. Luitjens
Executive Editor: Diana Faulhaber
Managing Editor: Ronald J. Liszkowski
Art Manager: Lucy Jenkins

© 1998, 1996, 1993, 1998 by Vernon Hoven.

Published by Real Estate Education Company®\Chicago
a division of Dearborn Financial Publishing, Inc.®
155 North Wacker Drive
Chicago, IL 60606-1719
(312) 836-4400
http://www.real-estate-ed.com

All rights reserved. The text of this publication, or any part thereof, may not be reproduced in any manner whatsoever without written permission from the publisher.

Printed in the United States of America.

98 99 2000 01 10 9 8 7 6 5 4 3 2 1

ISBN 0-7931-2785-8

DEDICATION

This book is dedicated to Willie Nelson, who more than anyone else exemplifies the philosophy that tax law is never to be taken too seriously, but is always taken.

How much should be taken by the government? Only the legal minimum! Therefore, this book also is dedicated to the ideal that *tax avoidance is a constitutional right . . . but tax evasion is "Sing-Sing time"* (with apologies to eminent Jurist Learned Hand).

Contents

PART IV—THE PASSIVE LOSS RULES

PART V—REAL ESTATE IN TROUBLED TIMES

Preface

The voluntary tax system, whether it is a flat tax system or an income tax system, will survive only if we understand and implement or supervise our own tax return preparation, a fact sadly forgotten by many members of the United States Congress! This book attempts to eliminate the aura of mystery surrounding the taxation of real estate. It is specifically written for the real estate investor, that occasional user of real estate tax knowledge, and not for real estate tax specialists.

In my lecturing travels throughout the United States, I discovered that confusion and fear of the Internal Revenue Code are widespread. This bewilderment and trepidation are unwittingly (and in some cases wittingly) promulgated by the two "specialists" in the tax field: Internal Revenue Service employees and their counterparts, independent tax preparers. As contents of most tax libraries demonstrate, numerous books and magazines have been written for the tax professional with advanced knowledge. Also, there are myriad books for taxpayers to help them prepare their tax returns. Very little has been written specifically for the real estate investor. This book meets that need.

You say, "I leave tax law to my tax professional!"

It is ludicrous to think of constructing a building without a strong foundation. Why do we accept the idea that we can invest in real estate without a strong understanding of the basics of real estate taxation?

This book's goal is to present the tax consequences of common types of real estate dealings in a clear and concise manner. The tax alternatives can be dramatic to the taxpayer. This book does not attempt to be a complete digest of every possible tax variation found in the Internal Revenue Code, its rules, regulations and court cases affecting the taxation of real estate. Instead, it takes the most commonly used areas and explains them fully and simply by use of examples, comments and tax planning tips.

The material in this book has been presented to thousands of casual sellers and buyers, professional real estate brokers and salespeople, CPAs and attorneys who are not real estate tax specialists. Mostly, though, it has been used by tax professionals, who are continually surprised at the number of planning tips and easy-to-use forms that make completing tax returns substantially easier. Throughout the book the materials and planning tips are backed up by court cases and tax citations.

After reading this book, share the information with your tax professional—do it as a favor to you! Do not assume that he or she knows all there is to know about real estate taxation. Tax law is too complicated today. This book is written so you will discover new tax planning ideas. Let the tax professional implement those ideas! The tax alternatives will dramatically affect you, the taxpayer.

Acknowledgments

Thanks to:

Karl Breckenridge . . . Exchanger and freelance real estate writer, whose extensive review resulted in more user-friendly chapters

Bradley Burnett, Attorney . . . Author and national lecturer whose extensive bankruptcy knowledge assisted in the chapter on real estate in troubled times

John J. Connors, CPA/Tax Attorney . . . National lecturer and author of the tax newsletter *Monthly Tax Update,* whose overall expertise and knowledge help ensure the accuracy of this book

Corey Hoven . . . My free spirit who made the fun computer graphics with the aid of Presentation Task Force, Harvard Graphics and PageMaker

Jill Hoven . . . Communication TA at the University of North Carolina who, having never prepared a tax return, reviewed this book with the reader in mind

Sharon Kreider, CPA . . . Author, national lecturer and tax practitioner from Santa Clara, whose insightful real estate examples forced me to write realistically . . . not theoretically, which is easier

Edith Lank . . . Author, and the sexiest lady to write real estate columns for the *Los Angeles Times Syndicate,* for reviewing the book with the real estate investor in mind

Bill Roos . . . A district manager of H&R Block, for all of his practical suggestions and for reading the materials with the taxpayer in mind

Roberta Schmalz, CPA . . . Author, lecturer and tax practitioner from Santa Clara, for reviewing every chapter and offering practical and technical suggestions throughout

Danny Santucci, Esquire . . . Mega-author and national lecturer, for his help in reviewing the §1031 materials

About the Author

VERNON HOVEN's book combines the real-life experience of a practicing CPA and a licensed real estate broker with essential down-to-earth tax materials. He coauthored two Prentice-Hall books and has written articles on taxation for numerous national publications.

Vern is a nationally recognized tax lecturer (averaging 100 days a year for EAs, CPAs, lawyers, and REALTORS® throughout the United States). Vern's powerful seminars on numerous tax topics, and his Master's Degree in Taxation from the University of Denver's School of Law, enable participants to quickly grasp recent tax changes. The Illinois, Indiana, and Nebraska CPA Societies have all honored him with their "tax instructor of the year" award. Vern's presentation skills earned him the coveted Certified Speaking Professional (CSP) from the National Speakers Association. There are only 274 CSPs out of 3,400 NSA members.

He has served on many national boards, including the National Association of REALTORS® Legislative Committee and Federal Tax Subcommittee, the Farm and Land Institute's Education Committee and Federal Tax Committee, and served for two years as National Treasurer and three years as National Director-at-Large for the National Real Estate Educators Association. He also has been active in his community, including serving as a publicly elected School Board Trustee for five years. He has a son, Corey, a daughter, Jill, and a son-in-law, Bill, and lives in the northern Rocky Mountain community of Missoula, Montana, with his partner and wife, Karen, also a CPA.

"Readers will double or triple their new tax planning ideas," Vern promises. "In addition, these concepts will be backed up with citations . . . when available."

Introduction

Many real estate investment strategies used prior to the middle of 1997 are not nearly as advantageous after the passage of the massive Taxpayers Relief Act of 1997. This book dramatically reveals the new tax do's and, as importantly, the new tax don'ts when investing in real estate . . . **which pre-1997 tax strategies are still relevant and which post-1996 new strategies should be adopted . . . now!**

Tax questions by real estate investors can be grouped into five areas of concern, which are listed in the order of importance as evidenced by the number of times each area is brought up in previous question-and-answer sessions:

1. Taxation at time of sale
2. Like-kind exchange rules
3. Tax solutions at purchase and during ownership
4. Living with the passive loss regulations
5. Real estate in troubled times

This book is divided into these five parts instead of the typical approach of starting with the acquisition and ending with the sale of real estate. It is designed to go directly to your questions, by topic, without the requirement of reading all the previous pages.

Even though this text focuses on successfully investing in today's real estate market after the passage of the Taxpayers Relief Act of 1997, real estate taxation and value is mostly influenced by the Tax Reform Act of 1986, the bill that promises us "fairness, growth and simplicity." Incidentally, tax practitioners have renamed that law "the complification act"!

The 1986 legislation, passed by Congress, with approval of President Reagan, devastatingly (1) increased from 40% to 100% the taxable portion of long-term capital gain on real estate and capital assets, (2) decreased from 50% to 39.6% (as amended subsequently) the government's maximum involvement in the taxpayer's tax loss,

(3) prolonged the depreciation of real property from 19 years to 29–39 years (as amended) and (4) restricted the current deduction of the operating losses for rental property. Having all four axes fall at the same time (Freddie Krueger style), why were Congress and the Resolution Trust Corporation surprised that so few investors were underwriting real estate?

With the advent of the Taxpayers Relief Act of 1997, this book argues that real estate is a better endeavor now than it has been in the last 10 years, but only if the speculator is using the revealed up-to-date investment tactics coupled with proper application of the enumerated new tax rules. A positive, upbeat book on real estate, it also dispels the negative tax image currently circulating about such investments. The real estate industry is not convincing the financing public that ownership of real property is still a marvelous tax venture.

For the first time, an understandable handbook, with appendixes, deciphers post-1996 tax simplicity as it applies to real estate investments. *The Real Estate Investor's Tax Guide* focuses, in a nuts-and-bolts manner, on the new tax ramifications found in the real estate field and lists the step-by-step, practical tax-planning strategies, with numerous sample forms, applicable to the modern-day real estate industry. For both the first-time buyer and the Certified Financial Planner, it is an ever-handy self-help tax book, not a shelf edition. It answers hundreds of common tax questions concerning real estate transactions, along with **suggesting numerous new tax planning ideas** that make real estate investments much more valuable.

1

Taxation of Profit—How Gains or Losses Are Computed

When an asset is sold, exchanged or disposed of in any income-taxable manner, the seller must calculate the gain or loss. After performing this calculation, numerous other code sections tell the taxpayer what to do with the gain or loss—that is, how much is taxable or nontaxable, what is deductible or nondeductible, what portion of the gain may be deferred, what portion of the gain may be rolled over or what portion of the gain may simply be excluded. Additionally, some property transfers need not be reported to the Internal Revenue Service. Why?

A sale or exchange is required before calculating gain or loss. Property *received* by gift or inheritance is *not taxable* because no sale or exchange occurred (but the giver may have to pay some gift or inheritance tax!). Even money received in a refinance is *not taxable* . . . no sale took place.

PLANNING TIP: When Dad gives Daughter the vacation cabin or Aunt Millie leaves Nephew the family plot, none of the four reports this transfer on his or her income tax return. Only sales or exchanges are reported, and this is a gift and an inheritance.

THE GAIN OR LOSS FORMULA

Once it is determined that the investor must tell the IRS he or she has sold an item, the amount of the gain or loss should seem easy to determine (that is, sales price less original purchase price, or basis). This complex computation should not be underestimated. To calculate gain or loss on *any* sale or exchange, use this basic formula:

Gain or Loss Computation

Sales price		+ $ _____
Less:	Selling expenses	− _____
Equals:	Net selling price	= $ _____
Less:	Adjusted basis	
	Original cost (or basis)	+ $ _____
	Plus: Improvements	+ _____
	Less: Accumulated depreciation	− _____
	Equals: Total adjusted basis	− $ _____
NET GAIN (OR LOSS) ON SALE		= $ _____

The easiest way to demonstrate each line of this formula is by using a series of examples that become progressively more difficult.

Example: Roberta purchases ten acres of land for $20,000 in 1988 and sells it to Joe in 1998 for $45,000. Her gain is $25,000 calculated as follows:

Gain or Loss Computation

Net selling price		+ $45,000
Less:	Adjusted basis	
	Original cost (or basis)	+ $20,000
	Equals: Total adjusted basis	− $20,000
NET GAIN (OR LOSS) ON SALE		= $25,000

Example: In the above example, assume that Roberta, after purchasing the ten acres of land in 1988, builds a home in 1989 for $150,000 and sells it to Joe in 1998 for $245,000. She pays the following expenses at the time of sale: $17,150 commission (7%); $450 title insurance; $300 attorney's fee; $200 accountant's fee; $4,900 two-point origination fee; and $200 closing costs for a total selling expense of $23,200. Her gain of $51,800 is calculated as follows:

Gain or Loss Computation

Sales price		+ $245,000
Less:	Selling expenses	− 23,200
Equals:	Net selling price	= $221,800
Less:	Adjusted basis	
	Original cost (or basis)	+ $20,000
	Plus: Improvements	+ 150,000
	Equals: Total adjusted basis	− $170,000
NET GAIN (OR LOSS) ON SALE		= $ 51,800

Example: Continuing with the previous example, assume that Roberta rents out the home continuously from January 1, 1995, until the property is sold in January 1998. She claims $16,136 of depreciation (discussed in Chapter 10) on her respective tax returns. Now Roberta's gain is calculated as follows:

Gain or Loss Computation

Sales price		+ $245,000
Less: Selling expenses		− 23,200
Equals: Net selling price		= $221,800
Less: Adjusted basis		
Original cost (or basis)	+ $ 20,000	
Plus: Improvements	+ $150,000	
Less: Accumulated depreciation	− $ 16,136	
Equals: Total adjusted basis		− $153,864
NET GAIN (OR LOSS) ON SALE		= $ 67,936

PLANNING TIP: Roberta's gain increases by $16,136 ($67,936 − $51,800) over the previous example, which is the exact amount of depreciation she deducted during her period of ownership. If accumulated depreciation increases gain (this portion of the gain is called depreciation recapture gain) at the time of sale by the same amount as the prior deductions, why take it? See Chapter 10 on depreciation for the answer.

The above examples leave many other questions unanswered when calculating gain or loss. Therefore, let's start at the beginning and examine each line in the basic formula. Below are the explanations of the terms used in the above calculations.

WHAT IS INCLUDED IN THE SELLING PRICE?

For tax purposes, the amount realized on a sale includes the amount of cash received plus the fair market value of any other property received [§1001(b)[1]]. The amount of the mortgages on the property sold that the purchaser either assumes or takes subject to is also figured into the sales price [§1.1012-1(a)].

When the selling or purchase price is not specifically stated or involves more than cash, the selling/purchase price is arrived at by the following formula:

Sales Price Computation

1. Cash down payment (earnest money deposit) $ _____
2. Cash brought to closing, cash used to pay selling and purchase $ _____
   expenses
3. Amount received for option to buy $ _____

---

[1] Throughout this book, the author refers by citation to the Internal Revenue Code, Tax Court decisions, Treasury regulations and rulings, and similar material. Why? It gives the investor a substantive position for taking tax positions suggested in this book, a great tool in a tax audit! As important, these citations save the tax professional research time.

    This citation—§1001(b)—refers to Internal Revenue Code section 1001, subsection b. The next citation refers to Department of Treasury regulation §1.1012-1(a), and court cases deciding tax issues are cited as *FRL Corp. v. U.S.* (see page 5).

4. Assumed mortgages or other encumbrances on the property
   (whether assumed or taken subject to by the buyer) generally at
   face value* $ _____

5. *Face* amount of two-party notes (e.g., between buyer and seller) $ _____
   given to seller (mortgage note or trust deeds) or *face* amount of
   buyer's contracted promise to pay (land contract or contract for
   deed)*

6. *Fair market value* of third-party obligations (e.g., U.S. Treasury $ _____
   bonds, AT&T debentures)

7. Face value of liens against property, whether or not buyer is $ _____
   personally liable for the liens (e.g., back taxes, etc.)†

8. *Fair market value* of property (other than cash) received from $ _____
   buyer (e.g., diamonds, free trips, value of services rendered in
   exchange for the property received, etc.)

ACTUAL SALES PRICE‡ $ _____

---

* The principal part of the mortgage cannot include interest because of the imputed interest rules or the
original issue discount rules [§483; §§1271-1274].

† Includes charges accrued against the property and assumed by the purchaser, such as taxes, mortgage
interest and liens.

‡ Commissions and other selling expenses paid or incurred by the seller do not reduce the selling price
even though they do reduce net profit.

PLANNING TIP: The selling price for tax purposes is the total assets transferred
from the seller to the buyer, whether they are, or are not, mentioned in the sales
contract. The contract price contained in the legal documents is normally, but not
always, the same as this calculation.

Example: Ruth purchased an office building from Gary, paying him $10,000 in
cash, assuming a $90,000 mortgage and giving Gary her note (a second mortgage)
for $50,000. The sales/purchase price for Ruth and Gary is computed below.

Sales Price Computation

1. Cash down payment (earnest money deposit) $ 10,000

4. Assumed mortgages or other encumbrances on the property
   (whether assumed or taken subject to by the buyer) generally
   at *face* value $ 90,000

5. *Face* amount of two-party notes (e.g., between buyer and seller)
   given to seller (mortgage note or trust deeds) or *face* amount of
   buyer's contracted promise to pay (land contract or contract for
   deed) $ 50,000

ACTUAL SALES PRICE $150,000

Example: Mary purchased an apartment building from Don, with a contract price of $150,000 ($10,000 in cash, $90,000 assumed mortgage and Mary's two-party note for $50,000). When Don started to back out of the transaction at closing, Mary gave Don her $10,000 diamond ring to keep the transaction together. Is the sales/purchase price the $150,000 that the legal documents state or the $160,000 in assets exchanged?

Sales Price Computation

1. Cash down payment (earnest money deposit)	$ 10,000
4. Assumed mortgages or other encumbrances on the property (whether assumed or taken subject to by the buyer) generally at *face* value	$ 90,000
5. *Face* amount of two-party notes (e.g., between buyer and seller) given to seller (mortgage note or trust deeds) or *face* amount of buyer's contracted promise to pay (land contract or contract for deed)	$ 50,000
8. *Fair market value* of property (other than cash) received from buyer (e.g., diamonds, free trips, value of services rendered in exchange for the property received, etc.)	$ 10,000
ACTUAL SALES PRICE	$160,000

PLANNING TIP: The buyer and seller *must* agree on the sales/purchase price. The IRS requires the seller's sales price to be the same as the buyer's purchase price. As silly as this statement sounds, when a buyer acquires more than one property at the same time (i.e., land and building), the purchase price must be allocated among the properties purchased to determine the basis of each [§1060; *FRL Corp. v. U.S.*, 74-2 USTC ¶9560; 33 AFTR2d 74-897 (D Mass 1974)].

There may be a *double* tax penalty if the parties don't agree. The sales/purchase price *of each component* is required to be the same for both parties, and if they are not, the IRS has the power to change the allocation *to the detriment of both parties*. The allocation must be done in a fair and equitable manner, i.e., based on the fair market value of the different assets on the date of purchase [§1.1060-1T(h); §1.61-6(a); see also Chapter 10 for details].

How to compute taxable gain on the sale of property sold on the installment basis.

Example: Paula purchases business property for $500,000, paying $150,000 in cash over a first mortgage in the amount of $350,000. Years later, she sells the property for $650,000. The terms are $200,000 cash, a purchase-money mortgage of $150,000 and assumption of the first mortgage, which at the time of sale has a balance of $300,000. Expenses of the sale amount to $30,000. During the period of ownership, Paula adds permanent improvements that cost her $50,000, and she is allowed depreciation deductions of $70,000. The gain on the sale is computed as follows:

Gain or Loss Computation

Sales price			
	Cash	$200,000	
	Purchase-money mortgage	$150,000	
	First mortgage assumed	$300,000	
Sales price			+ $650,000
Less:	Selling expenses		– 30,000
Equals:	Net selling price		= $620,000
Less:	Adjusted basis		
	Original cost (or basis)	+ $500,000	
	Plus: Improvements	+ 50,000	
	Less: Accumulated depreciation	– 70,000	
	Equals: Total adjusted basis		– $480,000
NET GAIN (OR LOSS) ON SALE			= $140,000

WHAT IS INCLUDED IN SELLING EXPENSES?

Example: Betty Broker instructs Sammy to spend $2,500 sprucing up his property to get it ready for sale. Is this a selling expense? Surprisingly, the answer is NO, even though Sammy would never have spent the money if Betty hadn't told him it was necessary to make the property saleable.

Selling expenses. These are all the expenses incurred to consummate the sales transaction. Selling expenses reduce the selling price. In other words, if a capital gain (defined in Chapter 2) on the sale is realized, the selling expenses reduce that gain; they are not deductible against ordinary income.

Selling expenses **do not** include the following:

1. *Any expenses that physically affect the property (e.g., repairs or improvements)* even if they are to prepare the property for sale
   Answer to above example: Sammy's $2,500 physically affected the home. Therefore, *it is not a selling expense.* (Maybe it is a repair or an improvement, as discussed later in this chapter.)
2. *Prorated items* such as prorated taxes, insurance, interest and rent
3. *Finance charges* paid by the buyer

Examples of deductible selling expenses include real estate sales commissions, points paid by the seller to the buyer's lending institution, attorney and accountant's fees, settlement charges, closing fees, appraisal fees, advertising, escrow fees, abstract or title search, title examination, title insurance binders, title insurance, title certificate (Torrens) and registration, document preparation, recording fees, transfer tax stamps, survey, pest inspection, and *any other expenses related to the sale other than those physically affecting the property.*

WHAT IS ADJUSTED BASIS?

Definition of adjusted basis when property is purchased for cash or with a mortgage. Adjusted basis is the *original cost* of property (or basis, if the owner didn't buy the property), *plus* the value of *improvements* made on the property, *minus depreciation* and losses taken while owning it. Original cost is usually the cash transferred and/or mortgage created or assumed at time of purchase. A more extensive formula follows [§1012; §1016].

Adjusted Basis of Property

Original purchase price (or basis) of property sold	+ $_____
Purchase expenses of property	+ $_____
Construction and/or reconstruction costs	+ $_____
Capital improvements subsequent to initial acquisition, construction and/or reconstruction	+ $_____
Special assessments, principal only (streets, sewer)	+ $_____
Less: Depreciation allowed/allowable in prior years	− $_____
Less: Casualty losses declared in prior years, if any	− $_____
Less: Demolition losses [§1.165(a)(1)], if any	− $_____
ADJUSTED BASIS OF PROPERTY SOLD	= $_____

What is meant by the phrase *or basis* in the above paragraph? The manner in which the property is acquired affects its basis. For example:

Inherited property. If property is inherited, the basis to the recipient is usually its fair market value at the time of the decedent's death (a step-up in basis) [§1014].

Gifted property or divorce settlement property. If property is received as a bona fide gift, the basis to the recipient is usually the donor's basis (called its carry-over basis) plus gift tax paid, if any, on the appreciation in value [§1015]. Any property received from a spouse during marriage or incident to a divorce is considered a transfer by gift [§1041].

Exchanged property. If the property is acquired in a tax-free exchange, the basis of the property received is the basis of the old property surrendered (called the substituted basis) decreased by the amount of *boot* received (money, non-like-kind property, etc.) and increased by gain recognized (or decreased by loss recognized) [§1031(d)].

Purchase expenses are added to basis. Common purchase price expenses include attorney fees [Rev. Rul. 68-528], escrow fees, recording costs, broker's and finder's fees, appraisal costs, surveys, charges for title search and title insurance, costs of acquiring any outstanding leases, inspection fees, and *any expenses related to purchase other than those physically affecting the property.*

PLANNING TIP: Surprisingly, tax practitioners often find that purchasers overlook the expenses incurred to purchase an asset (usually paid after closing) when calculating their adjusted basis. These acquisition expenses must be added to basis; they cannot be currently deducted. This unnecessarily decreases their depreciation and increases their subsequent gain. The investors commonly pay for these expenses after closing and simply forget.

Construction, reconstruction and capital improvements are added to basis. Any money spent to improve existing property or construct new property (or reconstruct if property is damaged) must be added to basis and depreciated. These *capital expenditures* are generally defined as amounts paid (1) to acquire property with a useful life in excess of one year, or (2) to permanently improve property [§263; §1.263(a)-1]. Capital expenditures cannot be currently deducted but must be recovered through annual expenses (called depreciation deductions) taken over the useful life of the depreciable property [§167; §168; see Chapter 10]. Tragically, if the tax rules state that a certain capital expense cannot be depreciated (e.g., land), the cost is only recovered at the time of sale.

Repairs and maintenance are not added to basis. Expenditures for repairs and maintenance are not capital expenditures and thus are generally deductible in the year paid or incurred. Repairs on business or investment property maintain the property in efficient operating condition. These types of repairs may be currently deducted so long as they do not materially add to the property's value or prolong its useful life. Repairs on personal residences are not deductible nor can they be added to the home's basis.

PLANNING TIP: Most taxpayers want expenditures on business property to be repairs so that they can currently deduct them. On the other hand, if those same expenditures are made on a personal residence, the taxpayer wants them to be capital improvements. Repairs on a personal residence are never deductible but capital improvements reduce the gain on a subsequent taxable sale.

The biggest tax question for owners of real estate: *What is the difference between repairs and capital improvements?* When deciding if an expenditure is a repair or an improvement, the following questions must be considered:

- Does the expenditure materially add to the property's value?
- Does it prolong the property's useful life?

If the investor answers yes to either question, the cost is generally a capital expenditure.

Casualty losses reduce basis. This occurs to the extent of the deductible loss allowable to the owner. Normally, the amount of the loss deduction equals the loss in value less any insurance proceeds recovered, but the loss deduction may not exceed the adjusted basis of the property prior to the occurrence [§1016(a)(1); 1.165-7(b)(1)]. Amounts expended after the casualty are normally added to basis; it is simply another improvement [Rev. Rul. 71-161, 1971-1 CB 76].

TAXATION OF OPTIONS

What is a real estate option? Sometimes an investor purchases an option to buy real property in the future instead of purchasing the property immediately. This allows the potential buyer to acquire the property within a designated future period of time without fear that the owner will sell it to someone else. Options are often used to allow the buyer enough time to arrange for financing or determine if he or she really wants to purchase the property. The optionee-buyer usually pays only a small fraction of the total purchase price for the right to buy the property in the future.

> ***Example:*** Mike, the optionee, pays Bernie, the owner, $5,000 cash for the right (option) to purchase property for an agreed price of $150,000 any time within the next three years.

The potential buyer also retains the right *not* to purchase the property at all; e.g., the receiver of the option may simply let the option "lapse." In this case, the optionee-buyer forfeits the option money as a "penalty" for failure to exercise. This compensates the seller for removing the property from the market.

A tax loophole: Option money is not immediately taxable. Options create unusual reporting requirements for both the seller of the option and the receiver (buyer) of the option, in that the initial receipt of option money is not a taxable event to either the seller or the buyer. An option is a different asset from the property covered by the option and is treated much the same as a deposit [§1234; *Lucas v. North Texas Lumber Co.*, 281 US 11 (1930)].

Tax ramifications of options. When real property is anticipated to be sold through the exercise of an option, the option payments do not become income to the potential seller until the option either lapses or is exercised. This creates the unusual situation that allows the seller to receive cash that is not immediately taxable [§1234].

PLANNING TIP: Therefore, the seller of an option does not immediately report the cash as taxable, and the buyer cannot immediately deduct the payments. How does the buyer report the money? What does the seller do?

First, the tax ramifications to the buyer.

- *When the option is exercised:* When real property is acquired through the exercise of an option, the buyer adds the cost of the option to the purchase price.
- *If the option is allowed to lapse:* If the buyer allows the option to lapse (e.g., the buyer decides not to exercise the option), the buyer is allowed to deduct the option payment as a loss, subject to all the loss restrictions, but only at the end of the option period [§1234(b)(2); §1.1234-1(b)].
- *The character of the loss:* If the option relates to real property, the option is generally considered either a capital asset, or a §1231 trade or business property. The character of the loss is determined by the property to which the option applies and therefore would be a capital loss or an ordinary business loss [§1.1234-1(a); §1234(a)(1); defined in Chapter 2].

COMMENT Tax practitioners commonly see buyers trying to disguise the option payment as a "lease" payment to accelerate the deduction. This seldom works as the IRS looks to the substance to see if an option actually exists.

Second, the tax ramifications to the seller.

- *Exercise:* If the option is exercised, the option money is included in the sales price of the property sold.
- *Lapse:* If the option is not exercised, the gain is ordinary income. Dealers in options are subject to special rules [§1.1234-1].

The selling of an option.

PLANNING TIP: After holding the option for over 18 months, sometimes investors sell their right to purchase property (i.e., the option) instead of purchasing the property with the option and immediately selling the property. The new owner of the option simply steps into the shoes of the old owner and exercises the option. *Why would a sophisticated investor want to sell the option instead of exercising the option and selling the property?*

The answer is to take advantage of the long-term capital gains tax rates (as discussed in Chapter 2). How long has the investor owned the option? Over 18 months, which is a long-term capital gain. If the investor exercises the option, how long has he or she owned the property? One day, which is a short-term capital gain. By exercising the option, the unsophisticated investor converts a long-term capital gain into a short-term capital gain. Not smart!

Options and related property. When property is acquired under an option to purchase, the holding period of the property begins on the day after the property is acquired, *not* on the day after the option is acquired. Investors cannot add the time an option is held to the time the property is held after exercising the option in order to satisfy the holding period requirement. However, if the option itself is held for the minimum holding period and then sold, the investor is eligible for capital gain treatment *if the property itself would have been a capital asset in the investor's hands*. Otherwise, the investor has ordinary income [§1.1234-1(a)(1)].

> **Example:** On January 1, 1997, Tom purchased, for $500, a two-year option to buy a minishopping center having an exercise price of $300,000. Two years later (January 1, 1999) Tom receives an offer of $400,500 for the building. He is willing to claim the whole gain in the year of the sale. On January 1, 1999, Tom exercises the option for $300,000 and the same day sells the building for $400,500. This results in a $100,000 *short-term* capital gain as Tom has owned the property for less than one day, not the required "more than 18 months." By not selling the option, Tom converted a long-term capital gain to a short-term capital gain. He did not know that the option is a different asset from the property it is optioning. Of course, the new buyer does not care what method is used. If Tom sells him the option for $100,500, the option price is added to the exercise price of $300,000, leaving him the same $400,500 basis as if he had purchased it directly from Tom.

CONCLUSION

Probably no tax formula is more misunderstood than the gain (or loss) calculation discussed in this chapter. Yet, as discovered in this section, a short methodical procedure makes this amount easy to determine accurately, even when an option to purchase is involved.

2

Capital Gains Taxation

After computing the gain or loss on the sale of real estate, the seller must decide what to do with that gain or loss. This chapter discusses the many special rules for calculating capital gain treatment at time of disposition and what tax rate to apply to that gain or loss.

In general, there are three different types of tax treatments for gains or losses realized on the sale or exchange of property. They are the

1. *capital gain or loss* method,
2. *ordinary gain or loss* method, and
3. *hybrid* method, capital gain and an ordinary loss.

Capital gain or loss treatment has the tax advantage of not requiring the gain to be totally taxable (or the disadvantage of the loss's not being totally deductible). Sadly, the capital gain calculation has ridden an uncertain roller coaster in the last decade, from extraordinarily positive tax treatment in the early 1980s, to extraordinarily negative tax treatment starting in 1987 (courtesy of the Tax Reform Act of 1986), followed by a potential softening of this negative tax treatment starting in 1991, again in 1993, and, in a most complicated manner, back toward positive in the Taxpayers Relief Act of 1997.

NET "CAPITAL GAINS" HAVE TAX RATE LIMITATION

In an attempt to counter the taxation of gain created by inflation (i.e., *real* tax on *phantom* income), Congress has rejected the simpler pre-1986 60% capital gain deduction method and greatly expanded the alternative tax computation method. This is the first capital gains tax rate cut since 1981.

Rate Cuts Lowered to 20% . . . And Even As Low As 10%!

These rate reductions for individuals, estates and trusts generally apply to sales and exchanges after May 6, 1997. If a taxpayer's tax year includes sales or exchanges before May 7, 1997, the taxpayer must determine net capital gain for the period prior to May 7, 1997, and for the period after May 6, 1997.

- The maximum tax rate on net capital gains is lowered to 20% from the previous 28% for sales after May 6, 1997. For individuals in the 15% bracket, the capital gains tax rate has been lowered to 10%.
- The gain element of installment-sale payments received after May 6, 1997, is taxed at the 10%/20% rate, even though the sale took place earlier.
- Depreciation on sales of real estate will be recaptured at a 25% rate.
- The same tax rates (e.g., 10%/20%/25%) apply to capital gains for alternative minimum tax (AMT) purposes. This may eliminate the concern that capital gains aggravate an AMT problem by virtue of being taxed at the generally effective 28% AMT rate instead of the new lower rate. However, a large capital gain often triggers the alternative minimum tax.

COMMENT: There were no rate reductions for corporations with capital gains in the Taxpayers Relief Act of 1997. A corporation's top rate stays at 35% and its holding period remains at 12 months. Interestingly, TRA 97 applies the alternative tax rate of 35% to the lesser of the corporation's net capital gain or its taxable income. But this alternative minimum tax rate only applies when the corporation's ordinary income tax rate *exceeds* 35%, resulting in no immediate advantage because of the top corporate tax rate being 35% [effective for tax years ending after December 31, 1997; Act §314(a); §1201(a)(2)].

Capital Gains Example

Smith family—1997 joint income over $41,200

Capital gain	$25,000			
Prior law tax:	$25,000	× 28%	=	$7,000
New law tax:	$25,000	× 20%	=	$5,000
Savings under new law:			=	$2,000

Jones family—1997 joint income under $41,200

Capital gain	$25,000			
Prior law tax:	$25,000	× 15%	=	$3,750
New law tax:	$25,000	× 10%	=	$2,500
Savings under new law:			=	$1,250

But a Hidden Rate Still Exists.

The personal exemption phaseout and the limit on passive losses and itemized deductions indirectly increases the taxable income.

PLANNING TIP: The actual individual "effective tax bracket" experienced by net capital gains may be 22% to 25% or higher because of the 2% personal exemption phaseout and the multiple limits on itemized deductions.

Example: Dick and Linda already have a $150,000 long-term capital gain in 1997 and anticipate a sale for an additional $2,500 long-term capital gain. This additional capital gain will experience a $500 tax ($2,500 × 20%), not potentially $900 ($2,500 × 36%). However, $79.50 of additional itemized deductions ($2,650 × 3%) and $106 of personal exemptions (2% of two $2,650 exemptions) will be lost. As a result, tax liability will be increased by $66.78 ($79.50 + $106 = $185.50 × 36%). Thus, the *effective* rate of tax on the additional long-term capital gain is 22.67% ($566.78/$2,500 capital gain), or 2.27% higher than the 20% "maximum rate" for 1997.

But . . . Holding Period Is Extended to 18 Months!

Long-term and short-term holding period. A capital asset is characterized as either a *long-term* or *short-term* capital asset, depending on the length of time the asset is owned (*holding period*), or deemed to have been held under the "tacking" and other rules [§1223].

After July 28, 1997, long-term capital gain or loss treatment is available only when capital assets are held for *more than 18 months,* and if the property is held for more than one year but not more than 18 months, the asset is characterized as a "mid-term" asset; prior to July 29, 1997, long-term was defined as *one year or more*. If property is held for a period of one year or less, the asset is characterized as a short-term capital asset. *The period is computed by excluding the day of acquisition and including the day of disposition* [§1222].

The lower capital gains tax rate applies only to assets held "long-term."

- For assets sold prior to May 7, 1997, the 15%/28% rates apply to assets held more than 12 months.
- For assets sold between May 7, 1997, and July 28, 1997, the 10%/20% rates apply to assets held more than 12 months.
- For assets sold after July 28, 1997, long-term means more than 18 months rather than 12 months.
- Assets sold after July 28, 1997, with a holding period of more than 12 months but less than 18 months will be taxed as "midterm gain" at the old 15%/28% rate. This is a new and complicated term and capital gain concept.

Example: On August 1, 1997, Julie, a 39.6% marginal tax bracket taxpayer, sold a one-acre residential lot and recognized a net capital gain of $10,000. She owned the lot for 13 months. She will **not** be able to use the 20% maximum capital gain rate because she sold the real estate after July 28, 1997, and did not hold it for more than 18 months. However, the gain is not taxed at her 39.6% ordinary income tax rate. Instead, she may use the "midterm gain" rate of 28% (the former maximum capital gain rate) when computing her tax due. Tragically, if she was in the 15% tax bracket, her tax would be computed by using the 15% rate, not the new 10% rate.

Mid-term gain is the amount that would be adjusted net capital gain for the year if (1) the adjusted net capital gain includes only the gain or loss from amounts received after July 28, 1997, from property held more than one year but not more than 18 months, and (2) capital loss carryovers and gain included in net investment income for purposes of the deduction for investment interest expense were not taken into account.

Note: Capital loss carryovers from mid-term property will reduce gain eligible for the 20% rate in later years.

Passthrough Entities

For gains attributable to a passthrough entity, such as a partnership, S corporation, or regulated investment company (RIC), the character of the gain (pre-May 7 or not) is determined by when the entity received the capital gains. For example, whether a capital gains distribution received from a mutual fund qualifies for the new lower tax rates in 1997 depends on when the fund received its capital gains, not when the investor received the distribution. Therefore, a gain taken into account before May 7, 1997, by passthrough entities is not eligible for the 10%/20%/25% capital gains rates.

Five Year Gains

Effective in 2001, a new rate structure has been created for assets held more than five years. This provision replaced the inflationary "indexing" proposal promulgated by investment proponents.

- The 20% rate drops to 18% for assets **purchased** after December 31, 2000, and held more than five years.
- For those in the 15% bracket the rate is 8% on assets **sold** after December 31, 2000. There is no requirement, however, that those assets be acquired after 2000.
- A special election to use the 18% instead of 20% rate: Taxpayers, other than corporations, may elect to treat capital assets, business assets and even readily tradable stock held on January 1, 2001, as if they had been sold for their fair market value so as to reset the acquisition date and qualify future appreciation

for the 18% rate. Gain from the deemed sale is subject to tax; however, any loss resulting from this election shall not be allowed [TRA §311(e)].

- In determining when the five-year holding period begins, taxpayers may "tack" the option (or other right or obligation to acquire property) holding period to the property. The holding period of property acquired pursuant to the exercise of an option (or other right or obligation to acquire property) shall include the period such an option (right or obligation) is held [§1(h)(2)(B)(ii)]. Under present law to calculate capital gains, the holding period for stock options begins on the day after the option is exercised, not the date the option is granted [§1.1234-1(a)(1)].

Example: On January 2, 2001, Diana, a 39.6% tax bracket taxpayer, purchases the Century Plaza office building. If she owns the commercial real estate more than five years and sells it for a gain, her net long-term capital gain is taxed at a maximum rate of 18%. However, if she owns the building for more than 18 months but not more than five years, her gain is only eligible for the 20% maximum capital gains rate.

CAPITAL GAIN FORMULA

The following types of gain are not eligible for the new 10% or 20% rates.

1. Gains on collectibles (as defined for purposes of IRAs) other than government-issued gold, silver, and platinum coins. The maximum rate on net capital gain on collectibles continues to be 28%.
2. Gain on section 1250 property (real property) to the extent the section 1231 (generally business property) gain would have been ordinary income under section 1245 (generally *all* depreciation taken on personal property and all previous accelerated depreciation taken on commercial real property) and was not recaptured under section 1250 (generally depreciation taken on residential rental property taken faster than straight-line).
3. Gain on qualified small business stock will be taxed at a rate of 28%. Small business stock is eligible for a 50% exclusion, so the maximum effective rate will be 14%.
4. Net capital gain treated as investment income for purposes of the deduction for investment interest expense.

Exception—Collectibles

The 10%/20% rates apply to most capital assets with the exception of collectibles, such as art, rugs, antiques, any metals, gems, stamps, coins and alcoholic beverages, which continue to be taxed at the 28% rate. Certain newly minted gold and silver coins issued by the federal government and coins issued under state law are subject to the lower capital gains rates, even though such coins generally qualify as "collectibles" [§408(m)(2), (3)].

Exception—Real Estate Depreciation Recapture

Not all gains from the sale of depreciable real property will benefit from the same low rate as gains from the sale of other assets. Specifically, the top rate on real property gain attributable to depreciation, but not already "recaptured," i.e., taxed at ordinary income rates, will be taxed at a top rate of 25% rather than the 20% top rate that applies to other capital gains.

Unrecaptured section 1250 gain is the amount of long-term capital gain that would be treated as ordinary income if the property were section 1245 property and, for gain property taken into account after July 28, 1997, only from property held more than 18 months. For 1997, only sales after May 6 are taken into account. This amount may not exceed the excess of the net section 1231 gain over the gain treated as ordinary income under the rules for nonrecaptured section 1231 losses from the five preceding years.

Note: It appears that this rule applies to installment payments received after July 28, 1997, from section 1250 property sold before July 29, 1997, if that property was held over 18 months.

> ***Example:*** John sold a residential rental building for $120,000. He paid $74,375 for it and claimed $67,561 regular ACRS deductions. The alternate ACRS deductions would have been $66,193. His section 1250 gain is $1,368 and his section 1231 gain is $111,818. The $1,368 section 1250 gain is taxed as ordinary income. $66,193, the amount of depreciation not recaptured under section 1250 and that would be recaptured under section 1245, is taxed at a 25% rate. $45,625 = $111,818 − $66,193 is taxed at the 20% rate. The tax on this sale (ignoring other factors and assuming he is in the top tax bracket) is $26,125, computed as follows:

		Gain	Tax Rate	Tax
Sales price		$120,000		
Original Cost	$74,375			
Less: Accumulated depreciation	−67,561			
Adjusted basis		− 6,814		
Total gain		113,186		
Less: §1250 ordinary income gain*		− 1,368 × 39.6%†	=	542
Less: Gain due to prior depreciation #		− 66,193 × 25.0%	=	16,548
Remaining capital gain		$ 45,625 × 20.0%	=	9,125
Total tax				$26,215

*Regular ACRS deduction:	$67,561	(Allowable accelerated depreciation)
Alternative ACRS deduction:	$66,193	(Straight-line depreciation)
§1250 gain (ordinary income):	$ 1,368	(Difference)
#Regular ACRS deduction	$67,561	
less §1250 gain recognized	$ 1,368	
§1245	$66,193	

†Assumes taxpayer in highest tax bracket

FIGURE 2.1   Rate Chart by Sales Date

Your Capital Gain Rate Is:	If Your Regular Tax Bracket Is:	And Your Holding Period Is More Than:	And Your Gain Is From:
For Sales Creating Individual's Long-term Capital Gains before May 7, 1997			
15%	15%	12 months	Net capital gains (including prior straight-line depreciation). The gains are treated as ordinary income up to the 28% tax bracket (i.e., the 15% tax bracket).
28%	28%–39.6%	12 months	Net capital gains (including prior straight-line depreciation). The gains are eligible for the alternative 28% maximum rate.

FIGURE 2.2   Rate Chart by Sales Date

Your Capital Gain Rate Is:	If Your Regular Tax Bracket Is:	And Your Holding Period Is More Than:	And Your Gain Is From:
For Sales Creating Long-term Capital Gains after May 6, 1997, But before July 29, 1997			
10%	15%	12 months	Net capital gains (including prior depreciation and collectibles). The gains are eligible for the alternative 10% maximum rate for non-corporate taxpayers.
20%	28%–39.6%	12 months	Net capital gains (other than prior depreciation and collectibles). The gains are eligible for the alternative 20% maximum rate for non-corporate taxpayers.
25%	28%–39.6%	12 months	Prior §1250 depreciation otherwise not subject to recapture.
28%	28%–39.6%	12 months	Collectibles (such as art, antiques, gems and stamps).

FIGURE 2.3   Rate Chart by Sales Date

For Sales Creating Long-term Capital Gains After July 28, 1997, But before January 1, 2001			
Your Capital Gain Rate Is:	*If Your Regular Tax Bracket Is:*	*And Your Holding Period Is More Than:*	*And Your Gain Is From:*
10%	15%	18 months	Adjusted net capital gains (excludes prior depreciation, qualified small business stock and collectibles). The gains are eligible for the alternative 10% maximum rate for non-corporate taxpayers.
7.5%–14%	15%–39.6%	60 months	Qualified small business stock issued after 8/10/93 and sold after 8/10/98 (without rollover).
15%	15%	12 months but not more than 18 months	Net capital gains (includes prior depreciation and collectibles). The gains are subject to the ordinary income tax rates as they are less than the "mid-term" capital gain rates.
15%	15%	18 months	Prior depreciation and collectibles.
20%	28%–39.6%	18 months	Adjusted net capital gains (excludes prior depreciation, qualified small business stock and collectibles). The gains are eligible for the alternative 20% maximum rate for non-corporate taxpayers.
25%	28%–39.6%	18 months	Prior §1250 depreciation otherwise not subject to recapture.
28%	28%–39.6%	12 months but not more than 18 months	Net capital gains (includes prior depreciation and collectibles). The gains are eligible for the alternative "mid-term" 28% maximum rate for non-corporate taxpayers.
28%	28%–39.6%	12 months	Collectibles (such as art, antiques, gems and stamps).

FIGURE 2.4   Rate Chart by Sales Date

For Sales Creating Long-term Capital Gains on or after January 1, 2001			
Your Capital Gain Rate Is:	*If Your Regular Tax Bracket Is:*	*And Your Holding Period Is More Than:*	*And Your Gain Is From:*
8%	15%	5 years	Adjusted net capital gains (excludes prior depreciation, qualified small business stock and collectibles). The gains are eligible for the alternative 8% maximum rate for non-corporate taxpayers.
10%	15%	18–60 months	Adjusted net capital gains (excludes prior depreciation, qualified small business stock and collectibles). The gains are eligible for the alternative 10% maximum rate for non-corporate taxpayers.
7.5%–14%	15%–39.6%	60 months	Qualified small business stock issued after 8/10/93 and sold after 8/10/98 (without rollover).
15%	15%	12 months but not more than 18 months	Net capital gains (includes prior depreciation and collectibles). The gains are subject to the ordinary income tax rates as they are less than the "mid-term" capital gain rates.
15%	15%	18 months	Prior depreciation and collectibles.
18%	28%–39.6%	5 years	Adjusted net capital gains from assets purchased after December 31, 2000, (excludes prior depreciation and collectibles). The gains are eligible for the alternative 18% maximum rate for non-corporate taxpayers.
20%	28%–39.6%	18–60 months	Adjusted net capital gains (excludes prior depreciation, qualified small business stock and collectibles). The gains are eligible for the alternative 20% maximum rate for non-corporate taxpayers.

FIGURE 2.4 Rate Chart by Sales Date *(Continued)*

Your Capital Gain Rate Is:	If Your Regular Tax Bracket Is:	And Your Holding Period Is More Than:	And Your Gain Is From:
25%	28%–39.6%	18 months	Prior §1250 depreciation otherwise not subject to recapture.
28%	28%–39.6%	12 months but not more than 18 months	Net capital gains (includes prior depreciation and collectibles). The gains are eligible for the alternative "mid-term" 28% maximum rate for non-corporate taxpayers.
28%	28%–39.6%	12 months	Collectibles (such as art, antiques, gems and stamps).

Section 1202 gain is gain from the sale of qualified small business stock that is eligible for the 50% exclusion.

When a taxpayer has net capital gain, the tax may not exceed the sum of the following five amounts:

1. The tax computed using the table or rate schedule on the greater of (a) taxable income reduced by net capital gain, or (b) the lesser of (i) the amount of income taxed at a rate below 28%, or (ii) taxable income reduced by the adjusted net capital gain (defined below).
2. 25% of the excess (if any) of (a) unrecaptured section 1250 gain (previously defined), or if less, the net capital gain, over (b) the excess (if any) of the sum of the amount that was taxed in item 1 plus the net capital gain over taxable income.
3. 28% of the amount of taxable income in excess of the sum of the adjusted net capital gain, and the sum of the amounts taxed in items 1 and 2.
4. 10% of the amount of the adjusted net capital gain (or, if less, taxable income) that is not more than the excess (if any) of (a) the amount taxable income that would normally be taxed at a rate below 28%, over (b) taxable income reduced by the adjusted net capital gain.
5. 20% of the taxpayer's adjusted net capital gain (or, if less, taxable income) in excess of the amount taxed in item 4.

Adjusted net capital gain is net capital gain determined without regard to

1. collectibles gain (previously defined),
2. unrecaptured section 1250 gain (previously defined),
3. section 1202 gain (previously defined), and
4. mid-term gain (previously defined).

CAPITAL GAIN TAX WORKSHEET

1. Taxable income	1. _____
2. Net capital gain	2. _____
3. Line 1 less line 2	3. _____
4. Enter 28% rate schedule amount* (e.g., for 1997: $24,650 single; $33,050 head of household; $41,200 married filing joint; $20,600 married separate)	4. _____
5. Adjusted net capital gain	5. _____
6. Line 1 less line 5	6. _____
7. Enter the lesser of line 4 or line 6	7. _____
8. Enter the larger of line 3 or line 7	8. _____
9. Enter the lesser of unrecaptured §1250 gain or line 2	9. _____
10. Enter line 2 plus line 8 less line 1. If zero or less, enter zero	10. _____
11a. Line 9 less line 10	11a. _____
11b. Line 1 less line 5 less line 8 less line 11a	11b. _____
12a. Enter the lesser of line 1 or line 5	12a. _____
12b. Line 4 less line 6. If zero or less, enter zero	12b. _____
12c. Enter the lesser of line 12a or line 12b	12c. _____
13. Line 12a less line 12c	13. _____
14. Tax on line 8 from the table or rate schedule	14. _____
15. Line 11a × .25	15. _____
16. Line 11b × .28	16. _____
17. Line 12c × .10	17. _____
18. Line 13 × .20	18. _____
19. Add lines 14 through 18	19. _____

CAPITAL GAIN OR LOSS

What is a capital asset? Before applying the advantageous capital gains treatment, it has to be ascertained if the property is actually a *capital asset*. Capital gain or loss is only available when a capital asset is sold.

Capital assets include *all* property, regardless of how long held, *with the following exceptions*. Capital assets do not include [§1221]

1. inventory or stock in trade of the taxpayer,
2. property held by the taxpayer primarily for sale to customers in the ordinary course of his or her trade or business (e.g., *dealer's realty*),
3. *depreciable property used in a trade or business* and
4. *real property used in a trade or business*.

AMT CAPITAL GAIN TAX WORKSHEET

1.	AMT taxable income less AMT exemption	1. _____
2.	Net capital gain	2. _____
3.	Adjusted net capital gain	3. _____
4.	Unrecognized §1250 gain (depreciation recapture)	4. _____
5.	Line 3 plus line 4	5. _____
6.	Enter the lesser of line 2 or line 5	6. _____
7.	Line 1 less line 6	7. _____
8.	Enter the lesser of line 4 or (line 1 less line 3 less line 7)	8. _____
9.	Enter the lesser of line 1 or line 3	9. _____
10.	Enter amount from line 12c of the regular tax capital gain worksheet	10. _____
11.	Enter the lesser of line 9 or line 10	11. _____
12.	Line 9 less line 11	12. _____
13.	Tax on line 7 using the 26% and 28% rates	13. _____
14.	Line 8 × .25	14. _____
15.	Line 11 × .10	15. _____
16.	Line 12 × .20	16. _____
17.	Add lines 13 through 16	17. _____

PLANNING TIP: Most investors are surprised to find that depreciable property (no. 3 above) and business real property (no. 4 above) *are not* capital assets! As will be seen in the "hybrid" method discussed later, most investors prefer *not* having property categorized as a capital asset when the property is to be sold for a loss.

Capital loss may be only partially deductible. A capital loss is a loss on the sale of a capital asset. The negative result of a capital loss is that both net short-term capital losses and net long-term capital losses are combined in offsetting ordinary income. Also, the pre-1986 rule that a maximum of $3,000 of ordinary income can be offset in any tax year is retained. Therefore, the only benefit is that both net long-term capital losses and net short-term capital losses offset up to $3,000 of ordinary income on a dollar-for-dollar basis instead of the previous two-for-one basis.

ORDINARY GAIN OR LOSS

Ordinary gains or losses are generally entirely taxable or entirely deductible. This includes "income from whatever source derived," including (1) compensation for services, such as fees, commissions, fringe benefits and similar items; (2) gross income derived from business; and (3) *gains derived from dealer's realty* (e.g., subdivider treating real property as if it is inventory) [§61(a)].

PLANNING TIP: Real estate investors may find their real estate holdings taxed as ordinary income if the IRS determines they purchased the property to sell it (e.g., dealer's realty). But isn't all property bought with the intention to eventually sell it?

Investors must make the argument that they hold property for other reasons than "for sale," such as for appreciation or for rental income. Careless use of technical tax terms can be very costly—ask Leona Helmsley!

Social Security increased the regular tax rate. Added to the maximum income tax rates (e.g., 39.6%), ordinary income *may* also have an additional 15.3% self-employment (also known as Social Security) "tax" rate imposed on it if the IRS determines the income is earned in the ordinary course of an active business, such as dealer's realty. This additional tax rate is not imposed if the property is considered a capital asset or a business asset, as discussed next.

HYBRID, CAPITAL GAIN AND ORDINARY LOSS (§1231 GAIN OR LOSS)

A great tax benefit. *Property used in a trade or business* is called *§1231 property*. It receives long-term capital gain benefits if there is a net gain; it receives ordinary loss benefits when there is a net loss. Therefore, business property sold for a gain may find only part of that gain taxed (a capital gain), whereas when business property is sold for a loss, it is *entirely* deductible—the best of both worlds!

What items are called §1231 items? *Property used in a trade or business,* subject to depreciation and held for more than one year, and *business realty* held for more than one year are called §1231 property. Therefore, most property used in a business is §1231 property (e.g., rental property and property used in the taxpayer's business). Real-estate-dealer realty and inventory property held primarily for sale to customers in the ordinary course of business are *not* §1231 property; they are ordinary income property [§1231(b); §61].

§1231 calculation. If the gains exceed the losses upon disposition of §1231 assets, then all the gains and all the losses are treated as capital gains and losses. If the net result is a loss, all the gains are taxed as ordinary gains and the losses are deductible in full as ordinary losses.

Example: Lance sells the following assets that are used in his business and held for more than one year:

	Gain	Loss
Raw land held for future building site	$7,000	$ 0
Automobile		300
Truck		3,700
Computer	2,000	
	$9,000	$4,000

As the §1231 gains exceed the §1231 losses, each gain and each loss is treated as long-term capital gain or long-term capital loss.

Most real estate investors find their real estate sales are eligible for the previously discussed hybrid method, wherein the gain receives the long-term capital gain benefits and the loss receives the ordinary loss treatment. As is fully discussed in the next chapter, most homeowners, though, find their long-term capital gain is not taxable, and their loss is never deductible!

3

The $250,000/$500,000 Exclusion Rule for Gain on Sale of Principal Residence

INTRODUCTION

Why the Change?

After Congress passed the principal residence rollover provision (i.e., buy up within 24 months) and later the exclusion rule (i.e., $125,000 of gain forgiven), its members slowly realized that although it adequately protected most taxpayers, it did not meet the needs of the retiree or empty nester who sells the large family residence and purchases a substantially less expensive home, the divorcee who subsequently rents an apartment, or the homeowner who moves from a high cost area into a low cost area (e.g., from Los Angeles to Casper, Wyoming). Congress concluded that the reinvestment requirement of the rollover provision was an undesirable burden and the $125,000 exclusion rule was not large enough. Therefore, effective for sales on or after May 7, 1997, they repealed both the §1034 rollover statute and the old §121 one-time over-55 exclusion rule and provided a new §121 relief provision applicable to principal residences (see the Taxpayers Relief Act of 1997).

This chapter describes various tax consequences when selling a personal residence and provides specific examples of the requirements necessary for homeowners to use the new §121 exclusion of gain rule.

WARNING: Any regulation or case citation in this chapter refers to previous Code §1034 and §121 that have been repealed by the Taxpayer's Relief Act of 1997. They are included in anticipation that future IRS positions will be similar. Any specific code section citation refers to the *new* Code §121!

WARNING: Always check with your tax practitioner as new IRS regulations are expected at any time!

DEFINITION OF PRINCIPAL RESIDENCE

As this large exclusion-of-gain rule only applies to the taxpayer's "principal" residence, the problems defining principal residence can be placed into four major categories: (1) types of qualified properties, (2) ownership requirements, (3) occupancy requirements and (4) residences used also for business. This definition of principal residence is the area in which most of the tax problems and IRS controversies arise.

Where Is Your Principal Residence?

Normally, this is easy to determine. A taxpayer's principal residence is the land and building where the taxpayer *principally domiciles,* based upon all the facts and circumstances in each case, including the good faith of the taxpayer. It may even be located in a foreign country [Rev. Rul. 54-611, 1954-2 CB 159].

Located where taxpayer is employed. The principal residence typically will be the home in the area where the taxpayer works [Rev. Rul. 60-189, 1960-1 CB 60; Rev. Rul. 83-82, 1983-1 CB 45]. Surprised? Most taxpayers think it is where they lay their heads, which is only true when the taxpayer doesn't have a job *and* under the circumstances described next.

If the taxpayer is retired or not working. In this instance, the principal residence is usually where the spouse and/or children reside, or where the taxpayer spends the most amount of time, votes, pays taxes, files his or her tax return and so forth [Rev. Rul. 71-247, 1971-1 CB 54].

Only one "principal" residence is possible. One taxpayer cannot own two principal residences simultaneously as principal is defined as "the most important" [*McDowell v. Comm.,* 40 TCM (CCH) 301 (1980)].

But each spouse may have a separate "principal" residence! Each spouse would be able to separately exclude $250,000 as long as each satisfies all the qualification requirements [new §121].

COMMENT: This allows spouses who both own homes to each exclude up to $250,000 in gain, just as if they are filing separately.

Examples of Property That Can Qualify

A personal residence may be a single-family house, condominium, cooperative, mobile home, boat, houseboat, a house trailer, or motorhome [previous §1.1034-1(c)(3)(i)].

REQUIREMENTS TO USE THE $250,000/$500,000 MFJ EXCLUSION RULE

Now, to the details of this provision!

DON'T WASTE TIME READING THIS CHAPTER, AS THE GAIN IS FREE, IF YOU CAN PROVE:

1. the sales price of the home was $250,000 or under ($500,000 if married and filing a joint return [MFJ]), OR
2. the costs of improvements ELIMINATE any *taxable* gain (i.e., above $250,000/$500,000 MFJ), AND
3. the original cost of the home sold (generally done by making available HUD Form 1 to the IRS auditor), AND
4. that no more than one home has been reported in the previous two years from the sale date, AND
5. that no prior depreciation has been taken on the home after May 7, 1997.

In General

This exclusion rule provides that up to $250,000 of gain ($500,000 for MFJ) realized on the sale or exchange of a principal residence on or after May 7, 1997, is not *taxable* (not just deferred) if certain prerequisites are satisfied. This permanent exclusion is allowed each time a homeowner meets the eligibility requirements, but generally no more frequently than once every two years [new §121].

PRIOR TAX PLANNING IDEAS THAT ARE NO LONGER RELEVANT!

Common "rules" under the previous tax provisions are no longer viable:

1. there is no requirement to reinvest the sales proceeds into another home, i.e., taxpayers do not have to buy equal or up within 24 months;
2. the requirement that the taxpayer must be at least aged 55 has been repealed;
3. fixing up expenses, including "conditions-of-sales" repairs, are no longer deductible *anywhere;*

4. the "moving at least 50 miles" requirement to avoid the once-every-two-years rule has been eliminated;
5. the nontaxable gain does not have to be "rolled over" into the new home; and
6. renting the home while trying to sell it generally will not cause tax problems.

COMMENT: This new exclusion eliminates most record-keeping requirements when home sellers ***absolutely know in the future*** they will not experience a home gain of more than $250,000 ($500,000 MFJ for married couples).

COMMENT: Starting for sales after May 6, 1997, the IRS will NOT receive notification of any home sale $250,000 or under ($500,000 MFJ for married taxpayers) via Form 1099-S by the real estate closing agent (e.g., the title company, real estate broker or mortgage company). The home seller will have to provide the agent "assurances" that: (1) the home was a "principal residence," (2) there was no federally subsidized mortgage financing assistance, and (3) the full gain is excludable from gross income (e.g., no depreciation recapture). The IRS has the authority to increase the dollar amount in the future [§6045(e)(5)].

It's an option! This exclusion rule is NOT mandatory, and the taxpayer(s) may elect out of this rule and have the gain taxable [§121(f)]. This provision is denied to disqualified expatriates [§121(e); §877(a)(1)].

COMMENT: Why would a taxpayer elect to have a gain taxable when it could be tax free? It took a little imagination, but how about this:

TAX PLANNING: Dolores marries Alfred on January 1, 1998. On May 15, 1999, they sell Alfred's old home for a $10,000 gain. On January 15, 2000, they sell Dolores's home for a $500,000 MFJ gain. It would be smarter for Alfred to elect to make his $10,000 gain taxable so that Dolores and Alfred can file jointly and use their combined $500,000 MFJ exclusion. If he uses it against the $10,000, he cannot again use the exclusion until two years after May 15, 1999, and Dolores could exclude only $250,000. Isn't that simple?

Wealthy homeowners may be forced to report gain! The amount in excess of the $250,000/$500,000 MFJ exclusion must be included in income even if all of the sales proceeds are reinvested in a new residence.

COMMENT: For those homeowners selling principal residences with gains in excess of $250,000/$500,000 MFJ, the repealed §1034 "rollover" provision was more beneficial.

What about an exchange? Instead of selling a principal residence, occasionally homeowners will exchange one personal residence for another personal residence (common in farm exchanges). Exchanges of personal residences are not eligible for tax-free exchanges, and, therefore, the rules of this chapter apply both to sales *and exchanges* of homes.

What about Those Taxpayers Who Previously Used Their "Once-in-a-Lifetime" Exclusion?

These lucky taxpayers get to use both the old and the new §121 without any penalty! "Pre-May 1, 1997, sales are not taken into account", and, therefore, the once-every-two-years rule is "applied without regard to any sale or exchange before May 7, 1997" [§121(b)(3)(B)].

TAX PLANNING: Those over-55 taxpayers who lived in their homes for at least two years and used the rollover provision within the last three years should consider filing an amended return for the year of that previous sale to exclude $125,000 of gain and roll over the remaining into the replacement residence. This results in eliminating $125,000 of future gain and still allows the taxpayer to eliminate $250,000/$500,000 MFJ under new §121! Generally, a taxpayer may make the old $125,000 election at any time before the expiration of the period (generally, back three years from the time the return is timely filed) for making a claim for credit or refund federal income tax for the taxable year in which the sale or exchange occurred [§121-4(a); §6511(a)]. See Form 2119 for the format. Thank you Duane Gomer, good idea.

Example: On January 1, 1994, Duane and Shirley sold their residence (used for over two years) in Mission Viejo for $1,625,000, experiencing a $625,000 gain. On May 1, 1994, they purchased a new replacement home in Hillsboro for $1,800,000. As they purchased equal-or-up-within-24-months, they "rolled over" the entire $625,000 gain into the new home, reducing the basis to $1,125,000 ($1,800,000 purchase minus $625,000 gain deferred). Therefore, when they sell the home after May 7, 1997, for more than $1,125,000, for example $1,800,000, at least $125,000 of gain will be taxed ($625,000 less $500,000 new exclusion). If they had used the $125,000 exclusion rule in 1994, they would have lowered the "rollover" gain from $625,000 to $500,000!

The §121 Qualification Requirements

To qualify for this tax break:

1. **"Own and occupy for two years" rule:** the taxpayer, with three notable exceptions discussed later, must own and use the home as his or her principal residence for a total of two years during the five-year period ending on the date of the sale or exchange [§121(a)], and
2. **"No more than once every two years" rule:** the taxpayer cannot report, during the 2-year period ending on the date of sale, other post-May 6, 1997, sales or exchanges to which §121 applies [§121(b)(3)].

When Does a Sale Occur?

The date of sale is generally the earlier of the date "a deed passes (the date of the delivery of the deed) *or* at the time possession and the burdens and benefits of ownership [from a practical standpoint] are transferred to the buyer" [Rev. Rul. 69-93, 1969-1 CB 139].

The Calculation

If the taxpayer meets the above qualifications, up to $250,000/$500,000 MFJ of gain may be excluded from gross income [§121(b)(1) and (2)].

> ***Example:*** Cindy sells her principal residence for $330,000. She had purchased the home twenty years earlier for $40,000 and had added a $25,000 recreation room to it. She pays commissions and other closing costs of $30,000. Her total gain is forgiven if she uses the $250,000 exclusion rule.

Gain or Loss Computation

Sales price			+ $330,000
Less:	Selling expenses		− $ 30,000
Equals:	Amount realized		= $300,000
Less:	Adjusted basis		
	Original cost (or basis)	+ $40,000	
	Plus: Improvements	+ $25,000	
	Equals: Total adjusted basis:		− $ 65,000
Gain realized on sale			= $235,000
Less:	**$250,000 Exclusion**		**− $250,000**
TAXABLE GAIN ON SALE			= NONE

The $250,000 Exclusion Doubles to $500,000 MFJ If Four Requirements Are Met:

1. A husband and wife make a joint return for the taxable year of the sale or exchange of the property,
2. *Either* spouse *owns* the property for two of the last five years,
3. *Both* spouses *use* the property as their principal residence for two of the last five years, and
4. Neither spouse is ineligible because more than one sale or exchange has been used during the previous two years [§121(b)(2)].

COMMENT: Therefore, if the above requirements are not met, a married couple will, at a minimum, be eligible for the $250,000 exclusion if *either* spouse meets all the requirements. Similarly, if a single taxpayer who is otherwise eligible for an exclusion marries someone who has used the exclusion within the two years prior to the marriage, the proposal would allow the newly married taxpayer a maximum exclusion of $250,000.

COMMENT: The two-year requirement does not prevent a husband and wife filing a joint return from each excluding up to $250,000 of gain from the sale of each spouse's principal residence provided that each spouse would be permitted to exclude up to $250,000 of gain if they filed separate returns.

COMMENT: This seems to allow a couple to have two principal residences if they are not living together, but are still filing jointly.

What Happens If One Spouse Qualifies and the Other Doesn't Qualify?

If a husband and wife make a joint return for the taxable year of the sale or exchange of the principal residence, the $250,000 exclusion rule and the proration of gain rule apply if *either* spouse meets the ownership and use requirements [§121(d)(1)].

COMMENT: Once both spouses satisfy the eligibility rules and two years have passed since the last exclusion was allowed to either of them, the taxpayers may exclude $500,000 MFJ of gain on their joint return.

TAX PLANNING: Has this tax provision created a new tax shelter, i.e., is a married housing contractor who builds and occupies his or her own principal residence and sells it two years after completion eligible to report up to $500,000 MFJ tax-free?

The determination of whether an individual is married shall be determined by the election to make a joint return, not as of the date of the sale or exchange [§1.6013-1(a)].

HUMOROUS TAX PLANNING! Single taxpayers with profits in excess of $250,000 may consider marriage to their over-two-years-live-in to gain an additional $250,000 tax shelter! On the other hand, the marriage better last more than two years for those single taxpayers who don't have live-ins! Tax law is now an incentive to keep the marriage together, but only for those taxpayers who didn't live together before marriage!

Owning a home with a "significant other." If two unmarried individuals jointly own and use one principal residence, the $250,000 exclusion provisions should apply independently to each upon a sale of the residence. The home is treated like a duplex owned by a joint venture partnership.

The Seller's Property Must Have Been Owned and Used as His or Her Principal Residence for at Least 2 of the Last 5 Years!

During the five-year period ending on the date of the sale or exchange, the taxpayer must have owned and used the property as a principal residence for periods aggregating two years or more. This two-year ownership and use requirement may be satisfied by establishing ownership and use for either 24 full months, or 730 days (365 days × 2) during the 60-month time period prior to sale [§121(a); previous §121-1(c)].

COMMENT: Therefore, the ownership and use requirement can be met in two years; if a homeowner *owns and uses the same home for two years,* he or she has automatically met the "two-of-the-last-five-years requirement."

Tacking of time prior to August 5, 1997, allowed. If a taxpayer acquired his or her current residence in a rollover transaction, periods of ownership and use of the prior residence can be taken into account in determining ownership and use of the current residence. Therefore, the holding and use periods prior to August 5, 1997, from a home that previously used the prior "rollover" provision may be "tacked on" or used in determining both the ownership and use test under the new exclusion provision [§121(g)].

COMMENT: All homeowners who owned and used a principal residence prior to May 7, *1995,* should automatically meet the two-year rule under this transition rule.

COMMENT: As the prior "rollover" provision could only be used to defer a gain, does this mean that the tacking rule cannot be used if the prior residence was sold for a loss? Maybe future regulations will clarify.

The ownership and use requirements do not have to be met simultaneously.

However, satisfaction of both conditions must occur within the five-year period ending on the date of sale or exchange. In other words, a tenant who purchases the home can count the time as a tenant as part of the use requirement. Also, a homeowner can rent out his or her home and still count that time toward the ownership requirements [Rev. Rul. 80-172, 1980-2 CB 56].

Flowcharting the ownership and use test:

The "Ownership" Test:

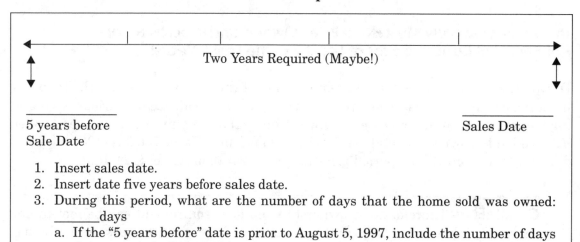

1. Insert sales date.
2. Insert date five years before sales date.
3. During this period, what are the number of days that the home sold was owned: _____ days
   a. If the "5 years before" date is prior to August 5, 1997, include the number of days the previous "rolled-over" home was owned [§121(g)].
4. If this number is either 24 full months or 730 days (365 days × 2) during the 60 months prior to sale, the taxpayer has met the required "ownership" test.

The "Use" Test:

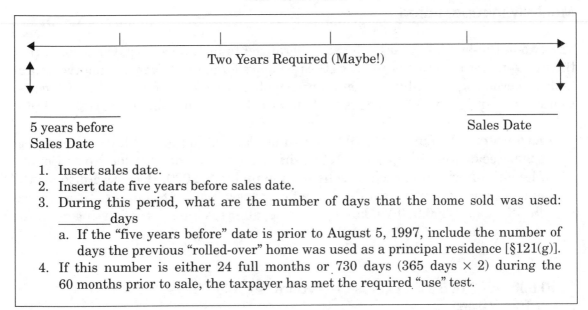

Two Years Required (Maybe!)

5 years before
Sales Date

Sales Date

1. Insert sales date.
2. Insert date five years before sales date.
3. During this period, what are the number of days that the home sold was used: _____days
   a. If the "five years before" date is prior to August 5, 1997, include the number of days the previous "rolled-over" home was used as a principal residence [§121(g)].
4. If this number is either 24 full months or 730 days (365 days × 2) during the 60 months prior to sale, the taxpayer has met the required "use" test.

Office-in-home. This requires the office-in-home to be converted back to personal use for two years before it is deemed to be "used" for two years.

Occasional absences. Short, temporary absences, such as vacations or other seasonal absences, even when accompanied by rental of the residence, are counted as periods of use [previous §1.121-1(c)]. A one-year sabbatical leave, however, is not considered a short, temporary absence [previous §1.121-1(d) (Example 5)].

No residence exists if the home is converted into a rental. A homeowner who converts a principal residence into a rental may be faced with a realized and taxable gain in a future sale. Once the personal residence has been rented for more than three of the last five years, the $250,000/$500,000 MFJ exclusion rule is not usable since the property is no longer deemed a principal residence. The taxpayer would be required to reoccupy the property as a principal residence for two of the last five years before the sale to reestablish the principal residence status.

PLANNING TIP: This is one of the most common questions asked tax practitioners, and the answer is *no exclusion for rentals!* Rentals may use the like-kind exchange rules to defer gain.

COMMENT: Unanswered is the question: "does this mean that for a taxpayer to convert a personal residence into a rental eligible for a like-kind exchange, it must be rented for more than three years?" Hum!

Only One Year Is Required for the Physically or Mentally Incapacitated

The two-of-the-last-five-years rule was liberalized to include a taxpayer who, during the five-year period (1) owns and uses the residence for at least *one year* (not two years) and (2) becomes physically or mentally incapable of self-care during the five years, thereafter residing in a state-licensed facility (including a nursing home) [§121(d)(6)].

> *Example:* On January 1, 1998, Edith purchased and moved into her new personal residence. On July 31, 1999, she moved into the Powder River County Memorial Nursing Home but sells it on January 1, 2000. Because Edith owned and occupied the principal residence for at least one year, she is entitled to use the $250,000/$500,000 MFJ exclusion rule, after residing in the nursing home for six more months (i.e., to meet the two-year rule).

$250,000/$500,000 MFJ Exclusion Available Only Once Every Two Years!

With some notable exceptions, the $250,000/$500,000 MFJ exclusion rule does not apply if during the two-year period ending on the date of sale or exchange there are any other sales or exchanges by the taxpayer in which the exclusion was previously used [§121(b)(3)(A)].

Exception to the two-year requirement. Pre-May 7, 1997, sales are not taken into account when calculating the "available only once every two years" restriction [§121(b)(3)(B)].

Flowcharting the requirement that the exclusion is only available once every two years.

The "Only-Once-Every-Two-Years" Test

Only One Home Sale Allowed (Maybe!)

LATER OF: 2 years before Sale Date or May 7, 1997

Sales Date

1. Insert sales date.
2. Insert LATER of either:
   a. May 7, 1997, or
   b. date two years before sales date [§121(b)(3)(B)].
3. If homeowners made NO other home sales in this time period, they qualify.

Example: Bill sold home #1 on January 1, 1997 (which he purchased on May 1, 1995), and rolled the $75,000 gain into home #2 purchased on February 1, 1997 (using the old §1034 provisions). He sells home #2 on May 30, 1997, with an accumulated gain of $100,000. He can use the new §121 on the entire gain even though he has sold more than one principal residence within the previous two-year period after the sale (between May 30, 1995, and May 30, 1997). Pre-August 5, 1997, sales are not taken into account when determining if more than one sale has occurred in the previous two years. Additionally, even though he only owned home #2 less than two years (from February 1, 1997, to May 30, 1997), he can tack on the previous §1034 home ownership and use (from May 1, 1995, to January 1, 1997) to exceed the two-year ownership and use requirement.

So What Happens If the Homeowner Can't Meet the Two-Year Rule? Not To Worry!

Three exceptions permit the homeowner to still exclude some of the gain. Only a portion of the gain is generally taxable even if the taxpayer (a) cannot meet the two-of-the-last-five-years-rule *ownership* test, (b) cannot meet the two-of-the-last-five-years-rule *use* test, or (c) has used this exclusion rule within the last two years. If the reason the homeowner cannot comply with the two-year rule is because of:

1. Change of place of employment,
2. Health, or
3. Other unforseen circumstances, to the extent provided in future IRS regulations [§121(c)(2)],

the taxpayer will still be able to exclude the fraction of the gain, the numerator being the shorter period of (1) the use period or (2) the period between the two sales dates, and the denominator being two years.

Major potential tax change. The Tax Technical Corrections Bill of 1997 (which has **not** passed as of the printing of this book) provides for a proration of the $250,000/$500,000 MFJ rather than the *gain*. This would permit $20,833 of the gain to be excluded for each **month** the homeowner meets the ownership, use and "not-two-year" rules! For example, a married contractor who builds his or her personal residence and moves out in six months for employment-related purposes would be permitted to exclude $125,000 of gain.

Here is how Code Section 121 says to compute the fraction: "the amount of excluded gain from the **last sale** shall not exceed the amount which bears the same ratio to the amount which would be so excluded if such requirements had been met, as the shorter of:

1. The aggregate periods, during the 5-year period ending on the date of such sale or exchange, such property has been owned and used by the taxpayer as the taxpayer's principal residence, or

2. The period after the date of the most recent prior sale or exchange by the taxpayer to which the exclusion rule applied and before the date of such sale or exchange,

bears to 2 years "[§121(c)(1)]. Really!

COMMENT: Does changing of employment within the same metropolitan area meet this compliance rule? What about moving back to the parent's hometown if they develop Alzheimer's disease? As this rule allows a percentage of a normally taxable gain to be excluded, creative reasons will be the norm! Watch for extensive regulations in the near future!

The formula to determine the "ratio factor amount" is:

$$\frac{\text{Own or use days \textbf{or} between-sales days}}{} \div \frac{\text{730 days (2 years)}}{} \times \frac{\text{total gain*}}{} = \frac{\textbf{excludable gain}}{}$$

* This may be $250,000 or $500,000 MFJ; check with a tax professional.

Example: Will sells home #1 on June 1, 1997, and excludes $70,000 of gain under new §121. He sells home #2 on January 1, 1999, for a $25,000 gain. As he has a previous sale within two years from the date of last sale (home #1 sold between January 1, 1997, and January 1, 1999), the $25,000 is entirely taxable, UNLESS the reason for the sale was because of change of employment, health, or other IRS sanctioned circumstance. Then, the only portion of the gain that is taxable is the amount exceeding the "ratio factor amount."

COMMENT: The previous employment requirements of moving "at least 50 miles" and "staying at least 75% of the first one- to two-years unless transferred or laid off" requirements have been eliminated. The "moving at least 50 miles" is still required to deduct employment-related moving expenses [§217(c)(1)].

Example: Jack, a single taxpayer working for AT&T, purchased his Atlanta home on July 1, 1993, and, after being transferred to Denver, sold it on August 1, 1997, for a $70,000 gain (nontaxable under §121). He buys a Denver home on July 1, 1997, but after only six months, he is transferred to New York City and sells his Denver home on January 1, 1998, for a $60,000 gain. As he has not owned and used his Denver home for at least two years, his excludable gain is capped by the ***shorter period*** calculated by the following formulas:

Alternative 1—the "own and use days" rule

Date of current sale:	January 1, 1998
Date five years prior to current sale:	January 1, 1993

Days Denver home owned and used during this period:
    July 1, 1997–Dec. 31, 1997   183 days

Ratio: 183 own and use days ÷ 730 total days (2 years) × $60,000 = **$15,041 excludable gain**

Alternative 2—the "days between sales" rule

Date of current sale:	January 1, 1998
Date of previous sale:	August 1, 1997
Total days in period	152 days

Ratio: 152 days between sales ÷ 730 days (2 years) × $60,000 = **$12,493 excludable gain***

Result: *The shorter period is 152 days. Therefore Jack may exclude $12,493 of the $60,000 gain. This excludable amount is capped at $250,000 for single taxpayers and $500,000 MFJ for married filing joint taxpayers.

Homeowner Must *Use* the Residence

Use of residence. As previously stated, for the residence to qualify under the exclusion provision, it must be *purchased and physically occupied* by the taxpayer for two years prior to the sale of the old residence. Previously, the IRS strictly construed this rule.

WARNING: No excuse is acceptable. Intent to actually occupy and a good faith effort to occupy are not acceptable *even if the delay past the two years is due to circumstances beyond the taxpayer's control* [*U.S. v. Sheahan,* 323 F2d 383 (5th Cir 1963); Rev. Rul. 69-434, 1969-2 CB 163; *Haydin v. Comm.,* 46 TCM (CCH) 518 (1983); *James A. Henry,* 44 TCM (CCH) 844 (1982)].

WARNING: Purchase but not occupy is not sufficient. If a homeowner purchases a house but does not significantly use the residence, and instead occupies a rental apartment, the rental apartment becomes the new principal residence [*William C. Stolk,* 40 TC 345 (1963)].

WARNING: And we mean occupy! This occupancy requirement is not satisfied by simply moving in furniture without personally occupying [*John F. Bayley,* 35 TC 288 (1960); *Anne Franklin Stanley,* 33 TC 614 (1959)], nor by using the residence on weekends or vacations [*William C. Stolk,* 40 TC 345 (1963)], nor by allowing a child of the taxpayer to occupy the property [Rev. Rul. 69-434, 1969-2 CB 163].

Tacking of a Deceased Spouses' *Ownership and Use* Allowed

WARNING: The exclusion reduces the next year. If one spouse dies, and the home is sold in the year of the deceased spouse's death, the surviving spouse can file as married filing jointly, with the $500,000 MFJ exclusion available. If the home is sold in a subsequent year, the spouse usually is required to file as single, with only the $250,000 exclusion available.

COMMENT: This may not be a severe problem, though, as under current estate taxation, the decedent's share of the principal residence usually experiences a stepped-up basis, eliminating one-half the gain [§1014]. And in a community-property state, the entire gain may be stepped up, depending on how title is held. Only couples with over $500,000 MFJ of gain might need this tax planning concept!

"Tacking" of ownership and use of deceased spouse permitted. When a surviving spouse sells the jointly used principal residence in a year following death, the surviving spouse must now file as a single taxpayer, but the surviving spouse's ownership and use period includes the deceased spouse's ownership period before death [§121(d)(2)].

Example: Don and Janice were married on January 1, 1998. At that date, Janice moved into Don's principal residence, which he had owned and used since 1967. Don dies on January 1, 1999, and Janice inherits the property. She continues to use the property as her principal residence until August 31, 1999, at which time she sells it (less than two years after she moved in). She may still make a $500,000 MFJ exclusion because, during the five-year period ending on the date of the sale (August 31, 1999), Don had previously satisfied the two-year ownership and use requirements. Janice can "tack" Don's ownership and use to her ownership and use. If she waits until January 1, 2000, she would not need to "tack" Don's time, but she would only be able to make a $250,000 election.

COMMENT: The marital invitation will *follow* the question, "Have you owned and used your home for at least two years?" Lock up the shotgun after marriage, Molly!

Tacking in a Divorce

Tacking of *ownership* in divorce. When property is transferred between spouses during marriage or transferred incident to a divorce, no gain or loss is recognized, and it is treated similarly to a gift [§1041]. The period such individual owns such property shall include the period the transferor owned the property [§121(d)(3)(A)].

COMMENT: Elizabeth marries and moves into Larry's longtime (over five years) home on January 1. One month later they divorce, and Elizabeth receives the home as part of her divorce settlement, which she immediately sells for $250,000 cash. Elizabeth's ownership period is deemed five years, not one month.

But what about the divorcee's use period? Tacking of a divorced spouse's previous use was not mentioned in the new exclusion rule. Therefore, it seems not to be permitted.

COMMENT: As Elizabeth, in the above example, is in possession of the residence at time of sale, she would probably have to establish her own *use* period.

Tacking of *use* in divorce allowed in one situation. It is fairly common for divorce courts to order the family home sold and the proceeds split between former spouses but that the parent granted custody of the children be given exclusive use of the house rent-free until sale. When this period extends beyond a reasonable time, e.g., two years, the IRS had successfully made the argument that the noncustodial parent was not "using" that home as his or her "principal residence" at the time of sale and taxed the noncustodial parent's gain [*D. D. Bowers,* Dec. 51,460(M); *C. B. Perry,* CA-9, 96-2 USTC ¶50,405].

The new rule change. An individual shall be treated as using property as a principal residence during any period of ownership while such individual's spouse or former spouse is granted use of the property under a divorce or separation instrument [§121(d)(3)(B)].

COMMENT: New §121 reverses a previously unfair court-created tax provision!

Danger: A Property Settlement in a Divorce May Move the Entire Gain to Just One Spouse.

Transfer of property in divorce is a tax-free gift. As previously mentioned, there is generally no gain or loss recognized for transfers of property between spouses. Further, there is no recognition of gain or loss on the transfer of property to a former spouse if the transfer is incident to a divorce [§1041].

> *Example:* Georgie Ann and Bob own a $490,000 home purchased 20 years before for $60,000 and a $490,000 condo in Aspen with a basis of $490,000. Neither property is encumbered with debt. They decide to get divorced. The divorce court awards the house (and children) to Georgie Ann and the condo to Bob. The following tax shifting occurs:
>
> | | Total | Georgie Ann | Bob |
> |---|---|---|---|
> | Fair market value | $980,000 | $490,000 | $490,000 |
> | Adjusted basis | 550,000 | 60,000 | 490,000 |
> | Total gain | $430,000 | $430,000 | $ 0 |
>
> This results in Bob's half of the inherent long-term capital gain being transferred to Georgie Ann. If both parties sell their divided properties the year after the divorce, Bob will pocket $490,000 tax-free and Georgie Ann will find $180,000 ($430,000 – $250,000 exclusion) of long-term capital gain on her single tax return!

The basic policy of Code section 1041 is to treat a husband and wife as one economic unit and to defer, but not eliminate, the recognition of any gain or loss on interspousal property transfers until the property is conveyed to a third party outside the economic unit. To that end, no gain or loss is recognized upon the transfer of property from one spouse to another. The property takes a transferred ("carryover") basis in the hands of the recipient spouse; the carryover basis preserves the gain (or loss) until the recipient spouse transfers the property to a third party in a taxable transaction.

> *Example:* Don and Debbie were recently divorced. Debbie owns raw land with a value of $100,000 and a basis of $10,000. Pursuant to the divorce instrument, Debbie transfers the raw land to Don for $100,000 cash. Because the transfer is incident to a divorce, Debbie does not recognize her realized gain of $90,000. However, Don's basis in the raw land is $10,000, the basis of the transferred property in the hands of the transferor (Debbie) immediately before the transfer [Temp. Reg. §1.1041-1T Q&A 1, 10, and 11].

Tenant-Stockholder Gets Same Benefits as Homeowner

The owner of an apartment in a cooperative is called a tenant-stockholder. The tenant-stockholder receives a "share of stock" as evidence of ownership, along with a proprietary lease of a specific unit, from the cooperative housing corporation. Sales of the tenant-stockholder's share of stock are eligible for the §121 exclusion. The holding requirements apply to the stock ownership, and the use requirements apply to the unit which the taxpayer is entitled to occupy [§121(d)(3)].

Involuntary Conversions of the Principal Residence

When the destruction, theft, seizure, requisition, or condemnation of the principal residence occurs, the taxpayer may use the §1033 rollover-of-gain rules after applying the $250,000/$500,000 MFJ §121 exclusion rules. The holding and use by the taxpayer of the converted property is tacked to the new property [§121(d)(5)].

A Sale of a Remainder Interest Is Eligible for this Exclusion

Occasionally homeowners will sell or transfer their principal residence but retain the right to possess the home until death (an interesting estate planning devise). This right of possession is called a "remainder interest," which can be sold, but the purchaser of a remainder interest can only maintain possession as long as the grantor of the remainder interest is alive. At the election of the taxpayer, the gain from the sale or exchange of the remainder interest (but no other type of interest) in a principal residence may use the $250,000/$500,000 MFJ exclusion, unless the sale is to a related party [as defined both by §267(b) and §707(b)], which includes both lineal decedents and over 50% owned corporations and partnerships [§121(d)(8)].

TAX PLANNING: Property can be held in a grantor-type trust [Rev. Rul. 95-84].

The Transition Rules—Opting To Use Prior Law after May 7, 1997

Even though the $250,000/$500,000 MFJ exclusion rules apply to home sales after May 6, 1997, homeowners may elect to apply prior law in these situations:

- when taxpayers **sold** their home **before** August 5, 1997; or
- when taxpayers **sold** their home **after** August 5, 1997, subject to a binding contract in effect on August 5, 1997; or
- when taxpayers **bought** a replacement residence on or **before** August 5, 1997, outright (or pursuant to a binding contract) and the prior-law rollover provisions would have applied [Act §314(d)].

COMMENT: Generally, the transition rules would be used for those taxpayers with gains in excess of $250,000/$500,000 MFJ. If the taxpayer elects to apply prior law, the ownership and use periods of the old home is added to the ownership and use periods of the new home.

Can We Rent the House During the Five-Year Period?

As long as the home is owned and used as a principal residence two out of the five years prior to the sale date, it retains its personal residence character and does not switch to a taxable rental property [§121(a)].

The problem with renting a personal residence. When a personal residence is listed for sale in a "down" or "slow" market, it is common to rent the house until it is sold. Under prior law, care was needed to ensure that the property retained its personal residence character and didn't convert to a rental (which wasn't eligible to use either the prior rollover provision or the prior exclusion rule). New §121 provides a definitive period of time, three out of five years, the home can be rented before it converts into a rental ineligible to use the $250,000/$500,000 MFJ exclusion rule.

TAX PLANNING TIP: This "tax loophole" allows homeowners to rent the house for up to three years while striving to sell it. Many taxpayers will be tempted to rent their residence and wait for someone to agree to their asking price instead of accepting a lower counteroffer. Additionally, there is no need to keep the property listed during the rental period, as was required under prior law [*Clapham v. Comm.*, 63TC 505 (1975)].

The Question Then Comes Up: Can We Depreciate the Home While It Is Being Rented?

Yes. We can depreciate a personal residence! In *Bolaris v. Comm.* (81 TC 840 (1983); 776 F2d 1428 (9th Cir 1985), the Tax Court held as proper the taxpayer's deduction of rental expenses and "residential" depreciation. The court held that a residence that qualifies for the principal residence provisions may also qualify as property held for the production of income and therefore allowed Bolaris to not only take depreciation but also to defer the ensuing (prior law) gain [see also *Grant v. Comm.*, 84 TC 809 (1985)].

WARNING: Depreciation taken after May 6, 1997, must be recaptured!

Any gain attributable to depreciation taken after May 6, 1997, with respect to the prior rental or business use of the principal residence must be recognized in the year of the sale (but interestingly not an exchange) [§121(d)(5)].

Note: Therefore, 65.753% of the 1997 depreciation must be recaptured. The period of May 7 through December 31, 1997, is 240 days.

> *Example:* Kim purchased a home on May 7, 1997, and sold it for a $30,000 profit on December 31, 1999. The accumulated depreciation on her office-in-home was $700. Therefore, $29,300 gain is excluded by §121 but the $700 must be reported on Form 4797 as depreciation recapture income, assuming the home office was converted back to personal use no later than December 31, 1997.

Home Used for Both Personal and Business Purposes

Some of the gain is taxable. When part of a property is used by the taxpayer as the principal residence and part of that same residence is used for other (business or investment) purposes, such as a basement rental, the basis and sales price must be divided between the home and the business property. Only the home gain may use the $250,000/$500,000 MFJ exclusion rule, and the business gain is taxable in the year of the sale [previous §1.1034-1(c)(3)(ii)].

What Happens If the Residence Is Sold for a Loss?

The loss is nondeductible. Even though the Internal Revenue Code requires the immediate recognition of all gain on the sale or exchange of property, including the gain on the sale of a personal residence that is not excluded, any loss on the sale of a personal residence is nondeductible as it is considered a "personal, living, or family" expense. The Internal Revenue Service takes a "heads I win, tails you lose" position to the treatment of a gain or loss on the sale of a personal residence [§1001(c); §262; §1.262-1(b)(4); §1.165-9(a)].

Converting a home into a rental makes the loss deductible. Can a personal residence be converted to a business use prior to the sale date and thereby convert the non-deductible personal loss to a deductible one? Theoretically, it is possible but difficult [§165(c)(1) and (2)]. It is not known what is the length of time before a personal residence becomes a rental, although the antithesis is known—if the home is rented for less than three of the last five years before sale, §121 considers it a personal residence.

One argument for the taxpayer: how a residence is being used *at the date of sale* is of major importance in determining whether property is business or personal [*U.S. v. Winthrop*, (5 Cir. 1969), 417 F2d 905]. Therefore, the taxpayer must prove that the property is a rental when sold, and the conversion is not done for tax purposes only [*William C. Horrmann*, 17 TC 903 (1951)].

What would be the basis in a conversion? The adjusted basis for determining loss for property converted from personal use is the *smaller* of (1) the fair market value of the property at the time of conversion, or (2) the adjusted basis of the property at the time of conversion. Therefore, the loss created prior to conversion is still not deductible, either at the time of conversion or at the time of sale [§1.165-9(b)(2)].

Here Is the Biggest Tax Problem Created by the New §121! How Much Land Can Be Sold with the Personal Residence?

Gain on land considered part of a personal residence can be excluded, but gain on land considered investment property held for appreciation, or business property held for profit, is taxable and may not use the exclusion provisions. How much land can be included when selling the principal residence?

> *Example:* Farmer McDonald, in contemplating a move to Florida, decides to sell his farm. He receives $1,200,000 for the house, farm buildings, outbuildings, and 500 acres, resulting in a $500,000 MFJ gain. Can he exclude the entire $500,000 MFJ gain? *We know he will try!*

> *Answer:* No. Only the gain of the personal residence and the land associated with the residence can be excluded. Unofficially, the IRS, in farm communities, considers one acre to be associated with the home unless the taxpayer proves that more than one acre is not used for income-producing purposes.

COMMENT: This is an appraiser's relief act! With up to $500,000 MFJ of gain at stake, valuation of multiuse property, such as farm property, will become one of the largest tax litigation areas in the near future!

It is a "facts and circumstances" test. An allocation has to be made when "property is used by the taxpayer as his principal residence and part is used for other (investment or business) purposes" [previous §1.1034-1(c)(3)(i); §1.1034-1(c)(3)(ii)].

So, how many acres? Prior IRS rulings and court cases have consistently allowed five to ten acres as part of the residence [*Estate of F. Russell Campbell,* 23 TCM (CCH) 508 (1964); Rev. Rul. 76-541, 1976-2 CB 246; *Bogley v. Comm.,* 263 F2d 746 (4th Cir 1959)].

PLANNING TIP: How much land qualifies when a personal residence is located on a 20-acre "ranchette"? Probably all 20 acres, as the entire acreage is being used for personal purposes.

On farm property, 43½ out of 51 acres allowed by Tax Court! [*J. D. Schlicher*, 1/97; Dec. 51, 839(M)]. An individual who sold his principal residence and purchased 51 acres of property of which he used only 7½ acres for his horse business was allowed to defer recognition of gain from the sale of the old residence in an amount equal to the cost of the new property that was *allocable* to the remaining 43½ acres. The taxpayer's use of the 43½ acres was "significant and constituted residential use." The taxpayer "credibly testified" that he moved to the property because he "appreciates nature, admires unobstructed views of the countryside, enjoys living in open spaces where he can hike and ride horseback, and desires to live the rest of his life there." The boarded horses were kept in the business portion of the property, and the taxpayer *neither* trained horses on the premises nor gave riding lessons there. Furthermore, he was *not* holding the property for investment.

The Calculations Required before Excluding the Gain

Once it has been determined that the sale of the home qualifies for the exclusion-of-gain provisions, the homeowner must calculate the realized gain and the taxable gain (if any). This requires a review of the gain (or loss) computation.

Amount of gain on sale of a personal residence. To calculate the amount of gain on a sale of a personal residence, subtract the selling costs and the adjusted basis from the sales price. The only time depreciation expense is subtracted is when part or all of the house has been used both for business and personal use (e.g., a deductible office-in-home converted back to personal use).

Gain or Loss Computation

Sales price			+ _____
Less:	Selling expenses		− _____
Equals:	Amount realized		= _____
Less:	Adjusted basis		
	Original cost (or basis)	+ _____	
	Plus: Improvements	+ _____	
	Less: Accumulated depreciation	− _____	
	Equals: Total adjusted basis		− _____
Less:	Deferred gain from prior home sale		− _____
GAIN REALIZED ON SALE			= _____

Selling price. The selling price of the personal residence is calculated using the following formula: the total consideration received, including the amount of cash received, any liabilities the purchaser either assumed or took the property subject to and the fair market value of *any* other property received [§1001(b)].

PLANNING TIP: In most residential sales, the selling price will agree with the Uniform Settlement Statement, HUD Form 1.

Personal property sold is not to be included in the sales price. The selling price of the residence does not include amounts received for personal property (e.g., refrigerator, stove, drapes, furniture, etc.). If personal property is acquired along with the real property, the personal property is assumed to have a zero value [previous §1034(c)(2); §1.1034-1(c)(3)(i)].

Selling expenses. The selling expenses associated with the sale of a personal residence include the expenses incurred to consummate the sales transaction, such as the real estate commission and title insurance. Selling expenses reduce the selling price to arrive at the *amount realized,* sometimes called *net sales price* [previous §1.1034-1(b)(4)].

> **PLANNING TIP:** These expenses are usually listed on the Uniform Settlement Statement, HUD Form 1.

Selling expenses do not include repairs or improvements to prepare the property for sale. They also do not include most prorated items, such as fire insurance, real estate taxes, advances on utilities, interest, and the like, even though these items may be "hidden" in the sales price.

Amount realized. The amount realized is the total selling price less the selling expenses.

Construction, reconstruction and capital improvements. Because capital expenditures are not depreciable on a personal residence, these costs are only recovered at the time of sale.

Examples of qualifying improvements include streets, sidewalks, many special improvement taxes, driveways, garages, basement recreation rooms, appliances, air conditioners, and the like.

Repairs and maintenance expenditures. These *nondeductible* items include painting and papering and other disbursements to keep the home in efficient operation.

> **PLANNING TIP:** Most taxpayers want expenditures made on a personal residence to be capital improvements and not repairs. Repairs on a personal residence are never deductible whereas capital improvements reduce the gain on a subsequent taxable sale.

> **PLANNING TIP:** To make use of any "conditions-of-sale" expenditures, (a) characterize the repairs as improvements, when possible; (b) anticipate the required

repairs prior to the signing of the contract-to-sell; or (c) have the seller give a price reduction allowance.

How long do we need to keep our receipts? Three to six years! Because improvements directly affect the gain of the primary residence sold, it is very important to retain property records and receipts of the improvements of the home owned. If the taxpayer does not retain the receipts on improvements of the home he or she purchases, the IRS may disallow this decrease in gain and therefore increase the taxable gain if the exclusion provision is not available to the homeowner.

COMMENT: State income tax law may dictate a longer retention period.

Cost means cost: "Sweat equity" is not allowed! When any part of the new residence is acquired other than by purchase, the value of the part so acquired may *not* be included in the cost of the new residence.

CONCLUSION

For some taxpayers, reporting home gain has become substantially simpler. For married taxpayers who sell their principal residence for less than $500,000, none of the capital gain is taxable as long as they have not excluded another home gain within two years and no depreciation has been taken (e.g., because they deducted an office-in-home) after May 7, 1997. But if homes are sold with gains in excess of $500,000, married taxpayers will, for the first time, **have** to pay taxes upon the sale of their principal residence, even if they purchase a more expensive home within two years. This chapter has guided you through the labyrinth created by the new sale of home tax rules.

CHAPTER

4

Installment Sales

A seller selling on the installment plan may report gain on the installment method. When a taxpayer sells property and some or all of the payments for sale are to be paid in the future (commonly by a purchase-money mortgage, a trust deed or a contract-for-deed), the transaction generally is called an *installment sale*. When installment reporting of the gain is available, it is an important financing and tax planning option for both the seller and the buyer.

>   **Example:** Jeanette sells investment property for $80,000. She had purchased this property four years ago for $50,000. She agrees to receive a 5% down payment ($4,000) in the year of the sale and a note for the other 95% to be received over ten years commencing the year after the sale.

Why use the installment method? To spread the taxable gain over multiple years. A taxpayer who sells real property on the installment plan is allowed to have a pro-rata portion of the total gain taxed *as each installment is actually received. Thus, the seller, instead of paying the whole tax in the year of the sale, may spread the tax on the gain over the period during which the installments are received* [§453].

Without the installment method of reporting gain, a taxpayer would be required to report the entire capital gain in the year of the sale, a severe tax hardship that in most cases would make owner financing economically unfeasible. If the tax cannot be deferred, the sale has created a cash liability against a paper profit.

>   **Example (continued):** In Jeanette's situation, she would owe the following:

Total gain:	$30,000
Times: 20% tax bracket	× 20% (assuming maximum capital gains rate)
Equals: Estimated tax due	$ 6,000

As can be easily seen, Jeanette must come up with an additional $2,000 just to cover her estimated tax bill! Congress realized that this was an undue tax burden and therefore permitted the installment method of accounting for tax due, allowing Barb to spread the estimated $6,000 tax due over the ten-year contract period.

WHAT ARE SOME OTHER IMPORTANT REASONS FOR USING, OR NOT USING, AN INSTALLMENT SALE?

1. Taking payments over a period of time may facilitate the sale and improve the price.
2. Deferment of a long-term capital gain may provide the opportunity to offset it with a loss realized in the future.
3. If a profitable sale takes place in the year of a business-operating loss, the investor may want to push the gain ahead and have it taxed at the taxpayer's regular tax rate rather than use it to reduce the amount of current loss that can be carried back against a previous year's ordinary income.
4. Taxpayers can save tax by deferring gain to years when their tax bracket may be lower.
5. Postponing the taxability of gain offers a speculation on the possible reduction in the rate of tax on capital gain. If the rate seems likely to be increased, the gain can be accelerated by sale of the installment obligation.

WHAT IS AN INSTALLMENT SALE?

One Payment in Year after Sale Occurs

An installment sale is the disposition of property when the seller receives at least one payment *after* the close of the taxable year in which the sale or exchange occurs [§453(b)]. Generally, when the seller finances the buyer's purchase, the transaction is an installment sale.

Installment reporting is mandatory (unless a proper "election out," discussed later in this chapter, is made). Installment reporting requires the taxpayer to report the gain from the sale over the period of time the proceeds will be received. Installment reporting is permitted regardless of the amount of payments received in the year, even if the entire purchase price is received in a lump sum in a year subsequent to the sale year [§15A.4453-1(b)]. The IRS rule that two or more installments payable in two or more taxable years were required to qualify any sale for installment reporting has been eliminated.

There is no limitation on initial payment. There is no minimum or maximum amount of payment required to be received in the year of the sale. Taxpayers may receive more than 30% down and still use the installment method of reporting. The requirement that "no more than 30% of the gross selling price may be received in the tax year of the sale" was eliminated in 1980.

May losses be reported on the installment basis? No, the entire loss must be reported in the year of the sale [Rev. Rul. 70-430, 1970-2 CB 51].

Is there an IRS tax form that is used when reporting installment gains? Yes, Form 6252 is used.

HOW MUCH OF EACH INSTALLMENT PAYMENT IS RECOGNIZED FOR TAX PURPOSES?

Gain Is Proportioned to Each Future Installment Payment

The following four formulas, in combination, explain how to calculate the gain to be reported on the taxpayer's tax return for each year the taxpayer receives principal payments on an installment obligation.

1. *Formula to Calculate Realized Gain*
    Selling price   + $ _____
    Less: Adjusted basis*   − _____
    Selling expenses   − _____
    Equals: Gross profit to be realized [§15A.453-1(b)(2)(v)]   = _____

2. *Formula to Calculate Contract Price*
    Selling price   + $ _____
    Less: Assumed mortgage†   − _____
    Equals: Contract price   = _____

3. *Formula to Calculate Gross Profit Percentage*
    Realized gain ($_____) ÷ Contract price ($_____) = %_____ Gross profit percentage
          (Formula 1)   (Formula 2)

4. *Formula to Calculate Recognized Gain Each Year*
    Gross profit percentage (_____%) × Payments ($_____) = $_____
               (Formula 3)   (Principal only) (Recognized gain)

---

* Ordinary income depreciation recapture is added to basis.
† This cannot exceed the adjusted basis.

Basis recovery. Under the installment method, generally only a portion of the amount received each year is taxable; the remainder is a tax-free recovery of basis. How is this done?

Gross profit percentage determines the amount that is annually taxable. The amount of each installment payment treated as income is determined by multiplying the payment received by a fraction called the *gross profit percentage*. The gross profit percentage is the ratio of the gross profit realized to the total contract price [§453(c); §15A.453-1(b)(2)(i)].

> ***Example (continued):*** Jeanette will receive a total of $80,000 over a ten-year period. Of this $80,000, $50,000 is a return of her capital investment and $30,000 is the gain she experiences on the sale. Therefore, every dollar that she receives involves ⅝ return of capital ($50,000 ÷ $80,000) and ⅜ gain ($30,000 ÷ $80,000).

Sales price	$80,000	(Contract price)
Less: Basis	–50,000	(⅝ of total contract price)
Equals: Total gain	$30,000	(⅜ of total contract price)

Therefore, Jeanette's pro-rata portion of the gain in the year of the sale and the subsequent tax are calculated as follows:

Principal payment received	$4,000	(Part of contract price)
Less: Basis	–2,500	(⅝ of $4,000 principal)
Gain reported in year of sale	1,500	(⅜ of $4,000 principal)
Times: 20% tax bracket	× .20	
Equals: Estimated tax due	$ 300	

Tax savings: The installment method of reporting gain results in reducing Jeanette's tax due from $6,000 to $300 in the year of the sale. Theoretically, the $6,000 tax bill is paid over the period of the contract (ten years). However, because we have a progressive tax system, and with proper tax planning, the estimated tax bill can be substantially decreased.

Five Basic Installment Sale Definitions

Before the gain to be recognized under the installment method of reporting can be calculated, the taxpayer must understand: (1) selling price, (2) selling expenses, (3) adjusted basis, (4) contract price, and (5) payments made by the buyer in the year of sale.

COMMENT: Luckily, some of these have been fully discussed previously in the book, so only a recapitulation is done here.

Selling price. Chapter 1 illustrates the formula for calculating the sales price when the selling or purchase price is not specifically stated or involves more than cash and/or the assumption of mortgages. The amount realized on an installment sale includes the amount of cash received plus the fair market value of any other property received and to be received. The amount of the mortgages on the property sold that the purchaser either assumes or takes subject to is also figured into the sales price. Commissions and other selling expenses paid or incurred by the seller do not reduce the selling price even though they do reduce net profit.

What happens if the note is reduced in the future? If the parties to an installment sale afterward agree to reduce the selling price, the gross profit percentage changes. The seller simply recalculates the gross profit ratio for the remaining payments and reports the now-correct remaining profit. The seller cannot amend any prior tax returns and file for a refund [§108(e)(5)].

How imputed interest affects selling price. Buyers and sellers may manipulate the tax consequences of an installment sale by varying the interest rate in seller-financed transactions. Previously this was done to convert ordinary interest income to long-term capital gain, but with the repeal of the capital gain deduction, this is no longer as large a tax issue. Nonetheless, it still is important as illustrated in the next planning tip.

PLANNING TIP: By decreasing the interest rate and increasing the sales price of depreciable property, the seller decreases the interest income and increases capital gain; the buyer normally will not care because all this does is decrease the interest expense and increase the depreciation expense. On the other hand, by increasing the interest rate and decreasing the sales price of property, the buyer increases the currently deductible interest expense; sellers won't care if they can offset this current interest income (e.g., with carryover net operating losses).

The IRS has, to a large extent, limited this tax plan with the imputed interest rules [§483] and the original issue discount rules [§1271-1274], by "imputing" an interest rate in the sales contract unless a statutorily set minimum rate of interest is expressed in the agreement.

> **Example:**   On May 21, 1998, D. J. Roberts sells a lot on Flathead Lake for $12,600. The contract provides for a down payment of $3,600 at the time of sale with the balance of $9,000 to be paid in three equal installments due yearly from the date of sale. The contract makes no provision for interest payments. Under §483, the total "unstated interest" under the contract is equal to the excess of the total payments over the total of the present values discounted at a 10% rate compounded semiannually. The present value of $9,000 discounted at 10% is $7,427.85. Therefore, the selling price is actually $11,027.85 ($3,600 + 7,427.85) and the unstated interest is $1,572.15. The interest ($1,572.15) will be taxed as ordinary income, not as a long-term gain.

PLANNING TIP: Care should be exercised by sellers to ensure that they do not generate excessive amounts of ordinary income because of unstated or imputed interest. Unstated interest is used to reduce the stated original sales price and, as noted before, the "selling price" is the amount used to determine the long-term gain.

What are selling expenses? Selling expenses are the expenses incurred to sell the property such as real estate brokerage fees, title insurance, transfer tax, recording fees and survey fees. Chapter 1 illustrates the selling expense computation.

What is "adjusted basis"? As explained in Chapter 1, the adjusted basis is the original cost (or basis) of the property plus the value of any improvements made on the property by the seller and minus accumulated depreciation and losses taken.

A new definition—what is total contract price? In most cases, the *total contract price* is equivalent to the amount that the seller will physically receive—cash and other property. The *total contract price* (not the *total selling price*) is important as it is used to determine the part of each installment payment to be included in income.

Example: Willy sells some land for $100,000 that he had purchased for $60,000 several years ago as an investment. There is a $20,000 mortgage on the property that the buyer assumes. Willy's gross profit percentage is calculated as follows:

Formula 2: Contract Price		*Formula 1: Realized Gain*	
Selling price	$100,000	Selling price	$100,000
Mortgage assumed	– 20,000	Basis of property	– 60,000
Equals: Contract price	$ 80,000	Equals: Gross profit	$ 40,000

Formula 3: Calculation of Gross Profit Percentage

$$\frac{\text{Realized gain (\$40,000)}}{\text{(Formula 1)}} \div \frac{\text{Contract price \$80,000}}{\text{(Formula 2)}} = \frac{50\%}{= \text{Gross profit percentage}}$$

In other words, Willy receives $80,000 (not $100,000) over the term of the contract. As $40,000 of the $80,000 to be received is gross profit, Willy's gross profit percentage is 50%; that is, 50% of each dollar received each year must be reported as capital gain. In this above example, Willy receives a $20,000 down payment in 1998 and collects the balance at $20,000 each year over the following three years. He will report taxable income (long-term gain) as follows:

1998	$20,000	×	50%	=	$10,000
1999	$20,000	×	50%	=	$10,000
2000	$20,000	×	50%	=	$10,000
2001	$20,000	×	50%	=	$10,000
Contract price =	$80,000				$40,000 = Gross profit

WHAT IS INCLUDED IN THE *"TOTAL PAYMENTS MADE BY BUYER IN YEAR OF SALE"*?

Payments made by the buyer in the year of sale include both cash and the fair market value of *any other property* received by the seller. All payments received by the seller on account of the sale during the year of sale are also included [§15A.453-1(b)(3)].

COMMENT: Strangely, it is more logical to first examine one item that is *not* to be included in the total payments made by the buyer before analyzing what is included. Therefore:

What is not included in the total payments made by the buyer in the year of sale?

Any notes between buyer and seller and any assumed mortgages are excluded from the buyer's total payments.

Mortgage liens are not considered a payment. The buyer's evidence of indebtedness, and the buyer's "assumptions of" mortgages and "taking property subject to" mortgages do not constitute payments made by the buyer in the year of the sale unless the evidence of indebtedness is payable on demand or readily tradeable or is secured by cash or cash equivalent (e.g., Treasury notes) [§453(f)(3); §453(f)(4); §15A.453-1(d)(3)(i)].

What happens when there is an excess of mortgage over basis?
As previously mentioned, mortgage liens are not included in the total contract price *unless they exceed the seller's adjusted basis.* When the assumed mortgage exceeds the seller's basis, the *excess* is considered an initial payment [§15A.453-1(b)(2)(iii)].

Example: On August 1, 1998, Lynn sells a lot in Phoenix for $100,000 that has an adjusted basis of $30,000 and on which she owes a mortgage balance of $40,000 (she refinanced it). Robin takes the property subject to the existing mortgage, paying $30,000 cash down, and agreeing to pay the remaining $30,000 in six equal annual installments, plus interest, starting December 31, 1998. The initial payments are calculated as follows:

Payments Made by Buyer in Year of Sale

Cash down payment	$30,000
Plus: Payment of any installment due during year of sale ($30,000 ÷ 6 years)	+ 5,000
Plus: Excess of mortgage assumed ($40,000) over seller's basis ($30,000)	+10,000
Equals: Total initial payments	$45,000

Note: Here the excess of the old mortgage over basis ($40,000 – $30,000 = $10,000) is treated the same as cash. The seller is treated as having received

$45,000 in the year of sale ($35,000 cash plus $10,000 excess mortgage over basis) and is taxed more gain than the physical cash on hand in the year of sale.

PLANNING TIP: Make sure that the excess of the existing mortgage over basis is added to the cash received when estimating the maximum amount of gain the seller is willing to include in taxable income. Use of a *wraparound mortgage* (to be discussed later) is one alternative to avoid this problem.

What happens to the gross profit percentage when the mortgage exceeds basis?

If the mortgage does exceed the seller's basis, only the basis is included in the total contract price and the gross profit will always be the same as the total contract price. The gross profit percentage will always be 100% and all payments received are to be included as income.

> **Example:** Willy sells some land for $100,000 that he had purchased for $60,000 several years ago as an investment. There is a $70,000 mortgage on the property, which the buyer assumes. Willy's gross profit percentage is:

Formula 2: Contract Price		*Formula 1: Realized Gain*	
Selling price	$100,000	Selling price	$100,000
Mortgage assumed*	− 60,000*	Basis of property	− 60,000
Equals: Contract price	$ 40,000	Equals: Gross profit	$ 40,000

*Not in excess of basis

In this case, Willy will receive $40,000 ($30,000 cash plus $10,000 excess of mortgage assumed over the seller's basis), which is the entire contract price.

> *Formula 3: Calculation of Gross Profit Percentage*
>
> Realized gain ($40,000) ÷ Contract price $40,000 = 100%
> (Formula 1)   ÷   (Formula 2)   = Gross profit percentage

Using a wraparound mortgage to avoid including in income the excess amount of mortgage over the seller's basis. As pointed out earlier, when mortgaged property is sold and the buyer either assumes or takes subject to the mortgage, the amount of the mortgage, to the extent it exceeds the seller's basis, is considered payment received by the seller in the year of sale.

PLANNING TIP: There is a way to arrange the sale that allows the seller to avoid reporting large amounts of the gain in the year of sale. With a *wraparound mortgage,* the buyer neither assumes nor takes subject to the mortgage, so the whole problem is neatly avoided. Following is a description of how this type of arrangement works:

The wraparound mortgage plan. Along with the down payment, the buyer gives the seller a mortgage *for the difference between the down payment and the selling price—* the total amount remaining to be paid. The wraparound mortgage payments should, of course, cover the seller's payments on the existing mortgage. The seller remains liable on any existing mortgages on the property, and no liability is transferred to the buyer. The wraparound mortgage can be deposited with an escrow agent, who collects the buyer's payments on the wraparound mortgage, makes the payments on the seller's mortgage and forwards the balance to the seller.

WARNING: The Internal Revenue Service has often attacked the wraparound method when it is used to "defer" the paying of taxes (such as in the above example). Their philosophy is that since the taxpayer has the money (because of the previous refinance) the taxpayer should have to pay the tax associated with the refinance at the time of sale. In all but the most blatant abuse cases the courts have overruled the IRS and have allowed the postponing of gain when the wraparound method is used [*Stonecrest Corp. v. Comm.,* 24 TC 659].

IRS regulations try to restrict "wraps." Even though the IRS has repeatedly lost its challenges to the use of wraparound mortgages in court, this does not discourage the IRS. In February 1981, the IRS issued regulations that treat the excess of mortgage over basis as a payment to the seller even when using the wraparound technique. In other words, whether the buyer legally assumes the mortgage or not, the IRS's position is that the buyer has assumed the mortgage (and therefore no wraparound mortgage exists) [§15A.453-1(b)(3)(ii)]. These proposed regulations have subsequently been overruled by the Tax Court, and the IRS has acquiesced to the decision [*Professional Equities, Inc.,* 89 TC 165, (1987); Acq. 1988-37 IRS 4].

PLANNING TIP: Even though the IRS agreed to the court decision without protest, it is also without enthusiasm, as the regulations dealing with wraparound mortgages have not been withdrawn or modified. In addition, it warns in the acquiescence that caution should be exercised in extending the application of the *Professional Equities, Inc.,* decision to any similar case unless the facts and circumstances are substantially the same (which is always a difficult standard). To avoid potential IRS penalties, conservative tax-planning advisors recommend that investors should disclose, by a Form 8275-R, that they are not abiding by the current regulations. This advice, of course, will also subject the tax return to an IRS audit!

PAYMENTS THAT MUST BE INCLUDED IN THE YEAR OF THE SALE

WARNING: Most taxpayers, and tax preparers, are stunned by the IRS's broad definition of the *first year total payments*. The importance of this calculation cannot be overemphasized as it determines the proper amount of income reported in the first and each subsequent tax year. Many tax practitioners simply subtract the assumed mortgage from the sales price to back into the amount of the total payments that must have been made in the year of the sale. This simplistic, though often accurate, calculation may leave out some rare "deemed" payments (e.g., some assumed mortgages do not qualify for this exclusion, such as no. 13 in the following list).

Payments made by the buyer in the year of sale (§15A.453-1(b)(3)). This list is followed by extensive examples.

1. Cash down payment or cash deposit, even if made in a year before the year of sale [Rev. Rul. 73-360]
2. Other cash, such as cash at closing
3. Option paid, even if received in a prior year, which is considered part of the down payment
4. Payment of any installment(s) due during year of sale (interest payments received on the installment note *are not reportable* here but are reportable as interest income)
5. Premature payments of a later year's installment
6. Fair market value of property (other than like-kind property) received from the buyer (e.g., boats, cars, etc.)
7. Notes or other evidence of indebtedness of *third* parties that are assigned to the seller as part of the consideration for the sale [§15A.453-1(b)(3)(i)]
8. Any obligation payable on demand [§453(f)(4)(A)].
9. Corporate or governmental bonds or other evidence of indebtedness issued by a corporation or governmental body either (a) with coupons attached or (b) in registered form unless taxpayer establishes that they are not readily marketable or (c) in any other form designed to render them readily tradeable in an established securities market [§15A.453-1(e)(1)]
10. Excess of mortgage assumed over seller's basis [§15A.453-1(b)(2)(ii)]
11. Cancellation of indebtedness owed by the seller to the purchaser
12. Selling expenses of seller paid by the purchaser in the year of sale, such as legal expenses
13. Charges accrued against the property and assumed by the purchaser (i.e., taxes, mortgage interest, and liens) which are paid by the purchaser in the year of sale and are directed to be paid out of the proceeds of the sale
14. When the taxpayer sells property to a creditor and the seller's indebtedness is canceled in consideration of the sale [§15A.453-1(b)(3)(I)]

15. Amounts paid by the buyer in discharging the mortgage if the buyer pays the seller's full mortgage in the year of sale instead of assuming it [*Ralph Sterling v. Ham,* (DC) 3 USTC 3 F. Supp. 386]

Commissions and other selling expenses paid or incurred by the seller do not reduce the payments made by the buyer in the year of the sale even though they do reduce the net profit.

What happens when the taxpayer sells an installment obligation? Instead of waiting to collect all or some of the buyer's obligations, the seller may choose to dispose of the debt instrument before maturity. When this is done, the gain or loss from disposing of the obligations must be reported in the year of the disposition. The gain or loss will be the difference between the seller's basis in the debt instruments and what is received for them. The seller's basis in the obligation is the unrecovered cost. If the seller disposes of the obligation other than by sale or exchange, the gain or loss is found by comparing the basis (unrecovered cost) with the fair market value at that time. The gain or loss retains its identity, that is, long-term, short-term, or ordinary income.

What happens when the buyer makes an earnest-money deposit and a subsequent down payment in different years?

Example: A contract for sale for $80,000 is signed in 1998 at which time Bob, the buyer, pays $10,000. The title is closed in 1999 at which time Bob pays another $15,000. Dennis, the seller, takes back a mortgage for $55,000.

Under these circumstances, the 1998 payment is treated as part of the payment in the year of sale (1999). It is not 1998 income. The seller has received $25,000 as the initial payment to be reported in 1999.

What happens when the buyer pays part of the purchase price in cash and the rest in securities and a promissory note?

Example: Bill pays $15,000 cash at closing and gives Sue securities (Microsoft stock) worth $10,000 and a note for $55,000. Sales price is $80,000 with no mortgage assumed.

Under these circumstances, the seller is treated as having received an initial payment of $25,000. This may cause a larger amount of the gain to be taxed in the first year then the seller has the cash to pay.

PLANNING TIP: Sue could take Bill's note for $65,000 secured in part by the pledge of the securities. This reduces the initial payment to $15,000.

What happens when the buyer makes a prepayment in the year of the sale?

> *Example:* An $80,000 sale occurs in 1998, and Cynthia, the buyer, pays $24,000 at the closing. Ken, the seller, takes back a mortgage for the balance, with the first $10,000 payment due on January 1, 1999. In December 1998, Cynthia prepays the first installment, which includes $1,000 principal amortization (she is trying to deduct $9,000 of interest!).

> *Note:* Unhappily, Ken must add the $1,000 to his other payment ($24,000) received in 1998, the year of the sale. In addition, the $9,000 interest also becomes taxable in 1998. This, of course, increases the tax he must pay.

PLANNING TIP: Make sure that the contract for sale and mortgage bond or note have a provision barring prepayment of installments. If the buyer tries to prepay, return the money.

May the seller have the buyer pay the full sales price in cash into an escrow and still use the installment method of reporting? No. With this type of escrow arrangement, the seller is no longer counting on the buyer for the remaining payments but the escrow itself [§15A.453-1(b)(5)(Example 8); §15A.453-1(b)(3)(I); Rev. Rul. 73-451, 1973-2 CB 158].

PLANNING TIP: In one rare case the sellers were given the option not to accept the buyer's offer to pay the full purchase price in cash and instead insist on installment payments using an escrow arrangement, solely to reduce the tax consequences of the sale. Evidently, the court decided that a substantial restriction of the seller's right to receive the sale proceeds existed [*E. Grannemann*, DC Mo. 87-1 USTC ¶9287, 649 F. Supp. 949].

Substitution of an escrow arrangement as security following an installment sale also ends the seller's ability to report the sale on the installment plan [Rev. Rul. 77-294, 1977-2 CB 173].

The cancellation of an installment obligation. If the installment obligation is canceled or becomes unenforceable, the cancellation or lapse will be treated as a disposition of the obligation resulting in taxation of the gain at cancellation.

The bequest of an installment obligation to the obligor. The decedent seller's estate is deemed to have made a taxable disposition of an installment obligation in any case where the obligation is transferred by bequest to the obligor or in which the estate allows the obligation to become unenforceable.

Example: Derrick purchases investment property from his father for $100,000 on July 1, 1998, agreeing to pay $10,000 (plus interest) on each anniversary date for ten years. Three years later Derrick's father dies and in his will forgives Derrick's $70,000 installment obligation. The father's estate must include this cancellation of installment obligation as income, the same as if Derrick paid the estate the $70,000 in cash.

WHAT OTHER ITEM IS NOT TO BE INCLUDED IN THE INITIAL PAYMENTS?

Like-kind Exchange Property Received Is Not Considered a Payment, Is Not Considered in the Total Contract Price and Reduces the Gross Profit.

As mentioned previously, another item not to be included in the total payments made by the buyer in the year of the sale is any like-kind property. An investor of real estate can take simultaneous advantage of both the tax-free exchange provisions (discussed in Chapters 5 through 8) and the installment gain provisions. Like-kind property is not treated as a payment when it is received in an installment transaction if the exchange of property qualifies under the like-kind exchange rules. In addition, the contract price computation disregards the value of the like-kind property; the contract price consists solely of the sum of the money received in the year of sale, the fair market value of other property received and the face amount of the installment obligations. It also requires that the gross profit is reduced by the amount not recognized by reason of the tax-free exchange [§453(f)(6); Reg. §1.1031(k)-1(j)(2)].

Example: In 1998, Sylvia sells an apartment house with an adjusted basis of $400,000 for an investment condominium in Martha's Vineyard worth $200,000 and an installment obligation for $800,000, with $100,000 payable in the year of the sale and the balance payable in 1999.

Selling price:
Fair market value of like-kind property received	$ 200,000
Installment obligation	+ 800,000
Equals: Sales price	= $1,000,000

Formula 2: Contract Price		*Formula 1: Realized Gain*	
Selling price	$1,000,000	Selling price	$1,000,000
Less: Fair market value of LKE property	– 200,000	Less: Basis of property	– 400,000
		Less: LKE property	– 200,000
Equals: Contract price	$ 800,000	Equals: Gross profit	$ 400,000

Formula 3: Calculation of Gross Profit Percentage

$$\frac{\text{Realized gain (\$400,000)}}{\text{(Formula 1)}} \div \frac{\text{Contract price \$800,000}}{\text{(Formula 2)}} = \frac{50\%}{\text{Gross profit percentage}}$$

Formula 4: Calculation of Recognized Gain Each Year

1998 gain to be reported		
Initial payment	$100,000	
Times: Gross profit percentage	× _____ 50%	
Equals: 1998 gain		= $ 50,000
1999 gain to be reported		
Subsequent payments	$700,000	
Times: Gross profit percentage	× _____ 50%	
Equals: 1999 gain		= 350,000
TOTAL GAIN REPORTED ON INSTALLMENT BASIS		$400,000

The *basis* of the like-kind property received is determined as if the obligation had been satisfied at its face amount. Thus, the taxpayer's basis in the property transferred is first allocated to the like-kind property received (but not in excess of its fair market value) and any remaining basis will be used to determine the gross profit ratio [Rev. Rul. 65-155, 1965-1 CB 356].

> ***Example (continued):*** In the previous example, Sylvia's basis in the like-kind property received, the condominium, is zero.

DEPRECIATION RECAPTURE: PROBLEMS WITH INSTALLMENT SALES

Ordinary income depreciation recapture. When the property sold is a depreciable asset, part or all of the gain *may* be required to be "recaptured" as ordinary income (called Section 1231/1245 depreciation recapture) that is totally taxable in the year of the sale. The ordinary income depreciation recapture is fully recognized in the year of the sale even if no payments are received in that year [§453(i)].

Capital gain depreciation recapture. Additionally, any prior "straight-line depreciation" taken must be "recaptured" at a 25% capital gain rate. As was covered in Chapter 2, this type of prior depreciation taken (called Section 1231/1250 depreciation recapture) is subject to the higher 25% capital gain rate, not eligible for the 2% capital gain rate.

Amount of the "ordinary income" depreciation recapture. Luckily, §1245 "ordinary income" depreciation recapture is generally defined as *excess* depreciation, or that depreciation taken over what normally is calculated on the straight-line basis for the same period of time. Since most real property placed in service before 1981 and after 1986 may *only* be depreciated using the straight-line method, there generally is only capital gains depreciation recapture [§1250(b)(1)].

WARNING: If commercial real property was purchased between 1981 and 1987 *and* the property was depreciated using the accelerated depreciation method, a disaster occurs as the *entire* accumulated depreciation must be recaptured [§1245(a)(3)(A); §1250(c)]!

PLANNING TIP: If the depreciation recapture amount is burdensome, the seller should demand a cash payment at closing substantial enough to pay the projected tax liability on the increased gain created by the recapture. Ordinary income depreciation recapture must be included in current income, whether or not enough cash payments are received by the seller.

Any "ordinary income" depreciation deductions that are recaptured are added to the basis of the obligation, regardless of the amount of principal payment received in that year [§453(i)].

Example: This illustrates the dangers of "ordinary income" depreciation recapture. Mark sells property for $20,000 cash and a note of $80,000, payable in four equal annual installments of $20,000, each bearing an adequate interest rate. Mark's adjusted basis is $30,000, with another $30,000 of ordinary income depreciation recapture (that must be fully recognized in the year of the sale).

Formula 2: Contract Price		*Formula 1: Realized Gain*	
Selling price:	$100,000	Selling price:	$100,000
Mortgage assumed:	– 0	Basis of property	– 60,000*
Equals: Contract price:	$100,000	Equals: Gross profit:	$ 40,000

*Ordinary income depreciation recapture of $30,000 is added to $30,000 basis.

Formula 3: Calculation of Gross Profit Percentage

Realized gain ($40,000)	÷	Contract price $100,000	=	40%
(Formula 1)	÷	(Formula 2)	=	Gross profit

Formula 4: Calculation of Recognized Gain Each Year

Gross profit percentage (40%)	×	Payments $20,000	=	$8,000
(Formula 3)		(Principal only)	=	(Recognized gain)

Total Gain To Be Reported in Year of sale:

Depreciation recapture (ordinary income)	$30,000
Installment gain (capital or §1231/§1250 depreciation recapture gain)	+ $ 8,000
Total gain to be reported in year of sale*	= $38,000

*Therefore, even though Mark received only $20,000 cash in the year of the sale, Mark is required to report a total gain of $38,000, of which $30,000 is ordinary income. The character of the other $8,000 of gain depends on whether the property is a capital asset or business (§1231) property.

Any depreciation deductions that are recaptured are added to the basis of the obligation. This happens regardless of the amount of principal payment received in that year [§453(i)].

ELECTING OUT OF THE INSTALLMENT METHOD IS OPTIONAL

The taxpayer may elect to report the entire gain in the tax year the sale occurs. When electing to report the entire gain in the year of the sale, the taxpayer must state on the appropriate tax form (Schedule D or Form 4797) "I elect out of the installment method" in addition to reporting *all* the gain. This election generally must be made on or before the due date (including extensions) for filing the taxpayer's return for the year of sale [§453(d)(1); §15A.453-1(d)(3)].

PLANNING TIP: Why accelerate reporting gain by electing out?

1. The seller may have another capital loss that can absorb this capital gain. Electing out of the installment reporting makes instant use of the loss and may reduce the current year's tax to zero.
2. The seller may have an expiring net operating loss.
3. This election is also recommended if the seller's tax rates are anticipated to increase, either by congressional action or if the seller anticipates escalating into a higher tax bracket.

WARNING: This election often "flags" a return for a future IRS audit!

A late election is normally not permitted. Unless the IRS District Director determines that the taxpayer has a good cause for failing to make the election on time, late elections are not allowed [§15A.453-1(d)(3)].

A change of mind after election is also normally not permitted. A valid election out of the installment method cannot be revoked without IRS permission [§15A.453-1(d)(4)].

PLANNING TIP: An election out can be especially damaging when, in a subsequent audit, the IRS redetermines income or expenses that now could be offset by the installment gain! The IRS says, "Tough bounce"—you should have done it correctly in the first place (as if they knew)!

WHO CANNOT USE THE INSTALLMENT METHOD?

Dealers, Certain Related Party Sales and Stock Sales

Sales of property by a real estate dealer [§453(b)(2)], certain sales of depreciable property to a controlled entity [§453(g)(1)(A)], sales or exchanges of marketable stock and securities [§453(k)(2)], and sales or exchanges between spouses [§1041] do not qualify for the installment method.

Tax planning for real estate dealers. A dealer is a taxpayer who buys real estate to sell it. An investor is a taxpayer who purchases real property for appreciation or income. Therefore, a real estate agent who treats his or her own property as an investment will normally not be a dealer to property he or she personally holds and may use the installment method on that property. Terminology is very important for this determination.

Sales of time-shares and residential lots *may* **be entitled to use the installment method.** The installment method is permitted for certain dealer-type sales to individuals of (1) time-share rights to use, or time-share ownership interest in, residential real property for not more than six weeks, (2) rights to use specified campgrounds for recreational purposes, and (3) residential lots, but only if the taxpayer (or related person) is not making any improvements to the lots [§453(i)(2)(B)].

The price to pay is interest on the deferred tax. In the case of sales of time-shares and residential lots, installment reporting is permitted only if the dealer elects to pay interest on the tax deferred by the use of the installment method. The interest rate is approximately the current federal rate; the interest amount is based on the tax that would have been paid in the year of sale without the installment method and is calculated from the date of sale to the date the payments are received. Even though it is added to the tax due, it is deductible by the dealer as an interest deduction [§453(i)(3)].

RESALE BY A RELATED BUYER—INSTALLMENT SALES

The Two-Year Rule

When the initial seller sells property to a related person on the installment method and the related person disposes of the property (for example, a sale for cash or by gift or exchange), generally within two years of the original sale, the initial seller will have to recognize the gain that would otherwise be deferred rather than continuing the installment reporting [§453(e)].

WARNING: This prevents one individual from selling property to a family member on the installment plan (and deferring the tax liability) and the family member then reselling the same property for cash. In essence, the related party is treated as the initial seller's agent when making a second disposition.

COMMENT: This does not prohibit installment sales between related parties. It only becomes applicable when the related party purchaser subsequently sells the property.

Who are related parties? Related parties include spouses, children, grandchildren, parents, grantor-fiduciary relationships and fiduciary-beneficiary relationship for trusts, corporations (if 50% or more of the value of the stock is owned directly or indirectly by such person), and partners in proportion to their share in the partnership interest [§453(f)(1)].

Example: Ty owns a condominium that has a fair market value of $300,000 and a tax basis of $100,000. On July 1, 1995, Ty sells the condominium to his son, Laird, for $300,000. Laird pays his father a cash down payment of $5,000 and gives him a note to pay the balance in ten annual installments of $29,500 each (plus interest), beginning September 1, 1996. On July 2, 1995, Laird sells the condominium for $300,000 cash.

Under the above resale rule, Ty is treated as receiving $300,000 from the installment sale in 1995. Ty must report all $200,000 gain from the sale on his 1996 income tax return even though he only received $5,000 in cash!

If Laird waits more than two years (July 2, 1997) after the initial installment sale, the resale rule will not apply to Ty.

Exceptions to the resale rule. These include a second disposition resulting after the death of the seller or related purchaser, certain involuntary conversions, or establishing to IRS satisfaction that one of the resale's principal purposes was not to avoid paying federal income tax [§453(e)(6), (7)].

RELATED PARTY SALES—SALES OF DEPRECIABLE PROPERTY

Penalty Is Conversion to Ordinary Income

When a sale of depreciable property is between specified related persons, the entire gain may be recharacterized as ordinary income [§1239], and when that happens the installment reporting is not permitted [§453(g)(1)(A)]. The seller must treat all payments to be received as received in the year of the sale. This prevents a sale to a related person, who starts depreciating the stepped-up full "fair-market-value" basis without a simultaneous reporting of income by the related seller [§453(g)(l)(B)(i)].

Who is a related party? In this case, the definition of related parties is generally (1) a taxpayer and a partnership or corporation in which the taxpayer has 50% ownership, (2) two or more partnerships in which the same persons own more than 50% of the capital or profits, and (3) a taxpayer and any trust in which such taxpayer (or spouse) is a beneficiary [§1239(b)].

Exception. A sale of depreciable property to a related person *may* use the installment method *if* the seller can establish to the satisfaction of the IRS that tax avoidance was not one of the principal purposes of the sale or that the seller did not derive any significant tax deferral benefits from the sale [§453(g)(2)].

SUMMARY

As the foregoing discussion illustrates, the installment method of reporting gains on real property sales provide an excellent mechanism for minimizing the tax costs. Figure 4.1 is a worksheet for calculating the gain of an installment sale. Again, a word of caution. The taxpayer must be careful to meet all the requirements for reporting under this method.

FIGURE 4.1 Installment Sale Worksheet

INSTALLMENT SALE WORKSHEET

PART I - GROSS PROFIT

1. Sales Price	$	
2. Adjusted basis of property sold	-	
3. Selling expenses	-	
4. Gross profit	....	$

PART II - CONTRACT PRICE

5. Cash downpayment	$	
6. Fair market value of other property received	+	
7. Face value of purchaser's note	+	
8. Excess of assumed mortgage over adjusted basis	+	
9. Contract price	....	$

PART III - GROSS PROFIT PERCENTAGE

10. Divide item 4 by item 9	%

PART IV - PAYMENTS RECEIVED IN YEAR OF SALE

11. Cash downpayment	$	
12. Fair market value of other property received	+	
13. Principal payments on purchaser's note	+	
14. Excess of assumed mortgage over adjusted basis	+	
15. Other payments	+	
16. Payments in year of sale	....	$

PART V - RECOGNIZED GAIN (YEAR OF SALE)

17. Payments received in year of sale (item 16)	$	
18. Gross profit percentage (item 10)	x	
19. Recognized gain	....	$

PART VI - RECOGNIZED GAIN (IN YEARS AFTER SALE)

20. Principal payments received in year	$	
21. Gross profit percentage (item 10)	x	
22. Recognized gain	....	$

hoven - copyright - 1997

5

Tax-Free Exchanges

INTRODUCTION AND HISTORY OF INTERNAL REVENUE CODE SECTION 1031

The advice "Don't put off until tomorrow what can be done today" was not written by a taxpayer. Advance tax planning often properly postpones until tomorrow what normally is considered today's tax liability. Better yet, with proper tax planning, taxpayers can take it (i.e., the tax due) with them when they die. Internal Revenue Code Section 1031 (commonly know as the like-kind exchange or LKE section) contains one method a taxpayer may use to defer today's tax bill. Although taxes on an exchange are actually deferred, not eliminated, the popular expression of "tax-free exchanges" is used in this chapter.

A gain occurring (i.e., realized) on a tax-free exchange will not be taxable (i.e., recognized) in the year of the sale. This is an exception to the taxing theory that all gains are taxable at the time of sale or receipt of money. As far back as 1921, the United States Congress felt, when it passed the like-kind exchange rules, it was inappropriate to recognize "theoretical" gains and losses. It concluded that evaluating all the different "horse trades" would not justify the potential revenues to be derived from them.

As a matter of fact, Congress stated in a later report that if taxpayers would be required to report all their theoretical gains and theoretical losses each year, the taxpayers' claims for theoretical losses "would probably exceed any profits" [H.R. Dept., No. 704, Revenue Act of 1934, 73rd Congress, 2d Sess.]. It is comforting to note that the taxpayers of the 1930s and the taxpayers of the 1990s are, in all probability, remarkably similar.

COMMENT: Throughout Chapters 5 through 8, which discuss the subject of like-kind exchanges, the materials and planning tips are backed up by court cases and tax citations. Why?

After reading the LKE chapters, share the information with your tax professional—do it as a favor to you! Do not assume he or she knows all there is to know about like-kind exchanges. Tax law is too complicated today. These chapters are written so you will discover new tax-planning ideas. Let the tax professional implement those ideas, some of which you will suggest after reading these chapters. These tax alternatives will be dramatic to you, the taxpayer.

What is an exchange? §1031 states: "No gain or loss shall be recognized on the exchange of property held for productive use in a trade or business or for investment if such property is exchanged solely for property of like kind which is to be held either for productive use in a trade or business or for investment" [§1031(a)(1)].

The tax difference between a sale and an exchange. Before discussing the ramifications of a tax-free exchange, let us examine the taxation of a taxable sale.

> *Example:* Debbie owns an apartment house (on leased land) in Atlanta, which she purchased for $100,000 on November 1, 1985. The property has a fair market value of $225,000 on December 1, 1998. She has taken 19-year straight-line depreciation since her purchase 13 years ago (75%, or $75,000 accumulated depreciation). She wants to sell it and buy an apartment house in Depoe Bay, Oregon, that has a fair market value of $225,000. Her taxable gain when she sells the Atlanta property would be $200,000 calculated as follows:

Sales price		$225,000
Less: Adjusted basis		
Original cost	$100,000	
Minus: Depreciation	– 75,000	
Adjusted basis		– 25,000
Equals: Long-term capital gain		$200,000

Tax due on sale: Debbie's tax, assuming she is in the 28% tax bracket, would be $43,750:

	Gain		Gain Rate		Tax Due
Depreciation recapture	$ 75,000	×	25%	=	$18,750
Long-term capital gain	$125,000	×	20%	=	$25,000
Total gain	$200,000				
Estimated tax					$43,750

A sale and subsequent reinvestment of proceeds, instead of an exchange, will result in Debbie's paying $43,750 of unnecessary taxes.

COMMENT: To be more dramatic, add your state tax rate to the federal rates and then calculate the tax savings!

Example (continued): **No tax due on exchange.** Instead of selling, Debbie trades her $225,000 Atlanta apartment house for the $225,000 Depoe Bay apartment. None of the $200,000 gain is recognized on Debbie's tax return; she would file a Form 8824 and report a §1031 tax-free exchange, *thereby currently saving $43,750 in federal taxes.* (This like-kind calculation is easy, as is demonstrated later in this chapter.)

Is the only benefit saving taxes? No! By exchanging, an investor not only saves taxes but can use this increase of their net worth, or "equity," to acquire additional real estate. Coupled with the magic of leverage, this creates dramatic results.

Example: Using an 80% loan-to-value ratio, Debbie can use the $43,750 tax savings as a 20% down payment to acquire $218,750 of additional real estate ($43,750 ÷ .20)! Of course, she would have to structure the acquisition as part of the above exchange.

May part of the gain be taxable in an exchange? Yes. Part of the total gain may be tax-free and part may be taxable. The allocation of the gain occurs when the investor receives unlike property (called "boot," which is defined more precisely later). As is discussed more thoroughly in Chapter 8, the like-kind exchange gain calculation may be summarized as follows;

Boot received		_____
Less: Exchange expense	−	_____
Plus: Net mortgage relief	+	_____
Equals: Gain recognized	=	_____ *

_____

*But not greater than the realized gain

PLANNING TIP: This means the exchanger is taxable to the lower of the gain or the boot! Don't worry—all the above terms are clearly explained in Chapter 8.

May a loss be recognized in an exchange? No. Loss from an exchange will not be recognized even though money or nonqualifying property is received [§1031(a)(1)]. Most investors generally try to avoid using an exchange when they are involved in a transaction that would create a tax loss if the property were sold (how to avoid an exchange is discussed later in this chapter).

What happens to the loss? The loss not recognized increases the basis of the property acquired. Hence, the loss is not eliminated, but instead is carried forward to the new property received in the exchange.

> ***Example:*** Helen exchanges her office building, which has an adjusted basis of $85,000, for an apartment building, which has a fair market value of $80,000. The $5,000 loss is a nonrecognizable loss affecting only the basis of the property received. Helen's new basis will be $85,000; that is, the fair market value of the new building plus the unrecognized loss ($80,000 + $5,000).

When a loss is recognized on a partially tax-free exchange because unlike property is transferred, the recognized loss decreases the basis of the property received. The sales price of the unlike property given is the fair market value of the property received.

CALCULATION AND REPORTING REQUIREMENTS

It is easy to calculate the gain that is tax-free! Most investors and tax preparers consider the like-kind exchange computation to be very difficult. After looking at the IRS's Like-Kind Exchanges Form 8824 (found as Figure 5.7 at the end of this chapter) and our worksheet (Figure 5.1), you may be inclined to confirm this misconception. Don't let the forms scare you. Nothing could be further from the truth.

This beginning like-kind exchange chapter allows the first-time exchanger to quickly hand-calculate the gain on *any* proposed exchange *without understanding the LKE requirements*. The calculation is the easy part. The hard part is answering the question, "Do we have a qualified like-kind exchange?" The subsequent chapters answer that question.

The examples in this chapter relate to the worksheet in Figure 5.1 and are labeled with line numbers from the worksheet where appropriate. So how easy is this calculation? Let's start from the beginning.

How exchanges are really put together.

Step 1: Negotiate the equity. Exchanges start with negotiating the financial economics, not the tax ramifications, of the transaction; that is, "Is the net equity in your property the same as the net equity in my property? If not, how much are you (or I) willing to add to the pot?"

Step 2: Determine the basis and expenses. Once the above equity figures are determined, only two other pieces of information are needed for the exchange calculation:

1. The exchange expenses
2. The adjusted basis of the property given

FIGURE 5.1   Sample Section 1031 Tax-Free Exchange Worksheet

Copyright - Hoven - 1998

**SECTION 1031
TAX-FREE
EXCHANGE
OF PROPERTY**

——————

WORKSHEET

exchangez.pm5

EQUITY CALCULATION Form 5.1		Gives		Receives	
E1. FMV of property exchanged E1		+$		+$	
E2. Less: Existing mortgages E2		−		−	
Equity (1 - 2).		=		=	
E3. Net boot added (plug figure**). E3		+	*	+	#
(**Difference between equities)					
Do equities balance? (1-2+3) [G = R]		=		=	
<u>Detail of boot added</u>					
Cash E4		*		#	
Other financing. E5		*		#	
Other unlike property E6		*		#	

PART I - BASIS OF PROPERTY GIVEN   EXCHANGE DATE:

Description:

1. Cost (or other basis) of property given - [date purchased:_____] 1	+$	
2. Depreciation allowed or allowable 2	−	
3. Adjusted basis of property given up (line 1 less line 2). 3	$	

PART II - REALIZED GAIN (LOSS)

4. FMV of qualifying property received (line E1-R) (Form 8824, Line 16) 4	$	
5. Cash received (line E4-R) 5	+$	**Proof: A Simple Check**
6. Less: Cash given (line E4-G) 6	−	FMV of Prop Exch:_____
7. Fair market value of other (boot) received (line E6-R) 7	+	Less: Adj. Basis: _____
8. Less: FMV of boot (other than cash) given up (line E6-G) 8	−	Gain (if sold): _____
9. Net liabilities assumed by other party (line E2-G less E2-R but not < zero) 9	+	
10. Exchange expenses. 10	−	
11.Total consideration received (add lines 5 thru 10) (Form 8824, Line 15) 11	$	
LESS:		
12. Adjusted basis of qualified property given up (line 3) 12	+$	
13. Net liabilities assumed by taxpayer (line E2-R less E2-G but not < zero) 13	+	
14. Total consideration given (add lines 12 and 13). . . . . . (Form 8824, Line 18) . . . 14	$	
15. GAIN REALIZED ON EXCHANGE (line 4 plus line 11 less line 14) (Form 8824, Line 19) 15	$	

PART III - RECOGNIZED TAXABLE GAIN

CASH AND BOOT

16. Cash and boot (other than cash) received (add lines 5 and 7) . . 16	+$	
17. Cash and boot (other than cash) given (add lines 6 and 8) 17	−	
18. Exchange expenses (line 10). 18	−	
19. Net cash and boot (other than cash) received (line 16 less lines 17 and 18) . . . 19	+/−$	

MORTGAGE RELIEF

20. Mortgage on property given (line E2-G) 20	+$	
21. Mortgage assumed on property received (line E2-R) 21	−	
22. Net mortgage relief (line 20 less line 21; if less than zero, enter zero). 22	+$	
23 GAIN RECOGNIZED (line 22 +/- line 19; line 23 cannot exceed) . . . .(Form 8824, Line 20). . . 23 line 15; if less than zero, enter zero	$	

PART IV - BASIS OF NEW PROPERTY   Description:

24. Adjusted basis of LKE property given (line 3). 24	+$	**Proof: A Simple Check**
25. Adjusted basis of boot property given (Form 8824, Line 13). . . . 25	+	FMV of Prop Rec'd: _____
26. Cash given (line 6). 26	+	Less: Gain *not* taxed:_____
27. Mortgage assumed on property received (line E2-R) 27	+	New Basis: _____
28. Subtotal (Plus) 28	+$	
29. Cash received (line 5) 29	+$	
30 Mortgage on property given (line E2-G). 30	+	
31. Subtotal (Minus) 31	−$	
32. Plus: Gain recognized on exchange (line 23) 32	+	
33. Plus: Gain recognized on boot given (line 8 less line 25 but not < zero) (Form 8824, Line 14) 33	+	
34. Less: Loss recognized on boot given (line 25 less line 8 but not < zero) (Form 8824, Line 14) 34	−	
35. Exchange expenses (line 10) 35	+	
36. BASIS OF ALL NEW PROPERTY RECEIVED (28,31,32,33,34,35) 36		
37. BASIS OF BOOT PROPERTY RECEIVED (FMV) (LINE 7) 37		
38. BASIS OF LIKE-KIND PROPERTY RECEIVED (LINE 36 LESS LINE 37) (Form 8824, Line 25) . 38	$	

Step 3: Calculate. We use an uncomplicated one-page worksheet to "number-crunch" the data accumulated, shown in Figure 5.1. This worksheet is divided into five parts:

1. Equity Calculation
2. Part I—Basis of Property Conveyed
3. Part II—Total Realized Gain (or Loss)
4. Part III—Recognized (Taxable) Gain
5. Part IV—Basis of New Property

It is easy. We only need to accumulate financial data for the equity calculation and Part I. Once we have these figures, the calculation (Parts II, III and IV) is a simple arithmetic exercise. This sum determines the nontaxable portion of the gain. So let's see the worksheet in action.

1. Equity calculation: As mentioned previously, the first step in preparing a transaction as an exchange is to ascertain the equities of each party and calculate which party, if any, must contribute additional assets. This is done by what has become known in the exchange field as the "napkin test" (FMV means fair market value):

			Gives	Receives
E1.	FMV of property exchanged	E1	_____	_____
E2.	Less: Existing mortgages	E2	_____	_____
	Equity (1–2)		=======	=======
E3.	Net boot added (Plug figure**)		_____ *	_____ #
	(**Difference between equities)		_____	_____
	Do equities balance? (1–2 + 3)[G = R]		======= =	=======
	Detail of boot added		_____ *	_____ #
E4.	Cash	E4	_____	_____
E5.	Other financing	E5	_____	_____
E6.	Other unlike property (B1)	E6	_____	_____

A "sweetener" or "evener" may be required to balance the exchange economically (line E3).

Example: Remember Debbie with her $225,000 apartment in Atlanta in the previous example? Let's prove that her exchange is fully tax-free.

Equity Calculation

		Debbie Gives Atlanta	and Receives Depoe Bay
E1. FMV of property exchanged	E1	$225,000	$225,000
E2. Less: Existing mortgages	E2	0	0
Equity (1–2)		$225,000	$225,000

COMMENT: Our "napkin test" determines that both equities are equal.

		Debbie Gives Atlanta	and Receives Depoe Bay
E3. Net boot added (Plug figure**)	E3	0*	0#
(**Difference between equities)			
Do equities balance? (1 – 2 + 3) [G = R]		$225,000 =	$225,000
Detail of boot added		*	#
E4. Cash	E4	0	0
E5. Other financing	E5	0	0
E6. Other unlike property (B1)	E6	0	0

2. Part I—Compute the adjusted basis of the property being given: The formula for calculating the adjusted basis of the property to be conveyed for an exchange is the same calculation as used in a sale. Each line in this formula is thoroughly discussed in Chapter 1.

Exchange Adjusted Basis Computation

Adjusted basis:

Original cost (or basis)	+	$
Plus: Purchase expenses	+	
Plus: Improvements	+	
Equals: Cost (or other basis) of property given	= 1	
Less: Accumulated depreciation	– 2	
TOTAL ADJUSTED BASIS (1 – 2):	= 3	$

COMMENT: The numbers in front of the dollar amounts refer to the Like-Kind Exchanges worksheet.

Example (continued):

Exchange Adjusted Basis Computation

Adjusted basis:

Original cost (or basis)	+		$100,000
Equals: Cost (or other basis) of property given	=	1	$100,000
Less: Accumulated depreciation	−	2	$ 75,000
TOTAL ADJUSTED BASIS (1 − 2):	=	3	$ 25,000

PLANNING TIP: This is all the information needed to calculate the tax ramifications of a tax-free exchange! To see all these numbers together, see the worksheet in Figure 5.2 and the IRS Form 8824 in Figure 5.3.

COMMENT: Debbie participates in a like-kind exchange and finds that the entire $200,000 gain is nontaxable, thereby saving her $43,750 of current taxes.

PLANNING TIP: *The basic rule in exchanges: Be the party who trades equal or up—both in fair market value and in debt—and don't receive any boot [§1031(a)(1)]!* This is what Debbie did in the previous example. This basic rule will be fully explained in the following chapter on requirements of like-kind exchanges, but next we will demonstrate what happens if the parties *do not* trade equal or up.

LET'S TRY A MUCH MORE COMPLICATED EXAMPLE

This is an actual example from the IRS's regulations [§1.1031(d)-2 (Example 2)]. Even though you may not understand the "why," you will be able to calculate the tax-free and taxable portion of the gain with the same ease as in the previous example.

Example: Donna owns an apartment with an adjusted basis of $100,000 and a fair market value of $220,000, but subject to a mortgage of $80,000. Edward wants to trade to Donna his apartment, which has an adjusted basis of $175,000 and a fair market value of $250,000, but is subject to a mortgage of $150,000. To even equity, Edward agrees to pay Donna $40,000 in cash [§1.1031(d)-2 (Example 2)]. Closing is January 1, 1998.

FIGURE 5.2 Sample Section 1031 Tax-Free Exchange Worksheet Completed

Copyright - Hoven - 1998

**SECTION 1031
TAX-FREE
EXCHANGE
OF PROPERTY**

WORKSHEET

exchange2.pm5

EQUITY CALCULATION Form 5.2	DEBBIE Gives	DEPOE BAY Receives
E1. FMV of property exchanged E1	+$225,000	+$ 225,000
E2. Less: Existing mortgages E2	−	−
Equity (1 - 2)...............	= 225,000	= 225,000
E3. Net boot added (plug figure**)...... E3	+ *	+ #
(**Difference between equities)		
Do equities balance? (1-2+3) [G = R]	= 225,000	= 225,000
Detail of boot added		
Cash E4	*	#
Other financing.............. E5	*	#
Other unlike property E6	*	#

PART I - BASIS OF PROPERTY GIVEN   EXCHANGE DATE:12/1/98

Description: DEBBIE'S ATLANTA APARTMENT

1. Cost (or other basis) of property given - [date purchased: 11/1/85] 1	+$100,000
2. Depreciation allowed or allowable 2	− 75,000
3. Adjusted basis of property given up (line 1 less line 2)........................ 3	$ 25,000

PART II - REALIZED GAIN (LOSS)

4. FMV of qualifying property received (line E1-R) (Form 8824, Line 16) 4	$ 225,000
5. Cash received (line E4-R) 5	+$
6. Less: Cash given (line E4-G) 6	−
7. Fair market value of other (boot) received (line E6-R) 7	+
8. Less: FMV of boot (other than cash) given up (line E6-G) 8	−
9. Net liabilities assumed by other party (line E2-G less E2-R but not < zero) 9	+
10. Exchange expenses................................10	−
11.Total consideration received (add lines 5 thru 10) (Form 8824, Line 15) 11	$
LESS:	
12. Adjusted basis of qualified property given up (line 3) 12	+$ 25,000
13. Net liabilities assumed by taxpayer (line E2-R less E2-G but not < zero) 13	+
14. Total consideration given (add lines 12 and 13)...... (Form 8824, Line 18) ... 14	$ 25,000
15. GAIN REALIZED ON EXCHANGE (line 4 plus line 11 less line 14) (Form 8824, Line 19) 15	$ 200,000

Proof: A Simple Check
FMV of Prop Exch:225,000
Less: Adj. Basis: 25,000
Gain (if sold):   200,000

PART III - RECOGNIZED TAXABLE GAIN

CASH AND BOOT

16. Cash and boot (other than cash) received (add lines 5 and 7) .. 16	+$
17. Cash and boot (other than cash) given (add lines 6 and 8) 17	−
18. Exchange expenses (line 10)......................... 18	−
19. Net cash and boot (other than cash) received (line 16 less lines 17 and 18) ... 19	+/−$ -0-

MORTGAGE RELIEF

20. Mortgage on property given (line E2-G) ....,..... 20	+$
21. Mortgage assumed on property received (line E2-R) 21	−
22. Net mortgage relief (line 20 less line 21; if less than zero, enter zero)......... 22	+$ -0-
23 GAIN RECOGNIZED (line 22 +/- line 19; line 23 cannot exceed) ....(Form 8824, Line 20)... 23	$ -0-
line 15; if less than zero, enter zero	

PART IV - BASIS OF NEW PROPERTY   Description: DEPOT BAY PROPERTY

24. Adjusted basis of LKE property given (line 3)............... 24	+$ 25,000
25. Adjusted basis of boot property given (Form 8824, Line 13).... 25	+
26. Cash given (line 6)................................. 26	+
27. Mortgage assumed on property received (line E2-R) 27	+
28. Subtotal (Plus) 28	+$ 25,000
29. Cash received (line 5) 29	+$
30 Mortgage on property given (line E2-G)................... 30	+
31. Subtotal (Minus) 31	−$
32. Plus: Gain recognized on exchange (line 23) 32	+
33. Plus: Gain recognized on boot given (line 8 less line 25 but not < zero) Form 8824, Line 14) 33	+
34. Less: Loss recognized on boot given (line 25 less line 8 but not < zero) Form 8824, Line 14) 34	−
35. Exchange expenses (line 10) 35	+
36. BASIS OF ALL NEW PROPERTY RECEIVED (28,31,32,33,34,35) 36	25,000
37. BASIS OF BOOT PROPERTY RECEIVED (FMV) (LINE 7) 37	
38. BASIS OF LIKE-KIND PROPERTY RECEIVED (LINE 36 LESS LINE 37) (Form 8824, Line 25) . 38	$ 25,000

Proof: A Simple Check
FMV of Prop Rec'd: 225,000
Less: Gain *not* taxed:200,000
New Basis: 25,000

FIGURE 5.3   Sample IRS Form 8824

Form **8824**	**Like–Kind Exchanges**	OMB No. 1545–1190
	(and nonrecognition of gain from conflict–of–interest sales)	**19**
Department of the Treasury Internal Revenue Service	▶ See separate instructions. ▶ Attach to your tax return. ▶ **Use a separate form for each like–kind exchange.**	Attachment Sequence No. **49**

Name(s) shown on tax return	Identifying number

Part I   Information on the Like–Kind Exchange

Note: If the property described on line 1 or line 2 is real property located outside the United States, indicate the country.

1 Description of like–kind property given up ▶ DEBBIE'S ATLANTA APARTMENT

2 Description of like–kind property received ▶ DEPOT BAY PROPERTY

3	Date like–kind property given up was originally acquired (month, day, year)	**3**	11/01/85
4	Date you actually transferred your property to other party (month, day, year).	**4**	12/01/98
5	Date the like–kind property you received was identified (month, day, year). See instructions	**5**	12/01/98
6	Date you actually received the like–kind property from other party (month, day, year)	**6**	12/01/98

7 Was the exchange made with a related party? If "Yes," complete Part II. If "No," go to Part III. See instructions.
  a ☐ Yes, in this tax year   b ☐ Yes, in a prior tax year   c ☒ No.

Part II   Related Party Exchange Information

8 Name of related party	Related party's identifying number
Address (no., street, and apt., room, or suite no.)	
City or town, state, and ZIP code	Relationship to you

9 During this tax year (and before the date that is 2 years after the last transfer of property that was part of the exchange), did the related party sell or dispose of the like–kind property received from you in the exchange? . . . . ☐ **Yes** ☐ **No**

10 During this tax year (and before the date that is 2 years after the last transfer of property that was part of the exchange), did you sell or dispose of the like–kind property you received? . . . . ☐ **Yes** ☐ **No**

If both lines 9 and 10 are "No" and this is the year of the exchange, go to Part III. If either line 9 or line 10 is "Yes," the deferred gain or (loss) from line 24 **must** be reported on your return this tax year, **unless** one of the exceptions on line 11 applies. See **Related Party Exchanges** in the instructions.

11 If one of the exceptions below applies to the disposition, check the applicable box:
  a ☐ The disposition was after the death of either of the related parties.
  b ☐ The disposition was an involuntary conversion, and the threat of conversion occurred after the exchange.
  c ☐ You can establish to the satisfaction of the IRS that neither the exchange nor the disposition had tax avoidance as its principal purpose. If this box is checked, attach an explanation. See instructions.

Part III   Realized Gain or (Loss), Recognized Gain, and Basis of Like–Kind Property Received

Caution: If you transferred **and** received (a) more than one group of like–kind properties, or (b) cash or other (not like–kind) property, see instructions under **Multi–Asset Exchanges.**

Note: Complete lines 12 through 14 ONLY if you gave up property that was not like–kind. Otherwise, go to line 15.

12	Fair market value (FMV) of other property given up	**12**		
13	Adjusted basis of other property given up	**13**		
14	Gain or (loss) recognized on other property given up. Subtract line 13 from line 12. Report the gain or (loss) in the same manner as if the exchange had been a sale	**14**		
15	Cash received, FMV of other property received, plus net liabilities assumed by other party, reduced (but not below zero) by any exchange expenses you incurred. See instructions	**15**		
16	FMV of like–kind property you received	**16**	225,000	
17	Add lines 15 and 16	**17**	225,000	
18	Adjusted basis of like–kind property you gave up, net amounts paid to other party, plus any exchange expenses **not** used on line 15. See instructions	**18**	25,000	
19	**Realized gain or (loss).** Subtract line 18 from line 17	**19**	200,000	
20	Enter the smaller of line 15 or line 19, but not less than zero	**20**	0	
21	Ordinary income under recapture rules. Enter here and on Form 4797, line 17. See instructions	**21**	0	
22	Subtract line 21 from line 20. If zero or less, enter –0–. If more than zero, enter here and on Schedule D or Form 4797, unless the installment method applies. See instructions	**22**	0	
23	**Recognized gain.** Add lines 21 and 22	**23**	0	
24	Deferred gain or (loss). Subtract line 23 from line 19. If a related party exchange, see instructions	**24**	200,000	
25	**Basis of like–kind property received.** Subtract line 15 from the sum of lines 18 and 23	**25**	25,000	

For Paperwork Reduction Act Notice, see separate instructions.   Form **8824** (1996)

Equity Calculation

		Donna Gives *Donna's Apt*	and Receives *Edward's Apt*
E1. FMV of property exchanged	E1	$220,000	$250,000
E2. Less: Existing mortgages	E2	− 80,000	−150,000
Equity (1 − 2)		$140,000	$100,000

COMMENT: Our "napkin test" determines that Donna has $40,000 more equity, and Edward needs to "sweeten the deal" by the difference between the two equities.

E3. Net boot added (Plug figure**)	E3	0*	$ 40,000#
(**Difference between equities)			
Do equities balance? (1 − 2 + 3) [G = R]		$140,000 =	$140,000
Detail of boot added		*	#
E4. Cash	E4	0	$ 40,000
E5. Other financing	E5	0	0
E6. Other unlike property (B1)	E6	0	0

Example (continued): Continuing with the example above, Donna's tax preparer informs us that she originally purchased the property for $228,583 on January 1, 1986, with $25,000 allocated to land and has accumulated $128,583 ($203,583 × 63.16%; see Chapter 10 for details) of depreciation during her twelve-year ownership. The exchange expenses are $5,000.

Exchange Adjusted Basis Computation

Adjusted basis:			
Original cost (or basis)	+		$220,000
Plus: Purchase expenses	+		8,853
Equals: Cost (or other basis) of property given	=	1	$228,583
Less: Accumulated depreciation	−	2	$128,583
TOTAL ADJUSTED BASIS (1 − 2):	=	3	$100,000

PLANNING TIP: This is all the information needed to calculate the tax ramifications of a tax-free exchange! To see all these numbers together, see the worksheet in Figure 5.4 and the IRS Form 8824 in Figure 5.5.

FIGURE 5.4 Sample Section 1031 Tax-Free Exchange Worksheet

Copyright - Hoven - 1998

SECTION 1031 TAX-FREE EXCHANGE OF PROPERTY

WORKSHEET

exchange4.pm5

EQUITY CALCULATION Form 5.4	DONNA Gives	EDWARD Receives
E1. FMV of property exchanged E1	+$ 220,000	+$ 250,000
E2. Less: Existing mortgages E2	− 80,000	− 150,000
Equity (1 - 2).	= 140,000	= 100,000
E3. Net boot added (plug figure**). E3	+ *	+ 40,000#
(**Difference between equities)		
Do equities balance? (1-2+3) [G = R]	= 140,000	= 140,000
Detail of boot added		
Cash E4	*	# 40,000
Other financing. E5	*	#
Other unlike property E6	*	#

PART I - BASIS OF PROPERTY GIVEN   EXCHANGE DATE:1/1/98

Description: DONNA'S APARTMENT

1. Cost (or other basis) of property given - [date purchased: 11/1/86] 1	+$ 228,583	
2. Depreciation allowed or allowable 2	− 128,583	
3. Adjusted basis of property given up (line 1 less line 2). 3	$	100,000

PART II - REALIZED GAIN (LOSS)

4. FMV of qualifying property received (line E1-R) (Form 8824, Line 16) 4	$ 250,000	
5. Cash received (line E4-R) 5	+$ 40,000	*Proof: A Simple Check*
6. Less: Cash given (line E4-G) 6	−	FMV of Prop Exch:220,000
7. Fair market value of other (boot) received (line E6-R) 7	+	Less: Adj. Basis: 105,000
8. Less: FMV of boot (other than cash) given up (line E6-G) 8	−	Gain (if sold): 115,000
9. Net liabilities assumed by other party (line E2-G less E2-R but not < zero) 9	+	
10. Exchange expenses. 10	− 5,000	
11.Total consideration received (add lines 5 thru 10) (Form 8824, Line 15) 11	$ 35,000	
LESS:		
12. Adjusted basis of qualified property given up (line 3) 12	+$ 100,000	
13. Net liabilities assumed by taxpayer (line E2-R less E2-G but not < zero) 13	+ 70,000	
14. Total consideration given (add lines 12 and 13). . . . . . (Form 8824, Line 18) . . 14	$ 170,000	
15. GAIN REALIZED ON EXCHANGE (line 4 plus line 11 less line 14) (Form 8824, Line 19) . . 15	$ 115,000	

PART III - RECOGNIZED TAXABLE GAIN

CASH AND BOOT

16. Cash and boot (other than cash) received (add lines 5 and 7) . . 16	+$ 40,000	
17. Cash and boot (other than cash) given (add lines 6 and 8) 17	−	
18. Exchange expenses (line 10). 18	− 5,000	
19. Net cash and boot (other than cash) received (line 16 less lines 17 and 18) . . . 19	+−$ 35,000	

MORTGAGE RELIEF

20. Mortgage on property given (line E2-G) 20	+$ 80,000	
21. Mortgage assumed on property received (line E2-R) 21	− 150,000	
22. Net mortgage relief (line 20 less line 21; if less than zero, enter zero). 22	+$ -0-	
23 GAIN RECOGNIZED (line 22 +/- line 19; line 23 cannot exceed) . . . .(Form 8824, Line 20). . . 23	$ 35,000	
line 15; if less than zero, enter zero		

PART IV - BASIS OF NEW PROPERTY   Description: EDWARD'S APARTMENT

24. Adjusted basis of LKE property given (line 3). 24	+$ 100,000	*Proof: A Simple Check*
25. Adjusted basis of boot property given (Form 8824, Line 13). . . . 25	+	FMV of Prop Rec'd: 250,000
26. Cash given (line 6). 26	+	Less: Gain *not* taxed: 80,000
27. Mortgage assumed on property received (line E2-R) 27	+ 150,000	New Basis: 170,000
28. Subtotal (Plus) 28	+$ 250,000	
29. Cash received (line 5) 29	+$ 40,000	
30 Mortgage on property given (line E2-G). 30	+ 80,000	
31. Subtotal (Minus) 31	−$ 120,000	
32. Plus: Gain recognized on exchange (line 23) 32	+ 35,000	
33. Plus: Gain recognized on boot given (line 8 less line 25 but not < zero) (Form 8824, Line 14) 33	+	
34. Less: Loss recognized on boot given (line 25 less line 8 but not < zero) (Form 8824, Line 14) 34	−	
35. Exchange expenses (line 10) 35	+ 5,000	
36. BASIS OF ALL NEW PROPERTY RECEIVED (28,31,32,33,34,35) 36		170,000
37. BASIS OF BOOT PROPERTY RECEIVED (FMV) (LINE 7) 37		
38. BASIS OF LIKE-KIND PROPERTY RECEIVED (LINE 36 LESS LINE 37) (Form 8824, Line 25) . 38	$ 170,000	

FIGURE 5.5 Sample IRS Form 8824

Form **8824**	**Like–Kind Exchanges**	OMB No. 1545–1190
	(and nonrecognition of gain from conflict–of–interest sales)	**19**
Department of the Treasury Internal Revenue Service	▶ See separate instructions. ▶ Attach to your tax return. ▶ Use a separate form for each like–kind exchange.	Attachment Sequence No. **49**
Name(s) shown on tax return		Identifying number

Part I   Information on the Like–Kind Exchange

Note: If the property described on line 1 or line 2 is real property located outside the United States, indicate the country.

1   Description of like–kind property given up ▶ DONNA'S APARTMENT

2   Description of like–kind property received ▶ EDWARD'S APARTMENT

3	Date like–kind property given up was originally acquired (month, day, year)	**3**	11/01/86
4	Date you actually transferred your property to other party (month, day, year)...................	**4**	1/01/98
5	Date the like–kind property you received was identified (month, day, year). See instructions......	**5**	1/01/98
6	Date you actually received the like–kind property from other party (month, day, year)	**6**	1/01/98

7   Was the exchange made with a related party? If "Yes," complete Part II. If "No," go to Part III. See instructions.
   a ☐ Yes, in this tax year   b ☐ Yes, in a prior tax year   c ☒ No.

Part II   Related Party Exchange Information

8 Name of related party	Related party's identifying number
Address (no., street, and apt., room, or suite no.)	
City or town, state, and ZIP code	Relationship to you

9   During this tax year (and before the date that is 2 years after the last transfer of property that was part of the exchange), did the related party sell or dispose of the like–kind property received from you in the exchange? .... ☐ **Yes** ☐ **No**

10   During this tax year (and before the date that is 2 years after the last transfer of property that was part of the exchange), did you sell or dispose of the like–kind property you received? .... ☐ **Yes** ☐ **No**

If both lines 9 and 10 are "No" and this is the year of the exchange, go to Part III. If either line 9 or line 10 is "Yes," the deferred gain or (loss) from line 24 **must** be reported on your return this tax year, **unless** one of the exceptions on line 11 applies. See **Related Party Exchanges** in the instructions.

11   If one of the exceptions below applies to the disposition, check the applicable box:
   a ☐   The disposition was after the death of either of the related parties.
   b ☐   The disposition was an involuntary conversion, and the threat of conversion occurred after the exchange.
   c ☐   You can establish to the satisfaction of the IRS that neither the exchange nor the disposition had tax avoidance as its principal purpose. If this box is checked, attach an explanation. See instructions.

Part III   Realized Gain or (Loss), Recognized Gain, and Basis of Like–Kind Property Received

Caution: If you transferred **and** received (a) more than one group of like–kind properties, or (b) cash or other (not like–kind) property, see instructions under **Multi-Asset Exchanges.**

Note: Complete lines 12 through 14 ONLY if you gave up property that was not like–kind. Otherwise, go to line 15.

12	Fair market value (FMV) of other property given up	**12**		
13	Adjusted basis of other property given up	**13**		
14	Gain or (loss) recognized on other property given up. Subtract line 13 from line 12. Report the gain or (loss) in the same manner as if the exchange had been a sale		**14**	
15	Cash received, FMV of other property received, plus net liabilities assumed by other party, reduced (but not below zero) by any exchange expenses you incurred. See instructions		**15**	35,000
16	FMV of like–kind property you received		**16**	250,000
17	Add lines 15 and 16		**17**	285,000
18	Adjusted basis of like–kind property you gave up, net amounts paid to other party, plus any exchange expenses **not** used on line 15. See instructions		**18**	170,000
19	Realized gain or (loss). Subtract line 18 from line 17		**19**	115,000
20	Enter the smaller of line 15 or line 19, but not less than zero		**20**	35,000
21	Ordinary income under recapture rules. Enter here and on Form 4797, line 17. See instructions................		**21**	0
22	Subtract line 21 from line 20. If zero or less, enter –0–. If more than zero, enter here and on Schedule D or Form 4797, unless the installment method applies. See instructions		**22**	35,000
23	**Recognized gain.** Add lines 21 and 22		**23**	35,000
24	Deferred gain or (loss). Subtract line 23 from line 19. If a related party exchange, see instructions		**24**	80,000
25	**Basis of like–kind property received.** Subtract line 15 from the sum of lines 18 and 23		**25**	170,000

For Paperwork Reduction Act Notice, see separate instructions.   Form **8824** (1996)

Note: Donna participates in a like-kind exchange and finds that $35,000 of her $115,000 gain is taxable. Can she avoid this gain? The answer to that question requires you to read the remaining like-kind exchange chapters!

COMMENT: Donna did not (1) "go equal or up" and (2) receive any boot as the LKE rules require for a fully tax-free exchange.

WARNING: There is no such thing as a tax-free "equity" exchange (e.g., I trade my $140,000 equity for your $140,000 equity) even though the equity calculation is exactly what we must calculate first before going to the exchange calculation. Once the equities are determined, we must ascertain the fair market values of all the properties, even the properties being exchanged tax-free, to calculate the realized gain or loss [Blatt, TC Memo 1994-64].

Figuring fair market value in an exchange is easy! Adding together the equity and assumed mortgages of each party equals the fair market value of the properties!

Example:

	Donna	Edward
Existing mortgage:	$ 80,000	$150,000
Plus: Equity	+140,000	+100,000
Equals: Fair market value	$220,000	$250,000

Let's try one more problem:

Example: What about the other party to the exchange—Edward? His tax preparer informs us that he originally purchased the property for $216,117 on January 1, 1991, with $30,000 allocated to land, and has accumulated $41,117 ($186.117 × 22.092%) of depreciation during his ownership. His exchange expenses were $4,500 [§1.1031(d)-2 (Example 2)]. Closing was January 1, 1998.

Equity Calculation

			Edward Gives Edward's Apt.		and Receives Donna's Apt.
E1.	FMV of property exchanged	E1	$220,000		$220,000
E2.	Less: Existing mortgages	E2	−150,000		− 80,000
	Equity (1 − 2)		$100,000		$140,000
E3.	Net boot added (Plug figure**)	E3	$ 40,000*		$ 0#
	(**Difference between equities)				
	Do equities balance? (1 − 2 + 3) [G = R]		$140,000	=	$140,000

Detail of boot added			*	#
E4. Cash	E4		$40,000	0
E5. Other financing	E5		0	0
E6. Other unlike property (B1)	E6		0	0

Exchange Adjusted Basis Computation

Adjusted basis:

Original cost (or basis)		+		$200,000
Plus: Purchase expenses		+		16,117
Plus: Improvements		+		
Equals: Cost (or other basis) of property given		=	1	$216,117
Less: Accumulated depreciation		–	2	$ 41,117
TOTAL ADJUSTED BASIS (1 – 2):		=	3	$175,000

PLANNING TIP: To see all these numbers together, see the worksheet in Figure 5.6 and the IRS Form 8824 in Figure 5.7.

NOTE: Edward participates in a like-kind exchange and finds that $25,500 of his $70,500 gain is taxable. Can he avoid this gain? Read on!

PLANNING TIP: *Isn't it easier than you first thought?* As can be seen, to calculate the taxable and non-taxable gain on an exchange, it is not necessary to know or understand any other terms or concepts, such as "what is *boot?*" "what do we do with *mortgage relief?*" and "what is the basis of the new property received?" To eliminate the gains for Donna or Edward, though, it is necessary to understand the minimum requirements for a tax-free exchange, *as are fully discussed in Chapter 8!*

§1031 IS MANDATORY

An exchange must be reported as an exchange. Section 1031 is not subject to election or waiver, and if all the exchange elements are present, the taxpayer must report the transaction as an exchange.

PLANNING TIP: However, §1031 and its associated nonrecognition of gain or loss can be intentionally avoided by evading one of the six exchange elements listed in Chapter 8 [Rev. Rul. 75-292, 1975-2 CB 333].

FIGURE 5.6   Sample Section 1031 Tax-Free Exchange of Property Worksheet

Copyright - Hoven - 1998

SECTION 1031 TAX-FREE EXCHANGE OF PROPERTY
——— WORKSHEET
exchange6.pm5

EQUITY CALCULATION	Form 5.6	EDWARD Gives	DONNA Receives
E1. FMV of property exchanged E1		+$ 250,000	+$ 220,000
E2. Less: Existing mortgages E2		− 150,000	− 80,000
Equity (1 - 2).		= 100,000	= 140,000
E3. Net boot added (plug figure**). E3		+ 40,000 *	+ #
(**Difference between equities)			
Do equities balance? (1-2+3) [G = R]		= 140,000	= 140,000
Detail of boot added			
Cash E4		* 40,000	#
Other financing. E5		*	#
Other unlike property E6		*	#

PART I - BASIS OF PROPERTY GIVEN   EXCHANGE DATE: 1/1/98

Description: EDWARD'S APARTMENT

1. Cost (or other basis) of property given - [date purchased: 1/1/91] 1	+$ 216,117	
2. Depreciation allowed or allowable 2	− 41,117	
3. Adjusted basis of property given up (line 1 less line 2). 3		$ 175,000

PART II - REALIZED GAIN (LOSS)

4. FMV of qualifying property received (line E1-R) (Form 8824, Line 16) 4		$ 220,000
5. Cash received (line E4-R) 5	+$	
6. Less: Cash given (line E4-G) 6	− 40,000	Proof: A Simple Check
7. Fair market value of other (boot) received (line E6-R) 7	+	FMV of Prop Exch:250,000
8. Less: FMV of boot (other than cash) given up (line E6-G) 8	−	Less: Adj. Basis: 179,500
9. Net liabilities assumed by other party (line E2-G less E2-R but not < zero) 9	+ 70,000	Gain (if sold): 70,500
10. Exchange expenses. 10	− 4,500	
11.Total consideration received (add lines 5 thru 10) (Form 8824, Line 15) 11		$ 25,500
LESS:		
12. Adjusted basis of qualified property given up (line 3) 12	+$ 175,000	
13. Net liabilities assumed by taxpayer (line E2-R less E2-G but not < zero) 13	+	
14. Total consideration given (add lines 12 and 13). . . . . . (Form 8824, Line 18) . . . 14		$ 175,000
15. GAIN REALIZED ON EXCHANGE (line 4 plus line 11 less line 14) (Form 8824, Line 19) 15		$ 70,500

PART III - RECOGNIZED TAXABLE GAIN

CASH AND BOOT

16. Cash and boot (other than cash) received (add lines 5 and 7) . . 16	+$	
17. Cash and boot (other than cash) given (add lines 6 and 8) 17	− 40,000	
18. Exchange expenses (line 10). 18	− 4,500	
19. Net cash and boot (other than cash) received (line 16 less lines 17 and 18) . . . 19	+/○$ 44,500	

MORTGAGE RELIEF

20. Mortgage on property given (line E2-G) 20	+$ 150,000	
21. Mortgage assumed on property received (line E2-R) 21	− 80,000	
22. Net mortgage relief (line 20 less line 21; if less than zero, enter zero). 22	+$ 70,000	
23 GAIN RECOGNIZED (line 22 +/- line 19; line 23 cannot exceed . . . . (Form 8824, Line 20). . . 23		$ 25,500
line 15; if less than zero, enter zero		

PART IV - BASIS OF NEW PROPERTY   Description: DONNA'S APARTMENT

24. Adjusted basis of LKE property given (line 3). 24	+$ 175,000	Proof: A Simple Check
25. Adjusted basis of boot property given (Form 8824, Line 13). . . . 25	+	FMV of Prop Rec'd: 220,000
26. Cash given (line 6). 26	+ 40,000	Less: Gain *not* taxed: 45,000
27. Mortgage assumed on property received (line E2-R) 27	+ 80,000	New Basis: 175,000
28. Subtotal (Plus) 28	+$ 295,000	
29. Cash received (line 5) 29	+$	
30 Mortgage on property given (line E2-G). 30	+ 150,000	
31. Subtotal (Minus) 31	−$ 150,000	
32. Plus: Gain recognized on exchange (line 23) 32	+ 25,500	
33. Plus: Gain recognized on boot given (line 8 less line 25 but not < zero) (Form 8824, Line 14) 33	+	
34. Less: Loss recognized on boot given (line 25 less line 8 but not < zero) (Form 8824, Line 14) 34	−	
35. Exchange expenses (line 10) 35	+ 4,500	
36. BASIS OF ALL NEW PROPERTY RECEIVED (28,31,32,33,34,35) 36		175,000
37. BASIS OF BOOT PROPERTY RECEIVED (FMV) (LINE 7) 37		
38. BASIS OF LIKE-KIND PROPERTY RECEIVED (LINE 36 LESS LINE 37) (Form 8824, Line 25) . 38		$ 175,000

FIGURE 5.7 Sample IRS Form 8824

Form **8824**	**Like–Kind Exchanges**	OMB No. 1545–1190
	(and nonrecognition of gain from conflict–of–interest sales)	**19**
Department of the Treasury Internal Revenue Service	▶ See separate instructions. ▶ Attach to your tax return. ▶ Use a separate form for each like–kind exchange.	Attachment Sequence No. **49**
Name(s) shown on tax return		Identifying number

Part I   Information on the Like–Kind Exchange

Note: If the property described on line 1 or line 2 is real property located outside the United States, indicate the country.

1 Description of like–kind property given up ▶ EDWARD'S APARTMENT

2 Description of like–kind property received ▶ DONNA'S APARTMENT

3	Date like–kind property given up was originally acquired (month, day, year)	**3**	1/01/91
4	Date you actually transferred your property to other party (month, day, year)	**4**	1/01/98
5	Date the like–kind property you received was identified (month, day, year). See instructions	**5**	1/01/98
6	Date you actually received the like–kind property from other party (month, day, year)	**6**	1/01/98

7 Was the exchange made with a related party? If "Yes," complete Part II. If "No," go to Part III. See instructions.

a ☐ Yes, in this tax year   b ☐ Yes, in a prior tax year   c ☒ No.

Part II   Related Party Exchange Information

8 Name of related party	Related party's Identifying number
Address (no., street, and apt., room, or suite no.)	
City or town, state, and ZIP code	Relationship to you

9 During this tax year (and before the date that is 2 years after the last transfer of property that was part of the exchange), did the related party sell or dispose of the like–kind property received from you in the exchange? .... ☐ Yes ☐ No

10 During this tax year (and before the date that is 2 years after the last transfer of property that was part of the exchange), did you sell or dispose of the like–kind property you received? .... ☐ Yes ☐ No

If both lines 9 and 10 are "No" and this is the year of the exchange, go to Part III. If either line 9 or line 10 is "Yes," the deferred gain or (loss) from line 24 **must** be reported on your return this tax year, **unless** one of the exceptions on line 11 applies. See **Related Party Exchanges** in the instructions.

11 If one of the exceptions below applies to the disposition, check the applicable box:

a ☐ The disposition was after the death of either of the related parties.

b ☐ The disposition was an involuntary conversion, and the threat of conversion occurred after the exchange.

c ☐ You can establish to the satisfaction of the IRS that neither the exchange nor the disposition had tax avoidance as its principal purpose. If this box is checked, attach an explanation. See instructions.

Part III   Realized Gain or (Loss), Recognized Gain, and Basis of Like–Kind Property Received

Caution: If you transferred **and** received **(a)** more than one group of like–kind properties, or **(b)** cash or other (not like–kind) property, see instructions under **Multi–Asset Exchanges.**

Note: Complete lines 12 through 14 ONLY if you gave up property that was not like–kind. Otherwise, go to line 15.

12	Fair market value (FMV) of other property given up	**12**		
13	Adjusted basis of other property given up	**13**		
14	Gain or (loss) recognized on other property given up. Subtract line 13 from line 12. Report the gain or (loss) in the same manner as if the exchange had been a sale		**14**	
15	Cash received, FMV of other property received, plus net liabilities assumed by other party, reduced (but not below zero) by any exchange expenses you incurred. See instructions		**15**	25,500
16	FMV of like–kind property you received		**16**	220,000
17	Add lines 15 and 16		**17**	245,500
18	Adjusted basis of like–kind property you gave up, net amounts paid to other party, plus any exchange expenses **not** used on line 15. See instructions		**18**	175,000
19	**Realized gain or (loss).** Subtract line 18 from line 17		**19**	70,500
20	Enter the smaller of line 15 or line 19, but not less than zero		**20**	25,500
21	Ordinary income under recapture rules. Enter here and on Form 4797, line 17. See instructions		**21**	0
22	Subtract line 21 from line 20. If zero or less, enter –0–. If more than zero, enter here and on Schedule D or Form 4797, unless the installment method applies. See instructions		**22**	25,500
23	**Recognized gain.** Add lines 21 and 22		**23**	25,500
24	Deferred gain or (loss). Subtract line 23 from line 19. If a related party exchange, see instructions		**24**	45,000
25	**Basis of like–kind property received.** Subtract line 15 from the sum of lines 18 and 23		**25**	175,000

For Paperwork Reduction Act Notice, see separate instructions.   Form **8824** (1996)

One-party exchanges common. An exchange may be taxable to one party and tax-free to the other; it need not be tax-free to both parties for §1031 to apply [Rev. Rul. 75-292, 1975-2 CB 333].

WHEN IS AN EXCHANGE NOT ADVISABLE?

Generally, real estate investors wish to avoid an exchange transaction in the following situations:

1. **When property could be sold for a loss.** This is because the loss on an exchange is not currently deductible, and the loss on a sale may be fully currently deductible as a §1231 ordinary business loss.
2. **When a taxable gain can be offset with other currently deductible losses that result in minimal tax due.** Exchanges generally cost more money to complete than sales transactions and, thus, current losses are normally more valuable than deferred losses.
3. **When liquidity is required.** This usually occurs at the time of retirement or for medical or other emergencies.
4. **When investors do not want any other property.** An example is when the individual wishes to discontinue managing the real estate and is tired of being a landlord.

Types of Simultaneous Exchanges

TWO PARTY EXCHANGES—A SWAP!

The two-party exchange (Figure 6.1) is the simplest to understand, but also the most difficult exchange to accomplish, because not only must both parties be willing to trade properties but the properties and equities must be of approximately the same value. In reality, this seldom happens.

MULTIPARTY OR THREE-LEGGED EXCHANGES

May a three-party exchange be arranged? What happens if one party in an exchange does not want any property owned by the other party but rather wants a third party's property? Exchanges involving three parties are about as common as two-party exchanges are rare, and a three-party exchange may turn a taxable sale into a nontaxable exchange.

Only one party need desire a tax-free exchange! Strange as it may sound, a multiparty exchange often involves only *one* party interested in an exchange, coupled with one buyer and one seller. Properly structured, the objectives of all parties can be accomplished in a multiparty or a three-legged exchange. The taxpayer, of course, is seeking to avoid recognition of gain in the disposition of the appreciated property.

Is a three-legged exchange a sham transaction? May the Internal Revenue Service pierce a multiparty or three-legged exchange on the grounds that it is being done for tax purposes only and therefore is a sham? *No,* according to *Alderson v. Comm.,* 317 F2d 790 (9th Cir. 1963) and many other subsequent cases; it is form over substance. The IRS also recognizes multiparty exchanges [Rev. Rul. 77-297, 1977-2 CB 304].

FIGURE 6.1 Two-Party Exchange

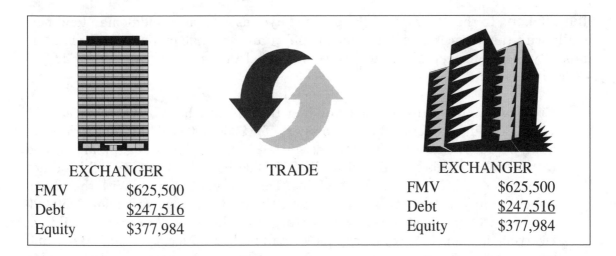

	EXCHANGER	TRADE		EXCHANGER
FMV	$625,500		FMV	$625,500
Debt	$247,516		Debt	$247,516
Equity	$377,984		Equity	$377,984

The *Starker III* case [*T. J. Starker v. U.S.*, 602 F2d 1341 (CA-9, 79-2 USTC ¶9451)] was considered an exchange for three reasons:

1. *Exchange, not sale, planned.* The taxpayer claimed that he intended from the outset of the transaction to receive nothing but like-kind property.
2. *Integrated plan exists.* All the recorded evidence indicated an exchange occurred.
3. *No actual or constructive receipt of cash.* The taxpayer never handled any cash in the course of the transaction.

THREE COMMON VARIATIONS OF A MULTIPARTY EXCHANGE

There are generally three varieties of multiparty exchanges. They are

1. the three-party "Alderson" exchange,
2. the three-party "Baird Publishing" exchange, and
3. the four-party "Accommodator" exchange.

All other types of exchanges are mere variations of these familiar types of exchanges.

Three-Party Alderson Exchange—Purchase First, Then Exchange

Why putting together an exchange is so difficult. What normally is found in exchange transactions is one seller who needs cash, one buyer with cash and our client, who wants an exchange, with none of the parties directly wanting what the other is offering.

The solution. In the Alderson exchange, the buyer assists, as a middleman (and normally with the services of a facilitator), to effect an exchange by first purchasing the property the exchanger wishes to receive by trade [*Alderson v. Comm.*, 317 F2d 790 (9th Cir. 1963)].

> ***Example:*** Moe owns a retail building that he purchased five years ago for $150,000. Curley offers to buy the property for $250,000 cash but Moe turns him down because he does not want to recognize $100,000 of capital gain. Moe would rather exchange his building for Joe's $250,000 diner. Joe wants to sell his diner for cash, not trade it for another building. The solution is simple. With the help of a facilitator, which is the usual practice, Curley buys Joe's diner for $250,000 cash. Now Curley exchanges his newly acquired diner for Moe's retail building. Everyone is happy! Curley owns Moe's retail building; Moe owns Joe's diner and because of the arranged exchange does not owe *any* taxes; and Joe has his $250,000 cash (less the taxes he must pay on his gain).

The mechanics. The Alderson exchange, illustrated in Figure 6.2, is consummated in two separate transactions, each of which should be accomplished by separate but dependent escrows, generally closed simultaneously with the help of the facilitator. First, in escrow 1 (the purchase/sale escrow), the buyer purchases the diner from the seller for cash. Second, in escrow 2 (the exchange escrow), the buyer transfers the diner to the exchanger in exchange for the store. In this case, the buyer is acting as a middleman or accommodator with the diner being transferred twice. Escrow 1 and escrow 2 normally close concurrently (resulting in the purchase of only one title insurance policy).

Buyer must report exchange portion of the transaction as a sale. The buyer of the diner has a taxable sale, not a tax-free exchange (even though the exchanger has a tax-free exchange) as the property is being acquired by the buyer for an exchange, not for business or investment purposes. However, normally the buyer does not care, as the purchase price and the sales price (fair market value) are identical [§1001; Rev. Rul. 77-297; Rev. Rul. 75-291].

Three-Party Baird Publishing Exchange—Exchange First, Then Purchase

The Baird Publishing exchange is a simple variation of the Alderson exchange, with the exchange step of the transaction occurring before the sale, the middleman being the seller instead of the buyer and again generally assisted by a facilitator. The transaction is illustrated in Figure 6.3 [*J. H. Baird Publishing Co. v. Comm.*, 39 TC 608 (1962)].

FIGURE 6.2   The Alderson Exchange—Purchase First, Then Exchange

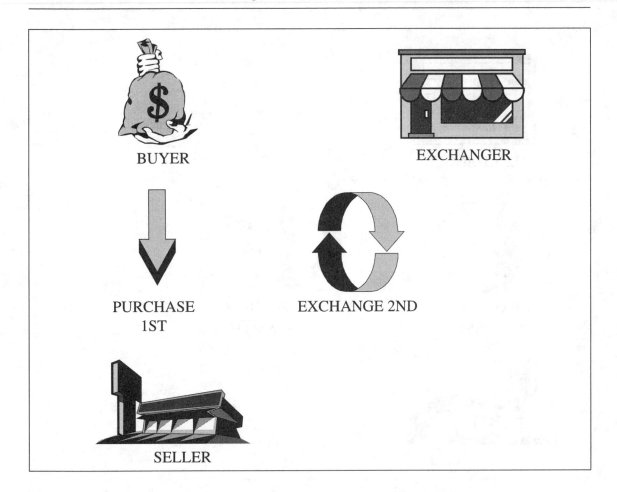

BUYER

EXCHANGER

PURCHASE 1ST

EXCHANGE 2ND

SELLER

The mechanics. As with the Alderson exchange, the Baird Publishing exchange is consummated in two separate transactions, each of which should be accomplished by a separate but dependent escrow, and again generally closed simultaneously with the help of the facilitator. First, in escrow 1 (the exchange escrow), the seller transfers the diner to the exchanger in exchange for the store. Second, in escrow 2 (the sales/purchase escrow), the seller sells the store to the buyer for cash. In this case, the seller is acting as a middleman or accommodator with the store being transferred twice. Escrow 1 and escrow 2 normally close concurrently. In this case the seller must report the sales transaction, reportable on Form 1040, Schedule D, Sale in the year of the exchange [§1001].

Other Essential Ingredients in an Exchange

Exchanger may direct what property he or she wants. In most cases, the exchanger may directly locate, negotiate, and assist in the acquisition of the property for which he or she wishes to exchange [*Rutland v. Comm.,* 36 TCM 40 (1977); Rev. Rul 77-297, 1977-2 CB 304; PLR 8110028].

FIGURE 6.3   Three-Party Baird Exchange—Exchange First, Then Purchase

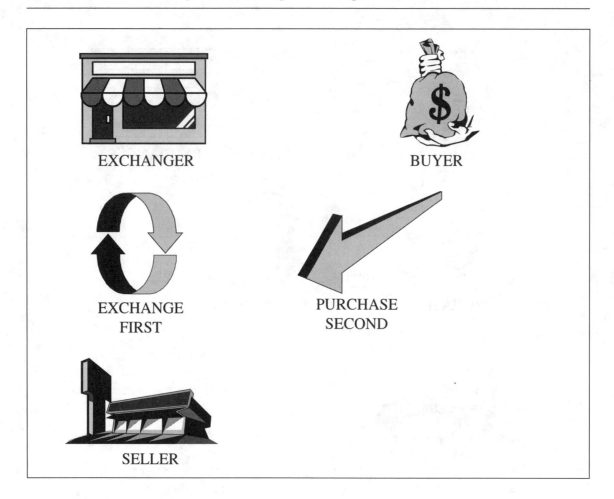

EXCHANGER

BUYER

EXCHANGE
FIRST

PURCHASE
SECOND

SELLER

WARNING: However, the exchanger should avoid executing any direct options and, in particular, purchase contracts directly with the seller. The property must be acquired through an exchange, not a purchase. See below.

Exchange property, not cash. Exchangers will recognize gain when the courts determine they actually "sold" property and then reinvested the money by purchasing like-kind property, even when there existed an intent for a tax-free exchange [*Carlton v. U.S.*, 385 F2d 238, (5th Cir. 1967)]. The opposite is also true.

Warning about seller *receiving property before* giving up property in a simultaneous exchange. It is often asked: "Can the exchanger purchase the seller's property *before* the buyer transfers his or her property to the exchanger?" No. This results in a purchase with a subsequent taxable sale, and the evidence is the title transfer [*Smith v. Comm.*, 537 F2d 972 (8th Cir. 1976); §1.1031(k)-1(a)].

PLANNING TIP: Some alternatives exist, though, that allow the exchanger to control disposition of the property prior to the time of the exchange without technically purchasing the property, such as the use of a lease or a purchase option. Another option is described below.

The "Reverse Starker" exchange—accommodators may purchase before exchange. Sometimes an outside party also is trying to buy the seller's property before the exchanger can secure it. An accommodator (which is discussed later) may acquire the seller's property in contemplation of the exchange, and subsequent to the closing time the accommodator can negotiate a transfer to the buyer, if desired. This is then followed by the buyer, accommodator and the exchanger affecting the exchange. Both the Tax Court and the Fifth Circuit conclude that a §1031 exchange is being properly completed in this situation. *And, the exchanger can loan the accommodator the money to acquire the seller's property.* The loan is repaid from the buyer's cash purchase [*Biggs v. Comm.,* 69 TC 905 (1978), *aff'd,* 632 F2d 1171 (5th Cir. 1981); *124 Front Street, Inc.,* 65 TC 6 (1975)].

COMMENT: It makes sense to use accommodators and facilitators, allowing flexibility that a normal exchanger doesn't have. These professionals are generally familiar with the unique requirements to maintain exchange status, such as those described below.

Contractual interdependence. The closing of each escrow (leg of the exchange) *should* be contingent on the closing of all escrows. However, contractual or mutual interdependence of the separate transactions in a multiparty exchange is not necessarily a critical factor so long as the exchanger never has actual or effective control of the cash [compare *Barker v. Comm.,* 74 TC 555 (1980), with *Brauer v. Comm.,* 74 TC 1134 (1980) and *Biggs v. Comm.,* 69 TC 905 (1978), *aff'd* 632 F2d 1171 (5th Cir. 1981)].

Exchange, not sale, must be planned. The escrows should be part of an *integrated plan* showing that the exchanger wishes to effect a §1031 exchange. This is evidenced by showing that an integrated plan for a like-kind exchange is conceived and implemented; the exchanger's actions are consistent with exchanging; the conditions required to effect that intent are met; the contracts providing for the necessary series of transfers are interdependent; and *no cash proceeds from the sale of the original property are actually or constructively received by the exchanger* [*Garcia v. Comm.,* 80 TC 491 (1983), *acq.* 1984-1 CB 1].

Exchanger must not actually or constructively receive cash. As a general rule, the problem with not using an accommodator is that a transaction will constitute a taxable sale and not an exchange if the exchanger *actually or constructively* receives money or other property (boot) for the relinquished property before he or she actually receives the like-kind replacement property. The result is that the exchange becomes a taxable sale and subsequent repurchase, not an exchange, even though the taxpayer desired an exchange from the inception.

Actual receipt. The taxpayer is in *actual receipt* of money or property *at the time* the taxpayer actually receives such money or property, or receives the economic benefit of such money or property (e.g., pledging the property as security for a loan) [§1.1031(k)-1(f)(2)].

Constructive receipt. The taxpayer is in *constructive receipt* of money or property at the time such money or property is credited to the taxpayer's account, set apart for the taxpayer, or otherwise made available so that the taxpayer *may* draw upon it at any time or so that the taxpayer can draw upon it if notice of intention to withdraw is given [§1.1031(k)-1(f)(2)].

> *Example:* Barb transfers a $100,000 fair market value (FMV) rental property to Carol in a deferred exchange on May 17, 1998. On or before November 13, 1998 (the end of the exchange period), Carol is required to purchase and transfer the property identified by Barb. At any time after May 17, 1998, and before Carol has purchased the replacement property, Barb has the right, upon notice, to demand that Carol pay $100,000 cash in lieu of acquiring the property.

> *Result:* *No §1031(a) exchange available.* It is a taxable sale followed by a subsequent repurchase because Barb has the unrestricted right to demand cash as of May 17, 1998. This is constructive receipt as of that date [§1.1031(k)-1(f)(3)].

Can we change to an exchange after we sign an offer-to-sell, i.e., in midstream?
Yes. The IRS allows the taxpayer to change a sale to an exchange *at any time prior to closing* [see the deferred exchange regulations, §1.1031(k)-1(a)]. The Tax Court looks at the form of the transaction over its substance [*Leslie Q. Coupe,* 52 TC 394 (1969)]. As long as an exchange is "intended," most court decisions find the details of the transaction are insignificant [*Rutland v. Comm.,* 36 TCM 40 (1977); *Biggs v. Comm.,* 632 F 2d 1171 (5th Cir. 1981), *aff'g* 69 TC 905 (1978); *Garcia v. Comm.,* 80 TC 491 (1983), *acq.* 1984-1 CB 1].

The qualified exchange may even contain the contingency that the transaction may, at the option of the exchanger, convert back to a cash sale [*Antone Borchard,* TCM 1965-297], or, alternatively, if the buyer cannot find a suitable property, the exchanger may demand cash [*Barker v. Comm.,* 74 TC 555 (1980)].

Four-Party (Neutral Accommodator) Exchange

Sometimes buyers of real estate want only to pay their money and be done with the deal. They have little interest in, or are unable to fund, the purchase of "replacement property" for the exchanger. The seller may also be uncomfortable in being the middleman. What happens if a buyer or a seller simply doesn't want to be bothered with

FIGURE 6.4 The Four-Party Accommodator

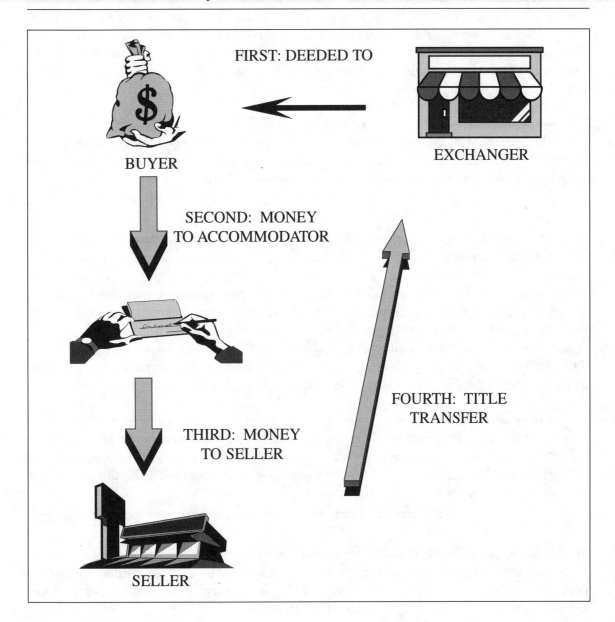

this complication and starts looking for other property? How can the exchanger or real estate agent keep the deal together?

When either the buyer or the seller is unwilling to act as the accommodator, a fourth-party escrow agent may act as a go-between to help facilitate the exchange [*Earlene T. Parker,* 74 TC 555 (1980)]. In such cases, "intermediaries" and "accommodators" have sprung up to facilitate regular exchanges—and now deferred exchanges. This is the same as a three-party exchange, except that a fourth-party accommodator assists all parties to effect the exchange (see Figure 6.4).

The mechanics. With the IRS blessing of direct deeding, the exchanger may deed the property directly to the buyer. The buyer then transfers the money to the accommodator (not to the exchanger). Finally, the accommodator pays for the seller's property, and the seller is permitted to deed the property directly to the exchanger. Before these IRS pronouncements, three or more separate escrows were required with the exchanger receiving each deed and subsequently granting each deed [Rev. Rul. 90-34, I.R.B. 1990-16; §1.1031(k)-1(g)(4)(iv)].

> **PLANNING TIP:** Again, the agreements between all the parties are encouraged to be mutually interdependent parts of one integrated plan with each contingent upon the successful completion of the other transactions.

Does the use of a fourth-party accommodator create constructive receipt via the principal-agent relationship? No. The use of a third-party or fourth-party accommodator may actually prevent actual or constructive receipt. According to the Tax Court, followed belatedly by the IRS, in the case of simultaneous transfers of like-kind properties involving a qualified accommodator, the qualified accommodator is not considered the agent of the taxpayer for purposes of the like-kind exchange rules. In such cases, the transfer and receipt of property by the taxpayer is treated as an exchange. This IRS position applies to transfers of property made by taxpayers on or after June 10, 1991 [*Brauer v. Comm.*, 74 TC 1134 (1980); §1.1031(b)-(2)].

> **COMMENT:** This rule does *not* imply that fourth-party accommodators *must* be used in simultaneous exchanges, i.e., buyers and sellers may still act as the middleman. This was confirmed by a telephone conversation with the authors of the deferred exchange regulations.

Who can be a fourth-party escrow agent? In numerous court cases, title companies, real estate agents and attorneys have all qualified as independent accommodators. In addition, the IRS has created a "safe harbor" qualified accommodator discussed next and more fully described in Chapter 7.

Using a qualified accommodator's participation. This practice prevents the taxpayer from constructively receiving the purchase money. The IRS has announced that both simultaneous and deferred exchanges are permitted (but not required) to be facilitated by the use of a *qualified intermediary* (clearly a new growth industry in the exchange field) *if* the exchanger's rights to receive the money or other property held by the accommodator are *substantially limited or restricted*. In this case the qualified accommodator is not considered the agent of the taxpayer (an agent is normally a disqualified person). The accommodator may actually purchase the property (even from money advanced directly by the exchanger) and then effect an exchange or simply assign the contractual right to purchase the property desired (see subsequent discussion on direct deeding) [§1.1031(k)-1(g)(4)(i),(vi)].

COMMENT: This does not mean that other parties (e.g., the taxpayer's present attorney or accountant) cannot be accommodators for simultaneous exchanges even though they are disqualified for deferred exchanges (as discussed in the next paragraph). It simply means that the IRS will look more closely at simultaneous exchanges when "safe harbor" accommodators are not used.

Who may be a "qualified" accommodator in an exchange? A qualified accommodator is one

1. who is not the taxpayer, related to the taxpayer or an agent of the taxpayer in the past two years (as discussed below) *and*
2. who acts to facilitate a deferred exchange by *entering into a written agreement (called the exchange agreement)* and, as required by the exchange agreement, *acquires* the relinquished property from the taxpayer, transfers the relinquished property, acquires the replacement property, and transfers the replacement property to the taxpayer [§1.1031(k)-1(g)(4)(iii)].

No agent of the taxpayer—within the last two years. Anyone who is the agent of the taxpayer at the time of the transaction is disqualified. For this purpose, *a person who has acted as the taxpayer's employee, attorney, accountant, investment banker or broker, or real estate agent or broker within the two-year period* ending on the date of the transfer of the first of the relinquished properties *is treated as an agent of the taxpayer* at the time of the transaction.

Real estate agents, escrow agents and title companies qualify. The performance of the following services will *not* be taken into account in determining who is an agent:

1. *Putting together an exchange.* Services for the taxpayer with respect to exchanges of property intended to qualify for nonrecognition of gain or loss under §1031
2. *Routine financial, title insurance, escrow or trust services* for the taxpayer by a financial institution, title insurance company or escrow company [§1.1031(k)-1(k)(2)]

COMMENT: The above means that normally the exchanger can safely use the real estate agent who is putting together the exchange but not his or her present lawyer or accountant. Evidently, the IRS writer of these regulations trusts real estate agents more than attorneys and accountants!

A further discussion on four-party accommodators and their required qualifications is found in Chapter 7, on deferred exchanges.

Direct deeding. Does "acquire" mean that the accommodator (e.g., buyer/seller/facilitator) actually has to momentarily take physical title to both properties? No. Some accommodators take momentary or "sequential" title for administrative purposes, but it is not necessary.

COMMENT: This "blink-of-the-eye" ownership can be potentially catastrophic for the buyer/seller/accommodator in light of the *hazardous waste liability* (i.e., Superfund or toxic waste liability). The liability to pay for cleanup costs in removing hazardous, toxic, or dangerous waste found on a property reaches *any* owner of a property even if that owner did not create such waste or cause its release into the environment.

To answer the above concern, the IRS came up with its own definition of the word *acquire,* probably to comply with previous judicial decisions [Rev. Rul. 90-34, I.R.B. 1990-16; §1.1031(k)-1(g)(4)(iv), *Biggs v. Comm.,* 69 TC 905 (1978); *Brauer v. Comm.,* 74 TC 1134 (1980)].

Acquiring. *Acquiring,* in the deferred exchange regulations, rejects the general tax principle definition of acquisition for deferred exchange purposes and treats accommodators *as if they acquired* and transferred title, if they

1. *actually acquire and transfer legal title* to that property (the least desirable option); *or*
2. *enter into an "agreement" (e.g., an assignment) with a person other than the taxpayer* (either on its own behalf or as the agent of any party to the transaction) *for the transfer of the relinquished property* to that person and, pursuant to that agreement, the relinquished property is transferred to that person; *or*
3. *enter into an agreement with the owner of the replacement property* (either on its own behalf or as the agent of any party to the transaction) *for the transfer of that property* and, pursuant to that agreement, the replacement property is transferred to the taxpayer [§1.1031(k)-1(g)(4)(iv)].

Assignment of contract permitted. Solely for these purposes, an accommodator is treated as entering into an agreement if the rights of a party to the agreement are assigned to the accommodator *and if all parties to that agreement are notified* in writing of the assignment on or before the date of the relevant transfer of property [§1.1031(k)-1(g)(4)(v)].

Example 1. **Direct deeding to accommodator.** The facts:

May 1:   Barb receives $100,000 cash offer-to-purchase from Danny on her office building. Danny hates exchanges and Barb hates paying taxes.

May 2:	Barb signs a qualified exchange agreement with qualified Acme Accommodators.
May 3:	Acme and Danny sign $100,000 offer-to-purchase/sell.
May 17:	Barb deeds office building to Acme.
May 17:	Acme deeds office building to Danny, and Danny delivers $100,000 cash to Acme; funds are placed in a qualified escrow.
June 3:	Barb identifies Eldon's $80,000 apartment house.
August 9:	Eldon deeds apartments to Acme, and Acme delivers $80,000 cash out of escrow to Eldon.
August 9:	Acme deeds apartments to Barb along with $20,000 cash.

Tax results: Barb is not in actual or constructive receipt of the $100,000, and Acme properly *acquired and transferred* both the office building and the apartments. Barb's transfer of the office building and acquisition of the apartments qualifies as a §1031 exchange. The $20,000 is taxable boot [§1031(b); §1.1031(k)-1(g)(8)(Example 3)].

The accommodator never has to take technical title! The transfer of property in a deferred exchange that is facilitated by the use of a qualified accommodator may actually occur via a *direct deed* of legal title by the current owner of the property to its ultimate owner [§1.1031(k)-1(g)(4)(iv)].

> ***Example 2.*** **Assignment of purchase agreement to accommodator.** The facts:

May 1:	Barb *signs* $100,000 cash offer-to-purchase/sell her office building to Danny. Danny hates exchanges and Barb hates paying taxes.
May 2:	Barb signs a qualified exchange agreement with qualified Acme Accommodators.
May 2:	Barb *assigns* her interest in Danny's offer to Acme.
May 17:	Barb notifies Danny of assignment.
May 17:	Barb deeds office building *directly* to Danny.
May 17:	Danny delivers $10,000 cash to Barb and $90,000 cash to Acme's qualified escrow.
June 1:	Barb identifies Eldon's $90,000 ranch.
July 5:	Barb *signs* $90,000 offer-to-purchase/sell on ranch.
July 5:	Barb *assigns* her interest in Eldon's ranch to Acme.
July 5:	Barb notifies Eldon of assignment.
August 9:	Acme delivers $90,000 cash out of escrow to Eldon.
August 9:	Eldon deeds ranch *directly* to Barb.

Tax results: Barb is not in actual or constructive receipt of the $100,000, and again Acme properly *acquired and transferred* both the office building and the ranch. Barb's transfer of the office building and acquisition of the ranch qualify as a §1031 exchange. Both state law on agency and general tax principles are disregarded. The $10,000 is boot, taxable under §1031(b) [§1.1031(k)-1(g)(8) (Example 4)].

Example 3. **How to do it wrong.** The facts:

May 1:   Barb *signs* $100,000 cash offer-to-purchase/sell with Danny on her office building. Danny hates exchanges and Barb hates paying taxes.

May 2:   Barb signs a qualified exchange agreement with qualified Acme Accommodators.

_____: Barb *doesn't assign* her interest in Danny's offer to Acme.

_____: Barb *doesn't notify* Danny of assignment.

May 17:   Barb deeds office building *directly* to Danny.

May 17:   Danny delivers $100,000 cash to Acme; funds are placed into qualified escrow.

June 1:   Barb identifies Milton's $100,000 trailer park.

August 9:   Acme purchases Milton's $100,000 trailer park.

August 9:   Milton deeds trailer part to Acme.

August 9:   Acme deeds trailer park to Barb.

Tax results: Because Barb transferred her office building directly to Danny under Barb's purchase/sell agreement with Danny, Acme did not acquire the office building from Barb and transfer the office building to Danny. Moreover, because Acme did not acquire legal title to the office building, did not enter into an agreement with Danny to transfer the office building to Danny and was not assigned Barb's rights in her agreement to sell the office building to Danny, Acme is not treated as acquiring and transferring the office building. Thus, Acme was not a qualified accommodator. Barb did not exchange the office building for the trailer park. Rather, Barb sold the office building to Danny and purchased, through Acme, the trailer park. Therefore, the transfer of the office building does not qualify for nonrecognition of gain or loss under §1031 [§1.1031(k)-1(g)(8) (Example 5)].

The pot exchange. Sometimes it is easier to have all the parties throw the assets brought to the exchange (i.e., cash or property) into one big escrow "pot" and have that escrow directly deed the property or cash to the ultimate recipient.

Problems with the pot exchange. The use of one escrow, instead of multiple escrows, may cloud the sale portion of the Alderson or Baird multiparty exchange. This exchange method is not specifically approved for simultaneous exchanges, even though Rev. Rul. 57-244 (1957-1 CB 247) does approve a three-party contract where there is a three-way exchange of property without the sale of any of the properties; it was successfully used in *W. D. Haden Co. v. Comm.,* 165 F2d 588 (5th Cir. 1948). For purposes of safety when using a pot exchange, there should exist contractual interdependence and a restriction of the receipt of cash by the exchanger.

WARNING: The pot theory is also questionable in deferred exchanges as indicated by the previous example on assignments, and, therefore, the use of a qualified accommodator is a more conservative option [§1.1031(k)-1(g)(8)(Example 5)].

CHAPTER

7

Deferred Exchanges

DOES THE EXCHANGE OF PROPERTY
HAVE TO BE SIMULTANEOUS?

Have you ever wanted to sell some of your, or your client's, property for cash with the plan to reinvest it in the future and during the interim deposit the money in an interest-bearing account *but* not pay the capital gains tax associated with the sale (i.e., defer the gain)? Until December 1979, most tax practitioners said "impossible"! We assumed that the trading of property had to be done concurrently. Then along came the *Starker* cases, commonly known as *Starker I, Starker II,* and *Starker III,* from Corvallis, Oregon, which has made the impossible a reality [*Bruce Starker v. U.S.* DC-Ore 75-1 USTC ¶9443; *T. J. Starker v. U.S.*, 432 F. Supp 864 (DC-Ore. 1977), 602 F2d 1341 (CA-9, 79-2 USTC ¶9451)].

The *Starker* facts: T. J. Starker (T. J.) owned $1,502,500 of timbered property that Crown Zellerbach Corporation (Crown) wanted to buy. T. J. wished to effect a like-kind exchange but, after viewing Crown's present land assets, found none to his liking. The two parties entered into an exchange agreement wherein T. J. would *immediately* transfer title to Crown. In return, Crown would record an unsecured $1,502,500 "exchange value credit" on its financial records. In addition, Crown would purchase property over the next five years that T. J. found acceptable and that he instructed Crown to purchase. After Crown's purchase, the corporation would transfer title to T. J. and reduce the "exchange value credit" by the purchase price of the property. If any cash was left at the end of the fifth year, the remaining cash would be transferred to T. J. as T. J. did not have the right under the contract to demand cash in lieu of property.

In addition, the account was credited with an annual 6% "growth factor" (some, including the courts, called it disguised interest), theoretically to reflect timber growth on the parcels conveyed by the taxpayer.

Although the taxpayer selected nine like-kind parcels to be conveyed, none of which was owned by T. J. at the time the exchange agreement was executed, the Ninth Circuit Court of Appeals found that the taxpayer did not have control over the cash used by Crown to purchase these parcels. The transaction was held by the Ninth Circuit to constitute a §1031 exchange and T. J.'s additional $301,000 tax assessment was refunded to him as the gain was declared not to be recognized.

Problem with *Starker* exchanges: How long? How long could Starker defer identifying and locating the property? Theoretically, if it was more than six years, the statute of limitations would have made any cash remaining exempt from taxes. This problem was solved by Congress in 1984 by the "deferred exchange" rules, followed by IRS interpretative regulations finalized on May 1, 1991.

Effective date: The effective date for the final regulations dealing with "Treatment of Deferred Exchanges" is for transactions on or after June 10, 1991. Transactions between May 16, 1990, and June 10, 1991, may rely on the proposed regulations [§1.1031(k)-1(o)].

WHAT DOES NOT QUALIFY AS A DEFERRED EXCHANGE?

As discussed previously concerning simultaneous exchanges: (1) a sale and subsequent purchase does not qualify as a deferred exchange; (2) a deferred exchange must be structured as an exchange, not a purchase; and (3) the taxpayer cannot receive the replacement property *prior to* the date on which the taxpayer transfers the relinquished property (e.g., no "receiving before giving up" exchanges) [§1.1031(k)-1(a)].

TIME LIMITS IMPOSED ON NONSIMULTANEOUS LIKE-KIND EXCHANGES

For any deferred exchanges after July 18, 1984, the following limits apply:

1. *Identified:* All properties to be received *must be identified within 45 days* after the taxpayer transfers the relinquished property.
2. *Received:* The exchange of titles must be *completed, or properties received, within strict time limits,* not more than 180 days (or, if earlier, the due date, including extensions, of the taxpayer's tax return for the tax year the relinquished property was transferred) after the transfer of the exchanged property [§1031(a)(3); §1.1031(k)-1(b)(1)].

The entire deferred exchange 45/180-day process is easily illustrated in Figure 7.1.

Filing a tax return on time can make a like-kind exchange taxable! A tax trap can occur by the 180 days "or, if earlier, the due date of the tax return" requirement. For example, if a calendar-year taxpayer gives property in a like-kind exchange on December 31, the 180 days would end on June 27 of the next year. But, if the

FIGURE 7.1   Deferred Exchange with Fourth Party Accomodator

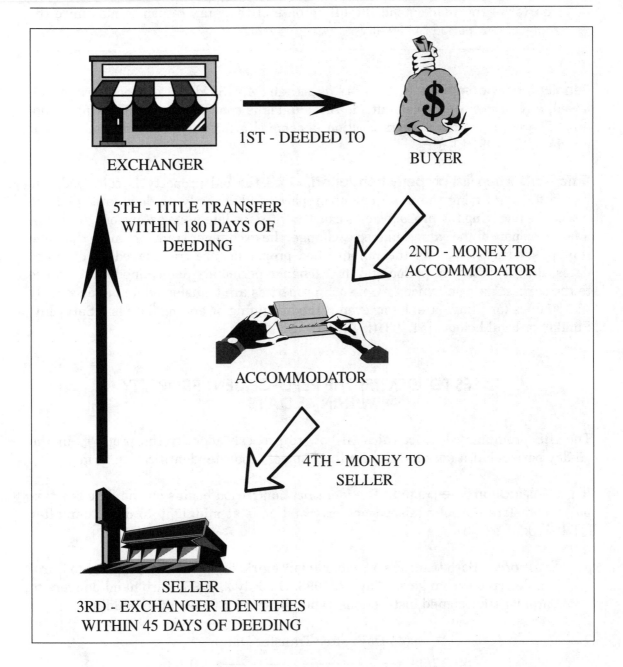

individual files on April 15, this shortens the allowable exchange period to 105 days. As corporations file on March 15, they would only have 74 days to complete an exchange! Luckily, the requirement adds "including extensions." In other words, if the taxpayer files on time, they lose the period of time from the filing date to the end of the 180 days. Investor Christensen received replacement property after filing his tax return but before the 180 days . . . *and no §1031 like-kind exchange was allowed* [*Orville E. Christensen*, TC Memo 1996-254]!

TAX PLANNING: Prudent investors participating in an exchange in the first quarter of the year extend the filling date of their tax return to maximize the replacement period to 180 days.

Penalty for noncompliance. If these dates (i.e., 45/180 days) are not strictly followed, any property received outside these dates is considered "not-like-kind" property. Therefore the tax-free transaction is deemed a taxable sale and a subsequent purchase [§1.1031(k)-1(a)].

Time starts when first property transferred. Once the old property is conveyed, the period for identifying the replacement property ends exactly 45 days later and the period for receiving the property ends exactly 180 days later—no extensions are available. If, as part of the same deferred exchange, the exchanger transfers more than one relinquished property and the relinquished properties are transferred on different dates, the identification period and the exchange period are determined by reference to the *earliest* date on which any of such properties are transferred and ends exactly 45/180 days (or filing date) later, even if the beginning or ending date is a Saturday, Sunday or legal holiday [§1.1031(k)-1(b)(1)(iii)].

RULES TO *IDENTIFY* THE REPLACEMENT PROPERTY WITHIN 45 DAYS

The IRS promulgated strict rules on how to properly identify the property in the 45-day period, but it does not require the filing of separate identification forms.

The identification time period. The identification period begins on the date the taxpayer transfers the relinquished property and ends at midnight 45 days thereafter [§1.1031(k)-1(b)(2)(i)].

> *Example:* Barb transfers a $100,000 fair market value rental property to Carol in a deferred exchange on May 17, 1998. On July 2, 1998, Barb hand-delivers to Carol written, signed instructions to purchase a $100,000 office building.

(45 Days after Transfer Date)

5 /17/98 ◄──────────────► 7/1/98

"Identification Period"

> *Tax result:* No §1031 exchange as the replacement property was identified outside the 45-day identification period [§1.1031(k)-1(c)(7)(Example 1)].

Not Timely Identifying Replacement Property Kills Tax-Free Swap

In this instance, an accountant sold two properties, intending to do a tax-free swap pursuant to the like-kind rules under Code §1031. Sales proceeds were held in an escrow account, and two weeks later, he found a building that needed renovation but otherwise suited his needs. However, he was too busy to carry on the necessary negotiations for acquisition of the building and never formally identified it as the replacement before eventually buying it more than 45 days later. Worse yet, on the IRS Form 8824, he "mistakenly" (or so he said), inserted an indentification date more than 45 days after the date the property was transferred. The Tax Court ruled that the exchange did not qualify under the like-kind rules. Even though he bought the building withing the overall 180-day limitation period, he did not otherwise satisfy the 45-day identification rule, thus making the transaction taxable [*Terry D. Smith;* TC Memo. 1997-109].

How to Properly Identify Property within the 45 Days

The identification must be in a written document, signed and delivered. Property must be designated as replacement property in writing, signed and delivered (either by hand or mailed, faxed or otherwise sent) to the person obligated to transfer the replacement property *or* to any other person involved in the exchange (other than the taxpayer or a "disqualified person," which is defined later), such as any of the other parties to the exchange, an accommodator, an escrow agent or a title company. A document signed by all parties prior to the end of the 45 days is also sufficient [§1.1031(k)-1(c)(2)].

COMMENT: There is no requirement that this identification be evidenced by a listing agreement or an option, but it probably is imprudent to identify three different properties without the permission of the present owner. Why? As is discussed later in this chapter, some or all of the identified properties *must* be received within the 180 days!

The property description must be unambiguous.

- *Describing real property.* Exchanger may use legal description, street address or distinguishable name (e.g., Trump Tower).
- *Describing personal property.* Description must be specific (e.g., truck must designate make, model, and year) [§1.1031(k)-1(c)(3)].

Example: Barb transfers a $100,000 fair market value rental property to Carol in a deferred exchange on May 17, 1998. On July 1, 1998, Barb hand-delivers to Carol written, signed instructions to purchase "unimproved land located in Powder River County with a fair market value not to exceed $100,000."

Tax result: No §1031 exchange, as the property description is not specific enough [§1.1031(k)-1(c)(7)(Example 3)].

Property that is to be produced or constructed in the future also qualifies but must follow special rules, which are discussed later in this material.

Limitations on how many replacement properties may be designated (the alternate and multiple property rules). Regardless of the number of relinquished properties in the same deferred exchange, the maximum number of replacement properties the taxpayer may designate is three; if more than three properties are identified, then property value may not exceed twice the aggregate fair market value of the property given up; and if both more than three properties *and* twice fair market value are identified, then the exchanger must purchase 95% of *all* the properties identified.

COMMENT: *All* property identified *must* be used in these calculations unless the property has been properly revoked [§1.1031(k)-1(c)(4)(iii)].

Test 1—The "three-property rule." The taxpayer may designate three properties of any fair market value [§1.1031(k)-1(c)(4)].

Example: Barb transfers a $100,000 fair market value rental property to Carol in a deferred exchange on May 17, 1998. On June 28, 1998 Barb hand-delivers to Carol written, signed instructions identifying real properties J, K and L as potential replacement properties (fair market values of $75,000, $100,000 and $125,000, respectively). On August 1, 1998, Barb informs Carol which of the three properties she wishes.

Tax result: §1031 exchange available, as no more than three properties are identified within the proper time frame [§1.1031(k)-1(c)(7)(Example 4)].

COMMENT: The dollar amount that must be designated is *not* the "net-equity" value even though the transaction may have been brought together as a "net-equity" exchange. The dollar amount is the fair market value without regard to liabilities secured by the property. So what is *fair market value* to the IRS? Uncertainty reigns as two appraisers seldom agree and that includes IRS appraisers.

What is a property? For example, Diana owns a ranch comprised of three separately purchased properties that are exchanged (one deed) with Charles for 20 commercial lots (again via one deed). Admittedly there are 23 separate parcels, but are there two or 23 properties?

Tax result: There is no specific answer in the §1.1031(k)-1 deferred exchange regulations. The "multiple-property" exchange regulations (discussed in Chapter 8) conclude that the three ranch properties are *one* "exchange group" and the 20 lots are *one* "exchange group" [§1.1031(j)-1(a)(2)(i)].

COMMENT: The author is certain this is not the answer the regulation writers wanted, with all the potential abuse provided by this conclusion! The use of a different street address for each commercial property may allow the IRS to dubiously argue that there are 20 properties, not one property [§1.1031(k)-1(c)(3)]. When appropriate, therefore, the taxpayer will want to avoid this type of "unambiguous" description. The *incidental property rule* probably is not applicable as it does not directly address the issue when similar properties are in the same group [§1.1031(k)-1(c)(5)(ii)]. Conclusion: no clear answer exists.

Test 2—The "200% rule." If the taxpayer designates more than three properties, the total fair market value of all the identified properties may not exceed 200% of the fair market value (on the transfer date) of the property given up [§1.1031(k)-1(c)(4)].

Example: Barb transfers a $100,000 fair market value rental property to Carol in a deferred exchange on May 17, 1998. Also on May 17, Barb hand-delivers to Carol written, signed instructions identifying real properties M, N, P and Q as potential replacement properties (with fair market values of $30,000, $40,000, $50,000 and $60,000, respectively). The written document provides that by July 2, 1998, Barb will orally inform Carol which of the identified properties Carol is to transfer to her.

Tax result: §1031 exchange available. Even though more than three properties were identified within the proper time frame, the aggregate fair market value ($180,000) does not exceed 200% of the property given up ($100,000 × 200%) [§1.1031(k)-1(c)(7)(Example 5)].

Test 3—Purchase 95% of all identified property. If the taxpayer purchases 95% of the aggregate fair market values of all properties originally identified, the three-property and the 200% limitation rules do not apply. For this purpose, the fair market value of each identified replacement property is determined as of the earlier of the date the property is received by the taxpayer or the last day of the exchange period [§1.1031(k)-1(c)(4)(ii)].

WARNING: Violation of all three tests makes the exchange fully taxable [§1.1031(k)-1(c)(4)(ii)].

Blanket 45-day exception. If all the property to be acquired is *received* within 45 days, the identification rule is waived [§1.1031(k)-1(c)(1)].

Segregating incidental property disregarded. For both the three-property rule and the 200% rule, property need not be separated if

1. in a standard commercial transaction, the property is typically transferred together with the larger item of property and
2. the aggregate fair market value of all such property does not exceed 15% of the aggregate total [§1.1031(k)-1(c)(5)(i)].

Example: Furniture, laundry machines and other miscellaneous items of personal property will not be treated as separate property from an apartment building with a fair market value of $1,000,000 if the aggregate fair market value of the furniture, laundry machines and other personal property does not exceed $150,000. In such case, for purposes of the three-property rule, the apartment building, furniture, laundry machines and other personal property are treated as one property. Moreover, when describing replacement property, the apartment building, furniture, laundry machines and other personal property are all considered to be unambiguously described if the legal description or street address of the apartment building is specified, even if no reference is made to the furniture, laundry machines and other personal property [§1.1031(k)-1(c)(5)(ii) (Example 2)].

Previously identified property may be revoked before the end of the 45 days. Taxpayers may change their minds and substitute other property they wish to identify at any time before the end of the 45-day identification period so long as the revocation is done in substantially the same manner as the original identification (i.e., written, signed and delivered revocation to the person originally notified) [§1.1031(k)-1(c)(6)].

Example: Barb transfers a $100,000 fair market value rental property to Carol in a deferred exchange on May 17, 1998. On May 20, 1998, Barb identifies real properties R and S as potential replacement properties by hand-delivering to Carol written, signed instructions. On June 4, 1998, Barb identifies real properties T and U as replacement property. On June 5, 1998, Barb telephones Carol and orally revokes R and S (fair market values of R, S, T and U are $50,000, $70,000, $90,000 and $100,000 respectively).

Tax result: No §1031 exchange available. Because the property was identified in writing, it must be revoked in writing—oral revocation is invalid. Thus, there are now four properties involved that exceed 200% of the fair market value of the property transferred. Barb is treated as if she did not identify *any* replacement property [§1.1031(k)-1(c)(7)(Example 7)].

COMMENT: Even though Barb identified four properties *during* the 45-day identification period, if she had revoked R and S in writing, we only test for more than three properties on the 45th day [§1.1031(k)-1(c)(4)(iii)]. Before that date, it is "flex" time. Therefore, Barb would have identified only two properties for this rule.

HOW TO PROPERLY RECEIVE PROPERTY WITHIN THE REQUIRED TIME FRAME

The regulations provide that replacement property is received before the end of the exchange period (i.e., the filing date or 180 days after transfer) if the replacement property received is "substantially the same" property as was identified [§1.1031(k)-1 (d)(1)].

COMMENT: An example in the regulations demonstrates that receiving at least 75% of the indicated property is substantial but does not indicate a lower limit [§1.1031(k)-1(d)(2)(Example 4)].

If the taxpayer identifies more than one replacement property, the receipt rules apply separately to each.

The exchange period. The exchange period begins on the date the taxpayer transfers the relinquished property and ends on the earlier of the 180 days thereafter or the due date (including extensions) for the taxpayer's tax return for the taxable year in which the transfer of the relinquished property occurs [§1.1031(k)-1(b)(2)(ii)].

Example 1: Microsoft, Inc., files its federal income tax return on a calendar-year basis. Microsoft and Chrysler enter into an agreement for an exchange of property that requires Microsoft to transfer Warehouse X to Chrysler. Under the agreement, Microsoft is to identify like-kind replacement property, which Chrysler is required to purchase and to transfer to Microsoft. Microsoft transfers Warehouse X to Chrysler on November 16, 1998.

The identification period ends at midnight on December 31, 1998, 45 days after the date of transfer of Warehouse X. The exchange period ends at midnight on March 15, 1999, the due date for Microsoft's federal income tax return for the taxable year in which the corporation transferred Warehouse X. However, if Microsoft, Inc., is allowed the automatic six-month extension for filing its tax return, the exchange period ends at midnight on May 15, 1999, 180 days after the date of transfer of Warehouse X [§1.1031(k)-1(b)(3)].

Example 2: Barb transfers a $100,000 fair market value rental property to Carol in a deferred exchange on May 17, 1998. On or before November 13, 1998 (the end of the exchange period), Carol is required to purchase and transfer the property identified by Barb. If the fair market value of the replacement property(ies') is greater or less than the rental property transferred in May, they both agree to pay the difference in cash the day after Barb receives the replacement property.

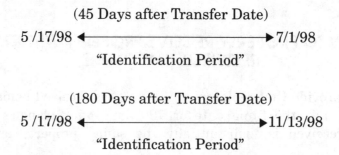

(45 Days after Transfer Date)

5 /17/98 ◄─────────────────────► 7/1/98

"Identification Period"

(180 Days after Transfer Date)

5 /17/98 ◄─────────────────────► 11/13/98

"Identification Period"

Barb identifies real properties J, K and L as potential replacement properties in the exchange agreement (fair market values of $75,000, $100,000 and $125,000, respectively). On July 26, 1998, Barb instructs Carol to acquire K for $100,000. On October 31, 1998, Carol purchases K and transfers it to Barb.

Tax result: *§1031 exchange available.* Property K was identified before the end of the identification period and received before the end of the exchange period [§1.1031(k)-1(d)(2)(Example 1)].

Example 3:   With the same basic facts as those described in example 2 above, Barb identifies real property P as replacement property in the exchange agreement (P is two acres of unimproved land with a fair market value of $250,000). On October 3, 1998, Barb tells Carol to purchase only 1.5 acres for $187,500 and transfer it to her, with Barb paying the $87,500 back to Carol.

Tax result: *§1031 exchange available.* The fair market value of the property *received* ($187,500) is 75% of the fair market value of P as of the date of receipt. Therefore, Barb is considered to have received substantially the same property she identified [§1.1031(k)-1(d)(2)(Example 4)].

THE *CONSTRUCTION EXCHANGE*—SPECIAL RULES FOR IDENTIFYING AND RECEIVING PROPERTY BEING PRODUCED OR CONSTRUCTED

In general. One of the strangest provisions in the final regulations permits, with limitations, the taxpayer to participate in an exchange even if the replacement property is not in existence, or is being produced, at the time the property is identified [§1.1031(k)-1(e)(1); PLR 9413006]. The tricky part is that the replacement property must still be properly identified (within the 45 days) and *received* within the proper time frame (i.e., 180 days). To produce includes to construct, build, install, manufacture, develop, or *improve* [§263A(g)(1)].

COMMENT: Exchangers smack their lips over this one. Imagine—the taxpayer can sell a business property for cash, have the money delivered to an accommodator, build another business property, and call it a tax-free exchange!

Replacement property being produced must be properly "identified." Identification must be as accurate as possible (e.g., for buildings to be constructed, use the legal description of the land and as much detail as practical) [§1.1031(k)-1(e)(2)(i)]. For the 200% rule and the incidental rule, the taxpayer must use the fair market value of the property as of the date it is expected to be received by the taxpayer [§1.1031(k)-1(e)(2)(ii)].

WARNING: Transfer of property for construction services is not an exchange [§1.1031(k)-1(e)(4); see also discussion on "services to be rendered" in Chapter 8].

The constructed property must be *substantially the same* as identified. If substantial changes are made after identification, the replacement property will *not* be considered substantially the same as identified and the exchange will be deemed a taxable sale and subsequent repurchase. Variations due to usual or typical production changes are not taken into account [§1.1031(k)-1(e)(3)(i)].

Receiving personal property. There is *no* extension of time (i.e., for the 180-day rule), and the property *must be finished* within the exchange period [§1.1031(k)-1 (e)(3)(ii)].

Receiving real property—it doesn't have to be finished! There is *no* extension of time (i.e., for the 180-day rule), *and* if the real property is in the construction phase (but not completed at time of receipt), the end product must be substantially the same as originally identified. However, real property does not have to be completed within the exchange period [§1.1031(k)-1(e)(3)(iii)].

Can we extend the 180 days through the back door? Probably. As the 180 days do not start to toll until after the *taxpayer transfers the relinquished property*, simply stalling the closing date results in extending the time [§1.1031(k)-1(b)(2)(ii)]. This should not be too risky if the legal contracts contain a "specific performance" clause and a large down payment.

COMMENT: A four-month postponement added to the 180 days equals almost ten months to complete the building!

WARNING: Possession, in lieu of deed transfer, by a new owner cannot take place as that is also considered to start the 180 days. Therefore, a rental agreement is recommended for this "extension" period.

THE SAFE HARBOR RULE TO AVOID CONSTRUCTIVELY RECEIVING MONEY

The problem—receiving too much security. After the exchanger has given the property, the exchanger typically is unwilling to rely on the buyer's *unsecured* promise to transfer the like-kind replacement property. Thus, exchangers often structure deferred exchanges where the buyer's obligation to transfer the like-kind replacement property to the exchanger is guaranteed or secured, typically using an escrow arrangement. But the exchanger *must* avoid actual or constructive receipt of the money (or other property). How?

The solution—restrictions on receiving the cash. If the right to demand the cash is subject to a "substantial limitation or restriction" [discussed below and at §1.1031(k)-1(g)(6)], there will not be actual or constructive receipt unless (or until) the limitations or restrictions lapse, expire or are waived. In addition to these "escrow instructions" (discussed in the next paragraph), the regulations provide three liberal safe harbors (discussed thereafter) wherein the taxpayer can be given security and still use the §1031 deferral of tax rules.

COMMENT: It is recommended that the next paragraph be included in the exchange agreement or escrow instructions required between the exchanger and the accommodator [see subsequent discussion on qualified accommodators and at §1.1031(k)-1(g)(4)(iii)].

Substantial limitations or restrictions exist if the taxpayer does not have the right to receive, pledge, borrow or obtain the benefits of, the money or other property until:

1. *after 45 days if no identification is made.* After the end of the (45-day) identification period, if the taxpayer has not identified replacement property before the end of the identification period, *or*
2. *after property is received.* After the taxpayer has received all of the identified replacement property to which the taxpayer is entitled (this will be the most common situation), *or*
3. *after 45 days and contingencies exist.* After the later of the end of the identification period and the occurrence of a material and substantial contingency that relates to the deferred exchange, is provided for in writing and is beyond

the control of the taxpayer or a "disqualified person" if the taxpayer identifies replacement property, *or*

4. *after the exchange period (e.g., 180 days)*. Otherwise, after the end of the exchange period [§1.1031(k)-1(g)(6)].

The above paragraph satisfies the requirement that the exchange agreement expressly limit the exchanger's rights to receive, pledge, borrow or otherwise obtain the benefits of the money or other property before the end of the exchange period until the exchange is completed or the exchange requirements can no longer be met.

COMMENT: Investors who don't specifically include the above wording in the exchange document run the risk of losing the advantages of the §1031 exchange rules. Investor Hillyer didn't use the above safe harbor rule and was *deemed* to have constuctively received the money. The exchange was taxable because he was *deemed* to have touched the money (*Michael Hillyer,* TC Memo 1996-214)!

What is this saying? Generally, the exchanger cannot touch the money until after he or she receives the property, or the 180 days lapse. But the exchanger may pay closing costs and pay or receive prorated items out of these funds in advance without the funds being deemed constructively received (e.g., commissions, prorated taxes and rent, recording or transfer taxes, and title company fees) [§1.1031(k)-1(g)(7)].

State law irrelevant. The regulations clarify that the terms of the agreement, rather than state law, determine whether the limitations imposed by a safe harbor with respect to a taxpayer's rights to receive, pledge, borrow or otherwise obtain the benefit of money or other property are satisfied [§1.1031(k)-1(g)(4)(vi)].

HOW TO PROPERLY STRUCTURE THE DEFERRED EXCHANGE

Because the above escrow instruction rules give little assurances as to how an exchanger can, or cannot, structure a successful transaction, the IRS suggests three safe-harbor entities to be used to close exchanges [§1.1031(k)-1(g)].

Follow These Rules and You Have a Tax-Deferred Exchange

Use of these safe-harbor rules results in a determination that the taxpayer is not, either directly or through an accommodator that may be an agent, in actual or constructive receipt of money or other property.

WARNING: *If the exchanger has a "right" to the money, even if he or she doesn't actually "use" the money, this "right" ruins these safe-harbor rules.* Even if a transaction is within the three safe-harbor rules, to the extent that the taxpayer has (or later receives) the ability or unrestricted right to receive money or other property *before* the taxpayer actually receives like-kind replacement property, the transfer of the property will not qualify for a tax-free exchange [§1.1031(k)-1 (g)(1)].

Red flag for audit if safe-harbor rules not used. If taxpayers go outside these safe-harbor rules, they may still argue against actual or constructive receipt of the cash based on all of the facts and circumstances. The IRS, however, states that transactions not structured to come within the safe harbors will be carefully scrutinized—a red flag for audit! Therefore, the biggest task for taxpayers is making sure that the transaction fits within the confines of the safe-harbor regulations.

Safe harbor 1—The buyer (not the seller!) continues to hold the money but with a security or guarantee arrangement. Once the exchanger has transferred the property (and now the buyer has both the property and the money!), he or she may secure the buyer's promise to pay with like-kind replacement property, or cash, by *one or more* of the following collateral arrangements:

1. A mortgage, deed of trust, or other security interest in property (other than cash or a cash equivalent) usually from the buyer
2. A standby letter of credit that satisfies all of the requirements of §15A.453-1 (b)(3)(iii) and that does not allow the taxpayer to draw on the standby letter of credit except upon a default of the transferee's obligation to transfer like-kind replacement property to the taxpayer
3. A guarantee of a third party [§1.1031(k)-1(g)(2)]

PLANNING TIP: Even though this is exactly the financial arrangement in *Starker*, this safe harbor is rarely used. Most exchangers shy away from this option as the buyer ends up with both the like-kind property *and* the money for a period of time.

Example: Barb transfers a $100,000 fair market value rental property to Carol in a deferred exchange on May 17, 1998, and the same day Carol secures her promise to purchase and transfer an office building suitable to Barb with a mortgage on the rental property.

Tax result: $1031 exchange available. There is no constructive receipt of cash. A mortgage used as collateral qualifies under the safe-harbor rules, and Barb does not have the unrestricted right to the money before she actually receives the replacement property.

Safe harbor 2—Cash put into qualified escrow accounts and qualified trusts. More commonly, the exchanger may require the buyer to deposit the cash (or its equivalent), into a qualified escrow account or a qualified trust, without the exchanger being considered in actual or constructive receipt of the cash. Rights conferred upon the exchanger under state law to terminate or dismiss the escrow holder of a qualified escrow account or the trustee of a qualified trust are disregarded for this purpose [§1.1031(k)-1(g)(3)].

A *qualified escrow account* is an escrow account in which the escrow holder is not the taxpayer or a disqualified person (defined later in this section) and the substantial-limitations-or-restrictions-must-exist rules apply against the cash deposited [§1.1031(k)-1(g)(3)(ii)].

A *qualified trust* basically follows the above escrow account rules [§1.1031(k)-1(g)(3)(iii)].

COMMENT: The escrow agreement *must* preclude the taxpayer from taking the cash unless and until he or she fails to designate the replacement property by a certain date. Therefore, if he or she designates property, the escrow agent (bound by the escrow instructions) is required to use the escrow funds to acquire the replacement property and transfer it to the taxpayer.

COMMENT: Be careful that the taxpayer does not *pledge* his or her promise to receive the property (e.g., the exchanger receives a cash loan from a lending institution and pledges the right in the escrow as security for the loan)! This can be a trap for the unaware!

Example 1: **Cash placed in escrow:** Barb transfers a $100,000 fair market value rental property to Carol in a deferred exchange on May 17, 1998, and Carol deposits $100,000 cash in escrow as security for Carol's obligation to perform under this contract. On or before November 13, 1998 (the end of the exchange period), the escrow is required to purchase and transfer the property identified by Barb. If the designated property's fair market value is above, or below, the $100,000, either Barb or Carol, as applicable, will make up the difference in cash one day after the replacement property is received by Barb.

Additional facts: The escrow agreement also provides as follows: The funds in escrow are to be used to purchase the replacement property. If Barb fails to identify replacement property on or before July 1, 1998, Barb may demand the funds in escrow at any time after July 1, 1998. If Barb identifies and receives replacement property, then Barb may demand the balance of the remaining funds in escrow at any time after she has received the replacement property. Otherwise, Barb is entitled to all funds in escrow after November 13, 1998. The escrow holder is not a related party. Pursuant to the terms of the agreement, Barb identifies replacement property, and Carol purchases the replacement property, using the funds in escrow, and transfers the replacement property to Barb.

Tax result: §1031 exchange available. There is no constructive receipt of cash as the escrow qualifies under the safe-harbor rules and as Barb does not have the unrestricted right to the money before she actually receives the replacement property [§1.1031(a)-3(g)(7)(Example 1)].

Example 2:   **Contingency released before property transferred:** Barb transfers a $100,000 fair market value rental property to Carol in a deferred exchange on May 17, 1998, and Carol deposits $100,000 cash in escrow as security for Carol's obligation to perform under this contract. Also on May 17, Barb identifies an office building as replacement property.

Additional facts: The escrow agreement provides the following stipulations: The funds in escrow are to be used to purchase the replacement property. Barb may demand the funds in escrow at any time after the later of July 1, 1998, and the occurrence of any of the following events: (1) the office building is destroyed, stolen, seized, requisitioned, or condemned, or (2) a determination is made that the regulatory approval necessary for the transfer of the office building cannot be obtained in time for it to be transferred to Barb before the end of the exchange period.

In addition, Barb may demand the funds in escrow at any time after August 14, 1998, if the office building has not been rezoned from residential to commercial use by that date. Otherwise, Barb is entitled to all funds in escrow after the earlier of November 13, 1998, and the time at which Barb has received all of the identified replacement property to which she is entitled. The escrow holder is not a disqualified person. The office building is *not* rezoned from residential to commercial use on or before August 14, 1998.

Tax result: *No §1031 exchange after August 14, 1998.* From May 17, 1998, until August 15, 1998, Carol's obligation to transfer the replacement property to Barb is secured by cash held in a qualified escrow account, and Barb does not have the immediate ability or unrestricted right to receive money or other property before she actually receives the like-kind replacement property. Therefore, Barb is determined not to be in actual or constructive receipt of the $100,000 in escrow from May 17, 1998, until August 15, 1998.

Because she had the unrestricted right to the money after that date, however, on August 15, 1998, Barb has the unrestricted right, upon notice, to draw upon the $100,000 held in escrow. Because Barb constructively receives the full amount of the consideration ($100,000) before she actually receives the like-kind replacement property, the transaction is treated as a sale and not as a deferred exchange. The result does not change merely because Barb chooses not to demand the funds in escrow and continues to attempt to have the office building rezoned and to receive the property on or before November 13, 1998 [§1.1031(k)-1(g)(7) (Example 2)].

Example 3: **Contingency not released:** If the office building had been rezoned on or before August 14, 1998, and Carol had purchased the building and transferred it to Barb on or before November 13, 1998, the transaction would have been a qualified exchange [§1.1031(k)-1(g)(7)(Example 2)(iii)].

A taxpayer may receive money or other property directly from a party to the transaction (other than the qualified escrow holder, trustee or accommodator) and not violate the *substantial limitations or restrictions* rules.

Example 4: **Part of sales proceeds can be paid to exchanger:** On May 17, 1998, Barb transfers a rental building to Carol. On the same day, Carol pays $10,000 to Barb and deposits $90,000 in escrow as security for Carol's obligation to perform under the agreement. The escrow agreement provides that Barb has no rights to receive, pledge, borrow or otherwise obtain the benefits of the money in escrow before November 14, 1998, except that

1. if Barb fails to identify replacement property on or before July 1, 1998, Barb may demand the funds in escrow at any time after July 1, 1998, and
2. if Barb identifies and receives replacement property, then she may demand the balance of the remaining funds in escrow at any time after she has received the replacement property.

The funds in escrow may be used to purchase the replacement property. The escrow holder is not a disqualified person. Pursuant to the terms of the agreement, Barb identifies replacement property, and Carol purchases the replacement property using the funds in escrow and transfers the replacement property to Barb.

Tax result: *§1031 exchange available.* Carol's obligation to transfer the replacement property to Barb is secured by cash held in a qualified escrow account because the escrow holder is not a disqualified person and the escrow agreement expressly limits Barb's rights to receive, pledge, borrow or otherwise obtain the benefit of the money in escrow. In addition, Barb does not have the immediate ability or unrestricted right to receive money or other property in escrow before she actually receives the like-kind replacement property. Therefore, for purposes of §1031, Barb is determined not to be in actual or constructive receipt of the $90,000 held in escrow before she receives the like-kind replacement property. The transfer of the rental property by Barb and her acquisition of the replacement property qualify as an exchange under §1031. Of course, the $10,000 gain is considered boot and may be taxable [§1.1031(k)-1(g)(8) (Example 1)].

Safe harbor 3—Qualified accommodators. Sometimes buyers of real estate want only to pay their money and be done with the deal. They have little interest in, or are unable to fund, the purchase of replacement property for the exchanger. What happens if a buyer simply doesn't want to be bothered with this complication and starts looking for other property? In such cases, *intermediaries* and *accommodators* have sprung up to facilitate regular exchanges—and now deferred exchanges.

Safe harbor 3 uses a qualified accommodator's participation in the exchange to prevent the taxpayer from constructively receiving the purchase money. Deferred exchanges are permitted to be facilitated by the use of a *qualified intermediary* **if** the taxpayer's rights to receive the money or other property held by the accommodator are limited by the previously discussed rules on substantial limitations or restrictions [§1.1031(k)-1(g)(4)(vi)]. In this case the qualified accommodator is not considered the agent of the taxpayer (an agent is normally a disqualified person) [§1.1031(k)-1 (g)(4)(i)].

> *Example:* **Using a qualified facilitator:** On May 1, 1998, Barb enters into an agreement to sell (not exchange) to Carol a $100,000 rental building on May 17, 1998. Prior to closing, on May 16, Barb retains Acme Accommodators to facilitate a deferred exchange by entering into a deferred exchange agreement. Acme is a qualified accommodator and is not a disqualified person. Under the terms of the deferred exchange agreement, on May 17, 1998, Barb will transfer the rental property to Acme subject to Carol's right to purchase it for $100,000 on that date. Barb has to identify the replacement property by July 1, 1998, and Acme must purchase that identified property by November 13, 1998, and transfer it to Barb. Barb's rights are limited by the substantial limitations discussed above and she is not related to Acme. Barb pays $1,000 to Acme for facilitating this transaction.

> *Additional facts:* On May 17, 1998, Acme acquires the rental property from Barb and simultaneously transfers it to Carol in exchange for $100,000 cash. For reasons unrelated to the federal income tax, the rental property's legal title is transferred directly from Barb to Carol (permitted by §1.11031(k)-1(g)(4)(iv) and Rev. Rul. 90-34). On June 1, 1998, Barb identifies an office building as replacement property. On August 9, 1998, Acme purchases the office building for $100,000 and transfers it to Barb.

> *Tax result:* *A §1031 exchange.* The transfer of the rental property by Barb is a qualified §1031 exchange. Even though Acme acquires the rental property subject to Carol's right to purchase the property on prearranged terms and conditions, and similarly acquires the office building, they both are deemed legitimate acquisitions. Barb is deemed not to be in constructive receipt of the money before she receives the office building [§1.1031(a)-3(g)(7)(Example 3)].

Who May Be an Accommodator in a Deferred Exchange?

A qualified accommodator is a person:

1. who is not the taxpayer or a disqualified person (discussed in the next section) *and*

2. who acts to facilitate a deferred exchange by entering into a written agreement (called the *exchange agreement*), and, as required by the exchange agreement, *acquires* the relinquished property from the taxpayer, transfers the relinquished property, acquires the replacement property, and transfers the replacement property to the taxpayer [§1.1031(k)-1(g)(4)(iii)].

WARNING: A legal document, generally called an exchange agreement, *must* exist evidencing the relationship between the exchanger and the accommodator.

PLANNING TIP: As previously discussed, the word *acquire* means either actual acquisition or assignment of the right to purchase.

Definition of a Disqualified Person

1. *Any agent of the taxpayer—within the last two years*. The person who is the agent of the taxpayer at the time of the transaction is a disqualified person. For this purpose, *a person who has acted as the taxpayer's employee, attorney, accountant, investment banker or broker, or real estate agent or broker within the two-year period* ending on the date of the transfer of the first of the relinquished properties *is treated as an agent of the taxpayer* at the time of the transaction.

   But the following will not be a disqualified agent:

   • *Putting together an exchange.* An agent providing services for the taxpayer with respect to exchanges of property intended to qualify for nonrecognition of gain or loss under §1031
   • *Routine financial, title insurance, escrow or trust services* for the taxpayer by a financial institution, title insurance company or escrow company [§1.1031(k)-1(k)(2)]

COMMENT: Therefore, most real estate agents putting together an exchange may be the accommodator so long as they have not represented the client in the last two years.

---

2. *A related party.* If a person and the taxpayer bear a relationship described in either §267(b) (e.g., family members, spouses, lineal descendants, a corporation and owner of 10% or more of the corporation, a fiduciary and beneficiary of a trust, a grantor and a fiduciary of a trust, etc.) or §707 (b) (e.g., a partnership and partner owning 10% or more of the partnership), determined by sub-

stituting in each section "10%" for "50%" each place it appears, he or she shall be a disqualified person [§1.1031(k)-1(k)(3)].

3. *A related agent.* If a person and a person who is an agent of the taxpayer at the time of the transaction bear a relationship described in §267(b) or §707(b), again substituting 10% for 50%, he or she shall be a disqualified person.

Examples: Unless otherwise provided, in the next group of examples the following facts are assumed: On May 1, 1998, Larry enters into an exchange agreement with General Business Services (GBS) whereby Larry retains GBS to facilitate an exchange with respect to his office building. On May 17, 1998, pursuant to the agreement, Larry executes and delivers to GBS a deed conveying his office building to GBS.

Example 1:   Taxpayer's accountant: GBS is Larry's accountant and has rendered accounting services to Larry within the two-year period ending on May 17, 1998, in addition to counseling him about the exchange of this property to qualify for nonrecognition of gain or loss under §1031.

GBS is a disqualified person because GBS has acted as Larry's accountant within the two-year period ending on May 17, 1998.

If GBS had not acted as Larry's accountant within the two-year period ending on May 17, 1998, or if GBS had acted as Larry's accountant within that period only with respect to exchanges intended to qualify for nonrecognition of gain or loss under §1031, GBS would not have been a disqualified person [§1.1031(k)-1 (k)(5)(Example 1)].

Example 2:   Escrow company: GBS, which is engaged in the trade or business of acting as an accommodator to facilitate deferred exchanges, is a wholly owned subsidiary of an escrow company that has performed routine escrow services for Larry in the past. GBS has previously been retained by Larry to act as an accommodator in prior §1031 exchanges.

GBS is not a disqualified person notwithstanding the accommodator services previously provided by GBS to Larry and notwithstanding the combination of GBS's relationship to the escrow company and the escrow services previously provided by the escrow company to Larry [§1.1031(k)-1(k)(5)(Example 2)].

Example 3:   Escrow company owned by exchanger's lawyer: GBS is a corporation that is only engaged in the trade or business of acting as an accommodator to facilitate deferred exchanges. Each of ten law firms owns 10% of the outstanding stock of GBS. One of the ten law firms that owns 10% of GBS is Snydley & Whiplash, Attorneys-at-Law. Barrister Bill is the managing partner of Snydley & Whiplash and is the president of GBS. Barrister Bill, in his capacity as a partner in Snydley & Whiplash, has also rendered legal advice to Larry within the 2-year period ending on May 17, 1998, on matters other than exchanges intended to qualify for nonrecognition of gain or loss under §1031.

Barrister Bill and Snydley & Whiplash, Attorneys-at-Law, are disqualified persons. GBS, however, is not a disqualified person because neither Barrister Bill nor Snydley & Whiplash own, directly or indirectly, more than 10% of the stock of GBS. Similarly, Barrister Bill's participation in the management of GBS does not make GBS a disqualified person [§1.1031(k)-1(k)(5)(Ex 3)].

How the Interest Earned in the Escrow Is Handled

Can the interest earned while the cash is controlled by the accommodator be paid to the exchanger? To compensate for the time value of money for the period between transfer and receipt of the replacement property, the taxpayer may charge interest, sometimes called a *growth factor,* during the exchange period, but only if:

1. the previously mentioned *substantial limitations or restrictions* exist [§1.1031(k)-1(g)(5)],
2. the interest time period is only the time between transfer of the relinquished property and receipt of the replacement property [§1.1031(k)-1(h)(1)] *and*
3. it is taxable as interest income, whether paid in cash or other property, *including like-kind property* [§1.1031(k)-1(h)(2)].

COMMENT: The exchanger must include the interest (or growth factor) in income according to the exchanger's method of accounting, (e.g., a calendar-year exchanger would include the interest income earned through December 31 even though the exchanger cannot remove the interest from the trust account because of the access-to-the-cash limitation rules) [§1.1031(k)-1(h)(2)].

COMMENT: Previously, small accommodators have retained any interest earned in escrow as partial compensation for services rendered. This new rule alerts the taxpayer(s), and their agents, that interest may be charged without risking the exchange, which will probably result in the more knowledgeable taxpayers requesting the interest for themselves. The effect of these regulations likely will be that either small accommodators will start charging flat fees or the majority of the work will be performed by banks and escrow companies.

8

Minimum Requirements for an Exchange

HOW TO USE THIS CHAPTER

The reader now knows how to calculate the tax results of a like-kind exchange and can pull together the parties for an exchange. The three previous chapters make like-kind exchanges sound fun, and they are fun—up to a point.

At some time in every exchange comes a technical question so crucial that potentially it can blow up the exchange. This chapter is written to supply the answer to that all-important deal killer. This part is not written to be read as a novel, but it does supply the nitty-gritty of the exchange requirements. Once the problem surfaces, look for the answer in this chapter. Generally, the answer is supported by tax citations and/or court cases.

As previously mentioned, §1031 provides that no gain (or loss) is recognized if certain qualifying property is exchanged solely for like-kind property. However, property qualifying for the nontax treatment is limited to *property held for productive use in a trade or business or for investment,* so long as the property is specifically not excluded (e.g., inventory, stocks and bonds cannot be traded tax-free) [§1031(a)(1)].

Six Basic Elements for an Exchange

To make searching for technical answers easier, this chapter has been divided into the six criteria necessary to meet the like-kind exchange prerequisites. Determine in what area your exchange question is and skip forward to find your answer.

The requirements of §1031(a)(1) involve the following six components:

1. *Property:* There must be property transferred and property received.
2. *Exchange:* There must be an "exchange" of properties.

3. *Qualified use:* Both the property transferred and the property received must be held for "productive use in a trade or business or for investment."

4. *Not excluded property:* The tax-free benefits of §1031 are not available to the transfers of stock-in-trade (e.g., inventory), stocks, bonds, notes, other securities or evidences of indebtedness or interest, interests in a partnership, certificates of trust or beneficial interests, or choses in action; and therefore exchanges of any of the enumerated properties are taxable transfers.

5. *Like kind:* The business or investment properties transferred must also be of a "like kind."

6. *No boot:* For the transaction to be entirely tax-free, the property received must be exchanged *solely* for qualified like-kind property.

1. The "Property" Requirement

Section 1031(a)(1) only applies "on the exchange of *property . . . for property*," not an exchange of property for something else (e.g., prepaid rent or services to be rendered). If nonqualifying property is included, §1031 may be partially or totally unavailable. Here is a list of some unusual items that may or may not qualify as property for like-kind exchange purposes.

Leasehold. A taxpayer who transfers a 30-year, or longer, leasehold on real property (e.g., land or building) is considered to have transferred qualifying property [§1.1031(a)-1(c)]; optional renewal periods are included when calculating the 30 years [Rev. Rul. 78-72, 1978-1 CB 258]. Leaseholds with a remaining duration of less than 30 years are of like kind to each other only but not to any other real property [Rev. Rul. 76-301, 1976-2 CB 241].

Prepaid rent. A leasehold is not considered real property if below-market rent is paid or when property reverts back to the exchanger at the end of the 30-year-plus lease [Rev. Rul. 66-209, 1966-2 CB 299].

Life estate. A taxpayer can exchange a life estate for real property so long as the property does not revert back to the exchanger. If the exchanger retains a remainder interest, the property received represents prepaid rent, not property [Rev. Rul. 72-601, 1972-2 CB 467].

Services to be rendered. A taxpayer cannot exchange property for services, including brokerage fees or production services [§1.1031(e)(4)]. This may lead to some bizarre results, as seen in the next two examples.

1. *The exchange of land for a building to be constructed on **presently owned** property is not a qualified exchange. Bloomington Coca-Cola Bottling Co.* [189 F2d 14 (9th Cir. 1950)] transferred property to a contractor in exchange for the construction of a building on some other Coca-Cola land. We know that the contractor cannot use §1031, but what about Coca-Cola? The court decided no exchange, as Coca-Cola was considered to have received building services

and materials, not qualifying property. (However, LTR 8008113 held that an exchange of improvements in a shopping center for a fee interest qualified for §1031). On the other hand:

2. *The exchange of land for a building to be constructed on a site **not presently owned*** is a qualified exchange [*J. H. Baird Publishing Co. 39* TC 608 (1962), acq., 1963-2 CB 4]. The taxpayer "sold" high-basis property to a contractor, then hired the contractor to build a building, and subsequently "traded" some low-basis property back to the same contractor—tax-free under §1031 (LTR 7823035)!

PLANNING TIP: As discussed previously in the "deferred exchange" rules, the taxpayer can clearly exchange existing property for property to be constructed but maybe not on their own property and definitely not for future services [§1.1031(e)].

---

2. The "Exchange" Requirement

There must be an *exchange* of property, not a sale of property followed by a subsequent purchase of other property. Ordinarily, a transfer will be considered an exchange if there is a reciprocal transfer of property for property but not a transfer of property for money [§1.1002-1(d)].

No simultaneous purchases allowed. The exchange requirement is not met when a cash sale of property is immediately followed by a cash purchase of like-kind property [*Halpern v. U.S.,* 286 F. Supp. 255 (N.D. GA. 1968)].

WARNING: Therefore, all documents used at closing must be *exchange documents* and not the typical purchase and sale agreements commonly associated with residential sales. It is not sufficient, in the author's opinion, to simply draw a line through the words *buy, sell, purchaser* and *seller* and substitute exchange verbiage, such as *exchanger* and *exchangee.*

May an exchange be arranged even though a contract for sale between two parties has already been signed? Yes, amazingly enough, by using an escrow arrangement. The Tax Court looks at the *form* of the transaction over its *substance.*

Example: In *Leslie Q. Coupe* [52 TC 394 (1960)], even though a contract to sell for a stipulated price had been signed with a second party, it was arranged that the second party deposit the money into an escrow account with instructions to the escrow agent that it be paid to the title holders of Coupe's property. Coupe then exchanges his property for like-kind property owned by a third party. The third party sells the Coupe property to the second party for the cash in the escrow account. This transaction was not considered a sham but rather a perfectly legitimate tax-free exchange.

Some sales will be treated as exchanges—trade-ins. A taxpayer may own property that has a basis higher than the trade-in value. Prudent tax planning would structure the transaction as a sale, followed with a subsequent purchase, to trigger the deductible loss. Tax planning professionals would *not* want to structure the transaction as an exchange, because this requires the loss to be currently nondeductible and adds the loss to the basis of the newly acquired property.

May a trade-in be structured as a sale? Probably not. If the sale and purchase is mutually dependent (i.e., both the sale and the purchase are from the same business—as is common in the automobile industry), the transaction may be deemed an exchange [Rev. Rul. 61-119, 1961-1 CB 395; *Redwing Carriers, Inc. v. Tomlinson,* (CA-5) 68-2 USTC ¶9540; 399 F2d 652].

> *Example:* George owns an apartment house with a central air conditioner that has a present depreciable basis of $12,000 (because it previously has only been allowed a depreciation rate of 27.5 years). This old air conditioner fails, and George decides to replace it with a new $42,000 Lenox. Dave (Lenox) allows a $2,000 trade-in on the old unit. Therefore George's *loss* is $10,000 ($12,000 basis—$2,000 fair market value).

> *Tax problem:* Is the $10,000 loss deductible? *No.* This is a like-kind exchange, and losses on like-kind exchanges are never deductible [§1031(a)(1); also discussed in Chapter 5]. Losses on exchanges are added to the purchase price of the new asset *and now will have to be depreciated over another 27.5 years* (also discussed in Chapter 10 on depreciation)! This is a terrible result. Are there any alternatives?

> *Tax solution:* One of the six like-kind exchange elements must be avoided. The most common solution is to not have an exchange in the first place by junking (abandoning) the old air conditioner and asking Dave for a $2,000 reduction in price for a cash purchase. In this situation, the $12,000 loss is currently deductible as an abandonment loss, normally reportable on IRS Form 4797.

Some exchanges will be treated as sales—cash received may create a deemed sale and reinvestment. If the taxpayer *constructively* receives the cash and subsequently uses it to purchase property, a structured exchange is treated as a sale, especially where a step-transaction analysis indicates that the substance (over the form) of the transaction is a sale [*Carlton v. U.S.,* 385 F. 2d 238 (5th Cir. 1967); *Crenshaw v. U.S.,* 450 F. 2d 472 (5th Cir. 1971)]. These problems can be easily avoided by using *qualified accommodators* as discussed in Chapter 7 on deferred exchanges.

3. The "Qualified Use" Requirement—What Property Qualifies for a Tax-Free Exchange?

Requirement. As mentioned previously, *both* the property given up and the property received by the taxpayer must be held for *productive use in a trade or business* **or** for investment [§1031(A)(1)]. For confusion's sake, §1031 does not define *business* or *investment;* therefore, conventional wisdom assumes that the terms have the same meaning as elsewhere in the code, which is discussed below.

COMMENT: The *qualified use* test is determined by the use of each property, both given and received, *in the taxpayer's hands*. Therefore, the use of either property in the hands of the other party involved in the exchange is irrelevant [Rev. Rul. 75-291].

"Held for productive use in trade or business." Qualifying property must be used in a trade or business in which the taxpayer is engaged [§162; §1231].

Examples of trade or business property include buildings owned and used by a business, office buildings, apartment houses, machinery and equipment, business trucks, and automobiles.

Confusion reigns—rental units are business property. For tax and exchange purposes, rental units are considered to be business property, *not* investment property. Most investors think rentals are investments, which is not true. Investment property has the negative result of creating a capital loss whereas business property creates a fully deductible ordinary loss (see Chapter 2 for more details). So what is included in the very limited definition of *investment* property?

"Held for investment." This probably refers to property held for future use or future appreciation in value [§212].

Examples of investment property include unimproved raw land, recreational property, vacation homes and condominiums.

COMMENT: As will be discussed further under requirement 5, real estate business property (e.g., an apartment) may be exchanged for real estate investment property (e.g., raw land or a vacation home being held for appreciation).

Personal residences and certain vacation homes don't qualify. A personal residence (or a vacation home not held for investment) is not *qualified use* property because it is being used for personal purposes, not *business or investment* purposes.

Personal residences cannot be included in an exchange: Therefore, when a personal residence is exchanged for any other property, the §121 residence exclusion rules apply (Chapter 3) and not the §1031 tax-free exchange rules.

WARNING: Vacation homes used personally cannot use §121 residence exclusion rules (as the home is not being used as the taxpayer's *principal* residence) and cannot use the §1031 rules (as the home is not being used for business or investment property). Personal-use vacation homes are normally fully taxable when sold.

Can we exchange a vacation home for a vacation home? The question is, at the date of exchange is the vacation home being used primarily for personal purposes or is it being held for investment purposes (e.g., for future appreciation)? An exchange of a personal-use vacation home for anything, even another vacation home, cannot use the §1031 exchange rules (and therefore it would be a taxable exchange). On the other hand, a vacation home held for investment (appreciation) or as a vacation home rental would fully qualify for a like-kind exchange. The date to determine personal, business or investment use is at the date of sale, and the previous use is relatively immaterial unless the conversion is for tax purposes only [*U.S. v. Winthrop*, 5 Cir. 1969, 417 F.2d 905; Rev. Rul. 82-26, 1982-1 CB 114].

PLANNING TIP: Can we convert a personal residence into property qualified for an exchange? Sometimes it may be desirable to use §1031 on the transfer of a personal residence, as when the taxpayer wishes to acquire, with separate funds, a less costly personal residence and the gain exceeds $250,000. Is it possible? Maybe, but with the changes to gains of sale on a principal residence and the ability to rent it for up to three years and still use the §121 exclusion, the law is unsettled in this area.

Residence into investment property. In Rev. Rul. 57-244, 1957-1 CB 247, the IRS addressed the facts of three taxpayers who purchase property for the construction of homes and later abandon that purpose for clearly established reasons and continue to hold the property for investment purposes (i.e., for appreciation in value). A subsequent exchange is held to qualify under §1031. Property constituting the taxpayer's principal residence will not concurrently qualify as investment property [*Starker v. U.S.*, 602 F2d 1341 (9th Cir. 1979)], even when the taxpayer argues that the residence is being held for appreciation.

Residence into rental property. Converting a personal residence into a rental would also change the use to qualified use. Given that the burden of proving conversion is on the taxpayer, the success of this tactic depends upon how long the property is rented before exchange, the documentation of rental efforts (e.g., newspaper for-rent advertisements, written rental agreements, retention of property managers, etc.), and the substance of the transaction.

Property received in exchange and immediately resold is not "held for" correct purpose. The purpose the taxpayer establishes for acquiring the property is important because property acquired by exchange for immediate sale is not *held for business or investment*. Rather it is acquired for resale (which is not one of the two qualified uses) and therefore cannot be exchanged tax-free. This is especially true when the taxpayer has entered into a binding contract *before the exchange* to sell the property after the exchange. The length of time the property must be held before sale or liquidation is uncertain [*Griffin v. Comm.*, 49 TX 253 (1967); *Black v. Comm.*, 35 TC 90 (1960); Rev. Rul. 75-291; Rev. Rul. 77-297].

Preexisting plan and contract. In one case, the taxpayer exchanged property for a commercial building and one month later initiated a plan of liquidation under which it would sell the building. The court held that the commercial building was *not* held for business or investment (but was held for trading or resale) and therefore the exchange did not qualify under §1031 [*Regals Realty Co. v. Comm.*, 43 BTA 194 (1940)].

Contributions or distributions involving corporations and partnerships. The law is unsettled concerning nonrecognition transfers to or from an entity soon before or after an exchange. The IRS argues that tax-free transfers (under §351 and §721) to the exchanger's own partnership or corporation soon before or after an exchange cause the taxpayer's exchange to fail the *holding for qualifying use* test [Rev. Rul. 75-292, 1975-2, CB 333; Rev. Rul. 77-337, 1977-2 CB 305].

In numerous cases, the Tax Court disagreed with the IRS's position in the previous paragraph and decided that each taxpayer *did meet* the holding-for-business-or-investment requirement. The court overruled the IRS opinion that the corporation or partnership will, by itself, have to reestablish business or investment use and could not attach the partner's/shareholder's use [*Magneson v. Comm.*, 81 TC 767 (1983), *aff'd* 753 F2d 1490 (9th Cir. 1985); *Bolker v. Comm.*, 81 TC 782 (1983), *aff'd* 760 F2d 1039 (9th Cir. 1985); *Mason v. Comm.*, 55 TCM 1134, *aff'd* 880 F2d 420 (11th Cir. 1989); and *Chase v. Comm.*, 92 TC 53 (1989); *Fredericks,* TC CCH Dec. 49,629(M), ¶47,543(M)(1994)].

Property acquired for exchange is also *not held* for correct purpose. In the reverse of the above situation, if the purpose for acquisition is to use the property for a future exchange, it also cannot be exchanged tax-free as it is not being *held for business or investment,* but rather it is being acquired for a future exchange. The length of time the property must be held before an exchange is uncertain [Rev. Rul. 77-337, 1977-2 CB 305; Rev. Rul. 84-121, 1984-2 CB 168].

4. The "Specifically Excluded Property" Requirement

Section 1031(a)(2) specifically states that the tax-free benefits are not available to the transfers of stock-in-trade (e.g., inventory), stocks, bonds, notes, other securities or evidences of indebtedness or interest, interests in a partnership, certificates of trust or beneficial interests, or choses in action. If an exchange involves any of these items, it is nonqualifying property.

> ***Example:*** Dean exchanged his 40-acre farm for Mary's 200 shares of Texaco stock, a $100,000 Commonwealth bond, and a personal note for $100,000. As all three assets received are specifically nonqualified property, the total gain must be recognized.

No like-kind exchange for "dealers" in real estate, as only "investors" qualify. Dealers in real estate may not use the like-kind exchange provisions regarding non-recognition of gain or loss on exchange of real property because they hold real property as stock-in-trade (inventory), and not for productive use in business or for investment [§1031(a)(2)].

PLANNING TIP: Often recently subdivided real estate may not be traded tax-free for other real estate, subdivided or otherwise, as the property being traded is *property held primarily for sale* and therefore is nonqualifying property. Special rules allow the investor to subdivide property and be exempt from dealer status [§1237].

Who is a dealer? In determining whether a person is a *dealer* to any property (as opposed to an *investor*), the facts and circumstances of each situation must be analyzed. The dealer-versus-investor issue must be decided on a property-by-property basis and not an individual-by-individual basis. There are no specific factors, or even combinations of them, that are controlling for deciding the dealer-versus-investor issue. The courts have traditionally used the following tests [*Winthrop, Ada Belle v. Tomlinson,* ¶(CA-5) 69-2 USTC ¶9686, 417 F2d 905]:

1. The reason and purpose the property was acquired and/or disposed
2. The length of time the property was held
3. The number and frequency of sales, usually annually
4. The continuity of sales or sales-related activity over a period of time
5. Overall reluctance to sell the property
6. The substantiality of the gain obtained on the sale
7. The extent to which the taxpayer or his or her agents engaged in sales activities by developing or improving the property, soliciting customers, or advertising
8. The substantiality of sales when compared with other sources of the taxpayer's income
9. The desire to liquidate unexpectedly obtained land holdings (such as by inheritance)

May a REALTOR® also be an investor? Yes. It is possible for the same person to simultaneously be a dealer and an investor in real estate. A dealer in real estate must be distinguished from a *REALTOR®* or a real estate agent. A dealer has ownership interest in property whereas a real estate agent brings together a buyer and a seller of property for a fee or commission [*Williford v. Comm.,* TC Memo 1992-430].

May we convert "dealer" property into property qualified for an exchange? Dealers have, with difficulty, converted a portion of their real estate inventory into business or investment property, but they must prove that the dealer intent has been abandoned and the property thereafter has been held for investment. The length of time the property must be held before sale or liquidation is uncertain, and the difficult evidentiary burden of proof has not been analyzed in any recent exchange cases by the courts [*Maddux Construction Co.,* 54 TC 1278 (1970); *Silversmith v. U.S.,* 79-1 USTC ¶9117 (D. Colo. 1979)].

Trading of partnership interests. The like-kind exchange rules do *not* apply to any exchange of interests in a partnership regardless of whether the interests exchanged are general or limited partnership interests or are interests in the same partnership or in different partnerships. The assets owned by the partnership are irrelevant [§1.1031(a)-(1)(a)(1)].

> *Example:* Edith owns a 50% partnership interest in a $500,000 rental office building in Syracuse and wishes to exchange it for a 50% partnership interest in a $500,000 rental office building in Orlando. Edith has been reporting her income or loss as partnership income or loss (Form K-1), and the rental office building has been reported on a partnership tax return, Form 1065. Edith's exchange would be a *taxable* exchange under these new regulations.

PLANNING TIP: Liquidation of a real estate partnership and transferal of the assets back into individual ownership allows Edith to use the like-kind exchange provisions. Therefore, if Edith first liquidated the partnership, she could use §1031 on her $250,000 half-interest in the rental office building.

Certain real estate joint ventures, and the like, are not considered partnerships. Mere co-ownership of property that is maintained, kept in repair, and rented or leased does not constitute a partnership. For example, if an individual owner or tenant in common of farm property lease it to a farmer for a cash rental or a share of the crops, he or she does not necessarily create a partnership [§1.761-1(a)].

Tenants-in-common, however, may be partners if they *actively* carry on a trade, business, financial operation or venture and divide the profits from the enterprise. For example, a partnership exists if co-owners of an apartment building lease space *and in addition provide services to the occupants,* either directly or through an agent [§1.761-1(a)].

Example: If Edith owns a 50% co-ownership interest in a $500,000 rental office building in Syracuse, she *could exchange tax-free* for a 50% co-ownership interest in a $500,000 rental office building in Orlando. If she really wants to protect herself, she could file a §1.761-2(b) election (discussed next) and not be considered a partnership.

Election to be excluded from partnership provisions available. An interest in certain investment and production partnerships that have made a valid §761(a) election [§1.761-2(b)] is excluded from the application of all of the partnership provisions and is treated as an interest in each of the assets of the partnership, not as an interest in a partnership [§1.1031(a)-(1)(a)(1)]. If the participants in the joint venture (1) purchase, retain, sell or exchange investment property, (2) own the property as co-owners, (3) reserve the right separately to take or dispose of their shares of any property acquired or retained, and (4) do not actively conduct business or use certain agents, then the participants may elect to be excluded from the partnership provisions [§1.761-2(a)(2)].

COMMENT: If the partnership has filed partnership returns for previous years, this election is probably not available as the election must be timely filed. When possible, consideration should be given to a partnership liquidation and a subsequent donation to a joint venture, which will timely file this election! The problem is that liquidation may be difficult.

Foreign real property. Real property located in the United States and real property located outside the United States are *not* property of a like kind. But exchanges of foreign real estate for foreign real estate and domestic real estate for domestic real estate are still permitted [1031(h)].

5. The "Like-Kind" Requirement

As mentioned previously, only like-kind trade, business or investment property owned and used may be traded for like-kind trade, business or investment property. In §1031, the words *like kind* refer to the nature or character of the property (and not to its grade or quality). Accordingly, "one kind or class of property may not . . . be exchanged for property of a different kind or class" [§1.1031(a)-1(b)].

Example: An exchange of a business office building (real property) for business machinery (personal property) will *not* qualify because the nature or character or the property is not like kind.

Like-kind real property exchanges. The Internal Revenue Service is quite liberal in interpreting that all real estate is similar in nature or character and does not have a different grade or quality. The fact that any real estate is improved or unimproved is not material. Also, unproductive real estate held for future use or appreciation in value is held for investment [§1.1031(a)-1(b)].

PLANNING TIP: Any business property for investment property qualifies. Therefore, any mixture of office buildings, apartment buildings, factory buildings, shopping centers, stores, hotels, motels, farms, ranches and parking lots is permitted.

Fee simple transfers. Exchanging fee simple ownership in real estate is virtually always of *like kind* to other fee interests in realty. Fee simple property may even be exchanged for leases in excess of 30 years [§1.1031(a)-1(b),(c)].

Mineral interests. Mineral and nonmineral real estate interests may be exchanged on a like-kind basis provided that the mineral interests are considered real property under state law and are of substantial equality with respect to the character and nature of title as the nonmineral property given. For example, oil and gas royalty rights are of like kind to ranch properties [Rev. Rul. 55-749, 1955-2 CB 95; LTR 7935126].

Leasehold. Thirty-year, or longer, leaseholds and real property (e.g., land or building) are considered to be like kind [§1.1031(a)-1(c)]. Optional renewal periods are included when calculating the 30 years [Rev. Rul. 78-72, 1978-1 CB 258]. Therefore, less-than-30-year leaseholds are not of like kind to a fee ownership in real estate [*Capri, Inc.,* 65 TC 162 (1975)]. Interestingly, leaseholds with a remaining duration of less than 30 years are of like kind to each other [Rev. Rul. 76-301, 1976-2 CB 241].

Sale coupled with a leaseback. A sale of property coupled with the seller leasing the property back for 30 years or longer is considered an exchange of like-kind property, according to the IRS [§1.1031(a)-1(c)(2)]. If the property being disposed of would have created a loss upon sale, this could be disastrous. The courts disagree with this regulation when both the sales price and the rent charged were fair market value [*Jordan Marsh Co. v. Comm.,* 269 F2d 452 (2d Cir. 1959), *nonacq.; Lesslie Co. v. Comm.,* 539 F2d 943 (3rd Cir. 1976), *nonacq.,* 1978-1 CB 3]. Losses have been allowed where the leaseback was for less than a 30-year term, as less-than-30-year leaseholds are not of like kind to fee estates [Rev. Rul. 78-72, 1978-1 CB 258; *Standard Envelope Manufacturing Co.,* 15 TC 41 (1950), *acq.,* 1950-2 CB 4].

Other examples of "like-kind" real property.

1. *Commercial building for lots* [*Burkhard Inv. Co. v. U.S.,* 100 F2d 642 (9th Cir 1938)]
2. *City real estate for a farm or ranch* [§1.1031(a)-1(c)]
3. *Developed property for undeveloped property* [§1.1031(a)-1(c)]
4. *Land subject to a 99-year condominium lease* [*Carl E. Koch,* 71 TC 54, 1978, acq.]
5. *Improved real property for unimproved real property* regardless of the locations [§1.1031(a)-1(c)], with the exception of foreign real estate [§1031(h)]
6. *Timberland for timberland* [Rev. Rul. 72-515; Rev. Rul. 76-253]

7. *A remainder interest in farmland for a remainder interest in other farmland* [Rev. Rul. 78-4]
8. *Perpetual water rights for a fee interest in land* [Rev. Rul. 55-749]
9. *Producing oil leases for a ranch* [Rev. Rul. 68-331]
10. *An easement on a farm for an unencumbered fee simple interest in another farm* [PLR 9215049]

Like-kind personal property exchanges. Normally, exchanges of real estate include furniture and fixtures. The exchange rules for personal property are much stricter than those for real property. Personal property used in a trade or business is considered exchanged for like-kind property *only if* the properties are either (1) like kind *or* (2) like class (e.g., one can't trade tax-free a business lawnmower for a business refrigerator even though both are being used at the same rental).

Each personal property exchange must be reported separately. Reporting like-kind exchanges has become substantially more complicated because disclosure of the exchange now goes on Form 8824 instead of Form 4797 or on Line 9a of Schedule D. To make matters worse, the final regulations [TD 8343] tell taxpayers *how* to report the "trading in" of personal property (e.g., automobiles, over-the-road trucks, office furniture and equipment) when replacing it with other similar personal property.

COMMENT: The final regulations contain *no exceptions* for items of personal property that have de minimis or minimum value! Therefore, every time a landlord trades in an old $50 refrigerator for a new $500 refrigerator, this will require the filing of a different Form 8824. Similarly, each time the real estate agent trades in his or her business automobile, another Form 8824 must be created! Each trade is a reportable like-kind exchange even though no tax may be due.

Multiple asset exchanges—analysis of underlying assets needed in business exchanges. When a taxpayer exchanges one business for a similar business, is the exchanged property the business for the other business? Can we exchange a Wendy's for a McDonald's, or a farm for a farm? According to the IRS, we cannot do a business-for-business exchange. It is an exchange of the separate assets of the businesses.

Example: Dennis exchanges his laundry business, comprising a building and seven washer and dryer units (fair market value of $1,000 per unit), to Evelyn for her laundry business, comprising a building, five washer and dryer units (fair market value of $1,000 per unit), and an old pickup truck. Can Dennis consider the exchange to be entirely tax-free? No.

As a general rule, real property may continue to be exchanged as one group, but personal property must be segregated into specific like-kind groups [§1.1031 (j)-1(a)(1); (§1.1031(j)-1(b)(2)(i); Rev. Rul. 89-121; Rev. Rul. 72-151]. The separation of the properties transferred and the properties received into *exchange groups* involves matching up properties of a like kind or like class to the smallest extent possible [§1.1031(j)-1(a)(2)]. For example:

1. *Personal properties* are accumulated into separate exchange groups of the same General Asset Class *or* within the same Product Class [as defined in §1.1031(a)-2(b)].
2. *All real properties* belong to one exchange group as they are of a like kind.
3. *Not-like-kind property*—if property exists that cannot be matched up like kind (or is unqualified property), it must be placed in the *residual* group.

How do the §1031 exchange rules apply to these exchange groups? The §1031 exchange rules apply *separately* to each exchange group to determine the amount of gain recognized in the exchange [§1.1031(j)-1(a)(2)(i)].

> **Example (continued):** Dennis and Evelyn have a tax-deferred like-kind exchange only to the extent of the first exchange group, consisting of the five washers and dryers being traded for five washers and dryers (Product Class 3633). But *both* have taxable boot (a non-like-kind exchange) to the extent of the second exchange group—that is, Dennis's trade of two washers and dryers (Product Class 3633) for Evelyn's pickup truck (ADR 00.22).

> **Example:** Paige owns a ranch comprised of three separately purchased properties that are exchanged (one deed) with Tyson for 20 commercial lots (again via one deed). Even though this exchange involves 23 separate properties, it is *one* separate exchange group for §1031 purposes, and the §1031 exchange rules apply to the group, not to each separate property.

Like-kind exchanges—rules for exchanges of goodwill. The goodwill or going-concern value of a business is not of a like kind to the goodwill or going concern value of another business. Therefore, the trading of goodwill is taxable [§1.1031(a)-2(c)(2)].

COMMENT: When exchanging business opportunities, the goodwill of either business is "boot" (or not-like kind property) and could create taxable gain. The IRS's theory is that goodwill comes from the business's customer base, and since most business's being exchanged are in different locations, it would be impossible to have the exact same customer base.

PLANNING TIP: When the different components of a business are being valued for exchange purposes, goodwill must also be identified and valued. In most cases, it would be desirable to establish the *lowest* fair market value. Establishing the lowest value would also be consistent with the §1060 regulations for valuing a business in non-like-kind exchanges even though §1060 is not applicable to exchanges [Reg. §1.1031(d)-1T].

Like-kind exchanges of other intangible personal property and nondepreciable personal property. An exchange of intangible personal property or nondepreciable personal property qualifies for nonrecognition of gain or loss under §1031 only if the exchanged properties are of a like kind. No like classes are provided for these properties. Whether intangible personal property is of a like kind to other intangible personal property generally depends on the nature or character of the rights involved (e.g., a patent or a copyright) and also on the nature or character of the underlying property to which the intangible personal property relates [§1.1031(a)-2(c)(1)].

> *Example:* Stephen King exchanges a copyright on a novel for a copyright on a different novel. The properties exchanged are of a like kind [§1.1031(a)-2(c)(3) (Example 1)].

> *Example:* Yanni exchanges a copyright on a novel for a copyright on a song. The properties exchanged are not of a like kind [§1.1031(a)-2(c)(3)(Example 2)].

> *Example:* Trading of a McDonald's franchise for another McDonald's franchise should be deemed like kind.

RELATED PARTY EXCHANGES

If a taxpayer exchanges property with a related party (as defined below), the original exchange will not qualify for tax deferral if either of the exchanged properties is sold or disposed of within two years of the transfer. Interestingly, the postponed gain becomes taxable at the time of the disqualifying disposition. It is important to note that exchanges between related parties may still use the tax-free benefits of §1031, provided the two-year waiting period and other requirements listed below are met [§1031(f) and (g)].

Who is a related party? Related parties include

1. *family members,* such as brothers, sisters, spouse, ancestors and lineal descendants as well as C or S Corporations and over 50% shareholders, corporate controlled members, and grantors and fiduciaries of trusts [§267(b)].
2. *partnership–partner.* The related party definition also includes over 50% partner-to-partnership attribution rules [§707(b)].

Two exceptions to the two-year rule.

1. *Dispositions due to death, involuntary conversion, or for non-tax-avoidance purposes* will not invalidate §1031 treatment. The Conference Report gives three examples of this non-tax-avoidance exception, which are (1) transactions

involving certain exchanges of undivided interests in different properties that result in each taxpayer's holding either the entire interest in a single property or a larger undivided interest in any of the properties, (2) dispositions of property in a compulsory or involuntary conversion (e.g., §1033), and (3) transactions that do not involve the shifting of basis between properties [§1031(g)(2)].

2. *Risk of loss diminished.* In addition, the running of the two-year holding period will be suspended during any period when a party's risk of loss with respect to the property is substantially diminished by §1031(g)(2), such as: (1) the holding of a put with respect to the property; (2) the holding by another person of a right to acquire the property; or (3) a short sale or any other transaction.

The penalty applies to both parties!

Example: Dan and George, who are brothers, exchange like-kind property in a §1031 transaction. The realized gain on the exchange is postponed. Dan sells the property he received 18 months after the exchange. The result is that an *unqualified* like-kind exchange is deemed to have occurred—as of the date Dan sold the property. When Dan disposes of the property, it causes all of the postponed gain to be recognized as of the date of the disposition. Not only does Dan have to recognize the gain, but George also has to recognize the gain he postponed.

Example (continued): What happens if Dan, 18 months after the exchange, enters into another §1031 exchange with an unrelated party? Even in this case, the second §1031 exchange is treated as a sale and will cause Dan *and George* to recognize the postponed gain from the first exchange.

Therefore, advance tax planning is required. Stronger controls must exist between the related parties to prevent unexpected tax consequences created by the unilateral actions of just one of the parties. The legal documents should include a provision specifying that if either of the parties triggers the recognition of the postponed gain within the two-year period, the innocent party will be reimbursed for the tax consequences.

Ouch—related parties who exchange must file IRS Form 8824 for the next two years! If the exchange is made with a related party, the taxpayer must file Exchange Form 8824 in the year of the exchange *and for the two following years* (Tax Management, Inc. (BNA) Portfolio, Vol. 61-5th, page C&A-2, A-31).

6. Boot—Receipt of Other Property or Money in Tax-Free Exchanges

May a tax-free exchange involve both qualifying and nonqualifying property?
Yes. A §1031 exchange is fully tax-free only if the taxpayer exchanges property *exclusively* for qualifying like-kind property. Nevertheless, if cash or any other type of nonqualifying property is received (commonly referred to as *receiving boot,* as in: "My property is worth more than yours and I will only trade you my apartment for your apartment if you give me $100,000 to boot"), this does not prevent the *partial* use of §1031, thereby finding part of the gain not currently taxable.

Definition of *boot*. The amount of boot received is the sum of any money and the fair market value of other nonqualified property the exchanger receives. Therefore, boot consists of money, liabilities assumed (or attached to the property received in exchange), non-qualifying property (such as cash, inventory, or stocks and bonds) and property that does not meet the like-kind definition (such as trading business property for personal property) [§1031(b); §1.1031(b)-1)]. It even includes cash received several years before the exchange for an option on the relinquished property, with the option money treated as boot during the year in which the exchange is completed [PLR 9413024]. However, there is a price to pay when receiving boot.

Receipt of boot—gain may be recognized to the lower of the gain or the boot. If nonqualifying property, or boot, is received in an exchange that otherwise consists of like-kind property, gain will be recognized (i.e., taxable) but not in excess of such money (and liabilities relieved of) and the fair market value of such other unlike property. This is basically saying that the taxpayer will not be required to pay more tax than would have been paid if the property had been sold for cash [§1031(b); §1.1031(b)-1(a)].

> ***Example:*** Jerry trades a building (fair market value of $500,000) and machinery (fair market value of $100,000) for Bill's building (fair market value of $600,000).
>
> Jerry does not recognize any gain on the exchange as he *did not receive* any nonqualifying property. (But watch out for giving nonqualifying appreciated property in an exchange as discussed in "giving of boot.")
>
> Bill, though, has a taxable gain, because *he did receive* nonqualifying property, the machinery. His gain is recognized but not in excess of the value of the machinery, $100,000 (unless Bill's realized gain is less than $100,000, e.g., if his adjusted basis were $550,000, the maximum taxable gain would, of course, be only $50,000).

Receipt of boot—but loss is not recognized. If a taxpayer receives, in addition to qualified like-kind property, either money or other property, any loss realized on the exchange is not recognized, that is, not deductible. This is true even if the loss on the exchange is created solely by the exchange brokerage commission. The loss is added to the fair market value of the property received (see basis-adjustment section for details on computation) [§1031(c); Rev. Rul. 72-456, 1972-2 CB 468].

Giving of boot—it's a regular sale for gain or loss purposes. Giving boot, or nonqualifying property (i.e., Jerry's machinery in the previous example), along with giving qualifying property in an exchange does not completely remove the transaction from §1031. Nevertheless, the transfer of non-money boot is treated as a sale of such property with respect to which any gain or loss is taxable. The taxpayer is deemed to receive in exchange for the nonqualifying property transferred an amount equal to its fair market value [§1.1031(a)-1(a); §1.1031(d)-1(e); §1.1031(d)-1(e)].

Formula. Therefore, the gain (or loss) is calculated under the general reporting rules of §1001(c), using the following formula:

Gain on Boot (B1 through B4) Calculation

Fair market value of boot property given	B1	+ _____
Less: Adjusted basis of boot property given	B2	– _____
Gain recognized on boot property given (1 – 2)	B3	_____
Loss recognized on boot property given (2 – 1)	B4	_____

> *Example:*   Joe trades in his old delivery truck for a new one. In addition, he gives the auto dealer 100 shares of stock as boot. Joe originally paid $1,000 for the stock, but at the time of the trade-in, the stock is worth $3,000. Joe has a $2,000 taxable gain because he has used the stock as boot.

Fair market value of boot property given	B1	+ $3,000
Less: Adjusted basis of boot property given	B2	– 1,000
Gain recognized on boot property given (1 – 2)	B3	$2,000
Loss recognized on boot property given (2 – 1)	B4	

Netting boot. In certain circumstances, the taxpayer may net the (taxable) boot received by any boot given (such as the netting of liabilities), thereby lowering the gain to be recognized.

Liabilities assumed. As mortgage relief is considered boot and treated as if it is money received by the taxpayer in the exchange, this can result in a disastrous tax consequence. Any mortgage assumed, or taken subject to, creates taxable gain for the party being relieved of the debt . . . to the extent of the total gain [§1031(d); §1.1031(b)-1(a)].

> *Example:*   Bob trades his $100,000 apartment house with a $60,000 mortgage (and a basis of $30,000) to Scott for a free and clear $40,000 bare lot. The $60,000 debt relief experienced by Bob is deemed *boot,* requiring that Bob pay tax on the gain to the extent of the boot. But Bob has no cash to pay the tax!

The mortgage napkin test. What happens if both parties bring a mortgage to the exchange? Fortunately, we can *net* the liabilities, as explained next. This calculation is similar to the computation used to balance equities when the transaction first started.

Mortgage given netted against mortgage received. If each exchange party assumes the liability of the other party, the parties are allowed to *net* their liabilities when calculating the amount of the taxable boot received. Even the issuance of the exchanger's own promissory note is considered boot given, which may be offset against mortgage relief. Therefore, only when taxpayers realize a *net* reduction in their debt do they experience taxable boot [§1.1031(b)-1(c); §1.1031(d)-2 (Example 2); Rev. Rul. 79-44, 1979-1 CB 265].

Example: Zane exchanges property with a fair market value of $150,000, which is subject to a liability of $60,000, for Willow's property, which has a fair market value of $190,000 and is subject to a liability of $100,000. Zane receives no mortgage boot because he experiences a net increase in indebtedness. But Willow receives $40,000 of boot, as she receives a net reduction of liability.

Note: The numbers in front of the dollar amounts in this example refer to the like-kind exchange worksheet in Figure 5.1.

Mortgage Relief—Zane

Mortgage on property given	20	$ 60,000
Less: Mortgage on property received	21	– 100,000
Net mortgage relief (but not below zero)	22	0

Mortgage Relief—Willow

Mortgage on property given	20	$100,000
Less: mortgage on property received	21	– 60,000
Net mortgage relief (but not below zero)	22	$ 40,000

PLANNING TIP: Trade up in debt!

Cash (and other property) **given** *may be netted against mortgage* **received.** The giving of cash and the fair market value of other nonqualifying property (property boot) is also netted against any relief of liabilities [1.1031(d)-2(Example 1); *Coleman v. Comm.,* 180 F2d 758 (8th Cir. 1950); Rev. Rul. 79-44].

Example: Zane exchanges $50,000 cash, stock worth $50,000 and property with a fair market value of $300,000 subject to a liability of $200,000 for Willow's property, which has a fair market value of $250,000 subject to a liability of $50,000. Even though Zane has a net mortgage relief of $150,000, he only receives $50,000 of net boot.

Cash and Boot

Cash received	5	0		
FMV of other (boot) property received	6	0		
Net cash and other boot received			16	0
Cash given	10	$50,000		
FMV of other (boot) property given	11	50,000		
Net cash and other boot given			17	– $100,000
Exchange expenses			18	– 0
Net cash and other boot received (16 – 17 + 18)			19	– $100,000
Mortgage on property given			20	$200,000
Less: mortgage on property received			21	– $ 50,000
Net mortgage relief (but not below zero)			22	$150,000
NET BOOT (Line 22 ± 19)				$ 50,000

But cash (and other property) **received cannot** be offset against mortgage given. Receipt of cash or other nonqualified property in a §1031 exchange *cannot* be offset by the assumption of liabilities. Therefore, the IRS prohibits netting when the exchanger both receives cash and receives a mortgage debt from the other party [§1.1031(d)-2 (Example 2)].

PLANNING TIP: Rather than receiving equalizing cash, it may be smarter to pay down each party's liabilities prior to the exchange. The cash received may also be used to pay exchange expenses.

Example: Zane exchanges property with a fair market value of $350,000 and subject to a liability of $150,000 for Willow's $100,000 cash plus property, which has a fair market value of $300,000 and is subject to a liability of $200,000. Zane receives $100,000 of boot because of the cash received. Although Zane may net boot given against boot received in the form of indebtedness, the increased debt cannot be offset by cash or property boot received.

Cash and Boot

Cash received	5	$100,000		
FMV of other (boot) property received	6	0		
Net cash and other boot received			16	$100,000
Cash given	10	0		
FMV of other (boot) property given	11	0		
Net cash and other boot given			17 –	0
Exchange expenses			18 –	0
Net cash and other boot received (16 – 17 + 18)			19	$100,000
Mortgage on property given			20	$150,000
Less: mortgage on property received			21 –	$200,000
Net mortgage relief (but not below zero)			22	0
NET BOOT (Line 22 ± 19)				$100,000

Note: For the opposite result, see *Barker v. Comm.*, 74 TC 555 (1980), in which a concurrent payoff through escrow of liabilities *was not* treated as cash received. The court stressed that there was an obligation to use the cash to pay off the mortgage, and hence the taxpayer did not at any time have the unfettered use of the cash.

What about netting cash given against cash received or other property given against other property received? Even though many exchanger parties make the assumption that this netting is permitted, it is uncertain whether, or to what extent, money (or other nonqualified property) given may be netted against money (or other nonqualified property) received, as no cases or IRS pronouncements currently give guidance.

Exchange expenses. Certain transaction expenses of the §1031 exchange, such as brokerage commissions paid, reduce the total consideration received and increase the basis of the exchange property received [Rev. Rul. 72-456, 1972-2 CB 468]. In *Westall v. Comm.,* 56 TCM 66 (1988), the court held that the taxpayer's cash received was off-set by *all* the taxpayer's selling expenses and did not delineate the type of selling expenses involved.

COMMENT: May exchangers create liabilities in anticipation of the exchange? The 1991 final regulations *do not include* the proposed amendment that liabilities incurred by the taxpayer in anticipation of a §1031 exchange will be considered taxable boot (i.e., §1031(b) "other property or money"). Whew! Therefore:

May We Refinance Just Prior to the Exchange?

Planning that the IRS doesn't like. In order to equalize their net equities, taxpayers sometimes place a mortgage on their property just prior to closing, with the result that they put cash in their pocket, tax-free. If the cash were paid at closing to that same taxpayer, the cash would be considered taxable boot. Needless to say, this "tax-planning device" is not favorably viewed by the IRS [Rev. Rul. 73-555, 1973-2 CB 159; *Long v. Comm.,* 77 TC 1045 (1981); PLR 8434015]. But can the IRS do anything but yell? See the following:

Refinancing before or after is OK. The Tax Court held, with an IRS acquiescence (i.e., complying without protest), that the assumption of a liability by a taxpayer in a like-kind exchange will be recognized even though the liability was placed on the property immediately *before* the exchange at the taxpayer's prompting so as to avoid the recognition of gain under the mortgage netting rule [*Garcia v. Comm.,* 80 TC 491 (1983), *acq.,* 1984-1 CB 1; PLR 8248039]. Any refinancing *after* the exchange should also be permitted [*Carlton v. U.S.,* 385 F2d 238 (5th Cir.) 1967].

WARNING: Refinancing *during* the exchange, if the taxpayer is allowed to touch the cash (i.e., be in actual or constructive receipt of the money), is not a safe option.

Refinancing is extremely helpful in the multiple (three or more) party exchanges, as illustrated in the next example.

Example: In an otherwise qualified exchange, Edwina wishes to exchange tax-free her free-and-clear (of debt) office building that has a fair market value of $400,000 for Sandy's office building that has a fair market value of $700,000 sub-ject to a $300,000 mortgage. Sandy wants to sell, not exchange, her office building as she needs $400,000 cash (she is willing to pay the tax due). Bobby has $100,000 cash and wishes to purchase Edwina's property.

Problem: Bobby does not have enough cash to buy Sandy's office building, which Bobby would subsequently exchange for Edwina's office building.

Solution: Bobby secures a new loan commitment on Edwina's property for the other $300,000, with Edwina having no immediate right to the money. The loan proceeds are then added to Bobby's existing $100,000 cash (i.e., now $400,000) and, coupled with the assumption of the existing loan, he can acquire Sandy's property through a cash-out (which is what Sandy wants). Bobby then exchanges his newly acquired property with Edwina. The result is that Bobby ends up with what he wants (i.e., Edwina's office building) and Edwina ends up with what she wants (i.e., Sandy's office building), acquired by using a tax-free exchange!

What about this new loan commitment? Many lenders realize that since Bobby will ultimately own Edwina's property and be responsible for paying off the mortgage, he can apply for the loan. This becomes clearer to the lender if all transactions are closed simultaneously in the lender's escrow department!

Reporting Gain on Boot—The Installment Method Is Available

Coordinating the exchange (§1031) and installment (§453) rules. When a taxpayer receives a promissory note instead of cash in addition to receiving like-kind property, the gain recognized in the like-kind exchange may be reported on the installment method (if the transaction otherwise qualifies as an installment sale). Furthermore, the like-kind property received in the exchange is not considered an installment payment in the year of sale [§453(f)(6)(C); §1.1031(k)-1(j)(2)].

Use escrows to hold installment note. The safe harbors relating to qualified escrow accounts, trusts and intermediaries apply for purposes of determining whether a taxpayer is in receipt of payment under the installment sale rules of section 453 [§1.1031(k)-1(j)(2)(i),(ii)].

Bona fide intent requirement. If at the beginning of the exchange period the taxpayer had a *bona fide intent* to enter into a deferred exchange and meets the safe-harbor rules of section 1031, the taxpayer then may report any gain recognized in the exchange under the installment method. A taxpayer will be treated as having a "bona fide intent" only if it is "reasonable to believe, based on all the facts and circumstances as of the beginning of the exchange period, that like-kind replacement property will be acquired before the end of the exchange period" [§1.1031(k)-1(j)(2)(iv)].

Certain other limitations also apply:

1. The gross profit from the exchange is reduced by the gain not recognized because of the exchange rules. Therefore, the gross profit is limited to the

amount of the gain that would be recognized on the exchange if the installment obligation had to be satisfied at its face value [§453(f)(6)(B)].

2. In addition, the total contract price does not include the value of the like-kind property. Therefore, the contract price will consist only of the money, face amount of the installment obligation and fair market value of the other boot received [§453(f)(6)(A)].

The taxpayer's basis in the property put into the exchange is allocated first to the like-kind property received to the extent of its fair market value. The effect of this allocation is to maximize the percentage of each payment received on the installment obligation to be reported as gain from an installment sale. Any remaining basis is used to calculate the gross profit ratio [§1.453(f)].

COMMENT: As a result of the above rule, if the property exchanged has a lower basis than the fair market value of the property received, the gross profit ratio will be 100%, and all payments on any installment obligation will be fully taxable. A more economically reasonable IRS alternative would have been to allocate the basis based on each property's relative fair market value.

Example: Dwight exchanges an office building with a fair market value of $1,000,000 and a basis of $200,000 for Jack's office building with a fair market value of $300,000 and Jack's note of $700,000. The sum of $100,000 is to be paid on the installment note each year, starting one year after the sale.

Even though the purported sales price is $1,000,000, the contract price for installment reporting purposes is $700,000 (since the fair market value of the like-kind property is ignored). The gross profit is also $700,000 since the realized gain of $800,000 is reduced by the $100,000 gain not recognized because of the exchange rules ($300,000 building received less $200,000 basis of the property given). Now the gross profit ratio is 100%, but as no "payment" is received in the year of the sale, no gain is recognized. Thereafter, 100% of each future payment must be included in income as gain!

Timing of gain recognition when exchange fails after cash deposited into escrow. From reading the above regulations, if a delayed exchange falls through, when is the gain from the sale of the relinquished property taxable? Is the gain taxable in the year of sale or in the year that money is received from the intermediary?

Example: Sharon transfers her apartment building to an exchange accommodator in 1998. The accommodator sells the property to a waiting buyer and holds the funds until Sharon can identify a replacement property. Sharon properly identifies a new property within 45 days but is unable to close the exchange within the required 180 days. Because the exchange fell through, the accommodator hands Sharon in 1999 all of the cash it held from the sale of the old property.

Tax Result: Because Sharon always intended to exchange, the sale is reported in 1998 but the gain is taxable as an installment sale with proceeds received in 1999.

What if the taxpayer does not want installment sales treatment? Sharon in the above example may prefer to have the gain taxable in 1998. Can she? Yes, by electing out of installment sales reporting. Remember that the exchange must be completed by the earlier of the due date of Sharon's return for the year of the exchange or 180 days from when she relinquished her property. If replacement property has not been found by the due date of Sharon's 1998 return, she must extend. The election out of installment sales reporting must be made on a timely filed return, including extensions. Regulation §15A.453-1(d)(3)(ii) states that late elections out of the installment method "will be permitted only in those rare circumstances when the IRS concludes the taxpayer had good cause for failing to make a timely election."

Exchanger receives a note. If the intermediary receives a note from the buyer of the relinquished property, can the note be passed on to the exchanger as a qualifying §453 installment obligation?

Example: Laura has a buyer, Beth, for Blueacre but Laura has not yet found a replacement property. Laura transfers Blueacre, pursuant to an exchange agreement, to a qualified intermediary, who then transfers it to Beth for $80,000 in cash and Beth's ten-year installment obligation for $20,000. Laura does not have an immediate ability or an unrestricted right to receive, pledge, borrow or otherwise obtain the benefits of the cash held by the qualified intermediary until the earlier of the date the replacement property is delivered to her or the end of the exchange period. Beth's obligation bears adequate stated interest and is not payable on demand or readily tradeable. Within 180 days the qualified intermediary acquires replacement property worth $80,000 and delivers it, along with the $20,000 installment obligation, to Laura.

Regulation §15A.453-1(b)(3)(i) provides that the term payment does not include the receipt of evidence of indebtedness of the person acquiring the property. Furthermore, the regulations state that payment does include evidence of indebtedness of a person other than the person acquiring the property from the taxpayer.

Example (continued):   Is Laura's receipt of Beth's installment obligation considered a current payment under the installment sale rules because Beth is not the person who acquired the property from the taxpayer (the qualified intermediary is)? No.

The regulations provide that, for purposes of the installment rules, the receipt of an installment obligation from the qualified intermediary's transferee is treated as the receipt of an installment obligation of the person acquiring the relinquished property.

BASIS, DEPRECIATION RECAPTURE, AND HOLDING PERIOD

The basis of property received. Computing the basis on the new property is simple when the exchange involves only property for like-kind property. The new basis of the property received in a tax-free exchange is the basis of the old property surrendered. This new *unadjusted* basis is known as the property's *substituted basis* and preserves the potential gain (or loss) on the disposed building for future recognition [§1031(d); §1.1031(d)-1(a)].

> *Example:* **Straight exchange.** Jennifer trades her office building, with a fair market value of $625,500 and an adjusted basis of $341,000, *straight across* for Hilary's office building. Jennifer's old remaining basis of $341,000 becomes her *substituted basis* in the new property.

This substituted-basis rule becomes complicated, though, when the exchange involves the paying or receiving of cash, netting of liabilities, giving or receiving of other boot, or if a loss is recognized because unlike property is transferred in the exchange along with the like-kind property.

The technical formula to calculate basis of property received. In a tax-free exchange, the new basis is the basis of the old property surrendered, increased by any money (including debt) given and the amount of any gain recognized, and decreased by the amount of money (including debt) received and any loss recognized on the exchange. Therefore, payment of cash and net mortgage debt assumed increases the new basis. Any brokerage commissions and other exchange expenses paid by the exchanger also increase basis [§1031(d); §1.1031(d)-1); Rev. Rul. 72-456, 1972-2 CB 468; *Westall v. Comm.,* 56 TCM 66 (1988)].

COMMENT: Said another way, if the exchange is tax-free, the exchanger's old basis is reduced by the cash received and mortgage relief (i.e., "cashed out") *and* increased by the cash given and the mortgage acquired (i.e., "cash in").

Note: In the following formula, the numbers in front of the dollar amounts refer to the like-kind exchange worksheet in Figure 5.1; B1-4 is the gain calculation on sale of boot property discussed previously in this chapter. "LKE" means like-kind exchange.

Formula for Calculating the Basis of the New Property

Adjusted basis of LKE property given	03 + $ _____	
Adjusted basis of boot property given	B2 + _____	
Cash given	10 + _____	
Mortgage assumed on property	12 + _____	
Subtotal (Plus)		28 + $ _____
Cash received	05 + $ _____	
Mortgage on property given	07 + _____	
Subtotal (Minus)		31 – _____
Plus: Gain recognized on exchange		23 + _____
Plus: Gain recognized on boot given		B3 + _____
Less: Loss recognized on boot		B4 – _____
Exchange expenses		13 + _____
BASIS OF ALL NEW PROPERTY RECEIVED (28, 31, 32, B, 35)		36 = $ _____
BASIS OF BOOT PROPERTY RECEIVED (FMV) (Line 6)		37 = $ _____
BASIS OF LIKE-KIND PROPERTY RECEIVED		36–37 = $ _____

Proving the basis of the new property: The "rule-of-thumb" proof to determine if the basis calculation has been properly computed is:

Fair market value of property received	E1	$ _____
Less: Gain not taxed	15–23 –	_____
New basis	34 =	$ _____

Basis when boot is given. As mentioned previously, the basis of the new property received in a tax-free exchange is the basis of the old property surrendered, increased by any money (including debt) given [§1031(d); §1.1031(d)-1].

> *Example:* **Giving of boot.** Jennifer trades her $625,500 office building and $100,000 cash for Hilary's office building. Jennifer's new substituted basis is her old remaining basis of $341,000 *plus* the $100,000 cash for a new substituted basis of $441,000 [§1.1031(d)-1(a)].

Formula for Calculating the Basis of the New Property

Adjusted basis of LKE property given	03 + $341,000	
Adjusted basis of boot property given	B2 + _____	
Cash given	10 + 100,000	
Mortgage assumed on property	12 + _____	
Subtotal (Plus)		28 + $441,000
Cash received	05 + $ _____	
Mortgage on property given	07 + _____	

Formula for Calculating the Basis of the New Property

Subtotal (Minus)	31 –	_____
Plus: Gain recognized on exchange	23 +	_____
Plus: Gain recognized on boot given	B3 +	_____
Less: Loss recognized on boot	B4 –	_____
Exchange expenses	13 +	_____
BASIS OF ALL NEW PROPERTY RECEIVED (28, 31, 32, B, 35)	36 =	$441,000
BASIS OF BOOT PROPERTY RECEIVED (FMV) (Line 6)	37 =	$
BASIS OF LIKE-KIND PROPERTY RECEIVED	36–37 =	$441,000

Basis when *cash* boot is received and gain is recognized. In a tax-free exchange, the exchanger's new basis is the basis of the old property surrendered, increased by any money (including debt) given plus the amount of any gain recognized and decreased by the amount of any money (including debt) received [§1031(d); §1.1031(d)-1].

> ***Example:*** **Receiving boot.** Jennifer trades her $625,500 office building for Hilary's office building and Hilary adds $50,000 cash. Jennifer's new *substituted basis* is her old remaining basis of $341,000 decreased by the $50,000 cash and increased by the $50,000 gain recognized [§1.1031(d)-1(b)].

Formula for Calculating the Basis of the New Property

Adjusted basis of LKE property given	03 +	$341,000	
Adjusted basis of boot property given	B2 +	_____	
Cash given	10 +	_____	
Mortgage assumed on property	12 +	_____	
Subtotal (Plus)			28 + $341,000
Cash received	05 +	$ 50,000	
Mortgage on property given	07 +	_____	
Subtotal (Minus)			31 – $ 50,000
Plus: Gain recognized on exchange			23 + $ 50,000
Plus: Gain recognized on boot given			B3 + _____
Less: Loss recognized on boot			B4 – _____
Exchange expenses			13 + _____
BASIS OF ALL NEW PROPERTY RECEIVED (28, 31, 32, B, 35)			36 = $341,000
BASIS OF BOOT PROPERTY RECEIVED (FMV) (Line 6)			37 = $
BASIS OF LIKE-KIND PROPERTY RECEIVED			36–37 = $341,000

Allocating basis when *property* boot is received and gain recognized. When the exchanger receives boot property and gain is recognized because of the receipt of the boot, the adjusted basis of the property given, decreased by the amount of cash received and increased by the amount of gain recognized, must be allocated to the properties (other than money) received on the exchange. The basis is *first* allocated to the boot property to the extent of the boot property's fair market value [§1.1031(d)-1(c)].

> ***Example:*** **Receiving boot.** Del trades her office building with a $125,000 fair market value but an adjusted basis of $100,000 for Hilary's $90,000 office building, an auto with a fair market value of $10,000 and $25,000 cash. Del realizes

$25,000 of gain (smaller of the $35,000 boot received or the total gain of $25,000), all of which is taxable [§1.1031(d)-1(c) (Example)].

Formula for Calculating the Basis of the New Property

Adjusted basis of LKE property given	03 + $100,000		
Adjusted basis of boot property given	B2 + _____		
Cash given	10 + _____		
Mortgage assumed on property	12 + _____		
Subtotal (Plus)		28 + $100,000	
Cash received	05 + $ 25,000		
Mortgage on property given	07 + _____		
Subtotal (Minus)		31 – $ 25,000	
Plus: Gain recognized on exchange		23 + $ 25,000	
Plus: Gain recognized on boot given		B3 + _____	
Less: Loss recognized on boot		B4 – _____	
Exchange expenses		13 + _____	
BASIS OF ALL NEW PROPERTY RECEIVED (28, 31, 32, B, 35)		36 = $100,000	
BASIS OF BOOT PROPERTY RECEIVED (FMV) (Line 6)		37 – $ 10,000	
BASIS OF LIKE-KIND PROPERTY RECEIVED		36–37 = $ 90,000	

Allocating basis when boot is received and nondeductible loss exists. No loss is recognized even when other property or money is received. The basis of the property(ies) (other than cash) received is the adjusted basis of the property given, decreased by the amount of money received. This basis is allocated to the properties received, and there must be allocated to such other property an amount of such basis equivalent to its fair market value [§1.1031(d)-1(d)].

Allocating basis when gain or loss on boot property is recognized. When an exchanger exchanges boot property and the boot property creates the recognized gain or loss (§1002), basis is first allocated to the boot property (other than money or liabilities) to the extent of its relative fair market on the date of the exchange, and the balance is allocated among the qualifying property received, based on its relative fair market value on the date of the exchange [§1.1031(d)-1(e)].

> *Example:* **Recognizing loss.** Angela exchanges raw land plus stock for a vacation home to be held for appreciation. The raw land has an adjusted basis of $100,000 and a fair market value of $110,000. The stock transferred has an adjusted basis of $40,000 and a fair market value of $20,000. The vacation home acquired has a fair market value of $130,000. Angela is deemed to have received a $20,000 portion of the acquired real estate in exchange for the stock since $20,000 is the fair market value of the stock at the time of the exchange. A $20,000 loss is recognized under §1002 on the exchange of the stock for real estate. No gain or loss is recognized on the exchange of the real estate since the property received is of the type permitted to be received without recognition of

gain or loss. The basis of the vacation home is determined as follows [§1.1031(d)-1(e), Example]:

Formula for Calculating the Basis of the New Property

Adjusted basis of LKE property given	03 + $100,000	
Adjusted basis of boot property given	B2 + $ 40,000	
Cash given	10 + _____	
Mortgage assumed on property	12 + _____	
Subtotal (Plus)		28 + $140,000
Cash received	05 + $ _____	
Mortgage on property given	07 + _____	
Subtotal (Minus)		31 – $ _____
Plus: Gain recognized on exchange		23 + $ _____
Plus: Gain recognized on boot given		B3 + _____
Less: Loss recognized on boot		B4 – _____
Exchange expenses		13 + _____
BASIS OF ALL NEW PROPERTY RECEIVED (28, 31, 32, B, 35)		36 = $ 20,000
BASIS OF BOOT PROPERTY RECEIVED (FMV) (Line 6)		37 = $120,000
BASIS OF LIKE-KIND PROPERTY RECEIVED		36–37 = $120,000

Loss on not-like-kind property given. Where loss is recognized on a partially tax-free exchange because unlike property is transferred by the taxpayer as part of the exchange, the recognized loss decreases the basis of the property received. For purposes of this rule, the amount regarded as having been received in exchange for the "other" property is its fair market value on the date of the exchange [§1.1031(d)-1(e)].

Example: Dave exchanges a parking lot with an adjusted basis of $15,000, together with equipment having a basis of $3,000 and worth $2,000, for farmland worth $17,000. His $1,000 loss on the exchange is recognized because he has transferred property that is not of a like kind. His basis for the farmland is $17,000, that is, the $18,000 basis of the properties transferred minus the $1,000 recognized loss.

Formula for Calculating the Basis of the New Property

Adjusted basis of LKE property given	03 + $15,000
Adjusted basis of boot property given	B2 + $ 3,000
Cash given	10 + _____
Mortgage assumed on property	12 + _____
Subtotal (Plus)	28 + $18,000
Cash received	05 + $ _____
Mortgage on property given	07 + _____
Subtotal (Minus)	31 – $ _____
Plus: Gain recognized on exchange	23 + $ _____
Plus: Gain recognized on boot given	B3 + _____
Less: Loss recognized on boot	B4 – $ 1,000
Exchange expenses	13 + _____
BASIS OF ALL NEW PROPERTY RECEIVED (28, 31, 32, B, 35)	36 = $17,000
BASIS OF BOOT PROPERTY RECEIVED (FMV) (Line 6)	37 = $ _____
BASIS OF LIKE-KIND PROPERTY RECEIVED	36–37 = $17,000

Allocation of basis when more than one property received. If more than one property is received in the exchange, the basis of the property given is allocated to the properties received in proportion to their fair market values on the date of the exchange [Rev. Rul. 68-36, 68-1 CB 357; §1.1031(j)-1(c); *Laster v. Comm.*, 43 BTA 159 (1940)].

Example: Natalie trades her office building worth $675,000, but with an adjusted basis of $140,000, for five residential rental properties. The $140,000 is spread among the five properties according to *their* fair market values.

Description	Fair Market Value	Percent	Basis Allocation
Rental A	$261,000	38.67%	$ 54,138
Rental B	$140,000	20.74%	$ 29,036
Rental C	$ 88,000	13.04%	$ 18,256
Rental D	$ 64,000	9.48%	$ 13,272
Rental E	$122,000	18.07%	$ 25,298
Total:	$675,000	100.00%	$140,000

What is done with the land in an exchange? The basis allocated to *each* rental must subsequently be allocated between the land and building, again on the basis of their relative fair market values [§1.61-6(a)].

Example: Natalie, in the previous example, determines that the land in Rental A is worth 20% of the entire fair market value (probably by using the property tax appraisal report). Therefore, $10,828 of the $54,138 is not depreciable, with the remaining $43,310 depreciable over 27.5 years. A similar allocation is made with properties B through E.

Allocation of basis when personal residence included. When an exchanger gives a personal residence as part of the boot in an exchange, the residence is treated separately from the exchange of the qualifying property. The basis in the personal residence is calculated under the §1034 rollover rules, not the §1031 like-kind exchange rules [Rev. Rul. 59-229, 59-2 CB 180].

Depreciation recapture. Real property capital gain may be converted into ordinary income if §1250 requires the taxpayer to calculate depreciation recapture. Under §1250, all realized gain is recognized as ordinary income to the extent that depreciation deductions exceed the allowable deduction under the straight-line method (or if the property is disposed of less than 12 months after acquisition).

No depreciation recapture exists if the real property is depreciated on a straight-line basis. Therefore, no depreciation recapture exists for property purchased and placed in service after 1986, as all residential and commercial real property must be depreciated on a straight-line basis. However, a taxpayer exchanging property purchased between 1981 through 1986 (Accelerated Cost Recovery System property) using an accelerated (faster than straight-line) method *may* have depreciation recapture.

Section 1250(d)(4) provides that the amount of realized gain recognized under §1250 is limited to the greater of the gain recognized under §1031 or the *excess* of the recapturable amount over the fair market value of any §1250 property acquired. Thus, when sufficient improved property (qualified as "§1250 property") is acquired, recapture does not occur. However, the recapture potential is transferred to the new property [§1250(d)(4)(A); §1.1250-3(d)(1)].

Calculation worksheet. To help you with this computation, we have included a depreciation recapture worksheet, Figure 8.5, at the end of this chapter. An extensive example can be found at IRS Regulations §1.1250-3(d)(1)(Example).

HOLDING PERIOD

The holding period of the new property acquired in a like-kind exchange *tacks,* or adds, onto the holding period of the property given, provided that (1) the property transferred was either a capital asset or §1231 trade or business property and (2) the basis of the property acquired is determined in whole or in part by the basis of the property exchanged [§1223(l)].

REMAINING CALCULATION AND
REPORTING REQUIREMENTS

As previously shown, the like-kind exchange worksheet is divided into five parts:

1. Equity calculation
2. Part I—Basis of property conveyed
3. Part II—Total realized gain (or loss)
4. Part III—Recognized (taxable) gain
5. Part IV—Basis of new property

We are now ready to calculate Parts II, III and IV. (The equity calculation and the basis of property conveyed were discussed in the previous chapter.) Again we will use a difficult IRS example to demonstrate how easy this computation is.

> **Example:** Bonnie owns an apartment house with a fair market value of $800,000, and an adjusted basis in her hands of $500,000, but it is subject to a mortgage of $150,000. Bonnie transfers the apartment house to Charlie, receiving in exchange $50,000 in cash and an office building with a fair market value of $600,000. The transfer to Charlie is made subject to the $150,000 mortgage. Bonnie pays $50,000 in exchange expenses. Bonnie realizes a gain of $250,000 on the exchange, computed as follows [§1.1031(d)-2(Example 1)]:

1. Equity Calculation

			Bonnie Gives Bonnie's Apt	and Receives Charlie's Apt
E1.	FMV of property exchanged	E1	$800,000	$600,000
E2.	Less: Existing mortgages	E2	−150,000	0
	Equity (1 − 2)		$650,000	$600,000
E3.	Net boot added (Plug figure**)	E3	0*	$ 50,000#
	(**Difference between equities)			
	Do equities balance? (1 − 2 + 3) [G = R]		$650,000 =	$650,000
	Detail of boot added		*	#
E4.	Cash	E4	0	$ 50,000
E5.	Other financing	E5	0	0
E6.	Other unlike property (B1)	E6	0	0

A $50,000 "sweetener" or "evener" is required to balance the exchange economically (line E3).

Once the equity calculation is completed, the only other information needed for the exchange calculation is:

1. the exchange expenses and
2. the adjusted basis of the property given.

2. Part I—Compute the Adjusted Basis of the Property Being Given

Exchange—Adjusted Basis Computation

Adjusted basis:			
Original cost (or basis)	+		$680,889
Equals: Cost (or other basis) of property given	=	1	$680,889
Less: Accumulated depreciation	–	2	$180,889
TOTAL ADJUSTED BASIS (1 – 2)	=	3	$500,000

Note: The numbers in front of the dollar amounts refer to the like-kind exchange worksheet in Figure 5.1.

3. Part II—Calculate the Total Realized Gain or Loss

The taxpayer must calculate the total gain on the property given before determining the amount of that gain that is not taxable and thereby determining the adjustment, if any, required to be made to the basis of the new property. Realized gain (Part II) is the profit on the property being exchanged as if the property had been sold for cash. Recognized gain (Part III) is the portion of the Part II realized gain that is taxable.

Formula for Calculating Realized Gain (Loss)

FMV of LKE property received	4 + $		
Cash received	5 +		
FMV of non-LKE boot property received	6 +		
Mortgage on property given	7 +		
Total consideration received (add lines 4 through 7)		8 + $	
Less:			
Adjusted basis of LKE property given	9 + $		
Cash given	10 +		
FMV of non-LKE boot property given	11 +		
Mortgage assumed on property received	12 +		
Exchange expenses	13 +		
Total consideration given (add lines 9 through 13)		14 – $	
GAIN REALIZED ON EXCHANGE (line 8 – line 14)		15 $	

Example (continued):   Bonnie's gain would be:

Formula for Calculating Realized Gain (Loss)

FMV of LKE property received	4 + $600,000	
Cash received	5 + 50,000	
FMV of non-LKE boot property received	6 + _____	
Mortgage on property given	7 + $150,000	
Total consideration received (add lines 4 through 7)		8 + $800,000
Less:		
Adjusted basis of LKE property given	9 + $500,000	
Cash given	10 + _____	
FMV of non-LKE boot property given	11 + _____	
Mortgage assumed on property received	12 + _____	
Exchange expenses	13 + 50,000	
Total consideration given (add lines 9 through 13)		14 − $550,000
GAIN REALIZED ON EXCHANGE (line 8 − line 14)		15 $250,000

The information required for Part II is very similar to the gain or loss formula found in Chapter 2. We use the formula below to prove that the information entered in Part II of our worksheet is correct.

Proof for Gain or Loss Computation

Fair market value of property given		E1 + $800,000	
Less:	Exchange expenses	13 − 50,000	
Equals:	Net selling price	= $750,000	
Less:	Adjusted basis		
	Original cost (or basis)	+ $500,000	
	Plus: Purchase expenses	+ _____	
	Plus: Improvements	+ _____	
	Less: Accumulated depreciation	− _____	
Equals:	Total adjusted basis	9 − $500,000	
NET GAIN (OR LOSS) REALIZED ON EXCHANGE		15 = $250,000	

4. Part III—Calculate the Recognized Taxable Gain (If Any)

As mentioned in the discussion of "receipt of boot," the amount of the gain that will be taxable is the smaller of the net gain or the boot received. Part III simply ascertains which one is smaller, the boot (calculated below) or the gain (line 15, above), and thereby establishes the amount of the gain taxable because of the exchange.

Formula for Calculating Recognized Taxable Gain

Cash and Boot

Cash and boot received (lines 5 and 6)	16	+ $_____
Cash and boot given (lines 10 and 11)	17	– _____
Exchange expenses (line 13)	18	$_____
Net cash and boot received (line 16 less 17 & 18)	19 ± _____
	(can be negative)

Mortgage Relief

Mortgage on property given (line 7)	20	$_____
Mortgage on property received (line 12)	21	– _____
NET MORTGAGE RELIEF (line 20 less 21, but not below zero)	22	$_____
GAIN RECOGNIZED (line 22 +/–line 19, but not in excess of actual gain [line 15]; if negative, put zero)	23	$_____

> **Example (continued):** **Receiving cash and net debt relief.** Assuming $50,000 of exchange expenses, of the total $250,000 gain realized in Part II, Line 15, Bonnie's recognized gain (because of the $50,000 cash received and the $150,000 net mortgage relief) is as follows:

Recognized Taxable Gain

Cash and Boot

Cash and boot received (lines 5 and 6)	16	+ $50,000
Cash and boot given (lines 10 and 11)	17	– _____
Exchange expenses (line 13)	18	– $50,000
Net cash and boot received (line 16 less 17 and 18)	19 ± 0
	(can be negative)

Mortgage Relief

Mortgage on property given (line 7)	20	$150,000
Mortgage on property received (line 12)	21	– _____
NET MORTGAGE RELIEF (line 20 less 21, but not below zero)	22	$150,000
GAIN RECOGNIZED (line 22 +/–line 19, but not in excess of actual gain [line 15]; if negative, put zero)	23	$150,000

5. Part IV—Calculate the *Substituted* Basis of the New Property

The technical formula to calculate the basis of property received in a tax-free exchange is the basis of the old property surrendered, increased by any money (including debt) given and the amount of any gain recognized and decreased by the amount of money (including debt) received and any loss recognized on the exchange [§1031(d); §1.1031(d)-1]. The formula for calculating the basis of the new property was discussed earlier in this chapter.

Example (continued): Bonnie's new substituted basis is her old basis less the $50,000 cash received and the $150,000 net mortgage relief plus the exchange expenses and the $200,000 gain recognized.

Formula for Calculating the Basis of the New Property

Adjusted basis of LKE property given	03 + $500,000	
Adjusted basis of boot property given	B2 + _____	
Cash given	10 + _____	
Mortgage assumed on property	12 + _____	
Subtotal (Plus)		28 + $500,000
Cash received	05 + $ 50,000	
Mortgage on property given	07 + $150,000	
Subtotal (Minus)		31 − $200,000
Plus: Gain recognized on exchange		23 + $150,000
Plus: Gain recognized on boot given	B3 + _____	
Less: Loss recognized on boot	B4 − _____	
Exchange expenses		13 + $ 50,000
BASIS OF ALL NEW PROPERTY RECEIVED (28, 31, 32, B, 35)		36 = $500,000
BASIS OF BOOT PROPERTY RECEIVED (FMV) (Line 6)		37 = $ _____
BASIS OF LIKE-KIND PROPERTY RECEIVED		36–37 = $500,000

The proof to determine if the basis calculation has been properly computed is:

Proof for Basis of New Property

Fair market value of property received	E1	$600,000
Less: Gain not taxed	15-23	− $100,000
NEW BASIS	34	= $500,000

(See Figure 8.1 and Figure 8.2.)

Lowering gain created by debt relief with other boot given. This example highlights the interaction of receiving cash and assuming liabilities. It also discloses the impact of mixing unlike property with like property in a tax-free exchange. Again we will use a difficult IRS example to demonstrate how easy this computation is. It is important to realize that a negative number is possible on line 19, the significance being that cash given can lower the amount of mortgage relief for gain purposes!

Example: **Giving cash and boot but receiving debt relief.** Zane exchanges $50,000 cash, stock worth $50,000 (with a basis to Zane of $30,000) and real property with a fair market value of $300,000 subject to a liability of $200,000 for Willow's property, which has a fair market value of $250,000 subject to a liability of $50,000. Even though Zane has a net mortgage relief of $150,000, he only receives $50,000 of net boot.

FIGURE 8.1   Sample Section 1031 Tax-Free Exchange of Property Worksheet

Copyright - Hoven - 1998

SECTION 1031 TAX-FREE EXCHANGE OF PROPERTY

WORKSHEET

exchange1.pm5

EQUITY CALCULATION Form 8.1	BONNIE Gives	CHARLIE Receives
E1. FMV of property exchanged E1	+$ 800,000	+$ 600,000
E2. Less: Existing mortgages E2	− 150,000	−
Equity (1 - 2)...............	= 650,000	= 600,000
E3. Net boot added (plug figure**)..... E3	+ *	+ 50,000#
(**Difference between equities)		
Do equities balance? (1-2+3) [G = R]	= 650,000	= 650,000
Detail of boot added		
Cash E4	*	# 50,000
Other financing.............. E5	*	#
Other unlike property E6	*	#

PART I - BASIS OF PROPERTY GIVEN   EXCHANGE DATE: 1/1/98

Description: BONNIE'S APARTMENT HOUSE

1. Cost (or other basis) of property given - [date purchased: 1/1/87] 1	+$ 680,889	
2. Depreciation allowed or allowable 2	− 180,889	
3. Adjusted basis of property given up (line 1 less line 2)..............3	$ 500,000	

PART II - REALIZED GAIN (LOSS)

4. FMV of qualifying property received (line E1-R) (Form 8824, Line 16)......4	$ 600,000	
5. Cash received (line E4-R) 5	+$ 50,000	
6. Less: Cash given (line E4-G) 6	−	Proof: A Simple Check
7. Fair market value of other (boot) received (line E6-R) 7	+	FMV of Prop Exch: 800,000
8. Less: FMV of boot (other than cash) given up (line E6-G) 8	−	Less: Adj. Basis: 550,000
9. Net liabilities assumed by other party (line E2-G less E2-R but not < zero)9	+ 150,000	Gain (if sold): 250,000
10. Exchange expenses................................. 10	− 50,000	
11.Total consideration received (add lines 5 thru 10) (Form 8824, Line 15)......11	$ 150,000	
LESS:		
12. Adjusted basis of qualified property given up (line 3) 12	+$ 500,000	
13. Net liabilities assumed by taxpayer (line E2-R less E2-G but not < zero) 13	+	
14. Total consideration given (add lines 12 and 13)..... (Form 8824, Line 18) ...14	$ 500,000	
15. GAIN REALIZED ON EXCHANGE (line 4 plus line 11 less line 14) (Form 8824, Line 19)......15	$ 250,000	

PART III - RECOGNIZED TAXABLE GAIN

CASH AND BOOT

16. Cash and boot (other than cash) received (add lines 5 and 7) .. 16	+$ 50,000	
17. Cash and boot (other than cash) given (add lines 6 and 8) 17	−	
18. Exchange expenses (line 10)......................... 18	− 50,000	
19. Net cash and boot (other than cash) received (line 16 less lines 17 and 18) ... 19	+/−$ -0-	

MORTGAGE RELIEF

20. Mortgage on property given (line E2-G) 20	+$ 150,000	
21. Mortgage assumed on property received (line E2-R) 21	−	
22. Net mortgage relief (line 20 less line 21; if less than zero, enter zero)........22	+$ 150,000	
23 GAIN RECOGNIZED (line 22 +/- line 19; line 23 cannot exceed) ....(Form 8824, Line 20)... 23	$ 150,000	
line 15; if less than zero, enter zero		

PART IV - BASIS OF NEW PROPERTY   Description: CHARLIE'S APARTMENT

24. Adjusted basis of LKE property given (line 3)............... 24	+$ 500,000	Proof: A Simple Check
25. Adjusted basis of boot property given (Form 8824, Line 13).... 25	+	FMV of Prop Rec'd: 600,000
26. Cash given (line 6)................................ 26	+	Less: Gain *not* taxed:100,000
27. Mortgage assumed on property received (line E2-R) 27	+	New Basis: 500,000
28. Subtotal (Plus) 28	+$ 500,000	
29. Cash received (line 5) 29	+$ 50,000	
30 Mortgage on property given (line E2-G).................. 30	+ 150,000	
31. Subtotal (Minus) 31	−$ 200,000	
32. Plus: Gain recognized on exchange (line 23) 32	+ 150,000	
33. Plus: Gain recognized on boot given (line 8 less line 25 but not < zero) (Form 8824, Line 14) 33	+	
34. Less: Loss recognized on boot given (line 25 less line 8 but not < zero) (Form 8824, Line 14) 34	−	
35. Exchange expenses (line 10) 35	+ 50,000	
36. BASIS OF ALL NEW PROPERTY RECEIVED (28,31,32,33,34,35) 36	150,000	
37. BASIS OF BOOT PROPERTY RECEIVED (FMV) (LINE 7) 37		
38. BASIS OF LIKE-KIND PROPERTY RECEIVED (LINE 36 LESS LINE 37) (Form 8824, Line 25) . 38	$ 500,000	

FIGURE 8.2   Sample IRS Form 8824

Form **8824**	**Like–Kind Exchanges**	OMB No. 1545–1190
Department of the Treasury Internal Revenue Service	(and nonrecognition of gain from conflict–of–interest sales) ▶ See separate Instructions. ▶ Attach to your tax return. ▶ Use a separate form for each like–kind exchange.	**19** Attachment Sequence No. **49**

Name(s) shown on tax return | Identifying number

Part I   Information on the Like–Kind Exchange

Note: If the property described on line 1 or line 2 is real property located outside the United States, indicate the country.

1 Description of like–kind property given up ▶ BONNIE'S APARTMENT HOUSE

2 Description of like–kind property received ▶ CHARLIE'S APARTMENT

3	Date like–kind property given up was originally acquired (month, day, year)	3	1/01/87
4	Date you actually transferred your property to other party (month, day, year)	4	1/01/98
5	Date the like–kind property you received was identified (month, day, year). See instructions	5	1/01/98
6	Date you actually received the like–kind property from other party (month, day, year)	6	1/01/98

7 Was the exchange made with a related party? If "Yes," complete Part II. If "No," go to Part III. See instructions.
a ☐ Yes, in this tax year   b ☐ Yes, in a prior tax year   c ☒ No.

Part II   Related Party Exchange Information

8 Name of related party | Related party's identifying number
Address (no., street, and apt., room, or suite no.)
City or town, state, and ZIP code | Relationship to you

9 During this tax year (and before the date that is 2 years after the last transfer of property that was part of the exchange), did the related party sell or dispose of the like–kind property received from you in the exchange? ☐ Yes ☐ No

10 During this tax year (and before the date that is 2 years after the last transfer of property that was part of the exchange), did you sell or dispose of the like–kind property you received? ☐ Yes ☐ No

If both lines 9 and 10 are "No" and this is the year of the exchange, go to Part III. If either line 9 or line 10 is "Yes," the deferred gain or (loss) from line 24 **must** be reported on your return this tax year, **unless** one of the exceptions on line 11 applies. See **Related Party Exchanges** in the instructions.

11 If one of the exceptions below applies to the disposition, check the applicable box:
a ☐ The disposition was after the death of either of the related parties.
b ☐ The disposition was an involuntary conversion, and the threat of conversion occurred after the exchange.
c ☐ You can establish to the satisfaction of the IRS that neither the exchange nor the disposition had tax avoidance as its principal purpose. If this box is checked, attach an explanation. See instructions.

Part III   Realized Gain or (Loss), Recognized Gain, and Basis of Like–Kind Property Received

Caution: If you transferred **and** received **(a)** more than one group of like–kind properties, or **(b)** cash or other (not like–kind) property, see instructions under **Multi–Asset Exchanges.**

Note: Complete lines 12 through 14 ONLY if you gave up property that was not like–kind. Otherwise, go to line 15.

12	Fair market value (FMV) of other property given up	12	
13	Adjusted basis of other property given up	13	
14	Gain or (loss) recognized on other property given up. Subtract line 13 from line 12. Report the gain or (loss) in the same manner as if the exchange had been a sale	14	
15	Cash received, FMV of other property received, plus net liabilities assumed by other party, reduced (but not below zero) by any exchange expenses you incurred. See instructions	15	150,000
16	FMV of like–kind property you received	16	600,000
17	Add lines 15 and 16	17	750,000
18	Adjusted basis of like–kind property you gave up, net amounts paid to other party, plus any exchange expenses **not** used on line 15. See instructions	18	500,000
19	**Realized gain or (loss).** Subtract line 18 from line 17	19	250,000
20	Enter the smaller of line 15 or line 19, but not less than zero	20	150,000
21	Ordinary income under recapture rules. Enter here and on Form 4797, line 17. See instructions	21	0
22	Subtract line 21 from line 20. If zero or less, enter –0–. If more than zero, enter here and on Schedule D or Form 4797, unless the installment method applies. See instructions	22	150,000
23	**Recognized gain.** Add lines 21 and 22	23	150,000
24	Deferred gain or (loss). Subtract line 23 from line 19. If a related party exchange, see instructions	24	100,000
25	**Basis of like–kind property received.** Subtract line 15 from the sum of lines 18 and 23	25	500,000

For Paperwork Reduction Act Notice, see separate Instructions.   Form **8824** (1996)

Formula for Calculating Recognized Taxable Gain

Cash and Boot

Cash and boot received (lines 5 and 6)			16 + $ _____	
Cash given	10 +	$50,000		
FMV of other boot given	11 +	$50,000		
Cash and boot given (lines 10 and 10)			17 – $100,000	
Exchange expenses (line 13)			18 – $ _____	
Net cash and boot received (line 16 less 17 and 18)				19 – $100,000
				(can be negative)

Mortgage Relief

Mortgage on property given (line 7)	20	$200,000
Mortgage on property received (line 12)	21 –	$ 50,000
NET MORTGAGE RELIEF (line 20 less 21, but not below zero)	22	$150,000
GAIN RECOGNIZED (line 22 +/–line 19, but not in excess of	23	$ 50,000

    actual gain [line 15]; if negative, put zero)

> ***Example (continued):*** Zane's tax preparer e-mails us the information that Zane originally purchased the property for $200,000 and has accumulated depreciation of $80,000. Only $50,000 of Zane's entire $180,000 gain is taxable! Remember, the stock is unlike property and therefore it is considered a taxable exchange!

See Figure 8.3 and Figure 8.4 for the entire solution.

REPORTING AN EXCHANGE TO THE IRS—FORM 8824

The Internal Revenue Service has issued Form 8824 for reporting like-kind exchanges. As the form is clumsy and confusing to prepare, we use the previously discussed worksheet (Figure 8.5). After completing the worksheet, we simply transfer the information to Form 8824. Form 8824 directs the taxpayer to transfer the taxable gain to the next appropriate form, either Form 4797, or directly to Form 1040, Schedule D.

FIGURE 8.3   Sample Section 1031 Tax-Free Exchange of Property Worksheet

Copyright - Hoven - 1998

**SECTION 1031
TAX-FREE
EXCHANGE
OF PROPERTY**
───
WORKSHEET
exchange3.pm5

EQUITY CALCULATION Form 8.3		ZANE Gives	WILLOW Receives
E1. FMV of property exchanged E1	+$	300,000	+$ 250,000
E2. Less: Existing mortgages E2	−	200,000	− 50,000
Equity (1 - 2).	=	100,000	= 200,000
E3. Net boot added (plug figure**). E3	+	100,000 *	+ #
(**Difference between equities)			
Do equities balance? (1-2+3) [G = R]	=	200,000	= 200,000
Detail of boot added			
Cash E4	*	50,000	#
Other financing. E5	*		#
Other unlike property E6	*	50,000	#

EXCHANGE DATE: 1/1/98

PART I - BASIS OF PROPERTY GIVEN

Description: ZANE'S APARTMENT			
1. Cost (or other basis) of property given - [date purchased: 1/1/87] 1	+$ 200,000	
2. Depreciation allowed or allowable 2	− 80,000	
3. Adjusted basis of property given up (line 1 less line 2). 3	$ 120,000	

PART II - REALIZED GAIN (LOSS)

4. FMV of qualifying property received (line E1-R) (Form 8824, Line 16) 4	$ 250,000	
5. Cash received (line E4-R) 5	+$	
6. Less: Cash given (line E4-G) 6	− 50,000	Proof: A Simple Check
7. Fair market value of other (boot) received (line E6-R) 7	+	FMV of Prop Exch:300,000
8. Less: FMV of boot (other than cash) given up (line E6-G) 8	− 50,000	Less: Adj. Basis: 120,000
9. Net liabilities assumed by other party (line E2-G less E2-R but not < zero) 9	+ 150,000	Gain (if sold): 180,000
10. Exchange expenses. 10	−	
11.Total consideration received (add lines 5 thru 10) (Form 8824, Line 15) 11	$ 50,000	
LESS:		
12. Adjusted basis of qualified property given up (line 3) 12	+$ 120,000	
13. Net liabilities assumed by taxpayer (line E2-R less E2-G but not < zero) 13	+	
14. Total consideration given (add lines 12 and 13). . . . . . (Form 8824, Line 18) . . . 14	$ 120,000	
15. GAIN REALIZED ON EXCHANGE (line 4 plus line 11 less line 14) (Form 8824, Line 19) 15	$ 180,000	

PART III - RECOGNIZED TAXABLE GAIN

CASH AND BOOT

16. Cash and boot (other than cash) received (add lines 5 and 7) . . 16	+$	
17. Cash and boot (other than cash) given (add lines 6 and 8) 17	− 100,000	
18. Exchange expenses (line 10). 18	−	
19. Net cash and boot (other than cash) received (line 16 less lines 17 and 18) . . . 19	+/−$ 100,000	

MORTGAGE RELIEF

20. Mortgage on property given (line E2-G) 20	+$ 200,000	
21. Mortgage assumed on property received (line E2-R) 21	− 50,000	
22. Net mortgage relief (line 20 less line 21; if less than zero, enter zero). 22	+$ 150,000	
23 GAIN RECOGNIZED (line 22 +/− line 19; line 23 cannot exceed) . . . . (Form 8824, Line 20). . . 23	$ 50,000	
line 15; if less than zero, enter zero		

PART IV - BASIS OF NEW PROPERTY   Description: WILLOW'S APARTMENT

24. Adjusted basis of LKE property given (line 3). 24	+$ 120,000	Proof: A Simple Check
25. Adjusted basis of boot property given (Form 8824, Line 13). . . . 25	+ 30,000	FMV of Prop Rec'd: 250,000
26. Cash given (line 6). 26	+ 50,000	Less: Gain *not* taxed:130,000
27. Mortgage assumed on property received (line E2-R) 27	+ 50,000	New Basis: 120,000
28. Subtotal (Plus) 28	+$ 250,000	
29. Cash received (line 5) 29	+$	
30 Mortgage on property given (line E2-G). 30	+ 200,000	
31. Subtotal (Minus) 31	−$ 200,000	
32. Plus: Gain recognized on exchange (line 23) 32	+ 50,000	
33. Plus: Gain recognized on boot given (line 8 less line 25 but not < zero) (Form 8824, Line 14) 33	+ 20,000	
34. Less: Loss recognized on boot given (line 25 less line 8 but not < zero) (Form 8824, Line 14) 34	−	
35. Exchange expenses (line 10) 35	+	
36. BASIS OF ALL NEW PROPERTY RECEIVED (28,31,32,33,34,35) 36	120,000	
37. BASIS OF BOOT PROPERTY RECEIVED (FMV) (LINE 7) 37		
38. BASIS OF LIKE-KIND PROPERTY RECEIVED (LINE 36 LESS LINE 37) (Form 8824, Line 25) . 38	$ 120,000	

FIGURE 8.4 Sample IRS Form 8824

Form **8824**	**Like–Kind Exchanges**	OMB No. 1545–1190
Department of the Treasury Internal Revenue Service	**(and nonrecognition of gain from conflict–of–interest sales)** ▶ See separate instructions. ▶ Attach to your tax return. ▶ Use a separate form for each like–kind exchange.	**19** Attachment Sequence No. **49**
Name(s) shown on tax return		Identifying number

Part I   Information on the Like–Kind Exchange

Note: If the property described on line 1 or line 2 is real property located outside the United States, indicate the country.

1 Description of like–kind property given up ▶ _ZANE'S APARTMENT_____

2 Description of like–kind property received ▶ _WILLOW'S APARTMENT_____

3	Date like–kind property given up was originally acquired (month, day, year)	**3**	1/01/87
4	Date you actually transferred your property to other party (month, day, year)........................	**4**	1/01/98
5	Date the like–kind property you received was identified (month, day, year). See instructions..............	**5**	1/01/98
6	Date you actually received the like–kind property from other party (month, day, year)	**6**	1/01/98

7 Was the exchange made with a related party? If "Yes," complete Part II. If "No," go to Part III. See instructions.

a ☐ Yes, in this tax year   b ☐ Yes, in a prior tax year   c ☒ No.

Part II   Related Party Exchange Information

8	Name of related party	Related party's identifying number
	Address (no., street, and apt., room, or suite no.)	
	City or town, state, and ZIP code	Relationship to you

9 During this tax year (and before the date that is 2 years after the last transfer of property that was part of the exchange),
did the related party sell or dispose of the like–kind property received from you in the exchange? .... ☐ Yes ☐ No

10 During this tax year (and before the date that is 2 years after the last transfer of property that was part of the exchange),
did you sell or dispose of the like–kind property you received? .... ☐ Yes ☐ No

If both lines 9 and 10 are "No" and this is the year of the exchange, go to Part III. If either line 9 or line 10 is "Yes," the deferred
gain or (loss) from line 24 **must** be reported on your return this tax year, **unless** one of the exceptions on line 11 applies.
See **Related Party Exchanges** in the instructions.

11 If one of the exceptions below applies to the disposition, check the applicable box:

a ☐ The disposition was after the death of either of the related parties.

b ☐ The disposition was an involuntary conversion, and the threat of conversion occurred after the exchange.

c ☐ You can establish to the satisfaction of the IRS that neither the exchange nor the disposition had tax avoidance as its principal purpose.
If this box is checked, attach an explanation. See instructions.

Part III   Realized Gain or (Loss), Recognized Gain, and Basis of Like–Kind Property Received

Caution: If you transferred **and** received (a) more than one group of like–kind properties, or (b) cash or other (not like–kind) property, see instructions under **Multi–Asset Exchanges.**

Note: Complete lines 12 through 14 ONLY if you gave up property that was not like–kind. Otherwise, go to line 15.

12	Fair market value (FMV) of other property given up...........................	**12**	50,000		
13	Adjusted basis of other property given up	**13**	30,000		
14	Gain or (loss) recognized on other property given up. Subtract line 13 from line 12. Report the gain or (loss) in the same manner as if the exchange had been a sale			**14**	20,000
15	Cash received, FMV of other property received, plus net liabilities assumed by other party, reduced (but not below zero) by any exchange expenses you incurred. See instructions			**15**	50,000
16	FMV of like–kind property you received			**16**	250,000
17	Add lines 15 and 16			**17**	300,000
18	Adjusted basis of like–kind property you gave up, net amounts paid to other party, plus any exchange expenses **not** used on line 15. See instructions			**18**	120,000
19	**Realized gain or (loss).** Subtract line 18 from line 17			**19**	180,000
20	Enter the smaller of line 15 or line 19, but not less than zero			**20**	50,000
21	Ordinary income under recapture rules. Enter here and on Form 4797, line 17. See instructions...................			**21**	0
22	Subtract line 21 from line 20. If zero or less, enter –0–. If more than zero, enter here and on Schedule D or Form 4797, unless the installment method applies. See instructions			**22**	50,000
23	**Recognized gain.** Add lines 21 and 22			**23**	50,000
24	Deferred gain or (loss). Subtract line 23 from line 19. If a related party exchange, see instructions			**24**	130,000
25	**Basis of like–kind property received.** Subtract line 15 from the sum of lines 18 and 23			**25**	120,000

For Paperwork Reduction Act Notice, see separate instructions.   Form **8824** (1996)

FIGURE 8.5   Like-Kind Exchange Depreciation Recapture Worksheet

LIKE - KIND EXCHANGE
DEPRECIATION RECAPTURE

Test #1: If straight-line depreciation has been used on the old like kind property, enter zero at Items g and l and go to the next schedule.

a. Gain recognized on like kind property. $ _____

b. Gain recognized on non-like kind property given up. $ _____

c. Total Gain Recognized on the Exchange (a + b). $ _____

Test #2: If the old like kind property is residential and accelerated depreciation or ACRS was used, fill out Part I. However, if the old like kind property is commercial and accelerated depreciation or ACRS was used, fill out Part II.

PART I - RESIDENTIAL PROPERTY RECAPTURE UNDER ß1250

d. Amount of ß1250 recapture (determined as if the property had been sold). $ _____

e. Fair market value (at the date of the exchange) of ß1250 property received in the exchange. $ _____

f. Excess of recapture over FMV of ß1250 property received (d - e, but not less than zero). $ _____

g. Section 1250 recapture recognized (as ordinary income) in the exchange (greater of c and f, but not in excess of d). $ _____

PART II - COMMERCIAL PROPERTY RECAPTURE UNDER ß1245

h. Amount of ß1245 recapture (determined as if property had been sold). $ _____

i. Fair market value of property received that is not ß1245 property. $ _____

j. Total gain recognized on exchange (Item c above). $ _____

k. Gain recognized plus FMV of non-ß1245 property received (i + j). $ _____

l. Section 1245 recapture recognized (as ordinary income) in the exchange (h - k, but not less than zero). $ _____

DEPRECAP.PM5

CHAPTER

9

The Home Mortgage Interest Deduction

INTRODUCTION

For most taxpayers, all mortgage interest expenses on the first and second personal residences remain fully deductible in spite of the elimination of the deduction for other personal interest expenses (e.g., interest on credit card purchases or personal automobile purchases).

Home mortgage debt must be secured by a security interest perfected under local law on the *qualified residence(s)*. In addition, the deductible portion of home mortgage interest is limited to the taxpayer's *qualified residence interest*. That is, the debt (within limits) must be incurred to buy, build or substantially improve these qualified residences [§163(h)(3)].

Because of the Tax Reform Act of 1986, home equity loans came into vogue. These loans allow the taxpayer to deduct interest on a loan secured by a principal residence even though it has no relation to the acquisition or substantial improvement of the residence.

> *Example:* Terry purchases a personal automobile on an installment contract and gives his home, instead of the automobile, as collateral. This converts a non-deductible personal interest expense to a deductible home mortgage interest expense.

The limitation on residential interest expense. To prevent abuse, as illustrated in the above example, "qualified residence interest" includes the aggregate amount of acquisition indebtedness not exceeding $1 million and the aggregate amount of home equity indebtedness not exceeding $100,000. This provision applies cumulatively to *both* the principal and the second residence of the taxpayer [§163(h)(3)].

FIGURE 9.1 Qualified-Residence Interest Deduction

Interest paid on *acquisition debt (1 below)*   + _____

Plus: Interest paid on *home equity debt (2 below)*   + _____

Equals: Qualified-residence interest deduction   = _____

(1) What is acquisition debt?

Pre-10/13/87 grandfathered debt (no dollar limitation)   + _____

Plus

Post-10/12/87 acquisition (or construction) debt   + _____

Substantial improvement debt   + _____

Divorce debt   + _____

Subtotal (cannot exceed $1,000,000 less grandfathered
  debt, but not below zero)   + _____

Equals: *Acquisition debt*   = _____

(2) What is home equity debt?

Fair market value of residence   + _____

Less: Acquisition debt (above)   − _____

Equals: *Home equity debt (cannot exceed $100,000)*   = _____

The above fill-in-the-blank formula, which helps arrive at the deductible portion of home mortgage interest, acts as a starting point for defining the new terms *acquisition* and *home equity indebtedness*. A line-by-line explanation follows.

WHAT IS ACQUISITION INDEBTEDNESS?

Acquiring or constructing a residence. Acquisition indebtedness is debt that is incurred in acquiring, constructing or substantially improving the principal residence or a second residence of the taxpayer *and* is secured by such property.

"Substantially improving" a residence. This term is not defined either by statute or by the Conference Report. It is hoped that future regulations will stipulate when an improvement is "substantial." Until then, uncertainty exists.

COMMENT: The word *substantial* as used in other Internal Revenue Code sections ranges in meaning from 15% to 35% or more of the fair market value. This would be unconscionable if applied to home loans; for a homeowner to deduct the interest on a home improvement loan, for example, the loan on a $100,000 home would have to exceed $15,000 to $35,000 or more. Most home improvement loans are not that large, and therefore *all* interest on the home improvement would not be deductible when using this definition; it would be a personal interest expense unless it qualifies as a home equity loan. The IRS will, it is hoped, be lenient in its future defining of the word *substantial*.

$1 million cap on level of acquisition debt. The total amount of acquisition debt that can give rise to qualified residence interest is $1,000,000. This cap applies to the combined debt on the principal and second residence. In the case of married persons filing a separate return, the limit is $500,000. Secured indebtedness created prior to October 14, 1987, is grandfathered and exempt from this limitation even if subsequently refinanced. For refinanced grandfathered debt to be considered pre-October 14, 1987, debt, the remaining term of the loan cannot be extended [§163(h)(3)(B),(D)].

A real problem for future refinancing. Acquisition indebtedness decreases as payments are made, and it cannot be increased if the loan is refinanced. In other words, a taxpayer's acquisition indebtedness eventually reduces to zero if the property remains the taxpayer's principal residence for the term of the mortgage.

> *Example:* Don purchases a principal residence for $250,000 in 1998, borrowing $200,000 on a 20-year mortgage note. In 1998, Don's acquisition indebtedness is $200,000 and the interest expense on that $200,000 is fully deductible. As Don amortizes his mortgage, the deductible amount of interest expense also decreases. In 2018 (20 years later), Don's acquisition indebtedness is zero, and any interest expense paid by Don on his home is nondeductible (with the exception of the interest expense on the home equity indebtedness).

Refinanced acquisition debt causes another problem. This is treated as acquisition debt *only* to the extent that it does not exceed the principal amount of acquisition debt *immediately before* the refinancing. In other words, the refinanced debt in excess of the debt just prior to refinancing is not qualified residence debt, and the interest expense created by the excess debt is generally not deductible (with the exception that it might qualify as home equity debt, business debt or investment debt).

> *Example:* Bill incurs $85,000 of acquisition indebtedness to acquire his principal residence and pays the debt down to $60,000. His acquisition indebtedness with respect to that residence cannot thereafter be increased above $60,000 (except for indebtedness incurred to substantially improve the residence).

> *Example:* Bill purchases a principal residence for $250,000 cash, and one year later needs to refinance $200,000. The acquisition debt *immediately before* the refinance is zero; therefore, the full $200,000 is excess debt, with only $100,000 eligible for home equity debt. Bill can only deduct 50% of his interest expense. Prior planning prevents poor performance.

PLANNING TIP: This law is economically strange as it creates a tax incentive for homeowners to (1) buy a new residence rather than improve an existing residence, (2) choose not to live and occupy their homes for long periods of time, (3) create as lengthy a loan as possible and (4) invest a minimal down payment. It is a pro-purchase, pro-borrowing but antisavings tax provision.

Relief for debt created at divorce. At divorce, it is often required that one spouse purchase the interest of the other spouse in the residence. The payor spouse must often create a second mortgage to accumulate the necessary funds. The problem is that the mortgage is not created at the time the home is purchased (not the typical acquisition debt), and it is not a typical substantial improvement loan (although the author has had taxpayers disagree with him on this as they think throwing out the spouse is a very substantial improvement). This new debt, even though not created at the original acquisition date, is also considered acquisition debt.

If an individual acquires the interest of a spouse in a qualified residence incident to a divorce, and such individual incurs indebtedness that is secured by such qualified residence, the individual's debt in such qualified residence may be increased by the amount of secured indebtedness incurred by the individual in connection with the acquisition of the spouse's interest in the residence. The amount of such debt, however, shall not exceed the fair market value of the interest in the residence that is being acquired [TAMRA of 1988, P.L. 100-203; Act. Sec. 1005(c)(14); also see House Committee Report].

WHAT IS HOME EQUITY INDEBTEDNESS?

Home equity indebtedness is debt (other than acquisition indebtedness) that is secured by the taxpayer's principal or second residence and does not exceed the fair market value of such qualified residence reduced by the amount of acquisition indebtedness for such residence(s) [§163(h)(3)(C)(I)].

In the following example, interest on qualifying home equity debt is deductible even though the money is used for personal expenses, such as purchasing a personal automobile.

Example: Lynn has a principal and second residence with fair market values and acquisition indebtedness as follows:

	Principal Home	*Second Home*
Fair market value	$150,000	$100,000
Less: Acquisition debt	−100,000	− 75,000
Equals: Home equity	$ 50,000	$ 25,000

Lynn has a maximum of $75,000 of home equity indebtedness available to her under this provision. If she purchases a BMW for $75,000 in 1998 and gives her two residences as collateral on the loan, she converts a nondeductible personal loan to a deductible qualified-residence interest loan.

What is fair market value? It is the price at which the property would change hands between a willing buyer and a willing seller, neither being under any compulsion to buy or sell.

$100,000 cap on home equity indebtedness. The amount of home equity indebtedness on which interest is treated as deductible qualified-residence interest may not exceed $100,000 ($50,000 for married persons filing separate returns). The amounts borrowed for educational or medical expenditures are included in the $100,000 limitation [§163(h)(3)(C)(ii)].

WHAT IS A RESIDENCE?

A residence *generally* includes a house, condominium, mobile home, boat or house trailer that contains sleeping space and toilet and cooking facilities. But whether a specific property qualifies as a residence shall be solely determined by all the facts and circumstances, including the good faith of the taxpayer [§1.163-10T(p)(3)(ii)].

> **COMMENT:** Does this mean a fishing cabin in the Rocky Mountains does not qualify as a second dwelling unit if it has only an outdoor toilet? The word *generally* might give relief, no pun intended. Most certainly, the primary residence with outdoor plumbing still qualifies as the principal residence.

Do motor homes qualify? Yes, motor homes have previously been held by the courts to be dwelling units [*R. L. Haberkorn,* 75 TC 259, Dec. 37,392; *J. O. Loughlin,* DC-Minn, 82-2 USTC ¶9543].

How many residences qualify? Only *qualified residences* are allowed a home mortgage interest deduction. The term "qualified residences" means the taxpayer's principal residence and/or the taxpayer's second residence [§163(h)(5)].

What is a principal residence? A taxpayer's principal residence is the land and building where the taxpayer principally domiciles, based upon all the facts and circumstances in each case, including the good faith of the taxpayer. The home must qualify for the exclusion provisions (see Chapter 3). It normally will be the home in the area where the taxpayer works; if retired or not working, it is usually where the taxpayer spends the most amount of time, votes, pays taxes, files his or her tax return, and the like. A taxpayer cannot have more than one principal residence at any one time [§1.163-10T(p)(2)].

What is a second residence? The second home, or vacation home, must (1) be a "dwelling unit" that (2) qualifies as a residence under the "use" requirements of §280A and that (3) the taxpayer elects to treat as a second residence [§163(h)(5)(A)(I),(II); §1.163-10T(p)(3)].

What qualifies as a second "dwelling unit"? A house, apartment, condominium, mobile home, boat or similar property qualifies as a dwelling unit. A dwelling unit does not include personal property, such as furniture or a television, that, in accordance with the applicable local law, is not a fixture [§280(f)(1); §1.163-10T(p)(3)(ii)].

PLANNING TIP: This definition allows the interest expense associated with the purchase of a yacht or motor home to be deductible if the taxpayer wishes to treat the yacht or motor home as a dwelling unit.

How much "use" must the taxpayer make of the vacation home? For a residence to qualify as a second dwelling unit, the taxpayer must either (1) not rent it out to anyone during the year or (2) personally use it at least two weeks a year or 10% of the number of days the residence is rented out to others, whichever period is greater. A residence will be deemed to be rented during any period that the taxpayer holds the residence out for rental, resale or repairs, or renovates the residence with the intention of holding it out for rental or resale [§280A(d)(1); §1.163-10T(p)(3)(iii)].

COMMENT: Interestingly enough, this 14-day use period could eliminate some or all of the vacation home expenses in excess of income, a catch-22 problem [§280A].

The taxpayer elects the two homes, not the IRS! In the case of a taxpayer who owns more than two residences, the taxpayer may designate *each year* which residence (other than the taxpayer's principal residence) is to be treated as the second residence. This election need not be disclosed to the IRS.

Exceptions to the "only-two-in-a-year" rule. A taxpayer may not elect different residences as second residences at different times of the same taxable year except as provided below [§1.163-10T(p)(3)(iv)]:

1. *Owning two homes and purchasing another.* If the taxpayer acquires a new residence during the taxable year, the taxpayer may elect the new residence as the taxpayer's second residence as of the date acquired.

   Example: Jeff owns vacation home A for the entire year and pays $3,000 interest expense. He acquires vacation home B on July 1 and pays $4,000 interest expense through December 31. Jeff may elect vacation home A as his second residence for the first half of the year (approximately $1,500 of interest) and vacation home B as his second residence for the second half of the year (the entire $4,000 of interest).

2. *Converting principal home into vacation home.* If a taxpayer moves out of his or her principal residence and converts it into a vacation home, the new vacation home becomes eligible as a second residence for interest deduction purposes.

Example: On July 1, Jeff decides to move out of his principal residence on St. Thomas, Virgin Islands, and purchase a principal residence in Aspen. The interest expense for the year on his St. Thomas home is $9,000 and for the half-year on his Aspen home is $4,000. Assuming Jeff does not convert the property into a rental, he may elect the St. Thomas home as a qualified second residence for the second half of the year. The tax result is that all $13,000 interest expense is deductible.

3. *Owning three homes and selling one in middle of year.* If property that was the taxpayer's second residence is sold during the taxable year or becomes the taxpayer's principal residence, the taxpayer may elect a new second residence as of that day.

Example: Jeff sold vacation home A on July 1, paying $4,000 interest expense from January 1 through the sale date. He elects A as his qualified second residence for the first half of the year. Jeff also owns vacation home B, paying $7,000 interest expense for the entire year. Jeff may elect vacation home B as his new second qualified residence starting July 1.

If the residence is also used for business, interest must be prorated. The interest expense must be allocated, based on their fair market values, between the residential use and the nonresidential use (e.g., business, rental or investment use) with the exception discussed below given to "certain residential rentals" [§1.163-10T(p)(4)].

Example: Tom uses 10% of his residence as an office in his trade or business. That portion does not qualify as a residence. Therefore, 10% of the interest *may* be deductible as business interest expense.

WARNING: See *secured* debt, discussed later, for a potential problem. Secured debt overrides the direct tracing rules. This requires that Tom deduct the 10% normal business expense as qualified-residence interest, an itemized deduction [§1.163-10T(p)(4)].

Special rule for "certain residential rentals." If the taxpayer rents out a portion of the principal or second residence, that portion may still be treated as residential use if

1. the tenant uses the rented portion primarily for residential purposes;

2. the rented portion is not a self-contained residential unit containing separate sleeping space and toilet and cooking facilities; and

3. the total number of tenants renting (directly or by sublease) the same or different portions of the residence at any time during the taxable year does not exceed two. If two persons (and their dependents) share the same sleeping quarters, they are treated as a single tenant [§1.163-10T(p)(4)(ii)].

The most common tax question—deducting interest on a residence under construction. A taxpayer may treat a residence under construction as a qualified residence for up to 24 months, but only if the residence becomes a qualified residence at the time the residence is ready for occupancy. This is an exception to the basic rule that the property must be *used* by the taxpayer as a residence [§1.163-10T(p)(5)].

WARNING: Make sure that the debt is also "secured" by the residence or this "relief" is irrelevant.

WARNING: If construction takes more than 24 months to complete, the interest after the 24th month and before occupancy is *not* deductible. The interest becomes deductible again as residence interest only after occupancy. What a strange regulation!

Interest on a vacant lot may be nondeductible. Frances Garrison's vacant lot, located in a recreational area, was determined to be neither the taxpayer's principal residence nor a second home; therefore, the interest on the debt was not qualified residence interest. Although the Garrisons never built a home on this property, they did avail themselves of camping privileges each year. The Tax Court cited Temporary Regulation §1.163-10T(p)(3)(A), which requires that a second residence generally include a house, condominium, mobile home, boat or house trailer containing sleeping space and toilet and cooking facilities (which this vacant lot did not). As the taxpayer didn't make the argument that the property was an investment since it was principally used as recreational property, Garrison's interest was treated as nondeductible personal interest [*Frances B. Garrison,* 67 TCM 2896; TC Memo. 1994-200].

Deducting interest on time-share purchases. Time-sharing arrangements are considered qualified residences as long as the taxpayer does not lease their use [§1.163-10T(p)(6)].

PLANNING TIP: Therefore, swapping personal-use time-share units should not jeopardize the qualified-residence status.

Joint return. In the case of a joint return, a residence includes property used by the taxpayer or spouse and is owned by either or both spouses.

WARNING (for newlyweds): Be careful with newlyweds if both previously owned personal residences and one also owned a vacation home! They did own two deductible homes but now own one nondeductible home.

HOW DOES A DEBT BECOME "SECURED DEBT"?

What does "secured" mean? In order for any interest to be deductible as *qualified-residence indebtedness interest,* the debt is required to be *secured by such residence.* The term *secured debt* means a debt connected with a security instrument (such as a mortgage, deed of trust, or land contract), and

1. the qualified residence is specific security for the payment of the debt;
2. in the event of default, the residence *could* be subjected to the satisfaction of the debt; and
3. *it is recorded* (or otherwise perfected under local or Texas law) [§1.163-10T(j)(1); §1.163-10T(o)(1)]. *(Observe the tax sucker-punch this administrative hassle causes, as illustrated in the next example!)*

Collateral must be correct. The "specific security" requirement compels the purchased property be pledged as collateral against the loan.

> *Example:* **The John Sununu provision.** As reported by the *Wall Street Journal* in 1991, the ex-governor of New Hampshire purchased a home in Georgetown for more than $400,000 when he became President Bush's chief of staff in 1987. He borrowed the $400,000 from a Republican banker, giving the banker *his New Hampshire home* as collateral. A mistake, John! The loan must be "specific security," therefore, the Georgetown home must secure the Georgetown loan. The estimated $40,000 per year interest is *not deductible* by John as it is personal interest! Query: how many think John amended his returns?

PLANNING TIP: Is this common? Yes! We have found numerous taxpayers purchasing vacation homes with loans secured by their primary residences. The result is that a loan normally considered acquisition debt of a second residence is now considered home equity debt of the primary residence. *Bad tax planning*!

Example: **Winning with a *home equity* debt.** Terry purchases a $75,000 BMW on an installment contract from the auto dealer and gives his home, in addition to the automobile, as collateral. This converts a nondeductible personal interest expense to a deductible home mortgage interest expense *if* the auto dealer records the house lien, along with the auto lien, with the local registrar.

Commercial property pledged against home loan. Borrowed money used to purchase a personal residence but secured by a commercial rental property is *not properly secured,* and therefore the interest is nondeductible personal interest [TAM 9418001].

Home pledged against commercial loan. Debt secured by a personal residence but used for business purposes is deductible as an itemized deduction, not a business expense. When the security for the borrowed funds is a mortgage on a first or second home, *the security,* not the way the funds are used, controls the treatment of the interest. This is the only exception to the rule that interest expense is deducted by tracing how the underlying debt is used [§1.163-8T(m)(3)].

WARNING: The IRS gets the taxpayer coming and going with this technical requirement!

Example: Dennis took out a $20,000 loan to purchase office furniture and computer equipment for his new business. The bank requires Dennis to give them a second mortgage on his personal residence as additional collateral. During 1998, Dennis earns $2,400 of income before deducting the $2,400 interest expense he paid on the home equity loan. Regulation §1.163-8T(m)(3) requires Dennis to report $2,400 of income on his business tax return and subsequently to pay $367.20 self-employment tax (15.3% of $2,400). The $2,400 interest expense is deductible on his Schedule A as an itemized personal deduction. But he is still out $367.20 for self-employment taxes.

PLANNING TIP: Can an election be made to treat the debt on a qualified residence as not "qualified-residence interest"? Yes, by attaching to the taxpayer's tax return a *§1.163-10T(o)(5) election out* of the qualified-residence interest rules. This election is effective for that taxable year and for all subsequent taxable years unless revoked with the consent of the Commissioner.

Example: (continued) Dennis attaches to his 1998 tax return a §1.163-10T (o)(5) election out. He traces the use of the $20,000 loan to the purchase of the business furniture and computer equipment, thereby legally deducting the interest expense on his business tax return [§1.161-8T(c)(1)]. The tax result is that the $2,400 of income is offset by the $2,400 interest expense and therefore no self-employment tax is due. A savings of $367!

Example: Pat owns a principal residence having a fair market value of $75,000 with an acquisition indebtedness of $45,000. She borrows an additional $25,000 to be used as a business loan, giving a second mortgage on her home to the lender. Later she borrows another $15,000 to purchase a personal automobile, giving both her home and the automobile as collateral. In the absence of an election to treat the business loan as unsecured, the applicable debt limit for the automobile loan would be only $5,000, the limit of her home equity amount (Option 1). A §1.163-10T(o)(5) election out would allow Pat to deduct all the business interest on her business tax return and all the interest on the automobile loan as qualified-residence interest (Option 1).

	Option 1	Option 2
Fair Market Value	$75,000	$75,000
Debt:		
Acquisition Debt	− $45,000	− $45,000
Business Loan	− 25,000	− 0
Automobile Loan	− 5,000	− 15,000
Home Equity Amount	$ 0	$15,000

Example: **Avoiding a tax problem with related-party loans.** On January 1, 1998, Chuck, Sr., sells to Chuck, Jr., the lake cabin for $65,000 on the installment plan with $1,000 down and the balance due over a 20-year contract. Chuck, Sr., does not record the sale as he doesn't want his son to think he doesn't trust him. As a result, Chuck, Jr., doesn't have an interest deduction on his second dwelling unit!

When is the debt treated as secured? A debt is treated as secured as of the date on which each of the three requirements detailed previously are satisfied, *regardless* of when amounts are actually borrowed with respect to the debt.

Example: (continued) On July 1, 1998, Chuck Sr. records the above lake cabin contract. Chuck, Jr., would be able to deduct only the interest paid for the last half of the year.

Unsecured liens, mechanics liens and general asset liens do not qualify. A debt will not be considered to be secured by a qualified residence if it is secured solely by virtue of a lien upon the general assets of the taxpayer or by a security interest, such as a mechanic's lien or judgment lien, that attaches to the property without the consent of the debtor.

GENERAL REQUIREMENTS FOR HOME MORTGAGE INTEREST AND POINTS TO BE DEDUCTIBLE

Interest is anything paid as compensation for the use of money. In order for interest to be deductible, though, there must be an existing, valid and enforceable obligation for the individual to pay a principal sum and to pay interest on it [§163; §461].

Cash-basis taxpayers can't deduct prepaid interest. They are automatically placed on the accrual basis. Taxpayers may only deduct interest in the year the interest represents a cost of using the borrowed money. Even if paid in cash in advance, it can never be fully deducted and must be charged to a capital account and deducted in the period to which it applies [§461(g)(1)].

> *Example:* Shane buys a piece of property for $50,000, paying $10,000 as a cash downpayment and assuming the mortgage of $40,000. He also pays five years of interest in advance at the time of purchase, amounting to $20,000. Shane must deduct the interest expense *monthly* over the next five years, approximately $4,000 per year. On the other side of the transaction, the seller must report the entire $20,000 as interest income in the year of the sale!

Points are deductible over the loan term. On the whole, points paid, generally at the time of purchase or refinance, are considered similar to a prepayment of interest and are to be treated as paid over the term of the loan. This also applies to charges that are similar to points, such as loan origination fees, loan-processing fees or premium charges, provided that they are to be paid for the use of the lender's money. Such payments are viewed as a substitute for a higher-stated interest rate [§461(g)].

> *Example:* Susannah paid $2,400 in points on a 20-year loan involving 240 monthly payments. Susannah may deduct only $10 for each payment that is due during the tax year. The remaining amount must be capitalized and deducted monthly over the remaining loan period.

What expenses are considered points? *Loan-processing-fee* points paid by a mortgagor-borrower as compensation to a lender solely for the use or forbearance of money is considered to be interest. *Loan-origination-fee points* paid by a borrower obtaining an FHA loan are normally considered deductible interest points [Rev. Rul. 69-188, 1969-1 CB 54, as amended by Rev. Rul. 69-582, 1969-2 CB 29].

What are not considered points? Charges for services, including the lender's services (such as appraisal fees, the cost of preparing the note and mortgage or deed of trust, settlement fees, etc.) are not interest. They are similar to acquisition costs even though the lender may characterize or refer to them as "points" [Rev. Rul. 67-297, 1967-2 CB 87].

In addition, items such as appraisal fees, inspection fees, title fees, attorney fees, property taxes, mortgage insurance premiums and other amounts ordinarily charged separately on the settlement statement cannot be disguised as points [Rev. Rul. 92-2].

But *home mortgage points* can be currently deducted. The entire amount of points paid for a mortgage note may be deducted in the year of payment if

1. the loan is incurred in connection with the purchase or improvement of a principal residence and the indebtedness is secured by that home;

2. the payments of points is an established business practice in the area where the debt is created; and
3. the points do not exceed the amount generally charged in the area [§461(g)(2)].

> ***Example:*** Susannah paid $2,400 in points on a 20-year loan involving 240 monthly payments when purchasing a principal residence. Susannah may deduct all $2,400 in the year of the payment of the home mortgage points.

The points paid on a loan in excess of the $1,000,000 qualified acquisition-indebtedness cap would not qualify [Rev. Rul. 92-2; Rev. Proc. 92-12].

Closing statement should designate points. The IRS, "as a matter of administrative practice," permits the current deduction of points incurred when purchasing a principal residence if the following conditions are satisfied:

1. The above three rules of §461(g)(2) are met.
2. The Uniform Settlement Statement, HUD Form 1, clearly designates the amounts as "points" incurred to procure the loan. Therefore, labels such as *loan origination fees, loan discounts, discount points, points, service fee points,* and commissions paid to a mortgage broker for arranging financing are acceptable [Rev. Rul. 92-2]. *Loan-origination-fee points paid by the borrower to obtain a VA or FHA mortgage are now also deductible as interest.*
3. The points must be stated as a percentage of the principal amount borrowed.
4. The amount must be paid directly by the taxpayer [Rev. Proc. 92-12, IRB 1992-26].

Points paid by seller are deductible by both buyer and seller! The IRS ruled that when a seller pays "points" on the sale of a principal residence, the *buyer* may deduct those points as interest, but both must subtract these points from the sales/purchase price. Seller-paid points are viewed as an adjustment to the purchase price of the home when certain requirements are met. This pro-home-buyer rule is retroactive for points paid by the seller after December 31, 1990 [Rev. Proc. 94-27; Reg. §1.1273-2(g)(5) (Example 3)]!

> ***Example:*** Danny Seller sells Roberta Buyer his principal residence for $101,600 and also agrees to pay two of the four points on Roberta's new $80,000 mortgage ($1,600.00). Danny must decrease his net sales price to $100,000 (which decreases his gain by $1,600). Roberta's purchase price is $100,000 and she gets to deduct all $3,200 of the mortgage points, just as if she had paid it personally!

The IRS requirements. So long as the previously mentioned requirements are met (i.e., computed as percentage, established business practice, not excessive, purchase points only, and paid directly), the deductible amount designated as mortgage discount points on HUD Form 1 may be shown as paid from either the borrower's or the seller's funds at closing!

PLANNING TIP: Therefore, points paid by the seller (including points charged to the seller) in connection with the buyer's loan will be treated as paid directly by the buyer from funds that have not been borrowed!

PLANNING TIP: For substantiation purposes, this requires the buyer to receive the seller's closing statement along with the buyer's closing statement, something generally not given to the buyer with the exception of HUD Form 1.

PLANNING TIP: Make sure the points are paid in cash. In order for points to be deductible, they must be paid from separate funds at the time of loan closing. They cannot be paid from borrowed funds. Points withheld by a lender from loan proceeds may not be deducted by a borrower in the year the points were withheld, because the withholding does not constitute payment within that tax year. Such withholding reduces the issue price of the loan, and thereby the amount of the deduction is governed by the original issue discount rules [§1271-1274] [*R. A. Schubel,* 77 TC 701, Dec. 38, 388 (1981)].

Points can be paid out of the earnest money deposit. So long as the funds are not borrowed, points may be deducted if they do not exceed the down payment, escrow deposit, earnest money applied at closing and other funds actually paid over at closing [Rev. Proc. 92-12; Rev. Rul. 92-2].

PLANNING TIP: Therefore, points do *not* have to be paid in cash at closing so long as the earnest money deposit exceeds the points.

Rental of large portion of residence does not hinder write-off of points. Russell rented a substantial portion of his principal residence (85%). The points he incurred to acquire the mortgage on the residence did not have to be amortized merely because the principal residence was also partially used for rental purposes. The Tax Court determined that there is "no exception in Code Section 461(g) for a principal residence which is also used (partly or substantially) for rental purposes." Therefore, the court held that the points Russell paid were deductible on Schedule A under Code Sections 163 and 461(g)(2) [*Russell,* TC Memo, 1994-96, 67 TCM 2347].

PLANNING TIP: The Tax Court's logic should also extend to a principal residence with a home office. The home office should not affect the write-off of the points.

This rule would not apply to the purchase of a duplex with one unit being used personally as that represents the purchase of two assets, a personal home and a business rental.

A big tax problem—points paid when refinancing are never currently deductible. Points paid in refinancing a mortgage are not deductible in full in the year paid, regardless of how the taxpayer arranges to pay for them. This is true even if the new mortgage is secured by the taxpayer's principal residence. According to the IRS, points paid to refinance an existing home mortgage are for repaying the taxpayer's existing indebtedness, and they are not paid *"in connection with"* the purchase or improvement of the home.

Therefore, taxpayers must deduct refinance points over the loan period. The IRS requires taxpayers to deduct these points monthly over the term of the loan. If part of the proceeds from the refinancing are used to improve the personal residence, the taxpayer may deduct a portion of the points in the tax year paid [IRS News Rel. IR-86-68, May 13, 1986; Rev. Rul. 87-22, IRB 1987-14,41].

> ***Example:*** Susannah paid $2,400 in points on refinancing a 20-year loan involving 240 monthly payments on her principal residence. Susannah may only deduct $10 for each payment that is due during the tax year.

Points paid to refinance a home mortgage loan may be currently deductible *if* advance planned—IRS doesn't agree. James and Zenith Huntsman bought a principal residence financed by a $122,000 mortgage loan with a balloon payment due in three years. Shortly thereafter, they obtained a $22,000 home improvement loan secured by a second mortgage. Within the three years, the Huntsmans obtained a 30-year variable-rate mortgage of $148,000 and paid off the prior loans with the proceeds.

When obtaining their new mortgage, the Huntsmans paid $4,440 in points and immediately deducted it as points paid *"in connection with"* the purchase of a principal residence [see the exact wording of §461(g)(2)]. In disagreeing with the IRS's and the Tax Court's disallowance of the current deduction, the U.S. Court of Appeals for the Eighth Circuit stated that "obtaining the short-term financing was merely an integrated step in securing the permanent financing to purchase the home." Judge Lay concluded that the statement *"in connection with"* should be "broadly construed" [*James Richard Huntsman v. Comm.*, CA-8 (rev'g TC) 90-2 USTC ¶50,340; 91 TC 917].

PLANNING TIP: This requires that the taxpayer plan the refinancing at the time of acquisition.

IRS nonaquiesces. The IRS has announced that it will *not* follow the *Huntsman* decision outside of the Eighth Circuit. The service warns that the test created by the

Eighth Circuit requires an examination of the facts of each case to determine whether a refinancing is sufficiently connected with the purchase or improvement of a principal residence. The IRS states that Congress enacted §461(g)(2) to eliminate the case-by-case approach to the deductibility of points [AOD No. 1991-02].

PLANNING TIP: This means that taxpayers should be warned of a possible disallowance at audit but not necessarily loss of deduction—if they are willing to go to court!

WARNING: Any fact pattern other than the facts in *Huntsman* will probably *not* be considered acquisition points. This includes refinancing to lower the interest rates [*Kelly v. Comm.*, TC Memo 1991-605, 62TCM 1406; *Dodd v. Comm.*, TC Memo 1992-341].

A tax pain—how to allocate points on home mortgages when they cannot be deducted in the year paid. The IRS provides for a monthly straight-line allocation of residential points over the loan period for those taxpayers who qualify. Generally, the method applies to an individual cash-basis taxpayer who is charged points on a loan secured by his or her principal residence if the loan period is no greater than 30 years. There are additional restrictions on loan amounts and number of points charged [Rev. Proc. 87-15; IRB 1987-14].

What happens to the points if the home is sold before the loan is paid off? They are fully deductible in the year of the sale. Whenever the property is sold or disposed of, any unamortized part of the financing expense can be charged off and deducted as interest expense. It makes no difference whether the purchaser assumes the mortgage, the property is simply sold subject to the mortgage or it is paid off by the seller at the time of the sale.

> *Example:*   David S. places a ten-year mortgage on an apartment building on July 1, 1995, using the proceeds to pay off an existing mortgage and to pay for repairs and operating expenses. He pays $1,000 in points at closing, of which only $50 is deductible in 1995 ($1,000 ÷ 10 years × .5 year). David sells the property on July 1, 1999. The remaining capitalized interest of $650 is triggered and becomes totally deductible as an interest expense in 1999. This would be true whether the mortgage is paid off at closing or the property is sold subject to the mortgage.

What happens to the points if the borrower prepays the loan? The points become fully deductible in the year of the payment of the loan. Refinancing, however, will not trigger this option. The loan must be paid off in cash or its equivalent [*B. L. Battlestein*, CA-5, 80-1, USTC ¶9225]. (But the IRS disagrees; see PLR 8632058.)

Points paid by the seller to help the buyer get financing. A loan charge of points or a loan replacement fee, paid by the seller of a residence as a condition to the arrangement of an FHA financing term for the buyer, is not deductible as interest; this charge is a selling expense that reduces the amount realized [Rev. Rul. 68-650, 1968-2 CB 78; Rev. Proc. 92-12A, IRB 1992-26].

FHA mortgage insurance premium (MIP) points. The IRS maintains that the insurance premiums on FHA loans are not interest. They are insurance and are therefore not deductible as interest.

CONCLUSION

Home mortgage interest is often the largest tax deduction for the average taxpayer. As this chapter showed, many technical traps exist that cause the homeowner to lose this valuable deduction. The material here helps the investor to maintain a legal deduction in case of an IRS audit.

10

Depreciation

INTRODUCTION

Depreciation expense is one of the major items of consideration when evaluating potential equipment or real estate acquisitions as it allows the investor to take an "imaginary" deduction even though the property may actually be *appreciating* in value. Depreciation is the periodic expending of an asset over the property's theoretical economic life. This tax deduction is intended to recognize the decrease in value caused by wear and tear, outdated interior improvements and neighborhood problems. Depreciation also provides a method of matching the income and related expense.

DEPRECIATION IS MANDATORY

If property qualifies for the depreciation expense deduction, the cost or other basis of property *shall* be decreased for depreciation at the end of each taxable year. This can create a financial disaster for the taxpayer.

> *Example:* **A tax problem.** Scott purchases a $100,000 rental building in 1998 (on leased land). He instructs his accountant not to take any depreciation on the building; he already has enough deductions to offset his income. In other words, he has no tax use for the depreciation deduction from the building. After holding the property for 39 years, he sells the building to Martin for $100,000. He reports to the IRS no gain on the sale because he never received any economic benefit from depreciation while owning the building. Wrong! He must report a $100,000 gain. Depreciation allowed *or allowable* is required in the capital gains computation.

Gain or Loss Computation

Sales price		<u>$100,000</u>
Less: Adjusted basis		
Original cost (or basis)	+ $100,000	
Less: Accumulated depreciation	− $100,000*	
Equals: Total adjusted basis:		− 0
NET GAIN (OR LOSS) ON SALE		= $100,000

* Depreciation allowed or allowable [§1.1016-3].

Here is a solution.

MISSED DEPRECIATION

"Missed Depreciation" Can Be Claimed Later—If Form 3115 Filed by December 31!

Allowable depreciation not taken? It is sometimes discovered, generally at the time of sale or the switching of tax preparers, that the taxpayer has deducted less depreciation than he or she is entitled, either because an asset was misclassified into a longer-life category (e.g., 15-year land improvements misclassified as 39-year commercial real property) or never placed on the return. The taxpayer cannot simply correct the mistake and take the missing depreciation without the IRS Commissioner's permission. The change in accounting method election, Form 3115, is required as miscalculating depreciation for two or more years is not an error, it is an accounting method, albeit an erroneous one [§1.167(e)-1(a); §1.446-1(e)(2)(ii)(b); Rev. Rul. 72-491].

Depreciation allowed or allowable increases gain. Even worse, the IRS requires the taxpayer to calculate the gain upon sale by subtracting from the basis the greater of accumulated depreciation allowed *or allowable* [IRC §1016(a)(2) and Regulation §1.1016-3]. Under this calculation, the taxpayer who improperly computes depreciation deductions may upon sale of the property end up paying tax on gain increased by a benefit never received (the prior depreciation).

Relief is on the way! This unfair provision was decidedly pro-IRS and antitaxpayer, one the present IRS administration evidentially wishes to correct. The IRS has essentially provided a back-door relief to the adjusted basis computation [Rev. Proc. 96-31 and Rev. Proc. 97-27].

COMMENT: Whether or not Rev. Proc. 97-37 discussed here is used, the taxpayer must still subtract from basis the depreciation allowed *or allowable.* As we will see later, all Rev. Proc. 97-37 does is to allow the taxpayer to take a current deduction for the previously unclaimed depreciation and all Rev. Proc. 97-27 does is extend the application deadline from June 27th to December 31.

___

Example: Elizabeth purchased a new apartment building (27.5 year life) on January 1, 1990, for $130,000, with the land value estimated at $30,000. Although the building was listed on her 1990 through 1996 depreciation schedules, no depreciation expense was taken because of a computer input error in her tax preparation software.

Year	Actual Depreciation	Allowable Depreciation	Accumulated Depreciation	Remaining Depreciation Basis
Purchase:				$100,000
1990:	$–0–	$3,485	$ 3,485	$ 96,515
1991:	$–0–	$3,636	$ 7,121	$ 92,879
1992:	$–0–	$3,636	$10,757	$ 89,243
1993:	$–0–	$3,636	$14,393	$ 85,607
1994:	$–0–	$3,636	$18,029	$ 81,971
1995:	$–0–	$3,636	$21,665	$ 78,335
1994:	$–0–	$3,636	$25,301	$ 74,699
1996:	$–0–	$3,636	$28,937	$ 71,063
1997:	$3,636	$3,636	$32,573	$ 67,427
1998:	$3,636	$3,637	$36,210	$ 63,790
1999:	$3,636	$3,636	$39,846	$ 60,154

New tax procedure—catch-up depreciation. A taxpayer who has claimed less than or none of the otherwise allowable depreciation (or amortization) can take a "catch up" current year deduction (as a §481(a) adjustment) for the understated amount, *including closed years,* by automatically electing (i.e., automatic IRS consent) to change his or her accounting method for that asset. The effective date of this change is May 13, 1996 [Rev. Proc. 96-31].

Example (continued): Elizabeth's unclaimed accumulated depreciation from 1990 through 1996 is $28,937. If she timely files Form 3115, she can claim the entire $28,937 as a §481(a) adjustment on her 1997 tax return, in addition to deducting her annual depreciation of $3,636. If the error is discovered in 1998, the $28,937 would have to be deducted on her 1998 return after filing Form 3115.

To obtain automatic IRS consent to catch up understated depreciation:

1. **File Form 3115 with the IRS national office timely:**
    (i) if filed after May 13, 1996, and before May 15, 1997, the form must be filed within 180 days of the beginning of the tax year in which the catch-up deduction will be claimed [Rev. Proc. 96-31];
    (ii) if filed on or after May 15, 1997, the form may be filed at *any time* during the year, *not* just during the first 180 days [§1.446-1T(e)(3)(i)(B); Rev. Proc. 97-37].

(a) Print on the top of Form 3115 *"Automatic Method Change under Rev. Proc. 97-37."*

(b) Complete on Form 3115 [see Rev. Proc. 97-37, Section 6.02(2)]:

(i) Part I, Eligibility to Request Change—lines 1, 2a and b, and 6;

(ii) Part II, Description of Change—line 8 and to the extent not provided elsewhere on Form 3115, lines 10, 11, 12, 13, 17, 18a and b, and 19;

(iii) Part III, Section 481(a) Adjustment—lines 20, 22, 23 and 25; and

(iv) Page 7, Schedule D, Part II, (Change in Depreciation or Amortization), and any other applicable forms.

(c) Mail to: Commissioner of Internal Revenue
Attn: CC:DOM: P&SI:6, Room 5112
P.O. Box 7604
Ben Franklin Station
Washington, DC 20044

(d) No user fee is required to be paid.

2. **Attach copy of Form 3115 to tax return** claiming catch-up deduction **[Rev. Proc 97-37; §5].**

WARNING: Adjustment only available in "the year of change." This new option only applies for any property held by the taxpayer as of the beginning of the *year of change* [Rev. Proc. 96-31; §3.06]. The year of change is the taxable year for which the original Form 3115 is considered **timely filed** with the national office [Rev. Proc. 96-31; §5.03]. Additionally, the taxpayer must take the entire negative §481(a) adjustment into account in computing the taxable income in the *year of change* (or spread over four years) [Rev. Proc. 97-37; §5.04(3)].

TAX PLANNING: Don't sell unless the election has been made. This means that if property is sold and no election has been made by December 31 (which will be a very common occurrence that will trap many an unwary taxpayer; e.g., tax preparers find out from their clients what assets were sold just before April 15th of the *next* year!), no catch-up depreciation is available.

This option does not apply to

1. any property held by a tax-exempt organization [§1016(a)(3)];
2. any intangible property except computer software, mortgage servicing rights, and certain interest or rights described in §197(e)(4)(B),(C), or (D);
3. any property for which a taxpayer is seeking to revoke a timely election or to make a late election under certain statutory provisions (a taxpayer may request consent to elect or revoke by submitting a ruling request);
4. except for property described in (2) above, any property subject to §167 for which a **taxpayer is changing only the estimated useful life,** which must be made prospectively;

5. **any property that changes use but continues to be owned by the same taxpayer;**
6. **any property for which a taxpayer has claimed depreciation in excess of the depreciation allowed;**
7. any change in accounting method involving a change from expensing a property's basis to capitalizing and depreciating that basis;
8. any change in accounting method involving a change from one permissible method to another permissible method (e.g., from S/L to income forecast for videocassettes); or
9. any change in accounting method other than depreciation even if a taxpayer's present method may have resulted in less than the allowable depreciation, e.g., when property is reclassified from inventory to depreciable property [Rev. Proc. 97-37; §3.02].

Even if the change is not allowed under Rev. Proc. 97-37, the taxpayer still has the option of requesting permission to make the method change under the general accounting method changes of Rev. Proc. 97-27. Transition rules are available for taxpayers who presently have a change pending under Rev. Proc. 92-20 and wish to avail themselves of Rev. Proc. 96-31 [Rev. Proc. 97-37; §8.02].

PROPERTY BECOMES DEPRECIABLE WHEN PLACED IN SERVICE, NOT WHEN PURCHASED!

Depreciation begins when the asset is *placed in service,* not necessarily when it is obtained. Depreciable real property usually is considered to be placed in service when it has been completed and is ready for occupancy [§1.167(a)-10(b)]. Business assets are not depreciable while out of service [*W. J. Walsh,* 55 TCM 994].

> ***Example:*** Sam purchases a fourplex apartment building on December 1, 1998, and spends the next three months getting it ready for occupancy. On March 1, 1999, he puts advertisements in the local newspaper and a "For Rent" sign in front of the building. Two of the units are rented on May 1, 1999, and the other two units are rented on July 1, 1999. Sam can start to depreciate the property on March 1, 1999 (not December 1, 1998), as that is the date the property is first ready for occupancy—the "placed-in-service" date.

WHAT KIND OF PROPERTY IS DEPRECIABLE?

Generally, depreciable property is

1. a capital expenditure in depreciable property,
2. used in a trade or business or held for the production of income, and
3. has a definite useful life of more than one year.

All three conditions must be met before the depreciation deduction is allowed.

Requirement 1: Capital expenditures in property. Qualified *capital expenditures* must be depreciated while qualified *repairs* must be currently expended. Capital expenditures include the acquisition costs of property as well as subsequent improvements that increase the property's value or prolong its useful life.

PLANNING TIP: Most taxpayers would want expenditures on business property to be repairs so they can currently deduct them. The tests to determine if an item is to be expended (as repairs) or depreciated (as capital expenditures) are

1. does it materially add to the property's value? or
2. does it prolong the property's useful life [§1.263(a)-1(b)] *unless*
3. substantial future benefit occurs (a facts and circumstances test) [*Indopco, Inc.*, SCt (*aff'g* CA-3), 92-1 USTC ¶50,133; 112 SCt 1039].

Therefore, improvements that have a more or less permanent value are capital expenditures that must be depreciated. Repairs, on the other hand, maintain the property in efficient operating condition and must be currently deducted [Rev. Rul. 94-12; see Chapter 1].

Requirement 2: Property used in a trade or business or for the production of income. Depreciation is allowed only for property that is used in a trade or business or that is held for the production of income [§167(a)].

WARNING: Personal property, such as a personal residence or personal automobile, may not be depreciated.

WARNING: Property that is held primarily for sale to customers (e.g., dealer's realty or inventory such as a model home) may also not be depreciated. If the taxpayer looks to the sale of the property rather than to its use in the taxpayer's business for the recovery of most or substantially all of the return of the investment, it does not qualify as depreciable property.

PLANNING TIP: Property used for both personal and business purposes. A personal residence containing an office-in-home is being used for both personal and business use and only the business portion may be depreciated. Another example: if the taxpayer owns a duplex apartment and rents out both units, it is fully depreciable, but if the taxpayer subsequently occupies one of the units as a principal residence, that unit becomes nondepreciable.

Requirement 3: Useful life of more than one year. The useful life of an asset is the period over which the asset is reasonably expected to be useful in a trade or business or for the production of income. In order to be depreciable, an asset must have a useful life of more than one year. If the life is less than one year, it is to be expended in the year placed into service (normally the year of acquisition).

LAND IS NOT DEPRECIABLE

Land cannot be depreciated because the taxpayers cannot calculate, with reasonable certainty, what would be the life of land.

Allocating purchase price between land and building. When improved property is purchased, the taxpayer *must* allocate the purchase price between the land, building and other improvements [§1.167(a)-5]. The allocation must be done in a fair and equitable manner, *based on the relative fair market values* at the time of purchase [§1.61-6(a)]. In other words, when improved real property is purchased, the lump sum price is divided between the depreciable property and the land in the same proportion of each to the total cost.

> ***Example:*** Randy acquires a piece of property for a $100,000 lump sum purchase price. An appraisal shows the land to be worth $50,000 and the building to be worth $150,000. The $100,000 is allocated as follows:

Land: $\dfrac{\$50,000}{(50,000 + \$150,000)} \times \$100,000 = \$\ 25,000$

Building: $\dfrac{\$150,000}{(50,000 + \$150,000)} \times \$100,000 = \underline{\$\ 75,000}$

TOTAL $100,000

DEPRECIATION METHODS

Historically, the calculation of depreciation has been determined under one of the following three methods: (1) economic life, (2) ACRS, or (3) MACRS. As the acquisition date of the property determines which of the methods are available, below are the alternative depreciation methods and related depreciable lives available to investors.

Real Property Placed in Service Date Between:	*The Depreciable Life Is:*
February 12, 1913, and December 31, 1980	Economic Life
January 1, 1981, and March 14, 1984	15 years—ACRS
March 15, 1985, and May 8, 1985	18 years—ACRS
May 9, 1985, and December 31, 1986	19 years—ACRS
January 1, 1987, and May 12, 1993	27.5/31.5 years*—MACRS
May 13, 1993, to present	27.5/39 years*—MACRS

* First life is for residential rental real estate; second life is for commercial real estate.

PLANNING TIP: Investors may be required to use all six methods. Taxpayers who have depreciable property placed in service before January 1, 1981, must continue to apply the economic-life depreciation method during their period of ownership. They cannot start using the ACRS method on property placed in service before January 1, 1981. As a result, both the economic-life method, for pre-1981 acquisitions, and the following ACRS and MACRS methods, for post-1980 acquisitions, are being used by most taxpayers.

The Economic Life Theory: Acquisitions Between 1913–1980

For assets placed in service before 1981, and for assets not eligible for ACRS or MACRS, property is depreciated over the asset's economically useful life (i.e., how long that asset is economically profitable) [§167].

Straight-line depreciation. This term means that the property is expensed evenly over the life of the property (e.g., a $100,000 building with an estimated life of 50 years would be depreciated at the rate of $2,000 each year).

Useful economic life is determined by all the facts and circumstances in each case. For eligible properties, depreciation expense is generally calculated by the intermixing of three major elements:

1. The method of depreciation to be used (e.g., straight-line, declining balance, sum-of-the-years digit)
2. The value of the property that is depreciable (land and salvage value is required to be subtracted)
3. The economic life of the property (buildings can be depreciated up to 60 years in length, depending upon the facts and circumstances)

As can be easily surmised, these three elements create many disagreements between the IRS and real estate investors.

The Accelerated Cost Recovery System (ACRS): Acquisitions Between 1981–1986

In an attempt to stop the disagreements about economic life, Congress completely revamped the depreciation calculation in the Economic Recovery Tax Act of 1981 (ERTA). Under ERTA, prior depreciation rules were discarded and replaced by a new simplified Accelerated Cost Recovery System (ACRS) for all property placed in service after December 31, 1980 (§168). This method is so radically different from the past that Congress even changed the word *depreciation* to *cost recovery*. Subsequently,

Congress passed numerous changes that repeal, limit and alter numerous ACRS deductions.

COMMENT: Real estate investors have experienced *five* different depreciation changes since the enactment of ACRS in 1981, averaging a different depreciation alternative every *three* years. Multiple changes create investor uncertainty, which directly impacts value. These changes clearly illustrate the problem when Congress continually interferes in the economic process, trying to mandate how long an asset will be economically useable. Congress's ACRS may be simple, but it is not fair!

The classes: ACRS places depreciable or recovery property into four classes with useful lives of 3, 5 or 10 years for personal property, and 15, 18 or 19 years for real property. The useful life for real property depends on the date the real property was placed into service.

Life. Under ACRS, investors have the choice of using one of two methods, a prescribed accelerated method using the regular recover period or the straight-line method, over either the ACRS assigned life or an extended-class life.

New versus used acquisitions. The ACRS abandons the "useful life" rules, the "salvage value" rules and even the "new versus used" rules for property placed in service after 1980. Therefore, it is irrelevant if the property is new or used. The percentage depreciation rate is exactly the same for both a new building and a newly acquired 50-year-old building.

COMMENT: This proves that something simple will inevitably be unfair somewhere!

Depreciation recapture—the wisdom of using the straight-line election for commercial real estate. Taxpayers were able to use the straight-line method of depreciation instead of the accelerated method for 15/18/19 real property. Most owners of non-residential (commercial) real estate made this election rather than the regular accelerated method. If they didn't, *all* accumulated depreciation (to the extent of the gain) would be subject to recapture as ordinary income *regardless* of how long the property is held and how the property is subsequently sold or exchanged. By electing the straight-line method of depreciation on the commercial real estate, *no* depreciation recapture is required. The depreciation recapture on residential real estate retains the §1250 rules—the amount of depreciation in excess of straight-line is recaptured as ordinary income in the year of the sale [§1245(a)(5)].

Rates. The rates used in computing depreciation for 3/5/10 property under the prescribed method is based on the 150% declining-balance method, switching to straight-line depreciation at the optimum time. For 18- and 19-year real property, the applicable percentage is based on the 175% declining-balance, switching to straight-line, method using a month-by-month convention. Before the enactment of TRA 84, a building placed in service during any part of the month was entitled to a full month of depreciation. However, TRA 84 changes this rule so that 18- or 19-year property in service for any part of a month receives only one-half-month cost recovery for that month.

IRS tables make calculating depreciation easy. IRS Publication 534 and IRS Form 4562 illustrate the applicable ACRS percentage rates for both personal and real property. If real property is not purchased in the first month, the first and last years' depreciation expense is based on the number of months the property was actually used.

THE MODIFIED ACCELERATED COST RECOVERY SYSTEM (MACRS) ACQUISITIONS AFTER 1986

Introduction. The Tax Reform Act of 1986 (billed as tax reform for fairness, growth and *simplicity*) substantially revises the ACRS for both personal and real property. In addition, it repeals the investment tax credit (ITC).

Beginning January 1, 1987, all tangible depreciable property purchased and used (placed in service) is expended using a straight-line or accelerated depreciation method over normally longer predetermined recovery periods [§168].

WARNING: This is a hidden tax rate increase. This Modified ACRS Method (MACRS) results in real property being depreciated at a substantially slower rate than in the past—as long as 27.5 to 39 years. Alternatively, investors and taxpayers may elect to use a 40-year recovery life on real property.

PLANNING TIP: Don't change the method previously used. These rules apply only to property placed into service after December 31, 1986. Investors continue with the depreciation method they started with when first placing the property on their depreciation schedule (e.g., commercial property purchased on December 31, 1986, would continue using a 19-year ACRS life in 1987 and thereafter. However, if that same property were purchased on May 13, 1993, the investor must use a 39-year MACRS life)! (And Congress wonders why real estate took such a nosedive starting in 1987!)

The eight MACRS classes.   All property is assigned to eight Modified Accelerated Cost Recovery System (MACRS) classes. The eight classes are titled for the number of years the property is to be depreciated.

The Internal Revenue Service prescribes the depreciation percentages to be applied to both personal and real property. A specially computed percentage is applied to these classes. These percentages, with the applicable half-year and half-month conventions, the declining balance percentages and the conversions to straight-line built in, are illustrated in Figure 10.1 and 10.2 reprinted from Rev. Proc. 87-57 [IRB 1987-42, 17].

FIGURE 10.1   Straight-Line Depreciation Percentages for "Real Estate"[1]

TABLE 1:   27.5 YEAR RESIDENTIAL REAL PROPERTY

The applicable percentage is: (Use the column for the Month in the First Year the Property is Placed in Service)

Recovery Year(s)	1	2	3	4	5	6	7	8	9	10	11	12
1	3.485	3.182	2.879	2.576	2.273	1.970	1.667	1.364	1.061	0.758	0.455	0.152
2–9	3.636	3.636	3.636	3.636	3.636	3.636	3.636	3.636	3.636	3.636	3.636	3.636
10,12, … 26	3.637	3.637	3.637	3.637	3.637	3.367	3.636	3.636	3.636	3.636	3.636	3.636
11,13, … 27	3.636	3.636	3.637	3.636	3.636	3.636	3.637	3.637	3.637	3.637	3.637	3.637
28	1.970	2.273	2.576	2.879	3.182	3.485	3.636	3.636	3.636	3.636	3.636	3.636
29	0.000	0.000	0.000	0.000	0.000	0.000	0.152	0.455	0.758	1.061	1.061	1.667
Total	100	100	100	100	100	100	100	100	100	100	100	100

TABLE 2:   31.5 YEAR RESIDENTIAL REAL PROPERTY

The applicable percentage is: (Use the column for the Month in the First Year the Property is Placed in Service)

Recovery Year(s)	1	2	3	4	5	6	7	8	9	10	11	12
1	3.042	2.778	2.513	2.249	1.984	1.720	1.455	1.190	0.926	0.661	0.397	0.132
2–7	3.175	3.175	3.175	3.175	3.175	3.175	3.175	3.175	3.175	3.175	3.175	3.175
8,10	3.175	3.174	3.175	3.174	3.175	3.174	3.175	3.175	3.175	3.175	3.175	3.175
9,11, … 31	3.174	3.175	3.174	3.175	3.174	3.175	3.174	3.175	3.174	3.175	3.174	3.175
12,14, … 30	3.175	3.174	3.175	3.174	3.175	3.174	3.175	3.174	3.175	3.174	3.175	3.174
32	1.720	1.984	2.249	2.513	2.778	3.042	3.175	3.174	3.175	3.174	3.175	3.174
33	0.000	0.000	0.000	0.000	0.000	0.000	0.132	0.396	0.661	0.925	1.190	1.454
Total	100	100	100	100	100	100	100	100	100	100	100	100

---

[1]Multiply depreciation percentages by original depreciation base.

Source: Rev. Proc. 87-57.

FIGURE 10.2   Straight-Line Depreciation Percentages for "Real Estate"[1]

TABLE 1:   39 YEAR NON-RESIDENTIAL REAL PROPERTY

*The applicable percentage is: (Use the column for the
Month in the First Year the Property is Placed in Service)*

Recovery Year(s)	1	2	3	4	5	6	7	8	9	10	11	12
1	2.461	2.247	2.033	1.819	1.605	1.391	1.177	0.963	0.749	0.535	0.321	0.107
2–39	2.564	2.564	2.564	2.564	2.564	2.564	2.564	2.564	2.564	2.564	2.564	2.564
40	0.107	0.321	0.535	0.749	0.963	1.177	1.391	1.605	1.819	2.033	2.247	2.461

[1]Multiply depreciation percentages by original depreciation base.
Source: Rev. Proc. 87-57.

Example: **The MACRS system.** John purchases an office building on January 1, 1998, for $500,000 with land valued at $50,000, leaving a depreciable basis of $450,000. His allowable depreciation expense for the first two years is:

Year	Unadjusted Basis	×	MACRS Percentage	=	Depreciation Expense
1998	$450,000	×	2.461%	=	$11,075

In the second year of ownership, John's depreciation expense is:

Year	Unadjusted Basis	×	MACRS Percentage	=	Depreciation Expense
1997	$450,000	×	2.564%	=	$11,538

John finds his MACRS depreciation percentage by first determining the MACRS class (39-year class in this case) and then finding the proper MACRS Table (39-year Nonresidential Real Property Table). Both the MACRS classes and MACRS Tables are explained below.

As mentioned previously, the Tax Reform Act of 1986 creates eight MACRS classes: six classes for depreciable personal property and two classes for real property.

MACRS classes for personal property. The first six MACRS classes—3, 5, 7, 10, 15, and 20 year—are the personal property classes.

Check IRS guidelines first. To determine property classifications within these six classes, the taxpayer must first refer to the properties "Class Life (in years)" under the IRS's Asset Depreciation Range (ADR) system [Rev. Proc. 87-56, IRB 1987-42,4]. This class life is the property's midpoint life and indicates the average useful life of an asset. The average lives are based on prior IRS research of broad industry classes of assets. The purpose of the class-life ADR system is to keep conflicts over individual useful lives at a minimum. In the past, ADR was an option.

A simplified finding list. The following list provides a quick synopsis of which ADR properties belong to which MACRS classes. It also indicates the depreciable life for each property for alternative minimum tax (AMT) purposes.

Items of depreciable property worth noting under MACRS: For investors in real estate, some items of real property are *not* real estate for purposes of the revised MACRS but instead receive the benefit of the substantially faster personal property depreciation rates. Real estate investors often use some of the below-listed personal property items.

- *Stoves, refrigerators, apartment furniture and similar items* are depreciable in the 5-year MACRS class (see 57.0 asset guideline ADR class).
- *Computers, adding machines, typewriters and photocopy machines* are depreciable in the 5-year MACRS class (see 00.12 and 00.13 ADR class).
- *Office furniture, fixtures and equipment* are depreciable in the 7-year MACRS class (see 00.11 ADR class).
- *Agriculture machinery and equipment* are depreciable in the 7-year MACRS class using the 150% declining-balance rate (see 01.1 ADR class).
- *Construction equipment* is depreciable in the 5-year MACRS class (see 15.0 ADR class).
- *Single-use agricultural buildings* (such as grain bins and silos) are in the 10-year MACRS class because of specific legislation (see 01.4 ADR class).
- *Land improvements* are in the 15-year 150% declining MACRS class and are described in ADR class 00.3 as follows: "includes improvements directly to or added to land, whether such improvements are section 1245 property or section 1250 property, provided such improvements are depreciable. *Examples of such assets might include sidewalks, roads (paving), canals, waterways, drainage facilities, sewers (not including municipal sewers in Class 51), wharves and docks, bridges, fences, landscaping, shrubbery, or radio and television transmitting towers*" (emphasis added).
- *Farm buildings* (but not special purpose) are in the 20-year class (see ADR class 1.3).
- *Municipal sewer pipes* are in the 20-year class (ADR class 51).

The ADR Class Life System allows the investor a certain amount of "component" depreciation.

> **Example:**   **Planning for a tax "loophole."** Zane wishes to purchase a piece of office property for $200,000. Zane has two options.

Investor

Asset Breakdown	Sophisticated	Unsophisticated	Life
Building	$100,000	$150,000	39-year Straight-line
Municipal Sewer	$ 5,000	0	20-year Accelerated
Land Improvements	$ 35,000	0	15-year Accelerated
Personal Property	$ 10,000	0	5-year Accelerated
Land	$ 50,000	$ 50,000	Not depreciable
Total	$200,000	$200,000	

Note: Allocating $50,000 of depreciable assets from 39-year straight-line depreciation to substantially faster 5-year to 20-year accelerated depreciation greatly changes the attractiveness of purchasing real property.

PLANNING TIP: The biggest problem with "component" acquisitions is proving to the IRS auditor that the allocation of the purchase price is fairly presented. It is recommended that the buyer break down the purchase price in the purchase-and-sale agreement. "Arm's-length" negotiations between buyer and seller are considered adequate evidence of value in many cases. Otherwise the IRS auditor can simply "reallocate" the purchase price to the detriment of the buyer.

TAX PLANNING: Investors can easily determine the value of components from professional appraisal books, such as Marshall & Swift's. Contact your local appraiser.

Real estate categories: The last two MACRS classes are for (1) residential rental real property and (2) nonresidential rental (commercial) real property.

27.5-year (straight-line) residential rental real property class. The IRS defines the property to be included in this class as residential rental property such as duplexes, apartment houses, condominium units and cooperative units used as personal residences, and the like. It specifically does NOT include hotels and motels [§168(b)(3),(c)].

Tax problem: One building containing both residential and commercial rentals must use the 80% gross rent test. The technical definition of residential rental property is a building in which 80% or more of the gross rental income comes from *dwelling units* [§167(j)(2)(B)]. The term *dwelling unit* is defined as a house or apartment used to provide living accommodations, but does not include a unit in a hotel, motor inn, or other establishment in which more than one-half of the units are used on a transient basis [§167(k)(3)(C)].

COMMENT: Many tax preparers erroneously think that a dual-use property is considered two properties. This is not true, as illustrated in the next example.

Example: Melvin owns a five-floor apartment complex with a grocery store on the first floor. In 1998, the residential tenants pay him $150,000 a year gross rent, and the commercial tenant pays him $50,000. Even though the residential portion of the building comprises 80% of the total floor space, it is irrelevant. The *total* building must be depreciated as a 39-year commercial building as the residential tenants' gross rent comprises only 75% of the total rental income. Better luck next year, Melvin!

COMMENT: This is a year-by-year test and could result in the taxpayer's being required to switch to the faster 27.5-year residential property method for those taxable years when the 80% test is met!

PLANNING TIP: For dual-use buildings, the use of "net, net, net leases" for commercial tenants coupled with "gross, gross, gross leases" for the residential tenants many time solves this problem and is becoming more common.

Example: The author is familiar with a large apartment complex that opened in Minneapolis recently with an exclusive health spa in the basement. All tenants received "free" membership (valued at $100 a month) in the spa *after* the landlord raised everyone's rent $100 per month. Their accountant had calculated that the spa's lease (with percentage lease payments) would exceed 20% of the annual gross rent from the building without this manipulation. [See Reg. §1.163(j)-3(b)(2) for the IRS's position on this "tax shelter."]

If any portion of a building or structure is occupied by the taxpayer, the gross rental income from such property shall include the rental value of the portion so occupied [§167(j)(2)(B)].

31.5-year or 39-year (straight-line) commercial real property class. Nonresidential real property is real property that is not residential rental property and that either has no ADR midpoint or does not have an ADR midpoint of less than 27.5 years [§168(b)(3),(c)].

Example: **Commercial property.** This category includes office buildings, shopping centers, and residential rental property failing the above-mentioned 80% test or dwelling unit test.

31.5-year life. For acquisitions between January 1, 1987, to May 13, 1993, this commercial (nonresidential) real estate must be depreciated over 31.5 years using the straight-line method.

39-year life. Effective for purchases after May 12, 1993, commercial real property must be depreciated over 39 years using the straight-line method. The alternative minimum tax depreciation rate of 40 years is unchanged.

Effective date: This law generally affects property placed in service on or after May 13, 1993. A transition rule exists: The 39-year rule does not apply to property placed in service before January 1, 1994, if (1) the taxpayer, or a qualified person, entered into a binding contract to purchase or construct the property before May 13, 1993, or (2) construction of the property commenced by or for the taxpayer, or a qualified person, before May 13, 1993. (A qualified person is anyone who transfers rights in such a contract or such property to the taxpayer without first placing the property in service.)

PLANNING TIP: Residential rental property stays at 27.5 years. Only commercial property was extended to 39 years.

PLANNING TIP: Investors must continue with the depreciation method used in the first year the property is placed into service. They are not required to switch to the 39-year life for property purchased before May 13, 1993. The useful life for real property depends on the date the real property was placed into service.

The depreciation rates—tables: Figure 10.1 and Figure 10.2 illustrate the applicable MACRS percentage rates for both personal and real property [Rev. Proc. 87-57, IRB 1987-42,17].

Improvements and Components—ACRS and MACRS

After investors reluctantly concede that an expenditure is a depreciable improvement and not a currently deductible repair, they want the improvement to be depreciated over the shortest period of time.

Component depreciation is no longer an advantage. The benefits of component depreciation used on personal or real property were eliminated by ERTA in 1981. *The depreciation expense on any component shall be computed in the same manner as the asset itself is being computed.*

> ***Example:*** Pete purchases a used commercial building for $500,000. He immediately rewires the building for $80,000 and replumbs it for $70,000. The $150,000 in improvements must use the same 39-year MACRS method as the building itself.

> ***Example:*** Maurice purchases a used commercial building for $250,000 in 1998, buying the components of the property for the following prices:

Building	$200,000
Land	$ 39,100
Air conditioner (a fixture)	$ 3,900
Personal property	$ 7,000
Total	$250,000

Because the building is being depreciated over 39 years, the air conditioner must also be depreciated over 39 years as it is a structural component of the building. Any personal property, (e.g., refrigerators and furniture) could be depreciated over five years.

Added improvements must be depreciated as if they are a new building. The life of any component of a building added after the acquisition shall be the same as the building, but the depreciation shall begin as of either the date the component starts to be used or the date the building starts to be used, whichever is later.

Example (continued):   Maurice, in the above example, is forced to replace the old air conditioner in 2001, after three years, and purchases a new air-conditioning system for $7,800. What is the depreciable life of the new air conditioner?

Answer: The new air conditioner, being a structural component, is considered a new building, not personal property. Therefore it must be depreciated as if Maurice purchased another building in that year. After May 12, 1993, acquisitions must be depreciated using a 39-year life!

COMMENT: Congress, this doesn't make economic sense!

Lessee leasehold improvements. Starting in 1987, leasehold improvements must be depreciated over the life of the property using the MACRS method and *not* over the life of the lease [§168(i)(6)].

Example: **A terrible tax problem.** Hayes leases bare office space in downtown Chicago for a five-year period, with no renewals, and spends $39,000 on improvements before occupancy. Hayes' amortization of the leasehold improvements is as follows:

	Under MACRS	*Under ACRS*
Year 1	$ 1,000	$ 7,800
Year 2	$ 1,000	$ 7,800
Year 3	$ 1,000	$ 7,800
Year 4	$ 1,000	$ 7,800
Year 5	**$35,000**	**$ 7,800**
Total	$39,000	$39,000

Note. The reason for the $35,000 in year 5 is that Hayes gets his normal $1,000 MACRS plus a $34,000 loss on abandoning his leasehold improvements! This is not a good deal! Economically Hayes has prepaid his taxes for years 1 through 4, and gets the prepaid taxes back in year 5.

THE ALTERNATIVE DEPRECIATION SYSTEM (ADS) FOR CERTAIN PROPERTY

This optional depreciation system, required for some types of property and electable by all taxpayers, is a straight-line method using substantially longer lives (with the half-month and half-year convention applicable and without regard to a salvage value) [§168(g)].

The ADS recovery period. Generally, the ADS class lives for most property will be as shown below:

In the Case of:	The Straight-Line Recovery Period Shall Be:
(1) Nonresidential real and residential rental property	40 years
(2) Personal property with no class lives	12 years
(3) Property not mentioned in (1) or (2) above	ADR midpoint*

---

* See column titled "Class Life (in years)" at Rev. Proc. 87-57, IRB 1987,42.

AT-RISK LIMITATIONS EXTENDED TO REAL ESTATE

General rule. The at-risk rules extend to real estate activities for all property placed in service after December 31, 1986. The at-risk rules will continue to be applicable only to individuals and certain activities of closely held corporations.

What are the at-risk rules? The at-risk rules of the current law reflect the fact that, as an economic matter, an investor cannot lose more than the amount that he or she has directly invested plus any additional amount for which the investor is liable. The purpose of the at-risk rules is generally to restrict the use of limited-risk transactions by individual taxpayers who artificially shelter their income from other sources.

> ***Example:*** Pat purchases a $100,000 building on leased land, paying a $5,000 cash down payment and giving the seller a $95,000 *nonrecourse* mortgage note for the remainder. At the end of five years, Pat pays another $5,000 on the principal. Assuming a 39-year life, Pat could have a total depreciation expense of $12,824 for the first five years. (Assume a zero cash flow and that the depreciation creates the total rental loss.) Since Pat has only *paid-in-cash or cash-like* $10,000 of the $100,000 owed, Pat's $12,824 depreciation deduction is limited to the *amount invested*—$10,000. If Pat had purchased the building with a $95,000 *recourse* note, he could have added the mortgage to the cash for a total amount invested of $100,000. In that case, the at-risk rules would not have limited any of the $12,824 depreciation deduction. Recourse notes are considered personal obligations and, therefore, for at-risk purposes can be added to the property's basis.

A real problem—trust deeds and contracts for deeds. In many states, trust deeds and contracts for deeds are considered nonrecourse financing. In case of default, the holder of the financing instrument can look only to the property for financial protection and cannot get a deficiency judgment in case of foreclosure.

PLANNING TIP: This makes trust deeds and contracts for deeds risky financing instruments to use in purchasing real estate. Even Congress admits, in the TRA 86 committee reports, that this tax change will require some states to statutorily change the legal concept of both these financing methods. Some states already make trust deeds recourse financing.

This will radically change the way farms and ranches will be sold in the future. To make trust deeds and contracts for deeds unavailable will eliminate most owner-financed sales.

Potential exception—third-party nonrecourse debt. A taxpayer is considered at risk for certain unrelated third-party nonrecourse debt incurred with respect to real estate. This should help large banks but not owner financing.

CONCLUSION

Depreciation is often calculated on property that is appreciating in value. It is one of the remaining tax shelters as it allows the investor to deduct a *phantom* expense against rental income. (But consult Chapter 12 on passive losses when a resulting loss is created.) This chapter illustrates that the depreciation computation, both annually and for the total amount accumulated during ownership, is ascertained simply by consulting a one-page tax rate schedule. Advance planning allows the investor to maximize the depreciation deduction even in light of the negative 39-year life.

New Office-in-Home Rules

THE OFFICE-IN-HOME REQUIREMENTS

A Taxpayer May Work out of His or Her Home

A new nontraditional trend in the business community finds many taxpayers working out of their personal residences. When a portion of a home is used for business purposes, a percentage of the total housing costs of these normally nondeductible personal expenses may be deducted as business expenses by a taxpayer who is an individual or an S corporation.

As Congress felt it necessary to prevent taxpayers from misusing the office-in-home deduction, it now requires stringent "exclusive, regular and principal" rules, discussed next, to be followed before this deduction is permitted.

THE OFFICE-IN-HOME REQUIREMENTS

Strict Office-in-Home Rules Prevent Abuse

For home-office expenses to qualify for a deduction, the portion of the home that is used for business must

1. be used *exclusively,* and
2. on a *regular* basis, in one of the following ways:
3. as the *principal place of business* for any of the taxpayer's trade or business; or

4. as a place of business for meeting or dealing with patients, clients or customers in the ordinary course of business; or
5. in connection with the taxpayer's trade or business if the taxpayer is using a separate structure that is not attached to the dwelling [§280A(c)(1)].

In the case of a home office used by an employee, the employee must establish that use of the home office is for the convenience of his or her employer [§280A(c)(1)(flush)].

WARNING: No "passive business" offices. These rules makes personal investment activities (e.g., reading financial periodicals, clipping bond coupons, etc.) ineligible for home-office deductions as they don't rise to the level of a "business" activity [*J. A. Moller,* CA-FC 83-2 USTC ¶9698, 721 F2d 810].

PLANNING TIP: *Renting room to an employer doesn't work.* A home-office deduction is barred when an employee leases a portion of his or her home to the employer. This rule also extends to an independent contractor who attempts to lease to the party for whom he or she perform services (e.g., a real estate agent should not lease office space located at home to his or her broker/owner) [§280A(c)(6)].

THE EXCLUSIVE RULE

The Room *Must* Be Exclusively Used for the Business

To qualify for business use of the home deduction, there must be a specific room or area that is set aside and used *exclusively* (no personal use during the year, including storage of personal items) on a regular basis as the principal place of any business. The exclusive rule will be met only if there is no use of the business portion of the dwelling unit *at any time during the year* other than for qualified business purposes. The mere absence of a wall, partition, curtain, or the like does not negate this deduction but does raise the level of inquiry by the IRS agent. Also, the act of walking through the home office to another room is not a violation of this rule [PR §1.280A-2(g); *Weightman,* 42 TCM 104, 1981-301; §1.280A-2(g)(1); *C. D. Hughes,* 41 TCM 1153, 1981-140].

PLANNING TIP: Don't take work home. Work from one business (e.g., college professor correcting student tests) brought home and taken into the office-in-home (that was the sole office of the professor's other business of being an actor) taints the room as a nonexclusive and therefore a nonbusiness room [*A. W. Hamacher v. Comm.,* 94 TC 348, No. 21, Dec. 46,444].

Example: Joan, a real estate agent, also operates an advertising agency from her personal residence. She may *not* make real estate brokerage calls from her advertising agency home office.

Operating Two or More Businesses Simultaneously out of the Same Home Office

The judge in *Hamacher* makes clear that two businesses may be exclusively operated out of the same office-in-home. But *each* activity must satisfy all the statutory requirements. For example, real estate brokers or businesspersons with a home office for managing property owned by themselves or others (e.g., a second business as a property manager) *may* be able to deduct an office-in-home.

PLANNING TIP: If any deduction, such as a home office, is first determined personal and, hence, nondeductible, the taxpayer cannot subsequently deduct any business office expenses. Unfortunately, there is not a clear dividing line between deductible business expenses that render passing personal benefits and nondeductible personal expenses that incidentally benefit business purposes [*S. A. Bodzin,* CA-4, 75-1 USTC ¶9190].

EXCLUSIVE USE RULE EXCEPTIONS: DAY CARE AND INVENTORY STORAGE

The exclusive use requirement does not apply when the home is used for qualified *day care* of children, handicapped or the elderly and to wholesale or retail sellers *regularly storing inventory in the home* (e.g., part-time Mary Kay or Shakley salespeople) and solely working out of their homes [§28OA(c)(4); §28OA(c)(2); §1.280A-2(e)].

Office-in-Home Deduction for Storage of Product Samples

The exception to the home-office deduction limitations for expenses related to space used to store inventory also applies to space used to store "product samples." The taxpayer must be in the trade or business of selling products at retail or wholesale, and the home must be the *sole* fixed location of such trade or business [§280(A)(c)(2)].

REGULAR USE TEST

Even though no home office case specifically defines regular use, this test implies that the home office is being used systematically throughout the year. Occasional or incidental business use of the home office will not be sufficient even though the room met the exclusivity requirement.

PATIENTS, CLIENTS OR CUSTOMERS

A deduction for home office will NOT be denied when a taxpayer in the normal course of his or her business meets or deals with patients, clients, or customers in his or her home as long as the space is used exclusively and regularly for this business activity. This exception applies even though the taxpayer may carry on business at another location. The IRS emphasizes that this exception applies only when the taxpayer is actually visited by clients or patients and will not apply to a room where only phone calls are received [§280A(c)(1)(B); IRS Pub. 587, p.3].

> *Example:* This would qualify doctors, dentists, attorneys, barbers, beauticians and even owners of small grocery stores who operate their business from their homes.

SEPARATE STRUCTURES

This exception applies to the freestanding structure apart from the taxpayer's residence if such structure is used exclusively and regularly in the taxpayer's trade or business. To qualify for the exception, it is not necessary that the taxpayer establish that the structure is his or her principal place of business or that it is a place where he or she meets patients, clients, or customers [§280A(c)(1)(C)].

> *Example:* A guest cottage used as a dentist's office or a separate garage converted into an artist's studio.

PRINCIPAL PLACE OF BUSINESS

Prior to 1997, neither the Internal Revenue Code nor congressional committee reports explained what was meant by *principal place of business* and left it to the administrative and judicial branches to define "principal place of business," which they did, much to taxpayers' chagrin in *Commissioner v. Soliman,* 113 SCt 701 (1993); IRS Notice 93-12; and Rev. Rul. 94-24.

How the Supreme Court Defined Principal Place of Business

Essentially, the Supreme Court and the IRS draconianly ruled that the principal place of business is where "client contact" occurs, as that is where the primary income-generation functions are performed. This eliminated approximately 95% of the previously deducted home offices. The legislative branch corrected this inequitable result, but only effective for tax returns filed starting in 1999.

COMMENT: This legislative correction gives small home-based businesses parity with those companies who choose to rent space and deduct the lease payments.

Political pundits also claim that it recognizes advances in technology that encourage operating a home-based business, helps cut down on commuting and conserves energy, provides a financial boost to these businesses, helps create jobs and even is profamily. At last, tax law with a moral purpose!

Applying the Principal Place of Business Test When the Taxpayer Has Only One "Regular" Business Location

If a taxpayer has only one place of business, this is considered the taxpayer's "regular" place of business, a location deemed superior to a principal place of business.

PLANNING TIP: If this regular place of business is in the home, the taxpayer would have a deductible office-in-home, assuming the exclusive and regular requirements are met.

IRS Example: **An author.** Danny is a self-employed author who uses a home office to write. He spends 30 to 35 hours of his work time per week writing in his home office. Danny also spends another 10 to 15 hours of his work time per week at other locations conducting research, meeting with his publishers and attending promotional events.

The essence of Danny's trade or business as an author is writing. Danny's research, meetings with publishers and attendance at promotional events, although essential, are less important and take less time than his writing. Therefore, Danny's office in the home is his principal place of business, and he can deduct expenses for the business use of the home [Rev. Rul. 94-24; IRB 1994-15,5].

Home Office Definition Expanded—Supreme Court's Opinion in Soliman Overturned!

Applying the principal place of business test when the taxpayer engages in business at multiple locations. To reverse the *Soliman* decision, Congress created a simple, two-step test to determine if the home office is the taxpayer's principal place of business. Starting in 1999, a home office qualifies as the taxpayer's "principal place of business" if

1. **the home office is used by the taxpayer for the administrative or management activities of any trade or business of the taxpayer,** and
2. **there is no other fixed location of the trade or business where the taxpayer conducts substantial administrative or management activities**

of the trade or business [new §280A(c)(1) flush language and effective for tax years after December 31, 1998].

TAX PLANNING: This liberal expansion restores the office deduction to the vast majority of the estimated 34 million businesspersons who work out of their homes, such as

- home-based employees who telecommunicate to the main office;
- doctors who perform their duties in hospitals but need to do their billings from their home office;
- salespeople who call at the customer's place of business;
- professional speakers who prepare at home but deliver the presentation at hotels and convention centers; and
- plumbers and other tradespeople who perform their duties at job sites away from the shop.

TAX PLANNING: Many taxpayers who have a second business conducted out of their home will be able to deduct their traveling to and from their "home office" to their main office (previously considered nondeductible commuting mileage) under this expanded definition. This topic is discussed later in this chapter.

Caution—the regular, exclusive requirements still valid. Of course, the home office deduction is only allowed if the office is also exclusively used on a regular basis as a place of business by the taxpayer [§280A(c)(1)].

Caution—the employer convenience requirements still valid. In the case of an employee, the home office is only deductible if such exclusive use is for the convenience of the employer. The question whether an employee chose not to use suitable space made available by the employer for administrative activities would be relevant to determining whether the "convenience of the employer" test is satisfied [§280A(c) (flush); Chairman's Mark, Revenue Reconciliation Bill of 1997].

Congressional examples are extraordinarily liberal. The House Committee Report provides the following examples of the types of taxpayers who will be able to use this new expanded definition of principal place of business:

- Taxpayers who carry out administrative or management activities at sites that are not fixed locations of the business (e.g., in a car or hotel room), in addition to performing those same activities in their home office;
- Taxpayers who do not conduct substantial administrative or management activities at a fixed location other than the home office, even if administrative or management activities (e.g., billing activities) are performed by other people at other locations;

- Taxpayers who conduct some administrative or management activities at a fixed location of the business outside the home, so long as the administrative or management activities conducted at any fixed location of the business outside the home are not substantial (e.g., the taxpayer occasionally does minimal paperwork at another fixed location of the business);
- Taxpayers who conduct substantial *nonadministrative* or *nonmanagement* business activities at a fixed location of the business outside the home office (e.g., meeting with or providing services to customers, clients, or patients at a fixed location of the business away from the home office); and
- Taxpayers who *in fact* do not perform substantial administrative or management activities at any fixed location of the business away from home will find the second prong satisfied, regardless of whether or not the taxpayer opted not to use an office away from home that was available for the conduct of such activities [see Chairman's Mark, Revenue Reconciliation Bill of 1997].

COMMENT: Therefore, taxpayers who perform administrative or management activities for their trade or business at places *other than* the home office are not automatically prohibited from taking this deduction. Additionally, in cases where a taxpayer's use of a home office does not satisfy the two-part test, the taxpayer nonetheless may be able to claim a home office deduction under the present-law "principal place of business" exception or any other provision of §280A [Chairman's Mark, Revenue Reconciliation Bill of 1997].

Applying the Principal Place of Business Test When the Taxpayer Engages in Business at Multiple Locations—Prior to Tax Years Beginning before January 1, 1999

In case the reader is under an IRS audit for years prior to 1999, or preparing a pre-1999 return, here is a synopsis of the *Soliman* decision and the tax ramifications it created.

When the business is engaged at multiple locations. When the taxpayer has multiple regular places of business (e.g., is engaged in a single trade or business at more than one location, such as a medical surgeon or concert pianist working out of his or her home), a *principal* place of business must be identified. Look what the Supreme Court did:

TAX PROBLEM: When taxpayers regularly meet clients/customers away from their home offices (e.g., part-time Mary Kay representatives delivering products to their customers), the Supreme Court ruled that *each* meeting location is a different "place of business" and each must be analyzed to determine which location is principal. The taxpayer was required to determine if the principal business location is where the product or service is designed, built, administered, stored, maintained, delivered or used.

The reversed Supreme Court test to determine "principal place of business." In *Soliman,* the Supreme Court identified two primary factors for determining whether a home office is the taxpayer's principal place of business for purposes of §280A(c)(1)(A):

1. The relative importance of the activities performed at each business location;
2. The amount of time spent at each location [*Commissioner v. Soliman,* 113 SCt 701 (1993); see also *Lynn Crawford,* TC Memo, 1993-192].

Using the "client contact" test to determine "relative importance." A comparison of the relative importance of the activities performed at each business location depends on the characteristics of each business. If the nature of a trade or business requires a taxpayer to meet or confer with clients or patients, or to deliver services or goods to customers, the place where that contact occurs must be given great weight in determining where the most important activities of the business are performed. If the nature of the business requires that its services are rendered or its goods delivered at a facility with unique or special characteristics (e.g., a hospital), this is a further and weighty consideration in determining where the most important activities of the business are undertaken.

Testing for time spent. In addition to comparing the relative importance of the activities performed at each business location, the Supreme Court also directed that a comparison be made of the time spent on business at home with the time spent on business at other locations. This time test is particularly significant when a comparison of the relative importance of the activities performed at each business location yields no definitive answer to the principal-place-of-business inquiry. This may happen when a taxpayer performs income-generating activities at both the office in the taxpayer's home and at some other location.

COMMENT: Apparently taxpayers previously needed a time log along with an auto log!

Under the previous "focal point" test, a comparison is required. Consistent with the Supreme Court's analysis in *Soliman,* the IRS first applied the "relative importance" test, comparing the activities performed at each business location to determine whether an office in the taxpayer's home is the taxpayer's principal place of business. If this test yields no definitive answer (which may occur, for example, if the taxpayer delivers services or goods to customers both at the office in the taxpayer's home and elsewhere), the IRS then relied on the "time" test.

Previously, the home office must have been the "principal" business location for an allowable office deduction. As the Supreme Court specifically noted in *Soliman,* in some cases the application of the relative importance and time tests may result in a determination that there is no principal place of business for purposes of §280A(c)(1)(A), and therefore no office-in-home deduction was available for the taxpayer.

PLANNING TIP: The harshness of this "focal point" test is a result of the rule that the home-office deduction is not available if any other business location is deemed more important than the office-in-home.

PLANNING TIP: But, you say, "The functions done at home are absolutely indispensable." No matter! The Supreme Court stated that even though the work done at the home office was necessary and essential to the success of the business, that was immaterial when determining if the home office was deductible: "Essential, then, is but part of the assessment of the relative importance of the functions performed at each of the competing locations."

The Supreme Court's "comparative analysis" of Dr. Soliman. Applying its test to the *Soliman* facts, the Supreme Court emphasized that the delivery location of the "goods and services" (the hospital in Dr. Soliman's situation) was more important than the preparation or manufacture of the goods or services and the general administration of the business. It stated: "In many instances, planning and initial preparation for performing a service or delivering goods are essential to the ultimate performance of the service or delivery of the goods, just as accounting and billing are often essential at the final stages of the process. . . . Even though these steps are important, it is not controlling."

COMMENT: The extensive analysis required by the Supreme Court is ridiculous. I can't imagine any Tax Court trying to decide sales, production or management the most important factor in the success of a business—yet, the Supreme Court states that "any particular business is likely to have a pattern in which certain activities are of most significance." This statement required taxpayers, and eventually the Tax Court, to make this impossible determination.

The IRS Required That the Home Office Must Be More Important than ALL the Other Places of Business Combined! [IRS Notice 93-12]

The Internal Revenue Service made the expansive argument that the hours spent at the home office must exceed the total time spent at *all* the business locations [IRS Notice 93-12, IRB 1993-8, Feb. 22, 1993].

PLANNING TIP: In essence, this interpretation requires that the majority (51%) of the total work time must be spent in the home office for a deduction to be allowed. This standard results in a much stricter, and new, "majority-place-of-business" requirement, replacing the old "principal place of business." The author doubted this was congressional intent, as proven by the 1999 legislative change.

The Following Are Examples from the IRS

Example 1:   **A plumber with full-time staff loses home office.** A is a self-employed plumber who installs and repairs plumbing in her customers' homes and offices. A spends approximately 40 hours of her work time per week at these customer locations and approximately 10 hours of work time per week in an office in her home talking with customers on the telephone, deciding what supplies to order, and reviewing business books. A also employs E, a full-time unrelated employee, in the home office to perform administrative services such as answering the telephone, scheduling A's appointments, ordering supplies and keeping A's books.

The essence of A's trade or business as a plumber requires her to perform services and deliver goods at the homes or offices of customers. The telephone activities, supply ordering and bookkeeping review that A performs at her home office, although essential, are less important and take less time than her service calls to customers. Therefore, A's office-in-home is not her principal place of business, and A cannot deduct expenses for business use of the home. The fact that E, A's employee, performs administrative activities at A's home office does not alter this result.

Example 2:   **The cottage industry craft artist keeps home office.** D is a self-employed retailer of costume jewelry. D orders the jewelry from wholesalers and sells it at craft shows, on consignment, and through mail orders. D spends approximately 25 hours of his work time per week at home filling and shipping mail orders, ordering supplies and keeping business books. D also spends approximately 15 hours of his work time per week at craft shows and consignment sale locations, generating a substantial amount of income from each type of sales activity.

Because the most important activity of D's business—sales to customers—is performed in more than one location, D's principal place of business cannot be determined definitively based on a comparison of the relative importance of the activities performed at his home office and at his other business locations. In this circumstance, the time spent on business activities at each business location assumes particular significance. D spends approximately 25 hours of his work time per week in the home office filling and shipping mail orders, ordering supplies, and keeping books. D also spends approximately 15 hours of his work time per week at craft shows and consignment shops. Accordingly, D's office in the home is the principal place of business, and D *can* deduct expenses for the business use of the home.

Example 3: **The outside salesperson calling on customers loses home office.** Joe Smith is a salesperson whose only office is a room in his house used regularly and exclusively to set up appointments, store product samples and write up orders and other reports for the companies whose products he sells.

Joe's business is selling products to customers at various locations within the metropolitan area where he lives. To make these sales, he regularly visits the customers to explain the available products and to take orders. Joe makes only a few sales from his home office. He spends an average of 30 hours a week visiting customers and 12 hours a week working at his home office.

The essence of Joe's business as a salesperson requires him to meet with customers primarily at the customer's place of business. The home-office activities are less important to Joe's business than the sales activities he performs when visiting customers. In addition, a comparison of the 12 hours per week spent in the home office to the 30 hours per week spent visiting customers further supports the conclusion that Joe's home office is not his principal place of business. Therefore, he cannot deduct expenses for the business use of his home [IRS Notice 93-12, Example 2].

Example 4: **The telemarketing salesperson keeps home office.** Fred Jones, a salesperson, performs the same activities in his home office as Joe Smith in the above example, except that Fred makes most of his sales to customers by telephone or mail from his home office. Fred spends an average of 30 hours a week working at his home office and 12 hours a week visiting prospective customers to deliver products and occasionally take orders.

The essence of Fred's business as a salesperson requires him to make telephone or mail contact with customers primarily from his office, which is in his home. Actually visiting customers is less important to Fred's business than the sales activities he performs from his home office. In addition, a comparison of the 30 hours per week spent selling to customers from the home office with the 12 hours per week spent visiting customers further supports the conclusion that Fred's home office is his principal place of business. Therefore, he can deduct expenses for the business use of his home [IRS Notice 93-12, Example 3].

TRANSPORTATION EXPENSES FROM HOME OFFICE

Commuting from a Home Office

A deductible home office often converts commuting mileage to business mileage! If a taxpayer has a home office that is the principal place of business, each of that taxpayer's business trips from home is considered a deductible transportation expense as he or she is traveling between different business locations. Because this may amount to a substantial annual tax deduction, it may pay to have an office-in-home.

However, if the principal office is at another location (e.g., a real estate office located downtown), the mileage from the home to the *first* business location is a nondeductible commuting trip [Rev. Rul. 190; Rev. Rul. 55-109].

TAX PLANNING: The liberalized definition of a principal place of business allows many more taxpayers to deduct their "commuting" costs. Financially, this is a much larger deduction for most taxpayers than the office-in-home deduction.

Example: Marianne is a real estate broker who is also a professional singer at the local jazz club. As she is the administrative manager of the brokerage firm, with a corner office, any brokerage office-in-home would not be deductible. But, as she has no other administrative office for her singing business, and as she conducts substantial nonadministrative and nonmanagerial business activities at a fixed location other than at the home office, her musical home office qualifies. Therefore, if every morning she first performs work duties at her home office before going to her second job site, she will be able to deduct the mileage between her home and her downtown brokerage office. But, if she only has *one* job, the trip from home to the real estate office is a nondeductible commuting trip.

A nondeductible office-in-home and the transportation deduction. May a taxpayer still call a nondeductible office-in-home a "principal place of business" and retain the transportation deduction by arguing that he or she is traveling between two places of business? The Tax Court, in one disturbing antitaxpayer case concluded "because the automobile expenses were incurred in commuting to and from a home office which does not qualify under section 280A(c)(1), the automobile expenses are not deductible" [*A. W. Hamacher v. Comr.,* 94 TC 348, No. 21]. We don't know if *Hamacher* made the argument that a nondeductible office may still be a principal place of business. We would have! At last, so did the attorneys in the following case.

A deductible office-in-home, even in the same metropolitan area, is irrelevant for determining if mileage is commuting [*Charles W. Walker and Cathe R. Walker v. Comm.,* 101 T.C. 537 (1993)]. In a more recent protaxpayer case, in which the court was clearly presented with the above argument, the court found that even though a taxpayer is not deducting (or cannot deduct) an office-in-home, this does not negate the fact that the office in the home is a regular place of business. Charles Walker did not establish that his residence was his "principal place of business" (a requirement to establish a deductible home office), but he did convince the court that his home was a "regular place of business" (a more liberal requirement). As Charlie was "going between two specific business locations," the mileage between his home and his next business location is a deductible business expense [Rev. Rul. 55-109, 1955-1 C.B. 261]. Charlie kept daily records showing that he spent approximately seven hours per week in the workshop adjacent to his residence maintaining and repairing his equipment even though no office-in-home deduction was taken.

Example: Charlie Walker was allowed a deduction from his nondeducted home office to his workplace, the forest, 90 miles one way from his home, as he regularly maintained his saws in his home shop. The IRS disagreed.

IRS disagrees with Walker: how they interpret a temporary assignment within metropolitan area with a regular place(s) of business [Rev. Rul. 94-47, 1994-29 IRB 1]. The IRS states that there are only two situations in which a transportation deduction is allowed for expenses incurred in traveling between a residence and a temporary place of business in the same metropolitan area. These situations are

1. when the taxpayer also has a regular place of business that is not located at the taxpayer's residence or
2. when the taxpayer's residence is his or her *principal* place of business.

Example: Charlie Walker (if the IRS had their way), who maintains an office/shop *away* from home, can deduct transportation expenses in going from home to a customer's location. However, if his office/shop is in his residence, the same trip is deductible *only* if that residence is also his deductible principal place of business. That is not fair!

TAX PLANNING: Starting in 1999, Charlie Walker will have no problem deducting mileage from his principal residence to the forest as he has only *one* home office—his garage.

THE IRS MAKES ACCOUNTING FOR HOME OFFICE EXPENSES MORE DIFFICULT

Individual Income Tax Form 1040, Schedule C, Line 30, Titled "Expenses for Business Use of Your Home (Attach Form 8829)." The reason for Form 8829: it is apparent that the IRS wants to prevent the home-office deduction from being hidden under some other heading (e.g., office expenses, miscellaneous expenses or spread throughout Schedule C as interest, taxes and utilities.) In addition, the agency wants to determine if the taxpayer is properly deducting these expenses.

Another reason for Form 8829 is that Congress believes taxpayers are abusing the office-in-home deduction and asked the IRS to analyze the potential misuse. The IRS wants to determine if the taxpayer is complying with the home-office limitations and if the calculation is being done correctly.

PLANNING TIP: Even though an office-in-home deduction may act as a red flag for audit, the author emphasizes that the taxpayer should take *all legitimate deductions*. A red flag doesn't mean an audit is imminent. This material is designed to examine proper tax reporting, and the author emphatically believes in the philosophy of eminent jurist Learned Hand, who said that "tax avoidance is a constitutional right." But also keep in mind the consequences faced by PTL Minister Jimmy Baker: "Tax evasion is 'Club Fed' time."

THE OFFICE-IN-HOME CALCULATION

The Formula

When a portion of the taxpayer's personal home is used for business purposes, the fill-in-the-blank worksheet shown next helps determine the business deduction for the office-in-home.

	Total	Personal Percentage	Schedule A*
Casualty losses	_____ ×	_____ % =	_____ *
Mortgage interest	_____ ×	_____ % =	_____ *
Property taxes	_____ ×	_____ % =	_____ *
Insurance	_____		
Repairs and maintenance	_____		
Janitor or maid services	_____		
Utilities	_____		
Depreciation (39 years)	_____		
Total	_____		
Multiply by business percentage ×	_____ %		
Office-in-Home deduction	_____ †		

* Deduct personal percentage on Schedule A, Form 1040
† Subject to §280A(c)

Calculating the allowable home-office deduction. Two types of expenses, direct and indirect, are deducted on Form 8829 when the home is used for business purposes. Any other expenses, such as salaries, supplies and business telephone expenses, are deductible elsewhere on Schedule C and should not be entered on Form 8829.

Direct expenses. These expenses benefit only the actual office itself, such as painting or repairs made to the specific area or room used for business. All of these expenses (100%) are entered on the appropriate expense line in column (a) of Form 8829.

Indirect expenses. These expenses are for keeping up and running the entire home. They benefit both the business and personal parts of the home, such as interest, taxes, roof repairs and utilities. Generally, 100% of these expenses are entered on the appropriate expense line in column (b) of Form 8829, totaled and deductible only to the extent of the business percentage.

Exception. If the business percentage of an indirect expense is more accurately determined separately, it is to be included as a direct expense. For example, if the electricity of the home office is on a separate meter, or the taxes are itemized between business personal property and home personal property, these normally indirect expenses should be considered direct expenses.

Calculation of business percentage. Previously, the business percentage was determined either by dividing the square footage of the office-in-home by the total square footage of the home (e.g., 200 square foot office ÷ 3000 square foot home = 6.67%) *or* by dividing the office room by the number of rooms in the house (e.g., 1 room ÷ 10 rooms = 10%) and using the percentage most advantageous to the taxpayer. No more!

Using the square-footage method as room-by-room allocation is no longer permitted. According to the newly released instructions of Form 8829, the room-by-room method is available only if "the rooms in the house are all about the same size" (i.e., each bathroom is the same size as the living rocm, etc.), which is a ridiculous requirement. In a recent court case, Edward Andrews claimed a deduction based on the ratio of rooms in the house, but the court determined that the home-office expenses should more reasonably be allocated on a square-footage basis [*E. W. Andrews v. Comm.*, 60 TCM 277, TC Memo. 1990-391; CA-1 91-1 USTC ¶50,211].

Home office deduction must be based on square footage, not rental value [*A. Swain,* CA-4, 96-2 USTC ¶50,480]. An engineer was *not* entitled to a home-office deduction in excess of the amount determined by the IRS. He used the home-office space to prepare for a course that he taught at a state university and to review students' homework. He did *not* allocate his expenses on the basis of the number of rooms in the house or by floor space (i.e., square footage). Instead, he *improperly* estimated the deduction based on an "approximation of the cost of renting comparable office space."

LIMITATION ON HOME-OFFICE DEDUCTION—NO LOSSES

A Home-Office Deduction Is Not Allowed to the Extent That It Creates or Increases a Net Loss of a Business

Any disallowed deduction is carried over to the next tax year, subject to the same limits in the carryover years, whether or not the dwelling unit is used as a residence during the tax year. Any unused carryover amounts are lost if the business closes.

COMMENT: For administrative purposes only, the IRS does allow the office-in-home deduction to create or increase a loss if that loss is created *solely* by otherwise deductible home mortgage interest and tax deduction. The following example demonstrates this exception, which increases the allowable loss from zero to a negative $1,000.

Example: The following example illustrates the office-in-home deduction as well as the proper use of the Form 8829 and Schedule C (see examples at the end of this chapter).

Jill, a real estate agent, operates an advertising agency from her 2,000-square-foot home and makes qualified business use of a 500-square-foot home office, i.e., a 25% business use.

Gross income		$25,000
Less: Expenses for operating agency but not home office		
(e.g., supplies, wages, taxes)		− 24,000
Tentative profit (or loss)		$ 1,000
Less: Home office expenses		
Total interest and taxes	$2,000†	
Total other expenses	$2,000*	
Total home office expenses	$4,000‡‡	
Limit on home office expenses		$ 2,000
Disallowed deduction	$2,000#	
Net profit **(or loss)** on Schedule C		($1,000)

Home office expenses	Total	Indirect (25%)
Interest and property taxes	$8,000	$2,000†
Insurance, utilities, repairs	$2,000	$ 500*
Depreciation (39 yrs.)	$6,000	$1,500*
		$4,000‡‡

\# Carried forward to next year, subject to same limitations.

HOME OFFICE ALSO CREATES GAIN WHEN RESIDENCE IS SOLD

No Rollover of Gain Allowed

A homeowner selling a residence in which he or she maintains an office-in-home really owns two types of assets, a personal residence real property and a business real property. Thus the gain associated with the office-in-home *cannot* be deferred. The gain will be prorated on a square-footage basis, and only the nonoffice footage is eligible for the *exclusion*-of-gain provision [*Poague, William W.,* DC-Va 90-2 USTC ¶50,539].

Example: Joan sells her personal residence, which contains her deductible office-in-home, for $100,000. She estimates that the office occupies 10% of her home. She is required to report a sale of a $90,000 rollover home and a $10,000 sale of a fully taxable office. Therefore, 10% of the total gain from the sale of her residence is taxable. If Jill closes her home office one year prior to the sale, she could have excluded the gain other than any depreciation recapture.

COMMENT: An office-in-home can only be converted back to personal use after two years of personal use.

Warning! Depreciation Taken after May 6, 1997, Must Be Recaptured!

Any gain attributable to depreciation taken after May 6, 1997, with respect to the prior rental or business use of the principal residence must be recognized in the year of the sale (but interestingly not an exchange) [§121(d)(5)].

COMMENT: Therefore, 65.753 percent of the 1997 depreciation must be recaptured. The period of May 7 through December 31, 1997, is 240 days.

Example: Kim purchased a home on May 7, 1997, and sold it for a $30,000 profit on December 31, 1999. The accumulated depreciation on her office-in-home was $700. Therefore, $29,300 gain is excluded by §121 but the $700 must be reported on Form 4797 as depreciation recapture income, assuming the home office was converted back to personal use no later than December 31, 1997.

FIGURE 11.1 Sample IRS Form 8829

Form **8829**	**Expenses for Business Use of Your Home**	OMB No. 1545-1266
Department of the Treasury Internal Revenue Service (99)	▶ File only with Schedule C (Form 1040). Use a separate Form 8829 for each home you used for business during the year. ▶ See separate Instructions.	**19** Attachment Sequence No. **66**
Name(s) of proprietor(s)		Your social security number

Part I   Part of Your Home Used for Business

1	Area used regularly and exclusively for business, regularly for day care, or for storage of inventory or product samples. See instructions...	**1**	500
2	Total area of home	**2**	2,000
3	Divide line 1 by line 2. Enter the result as a percentage......................................	**3**	25.00 %

● For day–care facilities not used exclusively for business, also complete lines 4–6.

● All others, skip lines 4–6 and enter the amount from line 3 on line 7.

4	Multiply days used for day care during year by hours used per day...................	**4**		hr.
5	Total hours available for use during the year (366 days x 24 hours). See instructions	**5**		hr.
6	Divide line 4 by line 5. Enter the result as a decimal amount	**6**		
7	Business percentage. For day–care facilities not used exclusively for business, multiply line 6 by line 3 (enter the result as a percentage). All others, enter the amount from line 3............................. ▶	**7**		25.00 %

Part II   Figure Your Allowable Deduction

8	Enter the amount from Schedule C, line 29, **plus** any net gain or (loss) derived from the business use of your home and shown on Schedule D or Form 4797. If more than one place of business, see instructions	**8**	1,000

See Instructions for columns (a) and (b) before completing lines 9 – 20.

			(a) Direct expenses	(b) Indirect expenses		
9	Casualty losses. See instructions	**9**				
10	Deductible mortgage interest. See instructions...............	**10**		6,000		
11	Real estate taxes. See instructions.........................	**11**		2,000		
12	Add lines 9, 10, and 11	**12**		8,000		
13	Multiply line 12, column (b) by line 7		**13**	2,000		
14	Add line 12, column (a) and line 13				**14**	2,000
15	Subtract line 14 from line 8. If zero or less, enter -0-..........				**15**	0
16	Excess mortgage interest. See instructions..................	**16**				
17	Insurance..	**17**		500		
18	Repairs and maintenance.............................	**18**				
19	Utilities..	**19**		1,500		
20	Other expenses. See instructions.........................	**20**				
21	Add lines 16 through 20...............................	**21**		2,000		
22	Multiply line 21, column (b) by line 7		**22**	500		
23	Carryover of operating expenses from 1995 Form 8829, line 41....................		**23**			
24	Add line 21 in column (a), line 22, and line 23................				**24**	500
25	Allowable operating expenses. Enter the **smaller** of line 15 or line 24...............				**25**	
26	Limit on excess casualty losses and depreciation. Subtract line 25 from line 15				**26**	
27	Excess casualty losses. See instructions		**27**			
28	Depreciation of your home from Part III below......................		**28**	6,000		
29	Carryover of excess casualty losses and depreciation from 1995 Form 8829, line 42.....		**29**			
30	Add lines 27 through 29...............................				**30**	6,000
31	Allowable excess casualty losses and depreciation. Enter the **smaller** of line 26 or line 30				**31**	
32	Add lines 14, 25, and 31.............................				**32**	2,000
33	Casualty loss portion, if any, from lines 14 and 31. Carry amount to **Form 4684**, Section B				**33**	
34	Allowable expenses for business use of your home. Subtract line 33 from line 32. Enter here and on Schedule C, line 30. If your home was used for more than one business, see instructions............................ ▶				**34**	2,000

Part III   Depreciation of Your Home

35	Enter the **smaller** of your home's adjusted basis or its fair market value. See instructions	**35**	
36	Value of land included on line 35....................................	**36**	
37	Basis of building. Subtract line 36 from line 35	**37**	
38	Business basis of building. Multiply line 37 by line 7	**38**	
39	Depreciation percentage. See instructions..................................	**39**	%
40	Depreciation allowable. Multiply line 38 by line 39. Enter here and on line 28 above. See instructions	**40**	6,000

Part IV   Carryover of Unallowed Expenses to 1997

41	Operating expenses. Subtract line 25 from line 24. If less than zero, enter -0-.............................	**41**	500
42	Excess casualty losses and depreciation. Subtract line 31 from line 30. If less than zero, enter -0-	**42**	6,000

For Paperwork Reduction Act Notice, see page 1 of separate Instructions.   Form **8829** (1996)

KFA

FIGURE 11.2   Sample IRS Form Schedule C

SCHEDULE C (Form 1040)	Profit or Loss From Business	OMB No. 1545-0074

SCHEDULE C (Form 1040)

Department of the Treasury
Internal Revenue Service

Profit or Loss From Business
(Sole Proprietorship)

▶ **Partnerships, joint ventures, etc., must file Form 1065.**
▶ **Attach to Form 1040 or Form 1041.**   ▶ **See Instructions for Schedule C (Form 1040).**

OMB No. 1545-0074

19
Attachment
Sequence No. **09**

Name of proprietor | Social security number (SSN)

A Principal business or profession, including product or service (see page C–1)	**B** Enter principal business code (from page C–6) ▶ **8888**
Tax Preparation	
C Business name. If no separate business name, leave blank.	**D** Employer ID number (EIN), if any
Associated Tax Preparation	11-1111111

E   Business address (including suite or room no.) ▶ 1040 Bankruptcy Lane _____
City, town or post office, state, and ZIP code   San Francisco, CA

F   Accounting method: (1) ☒ Cash   (2) ☐ Accrual   (3) ☐ Other (specify) ▶ _____

G   Did you "materially participate" in the operation of this business during 1996? If "No," see page C–2 for limit on losses .... ☒ Yes   ☐ No

H   If you started or acquired this business during 1996, check here .... ▶ ☐

Part I   Income

1	Gross receipts or sales. **Caution:** If this income was reported to you on Form W–2 and the "Statutory employee" box on that form was checked, see page C–2 and check here............ ▶ ☐	**1**	25,000
2	Returns and allowances	**2**	
3	Subtract line 2 from line 1	**3**	25,000
4	Cost of goods sold (from line 42 on page 2)	**4**	
5	**Gross profit.** Subtract line 4 from line 3..................................	**5**	25,000
6	Other income, including Federal and state gasoline or fuel tax credit or refund (see page C–2)............	**6**	
7	**Gross income.** Add lines 5 and 6 .... ▶	**7**	25,000

Part II   Expenses. Enter expenses for business use of your home **only** on line 30.

8	Advertising	**8**		**19**	Pension and profit–sharing plans	**19**	
9	Bad debts from sales or services (see page C–3)	**9**		**20**	Rent or lease (see page C–4):		
				a	Vehicles, machinery & equipment...............	**20a**	
10	Car and truck expenses (see page C–3)	**10**		**b**	Other business property	**20b**	
11	Commissions and fees	**11**		**21**	Repairs and maintenance	**21**	
12	Depletion	**12**		**22**	Supplies (not included in Part III)	**22**	
13	Depreciation and section 179 expense deduction (not included in Part III) (see page C–3)......	**13**		**23**	Taxes and licenses.......................	**23**	
				24	Travel, meals, and entertainment:		
				a	Travel..............................	**24a**	
14	Employee benefit programs (other than on line 19).........	**14**		**b**	Meals and entertainment		
15	Insurance (other than health) ...	**15**		**c**	Enter 50% of line 24b subject to limitations (see page C–4)........		
16	Interest:			**d**	Subtract line 24c from line 24b	**24d**	
a	Mortgage (paid to banks, etc.) ..	**16a**		**25**	Utilities	**25**	
b	Other	**16b**		**26**	Wages (less employment credits)...............	**26**	
17	Legal and professional services .	**17**		**27**	Other expenses		
18	Office expense	**18**			(from line 48 on page 2).....................	**27**	24,000

28	**Total expenses** before expenses for business use of home. Add lines 8 through 27 in columns .... ▶	**28**	24,000
29	Tentative profit (loss). Subtract line 28 from line 7.............................	**29**	1,000
30	Expenses for business use of your home. Attach **Form 8829**	**30**	2,000
31	**Net profit or (loss).** Subtract line 30 from line 29.		

● If a profit, enter on **Form 1040, line 12,** and ALSO on **Schedule SE, line 2** (statutory employees, see page C–5). Estates and trusts, enter on Form 1041, line 3.

● If a loss, you MUST go on to line 32.

} **31**   −1,000

32   If you have a loss, check the box that describes your investment in this activity (see page C–5).

● If you checked 32a, enter the loss on **Form 1040, line 12,** and ALSO on **Schedule SE, line 2** (statutory employees, see page C–5). Estates and trusts, enter on Form 1041, line 3.

● If you checked 32b, you MUST attach **Form 6198.**

} **32a** ☒ All investment is at risk.
32b ☐ Some investment is not at risk.

For Paperwork Reduction Act Notice, see Form 1040 Instructions.   Schedule C (Form 1040) 1996

KFA

CHAPTER

12

The Rules on Passive Activity

THE PASSIVE LOSS LIMITATION (PAL) RULES—IN GENERAL

Why? Prior to the Tax Reform Act of 1986 (TRA 86), no limitations were placed on the ability of a taxpayer to use deductions, losses or credits from one business or investment to offset the profits of another business or investment. This allowed the opportunity for taxpayers to offset, or "shelter," the income from one source with deductions and credits from another source.

> *Example:* **A pre-1986 tax shelter!** Brad is an attorney receiving a $150,000 salary. He is married with no children and has itemized deductions of $10,000. His limited partnership investments in real estate create a $140,000 loss. Brad owes no taxes as his real estate loss is fully deductible against his salary income. Without the real estate deduction, Brad would have approximately $37,500 of tax liability.

Congress has determined that the average taxpayer is losing faith in the federal income tax system because of abusive tax shelters. The congressional solution to limiting tax shelters without eliminating tax preferences to certain businesses and activities (such as the special tax benefits given to low-income housing, rehabilitation of older buildings, and farming) is to benefit and provide incentives only to taxpayers *actively involved* in their businesses.

Beginning in 1987, taxpayers must "materially participate" in the business to be eligible for most tax incentives. Tax preference benefits are directed primarily to taxpayers with a substantial and *bona fide* involvement in the activities to which the preferences relate. Therefore, even though Congress wants to continue giving tax preferences, it *does not* want those preferences used against unrelated income.

> *Example (continued):* **Kill the tax shelter!** Brad, in the above example, no longer can deduct the real estate loss against his salary income and his tax refund is reduced by approximately $37,500!

This congressional barrier is called the "Passive Loss Limitation Rules" (or PAL rules) and it is this attempt at balancing the halting of investments in tax shelters while encouraging savings and investments in active businesses that led to the vast complexity of the passive loss rules.

The §469 Passive Loss Rules—Overview

As a first giant step toward implementing a loss deduction limitation philosophy, Congress simply states that losses (and credits) from passive trade or business activities, to the extent they exceed income from all such passive activities generally, may not be deducted against other income, such as salaries and wages, or interest and dividends. The one major exception is the ability of middle-income taxpayers to deduct up to $25,000 of rental losses from "actively managed" real estate [§469(a)].

So what happens to these disallowed losses and credits? Are they lost forever? No. They are suspended and carried forward; they become deductible only against passive activity income in future years [§469(b)].

Additionally, they are "triggered" at time of sale. If the disallowed losses are not fully utilized when taxpayers dispose of their entire interest in the activity in a fully taxable transaction, the remaining losses are allowed (i.e., "triggered") in full, even against active income [§469(g)(1)].

> **PLANNING TIP:** For tax-planning purposes, it is *very* important to note that the PAL rules are only a "deferral-of-deductions" code section and not a "denial-of-deductions" code section. Theoretically, taxpayers will be able to use these deductions against *all* other income sometime in the future—and get their "prepaid" taxes back!

Passive losses continue to be currently deductible against passive income. With limited exceptions, the PAL rules continue to allow losses and credits from one passive activity to be applied against income for the taxable year from another passive activity. It also allows deductions against income subsequently generated by any passive activity.

These "simple" changes greatly influence the way we will conduct business in the future and require convoluted accounting of income and expenses, best demonstrated by an example. The taxpayer must divide his or her income into three separate "buckets," each of which is fully defined on the following pages and illustrated in Figure 12.1.

> ***Example:*** Dan is an accountant with a W-2 salary income of $40,000. He is married, has no children and claims $8,000 of itemized deductions. He invests $5,000, plus recourse notes, in a real estate *limited partnership* tax shelter at the

FIGURE 12.1   Passive Loss Categories

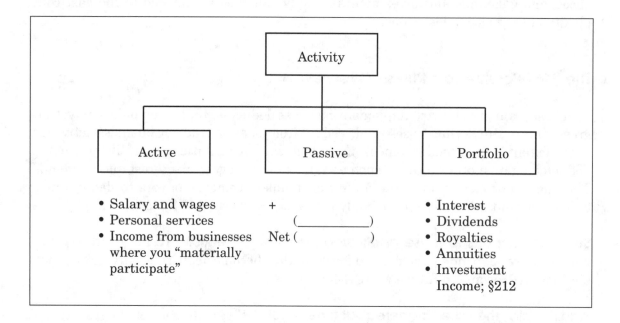

suggestion of his real estate broker. At the end of the year, he receives a "K-1" partnership tax schedule from the real estate company reporting that a $15,000 operating loss is allocated to him. Because of the "passive-limitation rule," the total $15,000 loss is nondeductible!

Active	Activity *Passive*	*Portfolio*
$40,000	($15,000)	

PLANNING TIP: Some relief may be possible. His $15,000 PAL amount *may* be annually deducted by the $25,000 relief provision granted to active participation rental real estate (but a limited partner cannot *actively* participate and therefore cannot use the $25,000 relief provision). In essence, this relief provision "reconverts" some or all of the PAL back to a current deduction.

IRS amends passive loss rules to allow casualty, theft losses. In response to questions about the treatment of losses resulting from recent natural disasters, the IRS announced that limitations on passive activity losses do not apply to earthquakes, fire, storm, shipwreck and certain other casualty or theft losses. In other words, losses from these occurrences are nonpassive deduction losses. These rules also exclude casualty and theft reimbursements from passive activity gross income and exclude capital loss carrybacks from passive activity deductions [Notice 90-21]. This exception does not apply if similar losses recur regularly in the business (e.g., shoplifting losses at Nordstroms or accident losses at Hertz).

Carryover of disallowed deductions and credits. Any PAL not currently deductible (disallowed) is suspended and becomes deductible in a subsequent year the taxpayer *either* has net passive activity income *or* completely disposes of the passive activity property in a taxable manner.

§469 applies after all other tax treatments: All other tax limitations apply first, such as the at-risk rules and the investment interest limitations rules and thereafter the passive loss limitation rules apply [Reg. §1.469-1T(d)(1)].

BACKGROUND OF DEFINING AN ACTIVITY

What is an activity? When applying the passive loss rules, the first, and most important, determination made by a taxpayer is defining how many different businesses (i.e., activities) that taxpayer must report to the IRS. (Remember, each business must have its own set of books!) Why? Defining separate activities either too narrowly or too broadly can lead to evasion of the passive loss rules.

For example, if two businesses are part of the same activity (e.g., a tire shop and a lingerie store), the taxpayer may offset the loss of one business against the income of the other business. (Generally a tire shop and a lingerie store would be considered two separate businesses and the PAL loss limitation restriction rules would apply to each separately.) At the other extreme, if one business is deemed two activities (e.g., a gas station and a grocery store), potential triggering of loss occurs by selectively disposing of portions of an activity where there has been a loss of value while retaining portions that experience appreciation. However, if the businesses are separate activities (as in the tire shop and the lingerie store), the taxpayer may have to establish material participation for *each* activity to offset the loss of one against the current income of the other.

Reasons for identifying each activity. It is also necessary to identify every separate activity of a taxpayer for each of the following purposes:

1. For determining whether the activity is a rental activity
2. For determining whether the taxpayer materially participates in the activity (if the activity is a trade or business)
3. For determining whether the taxpayer has completely disposed of his or her entire interest in the activity (to ascertain if the triggering of loss occurs)
4. For applying the transitional rules for pre-enactment interests in passive activities

"Activity" is not defined in the statute. In spite of the importance of this definition, §469 does not define the term *activity* (e.g., determining how many different businesses the taxpayer owns). Congress, in its infinite wisdom, left to the Department of the Treasury the definition of the term in regulations [Notice 88-94, IRB 1988-35, August 11, 1988; Temp. Reg. §1.469-4T and Prop. Reg. §1.469-4; Final Reg. §1.469-4, adopted October 3, 1994]. As a general rule, the legislative history suggests a definition of activity that entails dividing economic "endeavors" into fairly small units.

Four definitions of "activity" so far. As important as this basic definition is, the Department of the Treasury has defined activity four times since the enactment of the passive loss rules in 1987! The recently enacted *final* regulations permit substantial tax planning and are explained next.

THE FINAL SIMPLIFIED ACTIVITY REGULATIONS [REGULATION §1.469-4]

History. These streamlined regulations replace a series of mechanical rules [Temp. Reg. §1.469-4T] for determining a taxpayer's activities. Those rules were universally criticized as overly long (169 pages defining a business), complex and burdensome for small taxpayers, and mechanically inflexible.

In going back to the drawing board, the IRS asserts it has tried to address these concerns. The old 169-page definition of the word *activity,* requiring a determination of "operations" turning into "undertakings" combined or fractured into "activities," is replaced with a single "facts-and-circumstances" test allowing taxpayers to use any reasonable method when grouping their businesses. The new regulations are only seven pages long, are more flexible and easier to apply, but leave the investor with substantially more uncertainty when making the determination of "how many businesses do I have?"

Transition rules. The final regulations are effective for taxable years ending after May 10, 1992, although transitional rules are provided for taxable years that include May 10, 1992, through taxable years beginning before October 4, 1994 [§1.469-11; TD 8565, October 3, 1994]. Acquisitions prior to 1992 may substitute these simplified rules for the previous guidelines. On the other hand, acquisitions in tax years that include May 10, 1992, may continue to use the 169-page temporary regulations [Reg. §1.469-11(a); TD 8417].

WHAT IS AN ACTIVITY?

It is a "facts-and-circumstances" test. Taxpayers use a multiple-factor general facts-and-circumstances test to determine their "appropriate economic units" (non-bureaucrats more commonly call this determining their "different number of businesses"). The problem is that the IRS feels some test factors are more important than other test factors although they readily admit that there *may be more than one reasonable method* for grouping a taxpayer's activities after taking into account all the relevant facts and circumstances [§1.469-4(c)].

The five most important factors. The factors given the greatest weight when determining whether activities should be grouped together or kept separate are as follows [§1.469-4(c)(2)]:

1. *The similarities and differences in the respective types of businesses*

Example: A convenient food store combined with a gas station (e.g., a Circle K store) is commonly considered one business whereas a lingerie shop selling tires (e.g., a Corset & Chrome Store?) would normally be considered dissimilar.

2. *The extent of common control between the businesses*

Example: Billy is a partner in Video Variety, a partnership selling videotapes to grocery stores. Billy also is a partner in Madonna Movie Producers, a warehousing partnership principally supplying videotapes to Video Variety and whose largest customer is Video Variety. Both partnerships are located in the same industrial park and are under the same common control. Billy treats Video Variety's wholesale trade activity and Madonna Movie Producers' warehousing activity as one activity [§1.469-4(c)(3)(Example 2)].

3. *The extent of common ownership between the businesses*

Example: Charlene has a significant ownership interest in a bakery and a movie theater at a shopping mall in Baltimore and in a bakery and movie theater at a shopping mall in Philadelphia. Charlene may consider it reasonable to group these four businesses in any one of four combinations:

1. Combining the movie theaters and bakeries into *one single activity*
2. Separating the *movie theaters* into one activity and the *bakeries* into another activity
3. Separating the *Baltimore businesses* into one activity and the *Philadelphia businesses* into another activity
4. Segregating them all into *four separate activities* [§1.469-4(c)(3) (Example 1)]

PLANNING TIP: It is this extraordinarily liberal interpretation of business(es) that has tax planners salivating. But don't celebrate too early . . . the IRS has extraordinary powers to regroup those activities if the IRS agent feels the original grouping is inappropriate!

WARNING: Activities not "directly owned" by the taxpayer cannot be combined. For example, the activities of a partnership (or S corporation) cannot be combined with similar activities owned by one of the partners (or shareholders) [PLR 9722007]. This is true even when the two businesses are conducted at the *same* location . . . they are *not* owned by the *same* person [*Douglas. E. Kahle,* TC Memo 1997-90].

4. *The respective geographical locations of each business*

See the above "Charlene" example.

5. *The interdependencies between the businesses,* i.e., the extent to which the different businesses
   • purchase or sell goods between themselves,
   • involve products or services that are normally provided together,
   • have the same customers,
   • have the same employees, or
   • are accounted for with a single set of books and records [§1.469-4(c)(2)(v)].

   See the above "Billy" example.

6. *Remember, other factors may end up being important as the taxpayer may use "any reasonable method" to determine the number of activities* [§1.469-4(c)(2)]. The final regulations clarify that there *may be more than one reasonable method* for grouping a taxpayer's activities after taking into account all the relevant facts and circumstances.

Consistency rule. Once businesses are grouped together or kept separate, the taxpayer generally must be consistent in the treatment of these activities in subsequent years unless the previous determination was clearly in error (e.g., it was originally inappropriate, or there has been a material change in the facts and circumstances). Then the taxpayer must regroup the businesses and inform the IRS of the regrouping [§1.469-4(e)].

COMMENT: And this is simple?

Special rules for combining business and rental activities. Consistent with the previous pronouncements on activities, no grouping of business and rentals is allowed unless either is "insubstantial" in relation to the other. The problem is that the final regulations do not spell out *insubstantial*. The lapsed temporary regulations contained a "bright-line" 20% test (if the rental income is less than 20% of the combined business and rental income, the rental activity is "insubstantial," and vice versa). It is assumed that this test may be used to help determine if the rental may be an insubstantial part of the business or if the business may be involved in insubstantial rental activities without breaking them into two activities [§1.469-4(d)(1)].

Real property and personal property rentals. Real property rental activities and personal property rental activities may never be grouped together unless the personal property is provided in connection with the real property [§1.469-4(d)(2)].

PLANNING TIP: This allows most landlords to rent fully furnished apartments to tenants without dividing the business into two rental activities and maintaining two separate sets of financial records.

Grouping when taxpayers rent to their own businesses. The portion of a rental activity that involves the rental of items of property to a business activity may be "grouped" with the business activity regardless of whether one activity is insubstantial in relation to the other, *provided each owner of the business has the same proportionate ownership interest in the rental activity* [§1.469-4(d)(1)(i)(C)].

When the IRS can regroup your groupings. The IRS retains broad antiabuse powers "to prevent inappropriate aggregation of traditional shelter activities with other activities." This regrouping is to prevent tax avoidance. The IRS reserves the power to regroup a taxpayer's activities if his or her businesses have been *inappropriately* combined (whatever that means) *and* a principal purpose of the taxpayer's grouping is to circumvent the passive loss limitation rules (e.g., taxpayer possesses a dirty mind) [§1.469-4(f)(1)].

COMMENT: This seems to allow taxpayers to retain their groupings *if they honestly tried to comply* (i.e., a clean mind), even if the IRS auditor considers the groupings inappropriate (i.e., a dirty business)! One tax practitioner told the author that he must group appropriately as the IRS is convinced that tax planners already have dirty minds!

Example: Four medical doctors own rental property throwing off losses that are not deductible under the passive loss rules. They form a limited partnership that purchases and operates X-ray equipment at a fairly substantial profit. The doctors make sure of its profitability as this limited partnership primarily serves only their patients. Is the profit passive as none of the doctors materially participates in this limited partnership? If so, the doctors have lowered their active medical income by the money flowing to the limited partnership, and this money is converted into passive business income, which is offset by the passive rental losses (normally not currently deductible).

This proposed regulation determines that the limited partnership and the medical practice are one "appropriate economic unit," thereby making the X-ray operations active income, with the result that there is no passive income to offset the rental losses. In addition, if the IRS determines that it appears the limited partnership was created to circumvent the passive loss rules, the 20% (or more) substantial tax understatement penalties [§6662] may be imposed [§1.469-4(f)(2)]!

WARNING: This leaves a great amount of flexibility for the IRS agent at the time of audit. I doubt the IRS agent would have come to this same conclusion, i.e., one unit, if the rental business was generating a loss that the medical doctors wanted to offset against their active medical income! That is why this determination is inherently unfair.

Individual must follow corporation and partnership groupings. A corporation (including a personal service and a closely held corporation) or a partnership to which §469 applies must group its activities under these rules. Once the entity has grouped its activities, a shareholder or partner may group those activities with each other, with activities conducted directly by the shareholder or partner, and with activities conducted through other entities in accordance with these same activity rules. But a shareholder or partner may not treat activities grouped together by the entity as separate activities [§1.469-4(d)(5)(i)].

TAX PLANNING: Because of the last sentence, corporations and partnerships generally should create as many entities as possible. This allows the shareholder or partner the flexibility to combine activities in a manner most advantageous to the taxpayer.

The final regulations state that "an activity that a taxpayer conducts through a C corporation subject to §469 may be grouped with another activity of the taxpayer, but only for purposes of determining whether the taxpayer materially or significantly participates in the other activity" [§1.469-4(d)(5)(ii)].

Special rules when activity is conducted through limited partnerships. Limited partners and certain limited entrepreneurs may not group specifically designated activities with any other activities unless they are the same type of business or meet the "facts-and-circumstances" test [§1.469-4(d)(3)]. For limited partners in any of the following §465(c)(1) activities, these may only be combined with activities of the *same type of business* (whether or not these other activities are also owned as limited partnership interests) if appropriate under the facts or circumstances:

1. Holding, producing or distributing motion picture films or videotapes
2. Certain types of farming activities (commonly known as "tax shelter farm" activities)
3. Leasing any §1245 personal property
4. Exploring for, or exploiting, oil and gas resources
5. Exploring for, or exploiting, geothermal deposits

CONCLUSION

Once the taxpayer has determined how many businesses (i.e., activities) he or she must report to the IRS, the next step involves the actual calculation of the passive loss or passive gain. The next chapter analyzes these requirements.

CHAPTER

13

Application of the Passive Loss Rules

CALCULATING ACTIVITY INCOME OR LOSS—IGNORING THE ENTITY

Properly defining an activity is imperative, as it is required, for PAL purposes, to calculate the income and loss *of each activity conducted by the individual, partnership, S corporation or small C corporation.*

> **Example:** If a single taxpayer owns two real estate projects, it may be necessary to determine the income or loss of each separate activity.

> **Example:** If an active legal partnership rents part of its building to a massage parlor, it may be necessary to recognize part of the building as a passive rental activity.

WHAT IS AN ACTIVE ACTIVITY?

A business where a taxpayer materially participates is an active activity. An activity is determined to be active so long as the taxpayer materially participates in a trade or business and the business is not a rental activity [§1.469-1T(e)(1)].

The definitions of *material participation, trade or business* and *rental activity* are discussed later.

A business where a taxpayer provides personal services is an active activity. Personal service income is generally defined for passive loss purposes as gross income that is treated as "earned income" from the fields of health, law, engineering, architecture, accounting, actuarial services, performing arts or consulting [§911(d)(2)(A)]. Personal service income includes all amounts paid to an individual for services performed by the individual. It does not include an individual's share of partnership or S corporation income, even if a substantial portion of the income from the activity is attributable to services performed by the individual [§469(e)(3); Reg. §1.469-2T(c)(4)(i)].

WHAT ARE PORTFOLIO ACTIVITIES?

Portfolio income generally consists of income from investments other than those in trades or businesses. Portfolio activities normally give rise to income and are not likely to generate losses.

Why did Congress create a portfolio activity?   To permit interest and dividend income to be offset by passive losses would create the inequitable result of restricting sheltering by wage earners while permitting sheltering by those with investment portfolio income. It is for this reason that the §469 limitation rules restrict passive losses to be offset only against passive income and not against "active" or "portfolio" income.

What is "portfolio income"?   Amazingly, the term *portfolio income* is not even used in §469, but it is defined in the regulations at §1.469-2T(c)(3) as all gross income, other than income derived in the ordinary course of a trade or business, that is attributable to the following:

1. *Interest income* on debt obligations (including amounts treated as interest relating to certain payments to partners for the use of capital)
2. *Dividend income* from regular C corporation stock (e.g., AT&T stock) and S corporation stock as well as income (including dividends) from real estate investment trusts (REITs), regulated investment companies (RICs), real estate mortgage investment conduits (REMICs), common trust funds, controlled foreign corporations, qualified electing funds or cooperatives
3. *Royalty income,* including fees and other payments for the use of intangible property, but not "earned income" royalties (e.g., book and music royalties by original authors). Generally, taxpayers may not treat "mineral royalties" as derived in the ordinary course of a trade or business without obtaining a ruling.
4. *Annuity income* earned on funds set aside for future use in an activity (but not retirement annuity income)
5. *The gains (or losses) from sale of assets producing the above* interest, dividend or royalty income

Example: If a general partnership, such as a construction firm, owns a portfolio of appreciated stocks and bonds and also conducts a business activity, a part of the gain on sale of a partnership interest would be attributable to portfolio income and would, consequently, be treated as portfolio income.

6. *Gains (or losses) from the sale of §212 investment property,* such as unimproved raw land and vacation homes (but not the sale of active depreciable trade or business property nor the sale of passive activity property) [§469(e)(1)(A)(ii)]

7. *Dealer's investment gain or income.* Normally, dealer income is considered active income. But if a dealer held property as an investment *at any time* before the income or gain is recognized, the income will be considered portfolio income. Sadly, any loss from such property remains passive or active, depending upon the level of participation of the taxpayer [Reg. §1.469-2T(c)(3)(iii)(A)].

8. *Portfolio income from a passive activity* is taken into account separately from other items relating to the activity. For example, interest income earned from a business's setting aside funds for the future use of the business (e.g., interest earned on working capital funds) is portfolio income.

PLANNING TIP: Any gross income that is excluded from the passive activity classification because it is a portfolio activity is automatically taken into account as "investment income" for purposes of computing the §163(d) investment interest limitations [§163(d)(5)(A)].

PASSIVE ACTIVITIES: ONLY TWO ACTIVITIES ARE CONSIDERED PASSIVE

Generally an activity is a passive activity for a taxable year if the activity is

1. a *"rental activity"* without regard to whether or to what extent the taxpayer participates at all in such activity (therefore, a rental activity is treated as a passive activity regardless of the level of the taxpayer's participation) and

2. a *"trade or business activity"* in which the taxpayer does not materially participate for such taxable year.

A special $25,000 relief provision for rental real estate activities may permit a taxpayer to offset a portion of nonpassive income with losses from the rental real estate even though this is a passive activity.

PASSIVE ACTIVITY 1: RENTAL ACTIVITIES

A rental activity is any transfer of property for compensation. As most landlords and tenants know, common law defines a rental as a legal agreement, written or unwritten, transferring the right to exclusive possession and use of property for a definite period of time. The Internal Revenue Code defines the term *rental activity* as "an activity where payments are principally for the use of tangible property" [§469(j)(8)].

The IRS's definition of "rental activity" is more complex. With some major exceptions, the Regulations refine this definition, holding that an activity is a rental activity for a taxable year if

1. during the taxable year, tangible property held in connection with the activity is used by customers or held for use by customers; *and*
2. the gross income attributable to the conduct of the activity during the tax year represents amounts paid principally for the use of the tangible property [Reg. §1.469-1T(e)(3)].

When is a rental activity really a business? The real complexity of the passive loss rules, in light of the above definitions, is in making the determination whether a particular activity is a "rental activity," a "trade or business," or an "investment." The regulations exclude from the definition of a rental activity those activities in which the importance of providing services to customers outweighs the importance of providing tangible property to customers (i.e., normally a hotel is a business, not a rental activity). It is important to note that substance controls over form and use of a legal document stating that a relationship is a lease are irrelevant.

Six Exceptions—Activities That Are *Not* Rental Activities

If *any one* of the following six tests is met, the activity will not be treated as a rental activity even though it involves the rental of tangible property [Reg. §1.469-1T(e)(3)(ii)].

PLANNING TIP: The following definitions have no relief provision, as is granted to many of the other rules [Reg. §1.469-4(b)(2)].

Property is not a rental if any of the conditions discussed below apply.

1. When average tenant use is 7 days or less, it is a business. Rental of tangible property for an "average period of customer use" of seven days or less is not a rental activity.

PLANNING TIP: Because of this regulation, most vacation condominiums are considered a business, not a rental, which therefore makes them *ineligible* for the $25,000 relief provisions. Most tenant use of vacation homes averages less than seven days!

Average period of customer use is defined as the aggregate number of days of customer use (*not* the number of *days available for rent*!) during the taxable year divided by the actual number of periods of customer use. When rent varies during the year (e.g., a high season rate and a low season rate), a weighted average is calculated wherein the "average period of customer use" equals the *sum* of the average use of each class of property [Reg. §1.469-1(e)(3)(iii)].

Example: Jill uses her vacation condominium two weeks a year and leaves the property in the hands of a property manager for the other 50 weeks. The property manager rents it to five different families for a total of 30 days. The average period of customer use is 6 days (30 days divided by five periods.) Therefore, Jill does *not* have a rental—it is a trade or business—and the $25,000 real estate relief provision (discussed later in this chapter) is *not* available to her for that taxable year.

PLANNING TIP: Therefore, most hotels, motels, U-hauls, Hertz rent-a-cars, flea markets and the like are not rental activities. They are "trade or business activities."

2. When the average tenant use is greater than 7 days but not greater than 30 days and significant personal services are provided, it is a business.

Rental of tangible property for an average customer use of 30 days or less is not a rental activity if significant personal services (i.e., maid service, registration service, room service, etc.) are provided by the owner (or on behalf of the owner) in connection with making the property available for customer use.

PLANNING TIP: For vacation homes, if the average tenant use is less than 30 days but maid services are provided, vacation condominiums are still considered a business, not a rental, which therefore makes them *ineligible* for the $25,000 relief provision! The result is that most vacation homes probably do not qualify for the $25,000 annual deduction [*Floyd A. Toup*, 66 TCM 370, TC Memo 1993-359].

How "significant" must the personal services be? The term *significant* means that, at a minimum, the personal services must be (based on all the facts and circumstances) provided frequently, the type and amount of labor required to perform them must be significant, and their value relative to the rent charged for the use of the property must be significant [Reg. §1.469-1T(e)(3)(iv)].

What are personal services? Personal services include only services other than "excluded services," performed by individuals, not artificial entities such as corporations and partnerships. The term *excluded services* means

- services necessary to permit the lawful use of the property,
- services performed in connection with the construction of improvements (i.e., not repairs) and
- services commonly provided in connection with long-term rentals of high-grade commercial or residential real property (e.g., cleaning and maintenance of

common areas, routine repairs, trash collection, elevator services and security at entrances or perimeters) [Reg. §1.469-1T(e)(3)(iv)(B)].

PLANNING TIP: Therefore, most rentals of 30 days or longer will generally be considered long-term rentals and generally treated as rental activities, not business activities, unless extraordinary personal services are provided (discussed next) [TAM 9343010].

---

3. If extraordinary personal services are provided to the tenant, it is a business. Rental of tangible property (without regard to average period of customer use) when extraordinary personal services are provided is not a rental activity.

Extraordinary personal services are services provided in connection with making property available for use by customers only if the services are performed by individuals and the *use of the property is incidental* to the receipt of the services. A corporation or partnership cannot perform these extraordinary services [Reg. §1.469-1T(e)(3)(v)].

> *Example:* Hospital boarding houses and college dormitories are not deemed rentals as the rental activity is usually incidental to the supplying of medical or educational services.

4. If the rental is incidental to the business activity, the rental also is a business. The rental of tangible property that is simply incidental to a business activity will not be tainted as a rental activity. This "relief" provision applies only to the following *three* activities [Reg. §1.469-1T(e)(vi)(A)]:

> 1. *Rental property that is normally treated as an investment—a tax problem with renting out raw land.* The rental of property is treated as incidental to an investment activity if the principal purpose is to realize gain from its appreciation and the gross rental income is less than 2% of the *lesser* of the property's unadjusted basis or fair market value [§1.469-1T(e)(3)(vi)(B)].

> *Example:* Bill Sunpade owns unimproved land with an unadjusted basis of $200,000. The land has a fair market value of $300,000 in 1998 and a fair market value in 1999 of $325,000. Bill is holding the land principally for appreciation. The local chapter of The Future Farmers of America talk Bill into renting them the land at a nominal amount so that they can raise sheep for the annual county fair. The FFA members pay Bill $3,500 in lease payments in 1998 and $4,500 in 1999.

> In 1998, the lease is not a rental activity because $3,500 is less than $4,000 (i.e., 2% of $200,000). Any related interest and taxes on the unimproved land is generally deductible on Bill's Schedule A as an investment activity.

The tax problem. But in 1999, the FFA lease is now a passive rental activity separate from the holding of the land for appreciation because $4,500 is more than the maximum $4,000 allowable. If Bill has a large amount of interest and taxes on this unimproved "passive" property, he may find the amount in excess of the rental income as currently nondeductible and be required to carry it forward.

2. *The occasional renting out of idle business property—a tax problem with renting out occasional vacant office space.* The rental of property is treated as incidental to a trade or business activity if
   - the taxpayer owns an interest in the trade or business during the taxable year;
   - the property was predominantly used in the trade or business during the taxable year or at least two of the five preceding taxable years; *and*
   - the gross rental income is less than 2% of the *lesser* of the property's unadjusted basis or fair market value [Reg. §1.469-1T(e)(3)(vi)(C)].

Example: John Greathouse, owner of Greathouse Realty for the past five years, receives the resignation of one of his agent-employees. Instead of immediately hiring another agent, he decides to rent the space used by the departing agent to Bob Loblaw, attorney at law, for a temporary period of time. The gross rental income received from Bob for 1998 is $3,000 and for 1999 is $4,000. John's unadjusted basis in the office building is $200,000 and the fair market value is $250,000 in 1998 and $150,000 in 1999.

In 1998, the rental is incidental because the $3,000 gross rental income is less than $4,000 (i.e., 2% of $200,000). John would simply record the $3,000 as miscellaneous business income.

The tax problem. But in 1999, Bob's lease is a passive rental activity separate from John's real estate business because $4,000 is more than the maximum $3,000 (i.e., 2% of $150,000) considered incidental. If John has a large amount of expenses (e.g., taxes, insurance, repairs, janitorial, etc.) on this property, he may find the amount of prorated expenses in excess of the $3,000 rental income as currently nondeductible and be required to carry it forward.

3. *Lodging is furnished to tenant for convenience of employer.* Providing employee (or spouse) lodging supplied for the employer's convenience [see §119] is incidental to the business of the taxpayer in which the employee performs services [Reg. §1.469-1(e)(3)(vi)(D)].

The renting of dealer property—a problem if the property is sold during the year. Any rental income during the taxable year from property that is held primarily for sale to customers in the ordinary course of a trade or business [i.e., a dealer or developer as defined at §1221(1)] at the time it is sold (in a transaction in which gain or loss is recognized) will be deemed incidental to such sale. Therefore, the year a rental held primarily for sale to customers is sold or exchanged, the income is deemed active, not passive, rental income [Reg. §1.469-1T(e)(3)(viii)(Example 7)].

Example: Chuck Ells, a developer, finds himself in the unenviable position of having to rent out some buildings before being able to sell them. The fact that a developer, contractor or builder rents a building for 11 months before selling it does not alter the treatment of the building rental as incidental to the building sale and is therefore not a passive rental activity.

But what about renting it out the year before? This rental will probably *not* be considered incidental. Under this provision, the taxpayer is deemed involved in two activities, building rentals and building sales.

Example: In 1998, Ben Dover acquires vacant land for the purpose of constructing a shopping mall. Before commencing construction, Ben leases the land under a one-year lease to an automobile dealership, which uses the land to park cars held in its inventory. The taxpayer commences construction of the shopping mall in 1999.

Ben acquired the land for the principal purpose of constructing the shopping mall, not realizing gain from the appreciation of the property. The rental of the property in 1998 is *not* treated as incidental to an investment activity [see (1) above]. Also, the land has not been used in any taxable year in any of Ben's trade or businesses. Therefore, the rental of the property in 1998 is *not* treated as incidental to a trade or business activity [see (2) above.] The result is, the rental of the land in 1998 is a rental activity [Reg. §1.469-1T(e)(3)(viii)(Example 7)].

But be careful about the special rule (covered later in this chapter) that recharacterizes gross income from the rental of nondepreciable property to portfolio income [Reg. §1.469-2T(f)(3)].

5. When the business activity is renting to customers—the "Tools-R-Us" exception. Property customarily made available during defined business hours for nonexclusive use by various customers *is not a rental activity* [Reg. §1.469-1T(e)(3)(ii)(E)].

Example: The payment of greens fees or renting a golf cart at a golf course and the renting of beach towels and umbrellas at the ocean are all business activities, not rental activities.

6. When the owner provides property to a partnership or S corporation, the rental is a business—the "cropshare leasing" disaster. If the taxpayer owns an interest in a partnership, S corporation, or joint venture that is not conducting a rental activity, and provides property for use in the activity "in the capacity as an owner," the providing of such property will not be considered a rental activity. Answering the question of "capacity as an owner" is based on all the facts and circumstances [Reg. §1.469-1T(e)(3)(ii)(F)].

For example, if a partner contributes the use of property to a partnership, none of the partner's distributive share of partnership income will be considered as income from a rental activity [Reg. §1.469-1T(e)(3)(vii)].

WARNING: The taxpayer makes farmland available to a tenant farmer via a "cropshare lease." The taxpayer is obligated to pay 50% of the costs incurred in the activity (without regard to whether any crops are successfully produced or marketed) and is entitled to 50% of the crops produced (or 50% of the proceeds from marketing the crops). The taxpayer is treated as providing the farmland for use in a farming activity conducted by a joint venture in the taxpayer's capacity as an owner of an interest in the joint venture. Accordingly, the taxpayer is not engaged in a rental activity, without regard to whether the taxpayer performs any services in the farming activity [Reg. §1.469-1T(e)(3)(viii)(Example 8)]. What a disaster this can be for the retired farmer living in a retirement village 1,000 miles from the farm!

A rental activity that is not a passive activity—certain vacation homes. An activity involving the rental of a dwelling unit that is used as a residence by the taxpayer during the taxable year [within the meaning of §280A(c)(5)] is not a passive activity of the taxpayer for such year [Reg. §1.469-1T(e)(5); *Fudim,* TC Memo 1994-235; *Dinsmore,* TC Memo 1994-135].

PASSIVE ACTIVITY 2: TRADE OR BUSINESS ACTIVITY WHERE TAXPAYER DOES NOT MATERIALLY PARTICIPATE

As mentioned previously, only two activities are considered passive:

1. A rental activity without regard to whether or to what extent the taxpayer participates at all in such activity (therefore, a rental activity is treated as a passive activity, regardless of the level of the taxpayer's participation) and
2. A trade or business activity in which the taxpayer does *not materially participate* for the taxable year

The answers to three questions determine if a business activity is an active activity. An activity is determined to be an active activity if the taxpayer is able to answer yes to the following three questions [Reg. §1.469-1T(e)(1)]:

1. Is the business not a rental activity? (as previously defined)
2. Is the activity a trade or business?
3. Did the taxpayer "materially participate"?

A no answer to any of these questions may relegate the property to the passive classification.

What is a "trade or business"? An activity is a trade or business activity for a taxable year if

1. the activity involves the conduct of a trade or business (i.e., a §162 business that is not a §183 hobby business or a §212 investment business);
2. it is an activity in which research or experimental expenditures deductible under §174 [or §174(a)] are treated as a trade or business; *or*
3. future regulations deem the activity as a trade or business (e.g., certain §212 investment activities deemed trade or business); *and*
4. it is not a rental activity [Reg. §1.469-1(e)(2); Reg. §1.469-4(b)(1)].

What is "material participation"? *Material participation* in a trade or business activity is participation on a "regular, continuous, and substantial" basis. The regulations separately define the words *participation* and *material* [§469(h)(1)].

What is "participation"? *Participation* is any work done by an individual *in any capacity,* management or operations, in connection with an activity in which the individual owns an interest (directly or indirectly other than through a C corporation) at the time the work is done. Thus, work done by an individual in an activity in the individual's capacity as an employee of a related or unrelated employer is counted as participation in the activity [Reg. §1.469-5(f)(1)].

- *Owner can "tack" spouse's time.* Any participation by one spouse is attributed to the other spouse even if no joint return is filed and/or the participating spouse has no ownership interest in the activity. In effect, therefore, material participant status of both spouses is determined as though the two spouses were one individual [Reg. §1.469-5T(f)(3)].
- *When management does not count—work not customarily performed by an owner.* Management time is disregarded when determining participation if it is *not* a type "customarily performed" by owners (e.g., Leona Helmsley acting as a gift wrapper at Helmsley Palace) *and* one of the principal purposes of such work is avoiding the PAL rules [§1.469-5T(f)(2)(i)].
- *When management does not count—only counting the money.* If the total amount of the taxpayer's involvement is studying and reviewing financial statements, preparing or compiling summaries or analyses of the finances or operations of the activity for the individual's own use, and monitoring the finances or operations of the activity in a nonmanagerial capacity, this management time is ignored [Reg. §1.469-5T(f)(2)(ii)].

How do investors prove participation? Keep good time records. The extent of an individual's participation may be established by any reasonable means. Contemporaneous daily time reports, logs or similar documents are not required if the extent of such participation may be established by other reasonable means. Reasonable means include, but are not limited to, the identification of services performed over a period of time and the approximate number of hours spent performing such services during such period, based on appointment books, calendars or narrative summaries [Reg. §1.469-5T(f)(4)].

PLANNING TIP: Remember, the burden of proof is on the taxpayer to prove he or she did (or did not) work 500 hours a year! Taxpayers will find the courts difficult to convince without good records [*Goshorn v. Comm.*, 66 TCM 1499, TC Memo 1993-578; *Toups v. Comm.*, 66 TCM 370; TC Memo 1993-359]. The author guesses that the same number of taxpayers who fill in the auto log will keep this time log!

WARNING—for vacation home investors. The courts have consistently found that taxpayers cannot materially participate in a condominium hotel activity not located in their immediate vicinity. Because a vacation condominium usually has full-time staff, taxpayers have to prove they materially participated, other than as "investors," at least 500 hours (discussed next). Professor Scheiner was a board member, which constituted "investor participation," and failed to prove material participation (*Barry H. Scheiner*, TC Memo 1996-554). Also, a married couple could not deduct rental activity losses involving an out-of-state condominium partnership because the taxpayers did not "materially participate" . . . full-time condominium staff managed the day-to-day rental operations and the taxpayer's activities of preparing income tax returns, reviewing budgets, attending partnership meetings and paying bills were considered "investor activities" [*Robert Serenbetz*, TC Memo 1996-510].

ESTABLISHING MATERIAL PARTICIPATION

An individual is treated as participating "materially" in an activity for the taxable year if the individual's participation meets *one* of the following six tests or a seventh residual test based on all of the facts and circumstances [Reg. §1.469-5T(a)(1)-(7)].

How to "Materially Participate" (MP) Using Any of the Four "Time" Tests

1. Work 500 hours in the business. An individual participating in the activity for more than 500 hours during the taxable year is materially participating in that activity.

PLANNING TIP: There is no requirement that the 500 hours be spread throughout the year. Therefore it seems that the statutory language "regular and continuous" is not required.

---

2. Do substantially all the work—the "cottage industry" relief provision. When an individual's participation in the activity for the taxable year constitutes *substantially all* (e.g., more than 70% of the total business hours for the year are performed by the owner) of the participation in such activity (including nonowner employees) for such year, the individual is materially participating in the activity.

PLANNING TIP: This test does allow a taxpayer to materially participate in an activity even when participating less than 100 hours a year. But it's apparent that the regulations discourage joining with other partners or employees. Therefore, this is of restricted use—to those Schedule C taxpayers or independent contractors with limited staff.

---

3. Work 100 hours and no one in the firm does more. An individual participating in the activity for more than 100 hours during the taxable year is materially participating so long as such individual's participation in the activity for the taxable year is not less than the participation in the activity of any other individual (including nonowner employees) for such year.

Example: Bob and Carl are partners in a van conversion activity. The activity is conducted only on weekends because both partners hold full-time jobs during the week. Bob and Carl keep a daily log showing that Bob recorded 250 hours and Carl recorded 251 hours during the year. This example illustrates how capricious this rule is. As Carl worked one hour more than Bob, only Carl would be considered to "materially" participate. The result is that one partner is active while the other partner is passive in the same van conversion activity!

Tax problem. If both Bob and Carl work exactly 250 hours, would they both be deemed to materially participate as "no one did more?" Is there any IRS auditor who will accept two time logs reporting exactly 250 hours?

PLANNING TIP (with a weird twist): If, in the above example, Carl were an employee, Bob would *not* have materially participated. The employee did more work during the year than the owner.

PLANNING TIP: Most owners of time-share condominiums try to use this 100-hour argument to prove material participation but without much success [*Toups v. Comm.,* 66 TCM, TC Memo 1993-359; *Barry H. Scheiner,* TC Memo 1996-554; *Robert Serenbetz,* TC Memo 1996-510].

---

4. Working 500 hours in all the multiple small businesses owned. An individual is deemed to materially participate when the activity is a "significant participation activity" (SPA) for the taxable year, *and* the individual's aggregate participation in all SPAs during such year exceeds 500 hours.

COMMENT: This test is to be used by those taxpayers who have their fingers in many pies.

What is a "significant participation activity" (SPA)? A SPA is any trade or business in which the individual participates for more than 100 hours during the year but does not materially participate (i.e., for 500 hours) for the taxable year [Reg. §1.469-5T(c)].

> **Example:** Win Erluze owns interests in three trade or business activities, X, Y and Z. Win does not materially participate in any of these activities for the taxable year but participates in activity X for 210 hours, in activity Y for 160 hours, and in activity Z for 135 hours. Win has no other significant participation passive activities. Win's net passive income (or loss) for the taxable year from activities X, Y and Z is as follows:

	X	Y	Z	Total
SPA gross income	$600	$ 700	$900	$2,200
Less: SPA deductions	– 200	– 1,000	– 300	– 1,500
Equals: SPA income (loss)	$400	– $ 300	$600	$ 700

> As X, Y and Z are "significant participation activities" for the taxable year (Win participated for more than 100 hours but did not materially participate, i.e., for 500 hours), and Win's aggregate participation in all "significant participation activities" during such year exceeds 500 hours (505 hours), Win is considered to be materially participating in all three activities.

> *Tax problem:* If Win had not participated 500 hours in the three activities, he would have had to "recharacterize" the $700 net passive income as "active" income. The "recharacterization" rules are covered later in this chapter.

How to "Materially Participate" (MP) Using Either of the Two Long-Standing (or "Look-back") Participation Rules

1. Materially participate for five of the last ten years. An individual is treated as materially participating in an activity if that individual materially participates in it (without regard to this rule) for any five taxable years (whether or not consecutive) during the ten taxable years that immediately precede the taxable year (including taxable years before 1987). To determine whether an individual materially participated in any activity for a taxable year beginning before January 1, 1987, only the 500-hour rule (test 1 above) may be used [Reg. §1.469-5(j)].

> **Example:** In 1990, Robin Banks acquires stock in an S corporation engaged in a trade or business activity. For every taxable year from 1990 through 1994, Robin is treated as materially participating (without regard to the five-of-the-ten-

years rule) in the activity. Robin retires from the activity at the beginning of 1995 and does not materially participate in the activity during 1995 and subsequent taxable years. Under the five-of-the-ten-year rules, however, Robin is treated as materially participating in the activity for taxable years 1995 through 1999 because he materially participated in the activity for five taxable years during the ten taxable years that immediately precede each of those years. Robin is not treated as materially participating in the activity for taxable years after 1999 under the five-of-the-ten-years rule.

2. Materially participate in any three previous years in a "personal service activity." In the case of a personal service activity, an individual who materially participates in the activity for *any* three taxable years prior to the current taxable year is treated as materially participating in the activity for every year thereafter. For purposes of this three-year rule, a *personal service activity* is an activity involving the performance of services in

1. the field of health, law, engineering, architecture, accounting, actuarial science, performing arts or consulting [§1.448-1T(e)(4)] *or*
2. any other trade or business in which capital is not a material income-producing factor [Reg. §1.469-5T(a)(6); §1.469-5T(d)].

PLANNING TIP: This probably means that real estate agents, appraisers, and so on will be considered providing "personal services" but only for this three-year "look-back" rule. Although the regulations are silent about the definition of "material income-producing factor" as used previously, it would seem that the IRS auditors have a "blank check" on classifying activities as "personal service activities."

Example: Frank Phurter, attorney at law, had an interest in a real estate firm prior to completing his law degree. If he worked as a broker for three years before starting his legal practice, all future income paid to him by his real estate partners is "tainted" as trade or business income in which he materially participated.

The Last Way Taxpayers May Prove Material Participation Is by the "Facts-and-Circumstances" Test

A taxpayer who does not satisfy *any* of the previous six tests may try to convince the IRS that he or she is materially participating (or not materially participating if he or she wants the income to be determined passive) based on all the facts and circumstances. In this case the taxpayer *must* prove that he or she participated during the taxable year in the activity on a "regular, continuous and substantial" basis.

Hopefully, future IRS regulations will provide more details concerning the criteria needed to satisfy this seventh test. However, the IRS has established that the following three areas of participation will *not* be classified as material participation under the facts-and-circumstances test [Reg. §1.469-5T(b)(2)]:

1. *Paying self-employment tax is irrelevant.* This test does *not* care if the taxpayer has to pay FICA or self-employment tax, or satisfies any other participation standards established by Code sections other than the PAL rules. Therefore, the taxpayer may have to pay self-employment tax and still not be considered materially participating. One of the exceptions to this rule is granted to retired or disabled farmers if they were materially participating before their retirement or disability (or are a surviving spouse of an individual who was materially participating) [Reg. §1.469-5T(h)(2)].
2. *Management time may not count either.* The performance of management services will not be taken into account unless, for the taxable year, no other person who performs services in connection with the management of the activity receives "earned income" such as wages, salaries, professional fees and other compensation [described in §911(d)(2)(A)] *and* no other manager's hours exceed (by hours) those of the taxpayer for the year.
3. *The taxpayer must work at least 100 hours annually.* The facts-and-circumstances test will not apply unless the taxpayer participates at least 100 hours in the activity during the tax year [Reg. §1.469-5T(b)(2)(iii)].

A special material participation rule for partners and S corporation shareholders. For a holder of an interest in a pass-through entity, the general rule is that each item of gross income and deduction allocated to a taxpayer shall be determined, in any case in which participation is relevant, by reference to the participation of the taxpayer in the activity that generated that item. Such participation is determined for the taxable year of the pass-through entity (and not the taxable year of the taxpayer) [Reg §1.469-2T(e)(1)].

Even a limited partner *may* be able to materially participate. Generally, a limited partner is not considered as materially participating in any activity in which he or she is a limited partner. The regulations similarly adopt this rule but also provide four exceptions. The regulations provide that the general rule does not apply if the limited partner would otherwise be treated as materially participating for the taxable year

1. by participating *more than 500 hours,*
2. having participated for *five of the last ten years,*
3. having participated for *any three years in a personal service activity* or
4. if the limited partner *is also a general partner* at all times during the partnership's tax year that ends with or within the partner's tax year [§469(h)(2); Reg. §1.469-5T(e)(2); Reg. §1.469-5T(e)(3)(ii)].

RECHARACTERIZATION OF PASSIVE INCOME
IN CERTAIN SITUATIONS

According to the regulations, but not mentioned specifically in the Code itself, taxpayers are required to reclassify passive income to "active" income or "portfolio" income in certain situations.

Why do we have these recharacterization rules? Congress is concerned that taxpayers will purchase passive income generators (commonly known as "investing in a PIG"), thereby offsetting their previously owned, and now nondeductible, passive activity losses (commonly known as "holding a PAL").

> *Example:* Win Erluze owns interests in one trade or business activity, X, and one piece of real estate, Y. Win does not materially participate in business X and does not actively participate in real estate Y. Win has no other passive activities. Win's net passive income (or loss) for the taxable year from activities X and Y is as follows:

	Business X	Real Estate Y	Total
Passive activity gross income	$2,200	$1,500	$3,700
Less: Passive activity deductions	− 1,500	− 2,200	− 3,700
Net passive income (or loss)	$ 700	− $ 700	$ 0

> Win could, under the regular passive loss rules, offset PIG X against PAL Y.

	Active	Activity Passive	Portfolio
Passive activity X		$700	
Less: Passive activity Y		− $700	
Equals: Net passive loss		0	

It is this offsetting that, in certain situations, the IRS wants to stop. This is achieved, as is discussed below, via the recharacterization rules.

Where did the recharacterization rules come from? Congress gave the Department of the Treasury sweeping authority [§469(l)(3)] to prescribe regulations "requiring net income or gain from a limited partnership *or other passive activity* to be treated as 'not from a passive activity.'" Even though Treasury personnel state that the recharacterization rules are required "to maintain the integrity of §469," most tax practitioners look at these recharacterization rules as giving the IRS the right to say in audit, "Taxpayer—heads I win, tails you lose!"

COMMENT: In these cases, the taxpayer is involved in a new type of activity that is passive but whose income may be treated as active. This is the Department of the Treasury's attempt to eliminate these types of activities from becoming a PIG.

The recharacterization rules applicable to passive activities during the operational years may be divided into two major categories: (1) rules preventing the conversion of active business income into passive activity gross income, and (2) rules preventing the conversion of portfolio income into passive activity gross income [Reg. §1.469-2T(f)].

What is the theory of the recharacterization rules? The regulations provide that an amount of gross income generally equal to the "net income" is excluded from passive activity gross income. The result of these recharacterization rules is that the taxpayer will have a passive activity with no net income or loss as well as an amount of income that has been recharacterized as "active" or "portfolio" income. Needless to say, there are *no* recharacterization rules to convert passive activity deductions into "active" or "portfolio" deductions!

How to apply the recharacterization rules. Generally, each of the recharacterization rules treats as either "active" or "portfolio" an amount of gross income (which otherwise would be treated as passive activity gross income) equal to the net income from the activity to which the rule applies. This recharacterization of passive income is required regardless of whether the income is classified as passive income under the general passive activity rules [Reg. §1.469-2T(f)].

> ***Example (continued):***   Referring to the previous Win Erluze example, if the recharacterization rules apply to business property X, Win would be required to reduce the business's actual passive activity gross income of $2,200 by the business's net income of $700.

	Business X	Real Estate Y	Total
Passive activity gross income	$ 1,500	$1,500	$3,000
Less: Passive activity deductions	− 1,500	− 2,200	− 3,700
Net passive income (or loss)	$NONE	− $ 700	− $ 700

> Win, under the recharacterization rules, would now have $700 of taxable active income that came from a passive activity and $700 of nondeductible passive loss! (This isn't fair!)

	Active	Activity Passive	Portfolio
Passive activity X	$700	$3,000	
Less: Passive activity Y		− $3,700	
Equals: Net passive loss	$700†	$ 700‡	

---

† Recharacterized passive income that is current taxable
‡ Nondeductible passive activity loss

Recharacterizing Passive Gross Income to "Active" Income

There are four situations in which some or all of the taxpayer's gross income from a passive activity must be recharacterized as "active" income. They are:

1. Certain rental property developed by the taxpayer and sold for a gain may have to be recharacterized. A portion of a taxpayer's (e.g., a developer of commercial real estate) gross rental activity income for the tax year shall be recharacterized as active income if three tests are met:

- *Gain:* The gain (but not a loss) for the sale (exchange or other disposition) is included in the taxpayer's income for the taxable year;
- *Twelve months:* The use of the property in an activity involving its rental started less than 12 months before the date of its disposition; *and*
- *Participation and increased value:* The taxpayer materially participates or significantly participates for the tax year in the activity in which the performance of services enhances the value (e.g., construction, renovation, lease-up expenses and development) of the property (or any other item of property if its basis is determined by reference to the basis of the property whose value is enhanced by the performance of services) [Reg. §1.469-2(f)(5)(i)].

PLANNING TIP: This recharacterization rule requires many developers who rent out developed property to hold the property for 12 months or more before sale.

2. A taxpayer renting property to the taxpayer's own business will have to recharacterize income. Gross rental income equal to net rental income (including any income from a sale) is recharacterized as active income if the property is rented to a trade or business activity in which the taxpayer materially participates for the taxable year (without regard to the limited partner rules) so long as the property is not property rented incidental to a development activity [Reg. §1.469-2(f)(6); Reg. §1.469-2(f)(9)(iii)].

WARNING: This rule negatively impacts more taxpayers than any other recharacterization rule. It is intended to deter taxpayers from attempting to generate passive rental income and active business rental deductions by establishing rental arrangements between their own businesses. It does that and more.

Example: Wanda Dance, a senior partner in a ten-partner law firm, owns, with only two other lawyer-partners, the commercial building housing the law firm. The three-lawyer partnership leases the building to the law firm under a "net lease" arrangement at an arms-length, fair rental value of $48,000 per year. If the rental expenses, including depreciation, are $60,000 per year, Wanda's passive activity computation would be:

	Active	Activity Passive	Portfolio
Passive income		$16,000	
Less: Passive deductions		– $20,000	
Equals: Net passive loss		– $ 4,000	(a nondeductible net lease)

But if the partners' annual gross income and expenses are reversed, thereby generating a net passive income, the recharacterization rules require Wanda to reduce the passive activity gain to zero. Wanda's passive activity income *before* the recharacterization rules would be:

	Active	Activity Passive	Portfolio
Passive income		$20,000	
Less: Passive deductions		– $16,000	
Equals: Net passive loss		+ $ 4,000	(a nondeductible net lease)

The recharacterization rules force Wanda, now that the rental is profitable, to reduce the passive activity income by the amount of the $4,000 PIG. (This isn't fair! Now Wanda has $4,000 more *active* income and $4,000 less PIG.)

	Active	Activity Passive	Portfolio
Passive income	$4,000	$16,000	
Less: Passive deductions		– $16,000	
Equals: Net passive loss	$4,000†	– $ 0‡	

† Recharacterized passive income that is current taxable
‡ Nondeductible passive activity loss

Special effective date. This recharacterization rule does not apply to rental income from *written* binding contracts entered into before February 19, 1988 [Reg. §1.469-11(c)(1)(ii)].

WARNING: The regulations do not address the question of renewals contained in the lease agreement. However, it is clear that this type of regulation encourages taxpayers without written agreements to cheat by creating "Nixon-type" backdated contracts.

3. Significant participation passive activity net income will have to recharacterized. A special rule applies when a taxpayer satisfies the significant participation standards (the 100-hour but not materially participating rule—see definition previously discussed) but is still unable to satisfy the requirements of material participation in *all* these activities (e.g., the 500-hour material participation rule) [Reg. §1.469-2T(f)(2)].

PLANNING TIP: Income in excess of losses from significant participation activities cannot be used to offset other passive losses.

---

4. Qualified working interest in gas and oil. If a taxpayer used the qualified working interest exception to take any active losses with respect to an oil and gas property for a taxable year beginning after December 31, 1986, gross income from that property will be active income to the extent of the net income from it for such taxable year. Thus, even if the taxpayer converts his or her qualified working interest into an interest in a limited liability entity, gross income will be recharacterized as active income [Reg. §1.469-2(c)(6)(i)].

Recharacterizing Passive Gross Income to "Portfolio" Income

There are three situations in which some or all of the taxpayer's gross income from a passive activity must be recharacterized as "portfolio" income. They are described below.

1. Rental from nondepreciable property must be recharacterized—the "raw land" exception. If less than 30% of the "unadjusted basis" (i.e., do not subtract depreciation) of the property used, or held for use, by customers in a rental activity during the taxable year is subject to depreciation, an amount of the activity's gross income equal to the net passive income for the activity is treated as portfolio income. This rule comes from a suggestion in the Conference Report that "ground rents that produce income without significant expenses" are similar to portfolio income [H. Rep. 99-841, 99th Cong., 2d Sess. (Sept 18, 1986), at II-147); §1.469-2T(f)(3)].

> *Example:*   Pam Permie is a limited partner in a partnership. In prior years, the partnership acquired vacant land for $300,000, estimating the property now to be worth $500,000. Vacant land is considered a §212 investment, a "portfolio" activity. To change the property to a passive activity (and thereby creating a $200,000 PIG), the partnership constructs improvements on the land at a minimal cost of $100,000 and leases the land and improvements to a tenant. The partnership then sells the land and improvements for $600,000, realizing a gain on the disposition.
>
> *Applying the recharacterization rule to this example.* The unadjusted basis of the improvements ($100,000) equals only 25% of the unadjusted basis of all property

($400,000) used in the rental activity. Therefore, the $200,000 net passive income must be recharacterized as "portfolio" income.

2. Passive equity-financed lending activity. Some or all passive income is recharacterized as portfolio income if an activity is an equity-finance activity involving certain types of lending institutions [Reg. §1.469-2T(f)(4)].

3. Intangible property leased by a pass-through entity. With certain limited exceptions, net royalty income will be recharacterized as portfolio income if a taxpayer acquires an interest in a certain pass-through entity (e.g., partnership, S corporation, estate or trust) after it has either created an item of intangible property, performed substantial services, or incurred substantial costs. In other words, activities generating nonportfolio royalty income in cases of taxpayers investing in the activity after the royalty-producing property was developed must recharacterize the net royalty income as portfolio income. There is a "safe harbor" rule on what is deemed substantial services or costs [Reg. §1.469-2T(f)(7)].

THE $25,000 RELIEF PROVISION FOR RENTAL REAL ESTATE

In general. Under the general passive loss limitation rules, net losses from rental activities do not reduce taxable income unless the taxpayer has positive net income from other passive activities.

The rule. Under this relief provision for rental real estate, moderate-income individuals (but not corporations) may use up to $25,000 of excess losses (and deduction-equivalent credits) from all rental real estate activities against active, portfolio, and other nonpassive income if the individual actively participates (spouse's services also count) in the management of the property. This relief applies only if the individual does not have sufficient passive income for the year, after considering all other passive deductions and credits, to fully offset the losses and credits from such rental real estate activities.

> ***Example:*** Ellie is a real estate agent with a 1999 commission income of $40,000. She is married with no children and has itemized deductions of $8,000. She purchases a certified historic apartment house for $5,000, assumes an underlying mortgage, and rehabilitates the property. At the end of the year she receives a rental income schedule from her accountant reporting a $15,000 rental loss and $500 of rehabilitation tax credit. The $25,000 relief provision allows Ellie to offset her salary and commission income with the real estate losses and credits if she actively participates in the management of the apartment house.

It Is a $25,000 per Taxpayer Relief

A single $25,000 amount each tax year applies on an aggregate basis to deductions and credits. It is not a $25,000 relief provision for each rental owned.

$25,000 for single taxpayers. Each single taxpayer is eligible for this $25,000 relief provision each tax year.

$25,000 for married couples. This relief is a per-tax-return provision. Therefore, husband and wife on a joint return receive only a $25,000 relief.

$12,500 for married couples filing separate returns. If married individuals file separate tax returns *and* live separately *for the entire year,* this relief provision reduces to $12,500 for each [§469(i)(5)(B)].

Zero for married couples filing separate returns and living together at any time during the year. If married individuals filing separately live together *at any time* during the taxable year, the amount of the $25,000 relief reduces to *zero* [§469(i)(5)(B)].

COMMENT: This is weird tax planning by Congress. What a strange law—penalizing married couples getting divorced but allowing single couples living together $50,000 of relief!

Estates can also use the $25,000 deduction. The estate of a deceased taxpayer also qualifies for the $25,000 exception for the first two tax years following the death of the taxpayer if the decedent was actively participating in the rental real estate activity in the year of the death.

$25,000 for each partner. This provision is a $25,000-per-partner relief and not a per-partnership relief as long as the partner is an individual taxpayer.

WARNING: There is a phase-out of the relief provision! As mentioned previously, these losses generally apply only to middle-income taxpayers and are limited to $25,000 annually. But even this relief amount is phased out, in a 2:1 ratio, as the taxpayer's adjusted gross income (without regard to net passive losses, IRA contributions and taxable Social Security benefits) increases from $100,000 to $150,000. A taxpayer forfeits $1 of the $25,000 relief for each $2 of modified adjusted gross income (AGI) over $100,000. Therefore, a taxpayer earning $125,000 of modified AGI is permitted to deduct only half, or $12,500, of the loss created by the rental real estate. For low-income housing credits and rehabilitation credits, the $25,000 allowance (in deduction-equivalent credits) is reduced by one-half of the taxpayer's AGI in excess of $200,000 [§469(i)(3)].

Four Basic Requirements to Use the $25,000 Relief Provision

Certain rules *must* be followed before this $25,000 relief provision is available to an individual. The rules, in synopsis form (followed by a full explanation of each), are as follows:

1. It can only be *rental real estate.*
2. The taxpayer must have at least *10% ownership.*
3. The taxpayer must *actively participate* in the management.
4. The taxpayer must be an *individual* (not a corporation).

The relief is only available to rental real estate. The $25,000 exception to the limitation rule is available only to rental real estate and not to any other rental activity or other passive activity. Rental real estate is where payment is primarily for the use of real property. Apartment houses, commercial rental properties and similar properties are defined as passive rental real estate.

Tax problem with "net lease" property. Most net lease arrangements are considered rental real estate but can only use the $25,000 relief provision if the landlord also "actively manages" the net lease property—a task normally performed by the tenant.

This relief provision does not apply to active real estate (such as a vacation home in a rental pool). Passive real estate activities that are not treated as rental activities under this provision (e.g., hotel, motel, or a vacation home rental pool) may not use the $25,000 relief provision. Therefore, this relief provision is not available simply because the taxpayer owns real estate. For example, a hotel is treated neither as a rental real estate undertaking nor as consisting of two activities, only one of which is a rental real estate undertaking.

The 10% ownership rule. A taxpayer must (in conjunction with such taxpayer's spouse, even in the absence of a joint return) own 10% or more (by value) of *all* interests in the real estate activity for the entire year.

If the activity owns multiple buildings, does the taxpayer have to own at least 10% of each separate building? Separate buildings are treated as separate rental real estate activities if the degree of integration of the business and other relevant factors do not require treating them as parts of a larger activity (e.g., an integrated shopping center).

What about condominiums and cooperatives? A cooperative apartment in an apartment building, owned by a taxpayer unrelated to those owning the other apartments in the building, generally will qualify as a separate activity despite the fact that the ownership of the building may be shared with owners of other apartments in the building, and despite the sharing with owners of other apartments of such services as management and maintenance of common areas.

What about time-shares? By contrast, ownership of an undivided interest in a building (e.g., owning a two-week interest in a ski condominium) or of an area too small to be rented as a separate unit (or that is not rented as a separate unit) does not qualify as a separate activity.

PLANNING TIP—for vacation home investors: Therefore, most time-share arrangements do not qualify for the $25,000 relief provision [*Toups v. Comm.*, 66 TCM 370; *Fudim v. Comm.*, TC Memo 1994-235].

Active participation in the rental management is required. In the case of an individual taxpayer owning an interest in a rental real estate activity and meeting the 10% ownership requirement, *up to $25,000 of relief may be available, but only if the landlord actively participates in the activity.* Therefore, what is meant by "active participation"? To start, it is important to ascertain the following:

The difference between "active participation" and "material participation." The active-participation standard is designed to be less stringent that the material-participation requirement. Material participation requires the taxpayer to be involved in the operations of the real estate "in a regular, continuous and substantial manner." Active participation only requires the taxpayer to be involved "in a significant and bona fide sense."

So what is "active participation"? The determination of whether a taxpayer satisfies the "active participation" criteria of management of real estate is made by looking at all the facts and circumstances. Active participation occurs when a taxpayer participates in the making of management decisions or arranging for others to provide services (such as repairs) "in a significant and bona fide sense." Management decision that are relevant in this context include

1. approving new tenants,
2. deciding on rental terms,
3. approving capital or repair expenditures, and
4. other similar decisions.

Property managers may be used. Hiring a property manager will still allow the taxpayer to meet the "active participation" rule so long as the taxpayer "shares "in the management decision. But there is a warning to heed when using property managers. Services provided by an agent are not attributed to the principal, and a merely formal and nominal participation in management, in the absence of a genuine exercise of independent discretion and judgment, is insufficient.

> **Example:**   Tyson, who owns and rents out an apartment that formerly was his primary residence or that he uses as a part-time vacation home, may be treated as actively participating even if he hires a rental agent and others provide services such as repairs. So long as Tyson participates in a "significant and bona fide sense," a lack of participation in operations does not lead to the denial of relief.

PLANNING TIP: This should allow many rental vacation homes, other than vacation homes in rental pools and rented for seven days or less, to use the $25,000 relief provision.

Real estate owned in a limited partnership cannot use the $25,000 relief provision as, by state statute, a limited partner cannot participate in management at all!

Low-income housing. In the case of low-income housing and rehabilitation credits, the active participation requirements need not be satisfied and are exempt from the restrictive limited-partnership tests.

Net lease property, other than in the year of negotiation and the year of termination, probably cannot use the $25,000 relief provision. In most cases, the landlord will not be able to meet the active participation requirement.

Only individuals can use the $25,000 relief provision. No relief is provided to taxpayers other than individuals (e.g., a regular C corporation subject to the passive loss provisions).

Estates. If a taxpayer actively participated in a rental real estate activity in the taxable year in which he or she died, his or her estate is deemed to have actively participated for the two years following the death. This treatment applies to the taxpayer's estate during the two taxable years of the estate following death to facilitate the administration of the estate without requiring the executor or fiduciary to reach decisions about the appropriate disposition of the rental real property within a short period following the taxpayer's death [§469(i)(4)].

Trusts. A trust is not intended to qualify for the allowance of up to $25,000. As a result, individuals cannot circumvent the $25,000 ceiling or multiply the number of $25,000 allowances simply by transferring various rental real properties to one or more trusts.

Applying the Passive Loss Rules to Real Estate Professionals

REAL ESTATE PROFESSIONALS ARE EXEMPT FROM PASSIVE LOSS RULES!

One of the most unfair tax provisions contained in the passive loss rules is the general rule that all real estate rental activities must be treated passively, no matter what the owner's level of personal participation [§469(c)(2)].

> **Example (prior to relief provision):** Marilyn, a full-time real estate agent making $160,000 in commissions a year, purchased an apartment complex in 1991 throwing off a $40,000 loss. From 1991 through 1993, none of this $40,000 loss was deductible. (The $25,000 relief provision was not available to Marilyn as she makes over $150,000 in modified income.) She is carrying forward $120,000 of rental losses deductible against future income or deductible when the property is sold.

Real Estate Professionals Can Deduct Real Estate Losses Against Ordinary Income

The relief provision. Properly, Congress has made one exception to the general rule that all rental activities must be treated passively [Revenue Reconciliation Act of 1993]. Starting January 1, 1994, a taxpayer's rental real estate activities (RREAs) in which he or she materially participates are not subject to limitation under the passive loss rule *if* the taxpayer meets eligibility requirements relating to real property trades or businesses in which the taxpayer performs services. This means that those state investors who qualify are now permitted to deduct their rental real estate losses from their current commissions, wages, interest and dividends [§469(c)(7)]!

WHAT PROPERTY, WHAT INVESTORS, AND HOW DO THEY QUALIFY?

The general rule. The only RREAs that qualify for this exceptional relief provision are real property rentals in which the *qualified taxpayer materially participates* in the management and operation of the RREA.

PLANNING TIP: In other words, if real estate investors are not materially participating in their real estate rentals, there is no sense spending time calculating the complicated eligibility requirements!

Spending Enough Time as a Landlord?

Material participation. An individual is treated as participating "materially" for the taxable year if the individual's participation meets *one* of the seven enumerated material participation tests previously discussed in Chapter 13 [Reg. §1.469-5T(a)(1)-(7)]. The three most common ways real estate investors may meet this "material participation" test are by

1. managing and operating the rental real estate activity for more than 500 hours during the year,
2. doing substantially all the work required to manage and operate the rental real estate during the year (probably more than 70% of the total business hours are performed by the landlord) *or*
3. working more than 100 hours during the year with no one (including nonowner employees and independent property managers) participating more than the landlord [Reg. §1.469-5T(a)(1)-(3)].

PLANNING TIP: How will real estate investors be required to prove participation? The IRS encourages them to keep good time records based on appointment books, calendars or narrative summaries [§1.469-5T(f)(4)]. Apparently, landlords will carry these rental time logs along with their auto logs!

PLANNING TIP: "Participation" is an individual doing any work *in any capacity,* management or operations, unless (1) the total amount of the taxpayer's involvement is studying and reviewing financial statements or monitoring the finances or operations in a nonmanagerial capacity (e.g., acting as or being a limited partner), or (2) the work is management not "customarily performed" by owners *and* one of the principal purposes of such work is avoiding the passive loss rules [§1.469-5(f)(1)].

PLANNING TIP: For the material participation test only (not the 50% test and 750-hour test discussed below), an owner can "tack" a spouses's time for calculating the tests mentioned above (e.g., an owner/investor performing 51 hours could add a spouse's time of 50 hours to exceed the 100-hour requirement!) [Reg. §1.469-5T(f)(3)].

Aggregation of Rental Real Estate

Each rental is a separate activity, unless all rentals are combined. Each interest of the taxpayer in rental real estate is to be considered as a separate activity, but a taxpayer may elect to treat all interests in real estate including real estate held through pass-through entities, as one activity [§469(c)(7)(A)].

PLANNING TIP: The aggregation option permits the investor to meet the material participation test after *cumulatively* materially participating (e.g., working 100 hours or 500 hours) *in all the real estate rentals.* Without the aggregation option, the investor would be required to materially participate (i.e., spend 100 hours or 500 hours) in each activity, probably an impossible task for investors owning more than four rentals!

PLANNING TIP: When would investors *not* want to aggregate their rental real estate? When the rental real estate is throwing off passive income, and they purposely want to flunk this test! The rental real estate passive profit is then usable against other passive losses, such as other rentals in which they are not materially participating or vacation homes in rental pools in which they cannot materially participate.

The election must be properly made. The election to treat all interests in rental real estate as a single rental real estate activity is binding for all future years unless there is a material change in a taxpayer's facts and circumstances. The taxpayer makes the election by filing a statement with his or her original income tax return. This statement must contain a declaration that the taxpayer is a qualifying taxpayer for the taxable year and is making the election pursuant to section 469(c)(7)(A) [Prop. Reg. §1.469-9(g)].

Real estate owned by passthrough entities. If a taxpayer owns a 50% or greater interest in the capital, income, gain, loss, deduction or credit of a pass-through entity at any time during a taxable year, each interest in rental real estate held by the pass-through entity will be treated as a separate interest in rental real estate, regardless of the pass-through entity's grouping of activities. However, the taxpayer may elect to treat it as a single rental real estate activity [Prop. Reg. §1.469-9(g)].

THE TWO MAJOR REQUIREMENTS

How an Individual Satisfies the Two-Step Eligibility Requirements

1. The 50% test. More than 50% of the individual's personal services during the tax year must be performed in real property trades or businesses (defined below) in which the individual materially participates (defined previously), and

2. The 750-hour test. The individual must perform more than 750 hours of service in those same trades or businesses [§469(c)(7)(B)].

Restriction for employees. When this eligibility test is applied, the personal services of an employee are not counted unless the employee is also at least a 5% owner (i.e., owns more than 5% of the outstanding stock or more than 5% of the total combined voting power) [§469(c)(7)(D)(ii)].

Eligible corporations. A closely held C corporation satisfies the eligibility test if, during the tax year, more than 50% of the gross receipts of the corporation are derived from real property trades or businesses in which the corporation materially participates [§469(c)(7)(D)(i)].

PLANNING TIP: This relief provision does not apply to estates, trusts, or limited partnerships owning real estate rentals. It only grants relief to individuals and closely held C corporations.

Calculating 750 Hours

As mentioned previously, an individual must perform more than 750 hours of service in the real estate rental businesses.

Spouse's hours. In the case of joint returns, each spouse's personal services are taken into account *separately* when calculating the 50% test and the 750-hour test. But when determining "material participation," the participation of the spouse of the taxpayer is taken into account.

Example: A husband and wife filing a joint return meet the eligibility requirements of the provision if during the taxable year *one* spouse performs at least half of his or her business services in a real estate trade or business in which either spouse materially participates. The couple does not fail the eligibility requirements if less than half of their business services, taken together, are performed in real estate trades or businesses in which either of them materially participates, provided that more than half of one spouse's business services qualify.

PLANNING TIP: "Stay-home" spouses may now want to become active real estate agents. If they spend at least 750 hours cumulatively in selling and managing their family rentals, this converts the family rentals to *active* rentals!

Example (Marilyn continued):   Remember Marilyn, the full-time real estate agent making $160,000 in commissions a year, who purchased an apartment complex, throwing off a $40,000 loss? Assume she worked 1,000 hours in the brokerage business and only an additional 100 hours managing the real estate rental. The 50% test calculation is 550 hours (1,100 hours × 50%) and the 750 hour calculation is 1,100 hours, which is more than the minimum required and more than the 50% minimum required hours (550 hours). Therefore, starting in 1994, *all* the $40,000 loss is currently deductible against her commission income!

PLANNING TIP: This seems to be a fairly liberal relief provision for those taxpayers involved in the real estate profession who own rental real estate!

PLANNING TIP: The flowchart in Figure 14.1 titled "Rental Real Estate Activity Determination for Individuals" makes this calculation very easy.

The Real Estate Businesses That Can Be Combined!

Real property trade or business means any real property development, redevelopment, construction, reconstruction, acquisition, conversion, rental, operation, management, leasing, or brokerage trade or business [§469(c)(7)(C)].

PLANNING TIP: According to the new passive loss relief provision, the "blessed" businesses generally include most (1) real estate builders and contractors, (2) owners of rentals, (3) property managers and (4) participants in the real estate brokerage business—if they meet the 50% participation and the 750-hour requirements.

FIGURE 14.1   Rental Real Estate Activity Determination for Individuals Worksheet

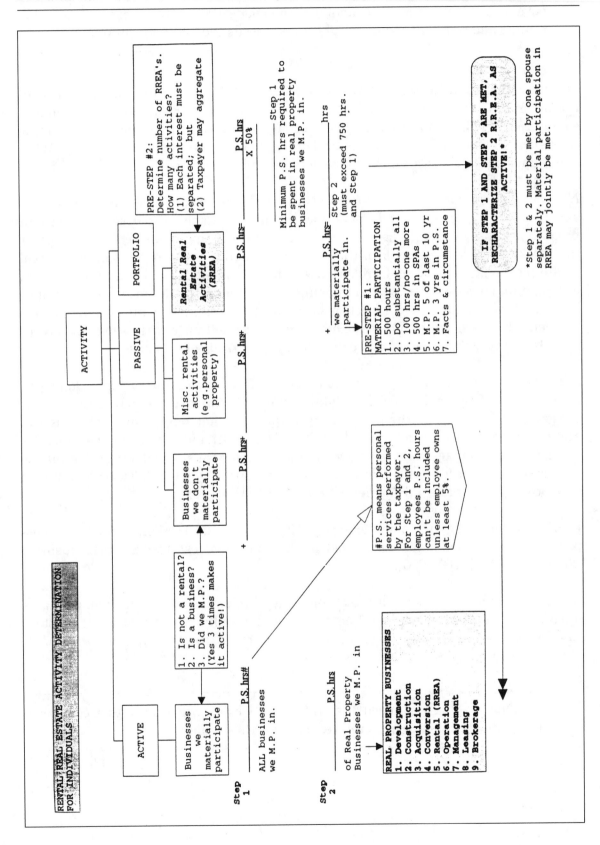

> **PLANNING TIP:** Any hourly combination in these four "blessed" businesses is permitted; a taxpayer, for example, who spends 100 hours managing his or her rentals and 651 hours selling real estate exceeds the 750-hour minimum!

What is included in "brokerage trade or business"? There is much discussion about the definition of *brokerage trade or business*. Do only brokers qualify, not agents or salespersons? (The *Kiplinger Letter* of February 11, 1994, asserts that the new relief provision applies only to real estate brokers and not agents and salespersons!) What about appraisers, real estate mortgage brokers and auctioneers?

Neither the law nor the IRS tells us. Neither the Internal Revenue Code section 469(c)(7)(C) nor the associated Conference Committee Report discusses the width or breadth of brokerage, and therefore neither specifically mentions real estate agents (i.e., brokers and salespersons) or those in the real estate financing business (i.e., real estate mortgage bankers and brokers). Nor do they mention real estate appraisers, although under most state laws appraising is included in the definition of brokerage. Many state real estate licensing acts also specifically exempt or require auctioneers to be licensed as real estate brokers. Therefore, we are left only with prior case law or state law for the definition of real estate "brokerage trade or business."

Real estate brokerages typically encompass brokers, agents and salespersons [*Robert C. Kersey,* 66 TCM 1863]; therefore, all should qualify. People involved in brokerage firms are generally "involved in the sale, leasing, acquisition, and development of industrial and commercial real estate" [*Alfred Rice,* 38 TCM 990] and may even specialize "in sales, property management, mortgage financing, appraisals, and insurance primarily on a commission or fee basis" [*Norman A. Grant,* CA-4 *aff'g* 64-2 USTC 9586, 333 F2d 603] or simply "appraisal" [*Charles W. Yeager,* 18 TCM 192].

Brokerage businesses hire salespersons [*FB Tippins, Jr.,* 24 TCM 521], and both salespersons and brokers may be involved in the same real estate brokerage business [*Floyd Wright,* 49 TCM 906].

Another place to find the definition of real estate brokerage is state law; all 50 states have real estate brokerage licensing acts, and generally states require real estate salespeople and brokers to be licensed under the same statutory provisions [*J. G. Mendoza,* 22 TCM 528].

> **PLANNING TIP:** It is hoped that future IRS rules will clarify this confusion. Regulation §1.469-4(h) has been reserved for these rules.

So What Can Be Done with the Rental Losses Previously Suspended?

As we can now fully deduct the current rental losses against our other current *active* income, can we also "trigger" the prior rental losses we have not deducted? Not easily!

Sadly, these suspended losses do not immediately convert to active losses. They maintain their passive status and may not be immediately deductible. The suspended nondeducted losses from an earlier year are treated as losses from a *former passive activity* [see §469(f)]. These previously suspended losses, however, unlike passive activity losses generally, *are* allowed against income realized from the activity after it ceases to be a passive activity. Thus, such suspended losses are limited to the income from that specific activity but are not allowed to offset other income. Of course, the matching-of-income burden of proof is on the taxpayer.

PLANNING TIP: When the taxpayer disposes of his or her entire interest in the activity in a fully taxable transaction with an unrelated party, any remaining suspended losses allocable to the activity are allowed in full.

Example (continued): Marilyn, in the above example, is carrying forward $120,000 of rental losses that were suspended from 1991 through 1993. These carry-forward losses are not immediately triggered but *are* deductible either against future income from this new real estate rental activity or deductible when sold.

Can we combine rental and business enterprises to get around these rules? In spite of the new rental real estate activity relief provision, no grouping of businesses and rentals is allowed unless either is "insubstantial" in relation to the other. The problem is that the proposed regulations do not spell out "insubstantial." The lapsed temporary regulations contained two "bright-line" insubstantial tests: (1) the 2% test (i.e., if the gross rental income is less than 2% of the smaller of the property's unadjusted basis or fair market value, the rental activity is insubstantial) and (2) the 20% test (i.e., if the rental income is less than 20% of the combined business and rental income, the rental activity is insubstantial). It is assumed that these tests may be used to help determine if the rental is an "insubstantial" part of the business . . . or if the business may be involved in "insubstantial" rental activities without breaking them into two activities [§1.469-4(d)].

PLANNING TIP: If the grouping of rental activities with the other real property businesses is permitted by the IRS, a large tax loophole for most real estate investors exists. But such aggressive tax planning is questionable!

Example (continued):   If Marilyn, in the previous example, can combine her two real property businesses (e.g., brokerage and RREA) into one activity, her $120,000 carry-forward rental losses can offset her $120,000 current brokerage income! This will bring her taxable income to zero for 1994! We seriously doubt that future IRS regulations will allow this type of activity grouping!

Stupid tax planning. What happens if the rental is sold for a large profit and the minimal annual losses were previously treated as an "active" rental loss? Rental properties treated as "active" rental losses in the year of the sale will create "active" gain at time of sale, with the result that this gain can only offset the carryover loss from that specific activity and is not available to offset any other passive losses.

PLANNING TIP: Any related gain on sale shall not be considered passive (it stays active) unless the property was used in a passive activity for either (1) 20% of the period owned *or* (2) the entire 24 months prior to the date of the signing of the offer-to-purchase agreement [§1.469-2T(c)(2)(iii)].

Example: Sandy purchases a large residential rental property with a large down payment. It throws off only a $4,000 per year rental loss. If she meets the 50% and 750-hour tests each year, after ten years she will have deducted $40,000 of "active rental losses." If she sells the property for a $1,000,000 profit, her gain is considered an active gain, unless she treated it as passive for 24 months prior to the signing of the offer-to-sell! Therefore, it is not available to be used against her other "limited partnership" passive losses.

Effective date. The provision is effective for taxable years beginning after December 31, 1993.

CONCLUSION

Real estate agents, contractors and developers who own rental real estate should be overjoyed over the return of the tax benefits previously enjoyed by everyone before 1987! But Congress exacted a price: to use this relief provision requires a time log and a few extra hours with a tax preparer!

CHAPTER

15

The Disposition of Passive Activities

The theory. Congress felt that only when a taxpayer disposes of the *entire* interest in a passive activity can the actual economic gain or loss on the investment be determined with total accuracy. Upon a taxable disposition, net appreciation or depreciation with respect to the activity can be finally ascertained. Prior to a disposition of the taxpayer's interest, it is difficult to determine whether there has actually been gain or loss with respect to the activity (e.g., allowable deductions may exceed actual economic costs or may be exceeded by untaxed appreciation).

Passive losses become deductible . . . eventually. Under the passive loss rules, upon a fully taxable, arm's-length disposition (i.e., taxable dispositions of the entire interest in the activity), any overall loss from the activity realized by the taxpayer is recognized (i.e., "triggered") and allowed against income (even against active or portfolio income) [§469(g)(1)].

Transfers other than by "taxable dispositions of the entire interest in the activity" are covered by special rules (discussed later), such as transfer by reason of death; transfer by gift; installment sales; activity ceasing to be passive; corporation changes from closely held (per §469) to nonclosely held; and nontaxable transfers.

WARNING: Tax credits (e.g., low-income housing and rehab credits) may be lost upon sale. Since the purpose of the disposition rule is to allow only "real" economic losses of the taxpayer to be deducted, credits (which are not related to the measurement of such loss) are not allowed at disposition. Therefore, credits are allowed only when sufficient passive income is generated.

TAXABLE DISPOSITIONS OF ENTIRE INTEREST IN ACTIVITY

The type of disposition that triggers full recognition of any loss from a passive activity is a fully taxable disposition of the taxpayer's entire interest in the activity. What does this definition entail?

Fully taxable disposition. A fully taxable disposition generally includes a sale of the property to a third party at arm's length and thus, presumably, for a price equal to its fair market value.

Abandonment. An abandonment constitutes a fully taxable disposition [if it gives rise to a deduction under §165(a)].

Worthlessness of security. Worthlessness is also a disposition [to the extent that §165(g) applies to a worthless security].

Entire interest. Originally, the taxpayer was required to dispose of the "entire interest" in the activity in order to trigger the recognition of loss. If less than the entire interest was sold, then the ultimate economic gain or loss computation in the activity remained unresolved [§469(g)(1)].

> *Example:* Charlene has a significant ownership interest in a bakery and a movie theater at a shopping mall in Baltimore and in a bakery and a movie theater at a shopping mall in Philadelphia. Even though Charlene may consider it reasonable to group these four businesses into any one of four combinations, the last option, four separate activities, generally will be the best of the following options:
>
> 1. Combining the movie theaters and bakeries into *one single activity*
> 2. *Separating* the *movie theaters* into one activity *and* the *bakeries* into another activity
> 3. *Separating* the *Baltimore businesses* into one activity *and* the *Philadelphia businesses* into another activity
> 4. Segregating them all into *four separate activities* [§1.469-4(c)(3) (Example 1)]

PLANNING TIP: Most taxpayers, therefore, try to create as many small activities as possible.

Exception: Triggering of carry-forward loss: A disposition of "substantially all" of an activity will trigger carry-forward losses so long as the taxpayer can establish with reasonable certainty the previous carry-forward losses of that specific segment of the activity and the segment's current year's gross income and expenses [§1.469-4(g)].

Proprietorship. A disposition of the taxpayer's entire interest involves a disposition of the taxpayer's interest in all entities that are engaged in the activity. To the extent that they are held in a proprietorship form, all assets used or created in the activity must be disposed.

Partnerships (general or limited) or S corporations. If a general partnership or S corporation conducts two separate activities, a fully taxable disposition by the entity of all the assets used or created in one activity constitutes a disposition of the partner's or shareholder's entire interest in the activity.

Grantor trust. Similarly, if a grantor trust conducts two separate activities and sells all the assets used or created in one activity, the grantor is considered to be disposing of his entire interest in that activity.

Records required. If losses are to be allowed in full upon disposition, the taxpayer is required to have adequate records of the suspended losses allocable to that activity that includes in income the gain (if any) allocable to the entire interest in the activity.

WHERE DOES THE GAIN (OR LOSS) GO?

Gain first offsets that activity's carry-forward losses. Gain recognized upon a transfer of an interest in a passive activity generally is treated as passive, and is *first* offset by the *suspended losses from that specific activity.* This accomplishes the purpose of recognizing net income or loss with respect to the activity when it can be finally determined [§469(g)(1)].

> *Example:* **Full recognition of suspended losses.** Terry sold an apartment house, which has an adjusted basis of $100,000, for $180,000. In addition, Terry has suspended losses associated with that specific apartment house of $60,000. The total gain, $80,000, and the taxable gain, $20,000, are calculated as follows:

Net sales price	$180,000
Less: Adjusted basis	− 100,000
Equals: Total gain	$ 80,000
Less: Suspended losses	− 60,000
Equals: Taxable gain	$ 20,000

The remaining ordering rules for any enduring (and "triggered") losses. If suspended losses exceed the gain recognized, the excess is allowed to offset income in the following order:

1. Net passive activity income or gains (if any)
2. Nonpassive income or gains (e.g., active and/or portfolio losses)

> *Example:* **Partial recognition of suspended losses.** Terry sold an apartment house with an adjusted basis of $100,000 for $150,000. In addition, Terry

has suspended losses associated with that specific apartment house of $60,000. The total gain, $50,000, and the *deductible loss,* $10,000, are calculated as follows:

Net sales price	$150,000
Less: Adjusted basis	– 100,000
Equals: Total gain	$ 50,000
Less: Suspended losses	– 60,000
Equals: Deductible loss	– $ 10,000

The $10,000 deductible loss can now be used against the taxpayer's other passive income. If any of the loss then remains, it may be used against ordinary income and portfolio income.

Loss from disposition. The loss on sale would simply be an additional deduction of the activity, added to the previously suspended losses, and the above rules would continue to be followed.

IS THE GAIN TREATED AS ACTIVE, PASSIVE OR PORTFOLIO?

The year of sale determines whether the gain is active, passive or portfolio. Any gain recognized upon the sale, exchange or other disposition (a "disposition") of property used in an activity, or of an interest in an activity held through a partnership or S corporation, is treated as follows:

1. The gain is treated as gross income from the activity for the taxable year or years in which it is recognized.
2. If the activity is passive in the year of disposition, the gain is treated as passive activity gross income for the taxable year in which it is recognized.
3. If the activity is not passive in the year of disposition, the gain is treated as nonpassive [§1.469-2T(c)(2)].

Example: A. J. owns an interest in a trade or business activity in which he has never materially participated. In 1998, A. J. sells equipment that is used exclusively in the activity and realizes a gain on the sale. The gain is passive activity gross income.

Example: B. J. owns an interest in a trade or business activity in which she materially participates during 1998. In 1998 B. J. sells a building used in the activity in an installment sale and realizes a gain on the sale. B. J. does not materially participate in the activity for 1999 or any subsequent year. As the year of the sale determines the character of the gain, none of B. J.'s gain from the sale (including gain taken into account after 1998) is passive activity gross income.

What happens when one asset that is being used for two purposes simultaneously is sold? In cases where a material portion of the property that was used at any time before the disposition in any activity in which the remainder of the property was not used, the material portion shall be treated as a separate interest in property. The amount realized from the disposition and the adjusted basis of the property must be allocated among the separate interests in a reasonable manner.

> ***Example:*** Sam sells a ten-floor office building for a $500,000 total gain. Sam owned the building for three years preceding the sale and at all times during that period used seven floors of the building in a trade or business activity and three floors in a rental activity. The fair market value per square foot is substantially the same throughout the building, and Sam did not maintain a separate adjusted basis for any part of the building. The seven floors used in the trade or business activity and the three floors used in the rental activity are treated as separate interests in property. The amount realized and the adjusted basis of the building must be allocated between the separate interests in a reasonable manner.
>
> Under these circumstances, an allocation based on the square footage of the parts of the building used in each activity would be reasonable. Therefore 70% ($350,000) of the total gain is active income and 30% ($150,000) is passive income.

DISPOSITION OF INTEREST IN PASSTHROUGH ENTITIES

Allocation among activities. If an interest in a partnership or S corporation (i.e., a passthrough entity) is sold or disposed of, a ratable portion of any gain or loss from the disposition is treated as gain or loss from the disposition of an interest in *each* trade or business, rental, or investment activity in which the passthrough entity owns an interest on the applicable valuation date (this date is generally either the sale date or the beginning of the tax year).

> ***Example:*** **Allocation of gain (or loss) when selling a partnership interest.** Abe owns a one-half interest in BobJoe, a calendar year partnership. In 1998, Abe sells 50% of his interest and the gain is determined as follows:
>
> | | |
> |---|---|
> | Sales price | $50,000 |
> | Less: Adjusted basis | − 30,000 |
> | Equals: Gain | $20,000 |
>
> BobJoe is engaged in one business and one rental in addition to owning marketable securities that are portfolio assets. A ratable portion of Abe's $20,000 gain is allocated to each appreciated activity in which BobJoe owns an interest on the applicable valuation date. The marketable securities are treated as owned by BobJoe as a single investment activity.

Gain. The ratable portion of any gain from the disposition of an interest in a passthrough entity that is allocable to each activity is

$$\text{Total gain} \times \frac{\text{Net gain from a specific activity on valuation date}}{\text{Sum of all activities net gain on valuation date}}$$

Loss. The ratable portion of any loss from the disposition of an interest in a passthrough entity that is allocable to an activity is

$$\text{Total loss} \times \frac{\text{Net loss from a specific activity on valuation date}}{\text{Sum of all activities net loss on valuation date}}$$

Optional allocation rule. If the gain or loss recognized upon the disposition of an interest in a passthrough entity cannot be allocated, the gain or loss is allocated among the activities in proportion to the respective fair market values of the passthrough entity's interests in the activities at the applicable valuation date, and the gain or loss allocated to each activity is treated as gain or loss from the disposition of an interest in the activity.

Gain allocated to certain passive activities may be deemed not from a passive activity. Recharacterization rules on substantially appreciated property sales exist for passthrough entity sales [§l.469-2T(e)(3)(iii)].

HOW THE RECHARACTERIZATION RULES APPLY TO SALES

Recharacterization of passive income when selling passive property. The last three recharacterization rules to be discussed relate to the sale of passive property by the taxpayer. As mentioned previously in Chapter 13, the basic rule for determining if property sold is passive or not passive is, "How is the property being used in the year of the sale?" The IRS is greatly concerned that taxpayers will use this rule to artificially create a PIG (passive income generator) by converting property to be sold for a gain into a passive activity immediately before sale. To prevent potential taxpayer abuse at time of sale, the regulations establish three major exceptions: (1) the "12-month rule," (2) the "20%/24-month rule" and (3) income from a dealer's investment property [§1.469-2T(f); §1.469-1T(f)].

COMMENT: Under the recharacterization rules, the "net income" from a sale is characterized as active or portfolio income, thereby eliminating much-needed "passive income" that could be offset by carry-forward passive losses.

The "12-month rule"—treatment of gain (or loss) when selling. If there is a sale within 12 months of conversion, a monthly allocation is required unless the gain is either (1) considered *de minimis* (i.e., under $10,000) or (2) subject to the next rule for "substantially appreciated property."

The "20%/24-month rule"—sale of substantially appreciated property formerly used in a nonpassive activity. Generally, if the fair market value of an interest in any property exceeds 120% of that property's adjusted basis (i.e., after subtracting accumulated depreciation) at the time of sale, it is deemed substantially appreciated. Therefore, any related gain shall not be considered passive (it's either active or portfolio) unless the property was used in a passive activity for either (1) 20% of the period owned *or* (2) the entire 24 months prior to the date of the signing of the offer-to-purchase agreement [§1.469-2(c)(2)(iii)].

> **Example:** On January 1, 1987, Scott purchases and moves his law firm into a new building. He materially participates in the law firm until March 31, 1997. On April 1, 1998, Scott leases the building to his former partners. On December 31, 1999, Scott sells the building. Assuming Scott's lease of the building to his old partners constitutes a rental activity under the passive loss rules, the building is used in a passive activity for 21 months (April 1, 1998, through December 31, 1999).

Thus, the building was not used in a passive activity for the entire 24-month period ending on the date of the sale. In addition, the 21-month period during which the building was used in a passive activity is less than 20% of Scott's entire holding period of the property (13 years, or 156 months).

Therefore, the gain from the sale is treated as not being from a passive activity (nor would it be portfolio income as the property was not held as an investment for more than 50% of its holding period as an investment). The result is that the gain must be recharacterized as an "active" gain [§1.469-2(c)(2)(iii)(D); §1.469-2T(c)(2)(iii)(A)].

The 20% / 24 Month Test

1. Was the asset used in the activity the entire 24 months?

        Yes   X* No

    *Rents to partnership   April 1, 1988
    Sells to partnership   December 31, 1999
    Total time used   21 months

or

2. Was the asset used in the passive activity for 20% of the holding period?

        Yes   X* No

    *Date acquired   January 1, 1987
    Date sold   December 31, 1999
    Total time owned   156 months × .20 = 31 months
    Total time used   21 months

PLANNING TIP: In essence, this creates another "holding period" for taxpayers. Therefore, in many cases taxpayers must hold passive property for a minimum of 24 months to convert active or portfolio gain to passive gain.

WARNING: The end of the 24-month period terminates on the day the offer-to-purchase-and-sell agreement is executed, *not* on the day of closing. Therefore, the seller cannot simply defer closing for 24 months!

Income from a dealer's investment property—another recharacterization rule. Normally, dealer income is considered active income. But if the dealer held the property as an investment *at any time* before the income or gain is recognized, the income will be considered portfolio income. Sadly, any loss from such property remains passive or active depending upon the taxpayer's level of participation [§1.469-2T(c)(3)(iii)(A)].

PLANNING TIP: Dealers should *never* call property "investment" property!

Example: Robin originally purchases 20 acres of land to be held for appreciation. He later subdivides the property for a $200,000 profit. Because of this recharacterization rule, this normally active income must be recharacterized as portfolio income. Paradoxically, if Robin sold the property for a $200,000 loss, the loss would be considered active or passive, depending upon whether Robin "materially participated" in the subdivision activity.

WHAT ABOUT TRANSFERS OTHER THAN ARM'S-LENGTH SALES?

As previously discussed, under the passive loss rules, only upon a fully taxable, arm's-length disposition (i.e., taxable disposition of an entire interest in an activity) is any overall loss from the activity realized by the taxpayer recognized (triggered) and allowed against income (even against active or portfolio income) [§469(g)(1)].

Suspended losses are not triggered when disposition is not *arm's length*. Where the taxpayer transfers an interest in a passive activity but the *form* of ownership merely changes, *suspended losses generally are not allowed* under the theory that the gain or loss realized with respect to the activity has not been finally determined. Of course, any losses created by the transfer could potentially be deductible by other passive income.

Transfers not considered "taxable dispositions of the entire interest in the activity" are covered by special rules. Examples include the following:

1. Transfers to related parties
2. Transfer by reason of death [§469(g)(2)]
3. Transfer by gift [§469(j)(6)]
4. Installment sales [§469(e)(3)]
5. Activity ceases to be passive [§469(f)(1)]
6. Corporate changes from closely held [per §469] to not closely held [§469(f)(2)]
7. Nontaxable transfers

The rules are discussed in the following sections.

RELATED-PARTY TRANSACTIONS

WARNING: The penalty is too high. In most cases, do not sell passive property with carryover losses to a relative. Why?

Losses are not triggered. As transfers between related parties (e.g., transactions between a partner and the partnership, a shareholder and the corporation or a mother and a daughter) are not "arm's-length," any carry-forward loss is *not* triggered. The investor is *not* treated as having disposed of his or her entire interest in a passive activity if it is sold to a related party [within the meaning of §267(b) or §707(b)(1)].

Keep the loss. Suspended losses are not triggered, remain with the investor, and may be utilized to offset passive activity income.

When do we get the loss? If the entire interest is later sold by the related party to an *unrelated* party in a fully taxable transaction, then any suspended losses remaining may be deducted.

TRANSFER BY REASON OF DEATH

WARNING: The penalty is usually too high. In most cases, do not die holding passive property with carryover losses. Why?

Congress says, "You can take it with you!" A transfer of an investor's interest in an activity by reason of death causes suspended losses to be allowed (to the decedent) only to the extent they exceed the amount, if any, by which the basis of the interest in the activity is increased at death under §1014. *Suspended losses are eliminated to the* *extent of the amount of the basis increase.* The losses allowed are generally reported on the final return of the deceased taxpayer [§469(g)(2)].

> *Example:*   **Transfer by death causes suspended losses to be lost.** Dad dies with passive property having an adjusted basis of $40,000, suspended losses of $10,000, and a fair market value at the date of death of $75,000. The basis increase is $35,000 (fair market value at date of death or alternative value), and therefore none of the $10,000 suspended losses is deductible by either Dad or his children. The total of adjusted basis ($40,000) and the suspended losses ($10,000) did not exceed the fair market value of the property ($75,000).

TAX PLANNING: The result is that Dad has reported $10,000 more in income during his lifetime than what economically occurred. If Dad had sold the property prior to his death, he would have had a $10,000 deduction (the suspended losses) in the year of disposition, a $35,000 gain, and the children would have inherited property (cash, notes, etc.) with a fair market value of $75,000, net of tax paid on the $25,000 net gain.

Alternative tax planning. It might be recommended, though, that taxpayers die holding passive property with suspended losses when the property's appreciation exceeds the suspended losses.

> *Example:*   **Transfer by death sufficient for a partial recognition of suspended losses.** Dad dies with passive property having an adjusted basis of $40,000, suspended losses of $10,000, and a fair market value at the date of death of $45,000. As the basis increase under §1014 is only $5,000 ($45,000 – $40,000), the suspended losses allowed are limited to $5,000 ($10,000 suspended loss at time of death minus $5,000 increase in basis). The $5,000 loss now available to Dad is reported on his last income tax return.

TAX PLANNING: In this case, Dad should not normally own appreciated passive property with suspended losses at time of death. This may not be true when the adjusted basis exceeds the fair market value of the activity. Compare the "loss" property in the following example with the "gain" property in the previous example.

> *Example:*   **Transfer by death creates a complete recognition of a passive activity loss.** Dad dies with passive property having an adjusted basis of $40,000, $10,000 of suspended losses, and a $35,000 fair market value at date of death. The basis decrease for the children is $5,000 to $35,000 (fair market value at date of death). The tax result: All $10,000 of the suspended losses are deducted on the final return; none of the losses are lost.

TAX PLANNING: This yields a much more favorable tax result than dying with appreciated passive property. Therefore, proper estate and income tax planning "in contemplation of death" now requires analyzing the type of property, active versus passive, that the taxpayer owns, the taxpayer's suspended losses, and the adjusted basis and fair market value of passive activity property.

TRANSFER BY GIFT

WARNING: The penalty with this transfer is the conversion of a potentially current deduction to a long-term deduction. Why?

A gift of all or part of the taxpayer's interest in a passive activity does not trigger suspended losses. However, §469 allows suspended losses to be added to the basis of the property immediately before the gift [§469(j)(6)].

Example: Dad gifts passive property having an adjusted basis of $40,000, suspended losses of $10,000, and a fair market value at the date of the gift of $100,000. Dad cannot deduct the suspended losses in the year of the disposition. Instead, the suspended losses transfer with the property.

In this example, the basis to a child when property is transferred by gift is the carryover basis, $40,000, plus the suspended losses immediately before the gift, $10,000, for a new adjusted basis to the child of $50,000. If this is business property, the child's new depreciable basis is $50,000.

TAX PLANNING: If Dad sells the property, he triggers the loss, which is a current deduction. He then can gift the cash to his child, and let the child purchase other commercial property for $40,000, which would have a 39-year life. A much smarter tax solution!

INSTALLMENT SALES

WARNING: The penalty on a sale of passive property with a carryover loss is that the loss must be spread over the contract period, and if it was sold for cash, the loss would be immediately and entirely deductible in the year of sale! Why?

An installment sale of the taxpayer's entire interest in an activity in a fully taxable transaction triggers the allowance of suspended losses. However, the losses are only allowed in each year of the installment obligation in the ratio that the gain recognized in each year bears to the total gain on the sale [§469(g)(3)].

Installment gains will continue to be reported by using the gross profit percentage and then offset by a proportionate amount of carry-forward losses.

Installment reporting of passive losses. The new provision requires the taxpayer to report passive losses (if any) on the installment basis when the property is sold at a loss or at a gain less than the carry-forward losses. This creates deferral of recognition of loss and is a radical change for those (passive) properties sold for a loss after adding back the carry-forward losses. Under the normal installment sales rules [§453], the total losses for business and investment properties are fully deductible in the year of the sale and cannot be reported on the installment plan over the life of the contract.

PLANNING TIP: This new change will probably require sophisticated investors to sell passive property for cash only.

Pre-1987 installment sales with gain reported after 1986. Taxpayers who sold or exchanged an interest in a passive activity in a pre-1987 tax year and who recognize gain during a post-1986 tax year under the installment method of accounting may treat this as income from a passive activity. However, the taxpayer must be able to prove that the activity would have been treated as a passive activity if the PAL rules had applied for the year of disposition and all succeeding tax years.

ACTIVITY CEASES TO BE PASSIVE

Sometimes the passive loss rules may cease to apply to a taxpayer even though a disposition does not occur.

> *Example:* Jim, an attorney, owns Northwest Travel Agency, which is managed by a full-time manager. It has been producing a $20,000 loss for each of its last five years that Jim has *not* been materially participating. Jim quits the legal profession to spend full time in the travel agency. What happens to the $100,000 of previously nondeducted carry-forward passive losses?

Material participation. An individual who previously was passive in relation to a trade or business activity that generates net losses may begin materially participating in the activity [§469(f)(1)].

So what happens with the previous passive losses? When a taxpayer's participation in an activity is material in any year after a year (or years) during which he or she is not a material participant, previously suspended losses remain suspended and continue to be treated as passive activity losses. These previously suspended losses, however, unlike passive activity losses generally, are allowed against income from the activity realized after it ceases to be a passive activity with respect to the taxpayer. Of course, the matching-of-income burden of proof is on the taxpayer.

The $25,000 relief provision. A similar rule applies to active participation. A change in the nature of the taxpayer's involvement does not trigger the allowance of deductions carried over from prior taxable years. If a taxpayer begins to actively participate in an activity in which, in prior years, he or she did not actively participate, the rule allowing up to $25,000 of losses (or credits) from rental real estate activities against nonpassive income does not apply to losses from the activity carried over from such prior years.

CORPORATION CHANGES TO NOT CLOSELY HELD

A similar situation arises when a corporation (such as a closely held corporation or personal service corporation) subject to the passive loss rule ceases to be subject to the passive loss rule because it ceases to meet the definition of an entity subject to the rule [§469(f)(2)].

PLANNING TIP: If a closely held corporation makes a public offering of its stock and thereafter ceases to meet the stock ownership criteria for being closely held, it is no longer subject to the passive loss rule.

NONTAXABLE TRANSFERS

WARNING: The penalty with transferring tax-free (such as by means of a like-kind exchange) is that the investor's carry-forward loss becomes frozen in limbo—maybe never to be seen again. Why?

Nonrecognition transactions. An exchange of the taxpayer's interest in an activity in a nonrecognition transaction, such as an exchange governed by §351 (tax-free transfers into a corporation), §721 (tax-free transfers into a partnership), and §1031 (tax-free exchange of property held for productive use or for investment), in which no gain or loss is recognized, *does not trigger suspended losses.*

To the extent the taxpayer does recognize gain on the transaction (e.g., boot in an otherwise tax-free exchange), the gain could be treated as passive activity income against which passive losses may be deducted.

So what happens to the suspended losses? The taxpayer keeps the suspended losses (they do not transfer with the property), and the suspended losses become "frozen" *and, in most cases, deductible in the year of the disposition of the received property!*

A second major penalty. Such suspended losses may not be applied against income from the property that is attributable to a different activity from the one that the taxpayer exchanged. There is no special rule permitting suspended losses from the prior interest to be offset by income from the new activity unless it, too, is a passive activity.

> *Example:* **Contributing passive property for partnership interest.** Donna exchanged a duplex for a limited partnership interest, using a §721 non-recognition transaction. The suspended losses from the duplex would never be deductible until the limited partnership interest is sold. Two separate activities exist, a rental real estate activity and a limited partnership activity. If Donna would have continued to own the duplex and the duplex had future taxable income, the suspended losses would have become deductible prior to the time of disposition.

> *Example:* **Exchanging for like passive property.** Donna exchanges, via a §1031 tax-free exchange, a duplex for an apartment house. The suspended losses from the duplex are deductible against future taxable income of the apartment house. The same activity exists.

> *Example:* **Exchanging for like, but active, property—a terrible penalty!** Donna exchanges, via a §1031 tax-free exchange, an apartment house for a hotel. The suspended losses from the apartment house would not be deductible since a "passive" for an "active" activity exchange occurred. *This is a real tax penalty!* Therefore, unless Donna can show that income against which suspended losses are offset is clearly from the passive activity (which she exchanged for a different form of ownership), no such offset is permitted. If Donna cannot clearly prove like-kind activity or passive activity, the suspended losses are not deductible.

If a passive activity conducted by a general partnership is contributed to an S corporation, followed by the dissolution of the partnership, subsequent income from the activity may be offset by suspended losses from the activity of a shareholder who was formerly a passive general partner. When the taxpayer disposes of his or her entire interest in the property received in the tax-free exchange, then the remaining suspended losses, if any, are allowed in full.

Cancellation of Debt, Bankruptcy and Repossessions

INTRODUCTION

Cancellation of debt by lenders, investor bankruptcy and repossession of collateral often cause taxable income to the borrower! How can this be averted? The problems in this chapter will be avoided if the investor pays cash for all investments. Real estate, though, is primarily purchased with a combination of equity financing (money from the investor) and outside financing (money from banks, savings-and-loans or insurance companies). The higher the ratio of debt is to the equity (commonly called leverage), the higher the repayment of debt and chance of financial stress.

Leverage may cause both financial and tax problems for the investor when (not if) future problems occur, such as low occupancy, inflation or changes in the tax rules. The interest and principal reimbursement may eventually be more than the investor can pay back.

When the investor realizes that a problem exists to pay back the debt, this usually causes additional tax problems with the Internal Revenue Service—the focus of this chapter.

Settlement of a mortgage debt at a discount may create cancellation of debt income for the borrower. On the other hand, if the lending institution is not willing to settle the debt voluntarily, foreclosure generally occurs and the borrower has essentially a taxable sale. Even a voluntary transfer to avoid foreclosure is considered a taxable sale. When property is financed by the seller, called a purchase-money mortgage, special benefits exist. Bankruptcy and insolvency provisions soften the income tax created.

COMMENT: It is impossible to cover all the tax ramifications of troubled financing in one chapter. On the other hand, it is derelict not to alert the reader to the tax concerns. If any of the following options are contemplated by the investor, the decision should be planned with a competent tax attorney and tax preparer.

Borrowing starts out nontaxable. Often investors borrow a substantial portion of the funds when purchasing real estate. It also is common to refinance real estate to enable the investor to "pull out the equity." These economic benefits received by the investor are not taxable as there is a future obligation to repay the debt, even when the mortgage is in excess of the basis [*Woodsam v. Comm.,* 198 F2d 357 (2nd Cir. 1952)].

> ***Example:*** Cathy bought her home for $80,000 *cash* in 1988. The home is now worth $130,000, and she takes out a refinanced loan of $110,000. Even though she has immediate use of $30,000 more in cash than her original investment, no gain is realized at the time of the loan as she must repay the entire amount in the future.

The loan is part of the sales price. If later this debt obligation is partially or totally eliminated (most commonly by a sale), the borrower *then* enjoys an economic benefit related to the earlier receipt of the money. The borrower is not being required to repay all the cash received, which, in theory, increases the taxpayer's net worth. When property is sold, the sales price is the cash, other property received *and the amount of the unpaid liability,* even if the liability debt is a nonrecourse mortgage involving no personal risk [§1001(b); §1.1001-2(a); *Crane v. Comm.,* 47-1 USTC ¶9217, 331 U.S. 1; *Estate of Franklin v. Comm.,* 544 F2d 1045 (9th Cir. 1976)]. See Chapter 1 for additional discussion.

> ***Example (continued):*** If Cathy later sells the property for $130,000 (payable with $20,000 in cash and assumption of the $110,000 mortgage), her sales price includes both the cash and the assumed mortgage. Thus, Cathy's gain is $50,000 ($130,000 sale price less her original $80,000 purchase price), even though she only will receive $20,000 in cash.

A mortgage placed on property after purchase does not increase the owner's basis [*Woodsam v. Comm.,* 198 F2d 357 (2nd Cir. 1952)]. A mortgage is not a taxable event.

COMMENT: The effect of this rule is that in spite of the earlier financial enrichment, the gain (or loss) is postponed from the time the mortgage is taken out to the time when the property is sold or exchanged.

A settlement of a loan *at a discount* may create income. This can occur either as a gain at time of sale *or* as cancellation of debt (COD) income [§1001(b); §61(a)(12)].

When is a loan cancellation a sale? When it is in connection with the surrender of the property. When property is deeded to a secured lender in satisfaction of the debt, this is considered, in whole or in part, a taxable sale (as discussed later in this chapter).

> ***Example:*** **Sale.** Cathy buys her home for $80,000 *cash* in 1988. When the home is worth $130,000, she takes out a refinanced loan of $110,000. The property subsequently reduces in value to $85,000 and she talks the lending institution into accepting a "deed-in-lieu-of-foreclosure" (i.e., the bank forgives the $110,000 current mortgage if Cathy voluntarily deeds the property to the bank.) In this case, Cathy has a taxable sale that *may* be accompanied by cancellation of debt income, even though she has no assets to pay the taxes associated with this "sale"!

When is a loan cancellation COD income? To many investors' surprise, any reduction in the principal amount of the debt at the time of, or prior to, sale or exchange may result in "cancellation-of-indebtedness income" [§61(a)(12)].

> ***Example:*** **Prudent financial planning with a nasty tax result.** Cancellation-of-debt income is most common when the investor wishes to prepay a mortgage *at a discount* (i.e., for less than the principal balance of the mortgage). Most investors erroneously think this is simply a reduction in the original purchase price. In many cases the investor "realizes" COD income, whether the mortgage is recourse or nonrecourse and whether it is partially or fully prepaid [Rev. Rul. 82-202, 1982-2 CB 35]!

Some COD income dodges tax. Whether this "realized" income converts to "taxable" income depends on a number of factors. Some COD income escapes taxation by exclusions enumerated next.

CANCELLATION OF DEBT (COD)

General rule: Cancellation of debt (COD) creates income. An investor's gross income, for tax purposes, includes income from discharge of indebtedness, or cancellation of debt (COD), in addition to the more common sources of income, such as salaries and commissions [§61(a)(12)].

Taxable ordinary income. Cancellation of indebtedness income is taxable ordinary income and results when any of the borrower's debt is reduced (by compromise, negotiation or otherwise) for less than the full amount due. COD income most commonly emanates when restructuring or settling a loan [*U.S. v. Kirby Lumber Co.*, 284 U.S. 1 (1931)].

COD income creates a tax problem for the solvent borrower. As discussed previously, the solvent borrower generally is subject to an immediate tax from the income created by the cancellation of debt. The problem is that this reduction in mortgage debt does not produce the immediate cash flow necessary to pay the tax associated with this "phantom" income.

Example: **Reduction in debt.** Instead of transferring the property to the Last Chance Savings & Loan, Cathy talks the lending institution into reducing the $110,000 refinanced debt to the fair market value of $85,000, with the promise that Cathy will restart making her monthly payments. In this scenario, Cathy has received a $25,000 economic benefit and still has possession of the property. Therefore, she has a $25,000 COD income tax problem.

Forgiveness of nonrecourse debt also creates COD income—not reduction in purchase price.   The lender's reduction of the principal amount of an undersecured nonrecourse loan (i.e., the borrower is not personally liable on the note and the lender looks to the property for security) results in COD income, not a purchase price reduction. The fair market value of the property is irrelevant when determining COD income or purchase price reduction [Rev. Rul. 91-31, IRB 1991-20].

In a 1934 case involving nonrecourse financing, the court decided that subsequent reduction in the debt *would* be a purchase price reduction and therefore not create an immediate income. Presently, the courts and the IRS disagree on this point [*Fulton Gold Corp. v. Comm.,* 31 BTA 519 (1934)].

Example: In 1998, wealthy Fran purchases an office building from Kukla for $1,000,000, borrowing the entire amount from Pioneer Federal S&L with a nonrecourse note (i.e., Fran has no personal liability with respect to the note) secured by the office building. In 1999, when the property's fair market value is $800,000 and the outstanding principal on the note is still $1,000,000, Pioneer agrees to reduce the note to $800,000. The $200,000 is taxable as COD income to Fran in 1999 (not a reduction in the purchase price) unless she is bankrupt or insolvent.

Exception to the COD income rule—a relief provision.   If the cancellation of debt (in whole or in part) occurs (1) in bankruptcy, (2) to an insolvent borrower, or (3) with qualified farm debt, this normally taxable income becomes *not* taxable [§108(a)(1)].

COMMENT: Many financially troubled transactions combine both sales *and* cancellation of debt. If the cancellation of a loan is part of the sales price and not a stand-alone cancellation of debt, it may *not* be excluded by this relief provision and is therefore taxable! This "short sale" is fully illustrated later in this chapter.

Excluding COD in a bankruptcy case.   Income from the discharge of debt incurred by a taxpayer in bankruptcy is excluded from income altogether, provided the bankruptcy case is not dismissed prior to debt discharge. However, to the extent available, a certain amount of a borrower's future tax benefits (called "tax attributes" and discussed later) will be reduced. This exclusion from income is allowed, though, regardless of whether the amount of such income exceeds the borrower's future tax benefits (tax attributes) available for reduction [§108(a)(1)(A); §108(b)].

What is bankruptcy? Bankruptcy is the status of a person on whose behalf a petition has been filed and proceedings are in progress in a federal bankruptcy court.

PLANNING TIP: Income from debt discharge *before* the filing of a bankruptcy petition does not qualify for this exclusion (and may not be entitled to either the insolvency or qualified farm-indebtedness exclusion). Thus, for tax-planning purposes, it is important for a borrower who will be involved in a bankruptcy to have the debt discharged through the bankruptcy court and not by voluntary action of the taxpayer.

Excluding COD when the taxpayer is insolvent. Gross income also does not include COD income when the borrower is insolvent. However, the amount excluded cannot exceed the amount by which the borrower is insolvent. Certain of the borrower's future tax benefits (i.e., tax attributes) must be reduced by the amount of income excluded under this insolvency exception. If the borrower remains insolvent after the discharge, all income from the discharge is permanently excluded regardless of whether the amount of such income exceeds the amount of future tax benefits (i.e., tax attributes) available for reduction [§108(a)(1)(B); §108(a)(3); §108(b)].

What is insolvency? Being insolvent means the investor's liabilities exceed the fair market value (FMV) of his or her assets determined immediately before the discharge (i.e., FMV assets less liabilities equals a negative number). Nonrecourse debt is included in this calculation only when it is involved in the debt discharge transaction itself, and in such cases only the amount discharged is counted [§108(d)(3); Rev. Rul. 92-53, 1992-27 IRB].

Excluding COD when discharging qualified farm debt. Cancellation of certain farm debt may also be excluded from COD income even if the farmer remains solvent! Debt is qualified farm debt if the taxpayer is directly operating a farm business and at least 50% of the farmer's gross receipts for the three tax years preceding the year of debt cancellation were from the farming business. Again, the penalty is the reduction of certain future tax benefits and the exclusion cannot exceed the tax benefits [§108(g)(3); §1017(b)(2)].

Reduction of certain future tax benefits (tax attributes). The price (or curse) for excluding COD from current gross taxable income under any of the above three exclusions is that the borrower loses certain future tax benefits, such as net operating loss carryover and future depreciation deductions [§108(b)]. However, prior to decreasing these future tax benefits, the borrower *may* elect to reduce the basis of his or her *depreciable* property. This reduction is done at the beginning of the tax year *following* the tax year of the debt discharge.

Election to reduce basis of depreciable property. The borrower may elect (on Form 982, which must be attached to the taxpayer's timely filed income tax return relating to the year of the discharge) to apply any of the COD income *first* to reducing the basis of depreciable property (but not below zero) *before* reducing any other future tax benefits. Depreciable property means any property subject to depreciation, but only if the basis reduction reduces future potential depreciation [§108(b)(5)].

> *Example:* **Why electing to first reduce depreciable basis might be good tax planning.** This election allows the borrower to reduce the depreciable basis (for commercial real property, an expense spread over the next 39 years) and preserve a net operating loss (potentially currently deductible).

The exclusion of COD as a result of bankruptcy or insolvency requires a corresponding reduction of future tax benefits [§108(b)].

In the absence of an election to first reduce depreciable basis, future tax benefits (tax attributes) of the borrower shall be reduced to the extent of debt discharge income (or its equivalent) in the following order:

1. *Net operating losses:* Reduce NOL dollar for dollar.
2. *General business credit:* Reduce at a 33.3% rate for each dollar of COD excluded.
3. *Alternative minimum tax credits:* Reduce the minimum tax credits as of the beginning of the tax year *immediately after* the tax year of the discharge.
4. *Capital losses:* Reduce dollar for dollar.
5. *Basis reduction:* Reduce, dollar for dollar, the basis of both depreciable and *nondepreciable* property. But this basis cannot be reduced below total liabilities immediately after the discharge [§108(b)(2)(D)].

PLANNING TIP: If the taxpayer makes the previously mentioned election to first reduce depreciated basis, then basis can be reduced below total liabilities all the way to zero [§108(b)(5)]. See the next example, which shows when an election is not smart.

---

6. *Passive activity losses (and credits):* Reduce the passive activity losses and credit carryovers from the tax year of the discharge.
7. *Foreign tax credit carryovers:* Reduce at a 33.3% rate for each dollar of COD excluded.

PLANNING TIP: The above-mentioned election to first reduce depreciable basis may cause tax benefits to be pointlessly eliminated when the total liabilities remaining after the COD are high in relationship to the property's basis.

> *Example:* **How electing to first reduce depreciable basis might be bad tax planning.** Mary is discharged of $350,000 of debt, which she excludes because she is insolvent even after the COD. Immediately after the cancellation,

her debts are $650,000 and the fair market value of her assets is $600,000 with a basis of $400,000 ($300,000 depreciable and $100,000 nondepreciable). Mary's tax benefits are a net operating loss (NOL) of $50,000 and the $400,000 property basis.

If Mary does not reduce her depreciable basis first, she must initially eliminate her NOL. However, her total after-discharge liabilities ($650,000) exceed her total after-discharge basis ($400,000), with the result that none of her basis need be reduced even though $350,000 of COD is excluded [§1017(b)(2)].

If Mary elected to reduce her depreciable basis first, she would have lost the entire $300,000 adjusted basis of her depreciable basis and would still be required to reduce her $50,000 NOL [§1017(b)(2)]!

The price of fun—basis reduction requires recapture (an increase amount of taxable gain) when the property is sold in the future. If the basis of a property is reduced and the property is later sold (or otherwise disposed of) at a gain, the part of the gain created by the COD basis reduction is taxable as ordinary income, not capital gain. This is Congress's way of giving the taxpayer a current benefit at the time of the COD but assuring recapture of that added benefit when the taxpayer later sells the property (preferably for cash, as this could result in 100% of the sales price being taxable as ordinary income)[§1017(d)].

Other common income exclusions when there is a cancellation of debt. *COD income is excluded if the payment of the liability would be deductible* [§108(e)(2)].

> **Example:** Cameron incurs $1,000 of deductible interest expense but talks his lender down to $600. Even though there has been a $400 cancellation of debt, Cameron may exclude the COD income because the payment for interest is a deductible expense. In addition, there is no reduction of any future tax benefits or tax attributes.

Other exclusions from COD income include (1) a lender's canceling a loan in exchange for a capital contribution to a corporation and (2) a borrower corporation's transferring stock to a creditor [§108(e)(6); §108(e)(8), (10)].

A wonderful relief for installment sales—a purchase price adjustment [§108(e)(5)]. If property is sold on the installment plan and the seller subsequently reduces the installment debt amount, the reduction to the buyer of this owner-financed debt (called a purchase-money mortgage) is a reduction of the purchase price, not COD income. This exception only applies if the buyer is neither bankrupt nor insolvent [§108(e)(5)(C),(B)].

> **Example:** Jeanette purchased her home from Shannon for $100,000 with Shannon "carrying the paper" in the amount of $85,000. After two years, the property value slipped to $80,000, with Jeanette still owing $84,000. Shannon reduced the

balance due to $80,000. This normally taxable $4,000 cancellation of debt is actually a nontaxable $4,000 reduction of the $100,000 purchase price.

WARNING: This relief is *not* available to buyers borrowing money from banks, savings and loan institutions, and mortgage companies unless these lending institutions are also the sellers—not a common situation except when you are buying from the Resolution Trust Corporation! Why?

Requirements to use the purchase price reduction. To use this purchase-price-reduction exception, the lender must also be the seller and the debt reduction must occur between the original buyer and the original seller of the property. It does not apply if (1) the purchase money debt has been transferred by the seller to a third party, (2) the buyer has transferred the property to a third party (but see PLR 9037003 that allowed a reduction of purchase price to a subsequent buyer upon the original seller's reduction of debt) or (3) the debt is reduced because of factors not involving direct agreements between the buyer and seller, such as the running of the statute of limitations on the enforcement of the debt.

> *Example:* Jeanette bought Shannon's home for $100,000, borrowing $85,000 from the Last Chance Savings & Loan. When the home's value dropped to $80,000, Cathy talked the lending institution into reducing the $84,000 remaining debt to the fair market value of $80,000, with the promise that Cathy would continue making her monthly payments. In this scenario, Cathy has received $4,000 of taxable COD income. It is *not* a purchase price reduction as the money came from a third-party lender, not the original seller!

Miscellaneous tax treatments of solvent borrowers. Some other COD income items that are excluded are described below.

The debt forgiveness is a gift. When the forgiveness or reduction of the loan is really a gift from the lender to the borrower, no COD income exists. But it is not a gift simply because the debt is reduced voluntarily by the lender. It must be coupled with an intent to "donate" with "detached generosity," a requirement almost impossible to meet in the financial community. Normally, the discharge of a mortgage for an amount less than the principal balance due is taxable as income to the borrower because the lender does not act with disinterested generosity but is motivated by sound economic reasons of ridding itself of problem or low-interest mortgages [*William DiLaura*, 53 TCM 1077, TC Memo 1987-291].

The debt is acquired by a related party. Can we get around this rule by having one of our relatives, or one of our corporate or partnership businesses, buy the loan at a discount? No. An outstanding loan acquired from an unrelated lender by a person *related to the borrower* is treated as if the borrower had acquired the debt. If the debt is acquired below face value, COD income exists.

DISCHARGE OF REAL PROPERTY BUSINESS DEBT

Introduction. As mentioned previously, the discharge of indebtedness generally gives rise to "phantom" income to the third-party debtor-taxpayer who is not bankrupt, solvent or a farmer. The newest exception to this general rule applies to certain real property business debt. The amount elected to be excluded cannot exceed the aggregate adjusted basis of the taxpayer's depreciable real property immediately before the debt discharge. Any amount excluded is treated as a reduction in the property's basis, which is similar to the §108(e)(5) purchase price adjustment allowed the buyer on owner-financed debt [§108(a)(1)(D); §108(c)].

COMMENT: Prior to 1987, the Code contained an elective exception for the discharge of qualified business debt [§108(c) was repealed by the Tax Reform Act of 1986]. This same §108(c) relief provision is back, in a more restrictive form, starting in 1993. This is recognition by Congress that the value of real property has declined, often below the underlying debt it secures.

New Exclusion for Debt Discharge Income

Debt relief on real property may not create COD income. Starting in 1993, Congress granted taxpayers, other than C corporations, the option of excluding from income the discharge of qualified real property business indebtedness. The price to pay is that the amount so excluded is treated as a reduction in the basis of that property (therefore, the future depreciation will be lower and the gain on sale will be larger) and the reduction cannot exceed the basis of certain depreciable real property of the taxpayer.

> *Example:* Robert purchases a $1,000,000 office building financed by a $900,000 nonrecourse loan from the Last Chance S&L and $100,000 of his own cash. Afterward, the value plummets to $700,000 and Robert goes to his friendly loan officer and says "You can have this pig back." The loan officer, as an alternative, offers to reduce his loan from $900,000 to $700,000 if he continues to make the agreed monthly payments. Robert accepts. Under prior law Robert would have had $200,000 of "phantom" taxable income from discharge of debt as he is not bankrupt, insolvent or a farmer. This new law allows an alternative—Robert simply reduces his depreciable basis by $200,000.

Required Qualifications

Qualified real property business indebtedness (QRPBI) is debt that meets the following three requirements:

1. The debt is incurred or assumed in connection with real property used in a trade or business (but qualified farm debt cannot be QRPBI).

PLANNING TIP: This is more restrictive than in the past; the old rules allowed *all* qualified business debt forgiveness to be excluded, not just real property business debt.

---

2. The debt is secured by that real property.

PLANNING TIP: This rule can be a real tax "sucker-punch" for the unwary businessperson! Secured debt is defined as a security instrument (such as a mortgage, deed of trust or land contract), and

(a) the qualified property is specific security for the payment of the debt;
(b) in the event of default, the property could be subject to the satisfaction of the debt; and
(c) *it is recorded* [§1.163-10T(o)(1)].

PLANNING TIP: It is very common for business debt (e.g., revolving credit line) to not be recorded, which means the investor's debt does not qualify for this relief provision . . . because of a sneaky technicality! Also, general liens on all business property would not qualify as no specific property is identified.

---

3. The taxpayer makes a proper election.

The election must be made on Form 982. New regulations provide that Form 982 must be attached to the return as originally filed for the year in which the discharge occurred. However, if the taxpayer can show reasonable cause, the taxpayer can file the election with an amended return. The revised form includes a new check box to make the election (box 1d) and a line (line 4) to indicate the amount to be applied against depreciable basis [IRS Ann. 94-11, 1994-3 IRB and Temp. Reg 1.108(c)-1T].

Post-1992 Debt Must Be "Acquisition" Debt

Real property business indebtedness does not include indebtedness incurred or assumed on or after January 1, 1993, unless it qualifies under one of two options.

PLANNING TIP: This is a grandfather clause that allows the investor to be exempt from the "tracing" rules for debt created prior to 1993.

---

1. Certain refinanced debt. QRPBI includes debt incurred to refinance qualified real property business debt incurred or assumed before that date (but only to the extent the amount of debt does not exceed the amount of debt being refinanced).

PLANNING TIP: The refinanced debt in excess of the debt just prior to refinancing is not qualified debt unless it is qualified acquisition debt.

COMMENT: Does this mean that as the debt is paid off, the "qualified" real property debt slowly becomes zero? Future regulations will tell!

---

2. Qualified acquisition indebtedness. QRPBI includes qualified acquisition indebtedness. Qualified acquisition debt is debt incurred to acquire, construct or substantially improve real property that is secured by such debt, *and* debt resulting from the refinancing of qualified acquisition debt to the extent the amount of such debt does not exceed the amount being refinanced.

PLANNING TIP: When is an improvement "substantial"? Until future regulations specifically define *substantial* in this context, uncertainty exists. Definition of the word *substantial* as used in other IRC sections ranges from 15% to 35% or more of the fair market value. On a $500,000 property, this would require an improvement to cost $75,000 to $175,000 before the debt would be qualified! Would this mean if the business borrows $50,000 for real property improvements that the business debt would not qualify? It would seem so.

Limitations on Exclusion from Income

Must take into account taxpayers' basis, outstanding debt and fair market value. The amount of income excluded because of the discharge of any QRPBI cannot exceed the taxpayer's basis in the property. In addition, it cannot exceed the excess of

1. the outstanding principal amount of such debt (immediately before the discharge) over
2. the fair market value (immediately before the discharge) of the business real property that is security for the debt.

COMMENT: For this purpose, the fair market value of the property is reduced by the outstanding principal amount of any other QRPBI secured by the property immediately before the discharge.

Example: On July 1, 1998, Dan owns a building worth $150,000 and used in his business that is subject to a first mortgage securing a $110,000 debt of Dan's and a second mortgage securing a $90,000 debt of Dan's. Dan is neither bankrupt nor insolvent and neither debt is qualified farm indebtedness. Dan agrees with his second mortgagee to reduce the second mortgage debt to $30,000, resulting in discharge of indebtedness income in the amount of $60,000. Under §108(c), assuming that Dan has sufficient basis in business real property to absorb the reduction, Dan can elect to exclude $50,000 of that discharge from gross income. This is because the principal amount of the discharged debt immediately before the discharge (i.e., $90,000) exceeds the fair market value of the property securing it (i.e., $150,000 of free and clear value less $110,000 of other qualified business real property debt, or $40,000) by $50,000. The remaining $10,000 of discharge is included in gross income.

Additional overall limitation. The amount excluded may not exceed the aggregate adjusted bases (determined as of the first day of the next taxable year or, if earlier, the date of disposition) of depreciable real property held by the taxpayer immediately before the discharge, determined after any reduction for insolvent or bankrupt taxpayers or solvent farmers. Depreciable real property acquired in contemplation of the discharge is treated as not held by the taxpayer immediately before the discharge [§108(c)(2)(B)].

Reduction in Basis

The amount of debt discharge excluded is applied (using the rules of §1017) to reduce the basis of business real property held by the taxpayer at the beginning of the taxable year following the taxable year in which the discharge occurs.

TAX PLANNING: There is no specific requirement that the basis to be reduced must be the property securing the debt.

Calculating Recapture as Ordinary Income

The recapture amount may disappear into the future. On a later sale of the property, the basis of which was reduced by this reduction-in-basis provision, the amount of the basis reduction that is recaptured as ordinary income is reduced over the time the taxpayer continues to hold the property, as the taxpayer forgoes depreciation deductions due to the basis reduction.

The exclusion is not limited to the basis of the particular real property secured by the discharged debt; rather, the aggregate adjusted bases of all depreciable real property (determined as of the first day of the next taxable year or, if earlier, the date of disposition) is available.

Partnerships and Partners

The election to use the exclusion is made at the partner level. However, the determination as to whether the debt is qualified real property debt is made at the partnership level [§108(d)(6)].

S Corporations and S Shareholders

All elections are at entity level. In applying this provision to income from the discharge of indebtedness of an S corporation, the election is made by the S corporation, and the exclusion and basis reduction are both made at the S-corporation level. The shareholders' basis in their stock is not adjusted by the amount of debt discharge income that is excluded at the corporate level [§108(d)(7)].

TAX PLANNING: As a result of these rules, if an amount is excluded from the income of an S corporation under this provision, the income flowing through to the shareholders will be reduced (compared to what the shareholders' income would have been without the exclusion). Where the reduced basis in the corporation's depreciable property later results in additional income (or a smaller loss) to the corporation because of reduced depreciation or additional gain (or smaller loss) on disposition of the property, the additional income (or smaller loss) will flow through to the shareholders at that time and will then result in a larger increase (or smaller reduction) in the shareholders' basis than if this provision had not previously applied. Thus, the provision simply defers income to the shareholders.

Effective date. The provision is effective with regard to discharges of indebtedness occurring after December 31, 1992, in tax years ending after that date.

TAX RESULTS WHEN BORROWER LOSES PROPERTY BY FORECLOSURE, DEED IN LIEU OF FORECLOSURE OR ABANDONMENT

As mentioned in this chapter's introduction, when an investor surrenders property to a lender in exchange for debt forgiveness, phantom income from the transaction may be created, either as "income from the discharge of debt" or as "income from the sale of property" or a combination of both.

Methods of Surrender of Property by Borrower to Lender

Property commonly is surrendered by a borrower to a lender by the following methods:

1. Foreclosure
2. Deed in lieu of foreclosure
3. Repossession
4. Abandonment

Foreclosure—A Forced Surrender of Property by the Borrower to the Lender

Definition. When a borrower fails to pay a mortgage on time, the lender generally starts legal proceedings to sell the property securing that debt. This involuntary sale normally causes adverse tax ramifications to the borrower.

Debt relief causes transfer of property to be a sale—and sale creates a gain (or loss). A foreclosure, even though the investor has no choice, is a *sale* for tax purposes (it is not a gift from the borrower back to the lender!) [*G. Hammel v. Helvering*, SCt, (*rev'g* CA-6), 41-1 USTC ¶9169, 311 U.S. 504, 61, S. Ct 368].

Review on calculating gain. As with any sale, the gain or loss is calculated by subtracting the taxpayer's adjusted basis from the "amount realized" (as discussed in Chapter 1).

Personal liability (recourse debt) versus nonpersonal liability (nonrecourse debt). Strangely, the amount realized, which is usually the debt forgiven in these situations, may be different, depending on whether the taxpayer is personally liable on the mortgage (i.e., a recourse mortgage) or not personally liable on the mortgage (i.e., a nonrecourse mortgage) [*J. G. Abramson*, CA-2, 42-1 USTC ¶9200, 124 F2d 416].

A foreclosure when the borrower is personally liable (a recourse mortgage) requires a two-step calculation. Generally the deemed "sales price" when a recourse mortgage is turned back to the lender is the actual debt relief as a result of the foreclosure. But this sales price cannot include any COD income. Therefore, a foreclosure involving a recourse debt must be bifurcated or divided into two parts: (1) gain (or loss)

FIGURE 16.1   Cancellation of Debt Formula

$\underline{\$\hspace{2.5cm}}$
Recourse debt

$\underline{\text{\$ Ordinary income (A)(B)}}$ Step 2
Income from discharge of debt

$\underline{\$\hspace{2.5cm}}$ (C)
Sales proceeds

$\underline{\text{\$ Capital gain or loss}}$ Step 1
Gain (or loss) from foreclosure

$\underline{\$\hspace{2.5cm}}$
Adjusted basis

(A) COD income can be offset if bankrupt or insolvent (§108)
(B) Taxable only in the year lender releases liability
(C) Sales price at sheriff's sale or fair market value

created by foreclosure and (2) income from the discharge of indebtedness [§1.1001-2(a)(2), and (c)(Example 8); Rev. Rul. 90-16, 1990-1 CB 12; *Bressi v. Comm.*, TC Memo 1991-651, 62TCM 1668].

The income on the surrender of secured property in exchange for the discharge of recourse debt is calculated as follows:

Step 1. Gain or loss from foreclosure. The sales price (or fair market value when there is no sale) of property surrendered less the property's adjusted basis is the gain or loss from the disposition of property (generally capital gain or loss).

Step 2. COD income. The excess of the amount of the debt discharge over the property fair market value, if any, is income from the discharge of indebtedness (ordinary income). This is the only amount that may be sheltered by bankruptcy and insolv relief provisions. Of course, there is no COD income if the borrower remains liable the deficiency [§1.1001-2(a)(2); Rev. Rul. 90-16, 1990-1 CB 12].

The formula when surrendering secured property in exchange for the disch recourse debt is shown in Figure 16.1 above.

> *Example:* **Recourse debt.** Sharon purchased property for $85,000 $80,000 30-year mortgage (recourse debt). After eight years, she has a of depreciation of $35,000 (using a 15-year life), leaving her an adjusned $50,000, but she has paid down the mortgage to only $75,000. Liferty Sharon stops making payments. The lending institution forecloses ain-is sold at sheriff's sale for $60,000 and *the lending institution forgi*

ing amount due as it determines there "tain't no blood left in that turnip." Even though Sharon is broke, the IRS doesn't care—she has both capital gain and ordinary income.

$75,000
_____
Recourse debt

$15,000 Ordinary income (A)(B)   Step 2
_____
Income from discharge of debt

$60,000   (C)
_____
Sales proceeds

$10,000 Capital gain or loss   Step 1
_____
Gain (or loss) from foreclosure

$50,000
_____
Adjusted basis

(A) COD income can be offset if bankrupt or insolvent (§108)
(B) Taxable only in the year lender releases liability
(C) Sales price at sheriff's sale or fair market value

PLANNING TIP: Only the COD income can be offset if Sharon is bankrupt or insolvent. She still is taxed on the $10,000 capital gain.

---

foreclosure when the borrower is not personally liable (a nonrecourse mortgage) requires only a one-step approach. In a nonrecourse debt, the lending institution looks only to the property for recovery of the mortgage and cannot additionally look to the borrower's other assets. In effect, the investor never owes more than the fair market value of the asset securing the loan! Therefore, the sales price is the entire nonrecourse debt even if the fair market value is less than the amount of the loan. The result here will never be COD income in a nonrecourse debt [§1.1001-2(b); *Comm., v. Tufts,* SCt, 83-1 USTC ¶9328, 461 U.S. 300 (1983)].

The gain or loss on the surrender of secured property in exchange for the discharge of nonrecourse indebtedness is calculated as follows:

Gain or loss from foreclosure (the one and only step). Subtract the adjusted basis from the mortgage relief. Foreclosure results in income to the borrower when the mortgage loan exceeds the borrower's adjusted basis in the secured property [§7701(g)].

Nonrecourse debt. Sharon purchases property for $200,000 with a 20-year mortgage (nonrecourse debt). After eight years she has accumulated depreciation of $35,000 (using 15-year life), leaving her an adjusted basis of $165,000. But she has paid down the mortgage to only $190,000. Life is tough and Sharon stops making payments. The lending institution forecloses and the property is sold at a sheriff's sale for $150,000 (which is irrelevant as Sharon is not personally responsible for any deficiency judgment).

The formula when surrendering secured property in exchange for the discharge of non-recourse debt is as follows:

$N/A
_____
Recourse debt

$ N/A   Step 2
_____
Income from discharge of debt

$190,000   (C)
Sales proceeds are
    nonrecourse debt

$10,000 Capital gain or loss   Step 1
_____
Gain (or loss) from foreclosure

$165,000
_____
Adjusted basis

COMMENT: The calculation is the same even if the property is voluntarily transferred by a deed in lieu of foreclosure, discussed later in this chapter [§1.1001-2(c)(7)].

Character of the gain or loss in a foreclosure. Foreclosure gain or loss is governed by the normal gain or loss rules; that is, a capital asset creates a capital gain or loss, business assets create capital gain and ordinary loss, and dealer realty creates ordinary gain and loss. Tragically, foreclosure on a personal residence may create a taxable gain or a nondeductible loss! The $250,000/$500,000 MFJ exclusion rule is available (see Chapter 3 for the general rules).

Year to report the gain or income. Gain or loss on foreclosure is generally reportable in the year the foreclosure sale and debt discharge takes place unless state law allows the borrower a right-of-redemption period (e.g., one-year right of redemption). Then the gain is reported after the right-of-redemption period lapses [*William A. Belcher, Jr. v. Comm.*, 24 TCM 1; TC Memo 1965-1; *Derby Realty Corp. v. Comm.*, 35 BTA 335 (1937)].

PLANNING TIP: If the investor needs the loss, or can use the gain in a specific tax year, this loss can be deferred or accelerated by voluntarily quitclaiming his or her right of redemption to the lender [*Atmore Realty Co.*, BTA Memo, Dec. 12,517-A, April 30, 1942].

Deed in Lieu of Foreclosure—A Voluntary Transfer of Property to the Lending Institution

Definition. In a deed in lieu of foreclosure, a borrower voluntarily delivers the property deed to the lender before the lender starts foreclosing on the property (normally to avoid the embarrassment and/or the legal fees involved in a foreclosure).

> **COMMENT:** What a surprise, because:

It is a taxable sale. A voluntary transfer by a deed in lieu of foreclosure is a sale for tax purposes [§1.1001-2(a)(4)(iii); Rev. Rul. 78-164, 1978-1 CB 264; Rev. Rul. 90-16, 1990-1 CB 12].

Recourse debt. Similar to a foreclosure, a deed in lieu of foreclosure involving a recourse debt must also be bifurcated, or divided into two parts: (1) gain (or loss) created by the transfer and (2) income from the discharge of indebtedness [§1.1001-2(a)(2); Rev. Rul. 90-16, 1990-1 CB 12].

The two-step approach formula. The income on the surrender of secured property in exchange for the discharge of recourse indebtedness is the same as is used in a foreclosure (previously discussed).

> **PLANNING TIP:** When the investor is insolvent (or bankrupt), keep the capital gain on sale (step 1) low and the COD income (step 2) high. COD income may end up being excluded from income. The gain on sale will never enjoy this exclusion.

How? This may be done by obtaining a credible *low* fair market value appraisal of the surrendered property.

> *Example:* **Recourse debt.** As in the prior example, Sharon finds herself owing $75,000 on a property worth $60,000 that has an adjusted basis of $50,000. Instead of Sharon's going through foreclosure proceedings, she agrees to voluntarily transfer the property by a deed in lieu of foreclosure.

$75,000
Recourse debt

$15,000 Ordinary income (A)(B)   Step 2
Income from discharge of debt

$60,000 _____ (C)
Fair market value

$10,000 Capital gain or loss   Step 1
Gain (or loss) from foreclosure

$50,000
Adjusted basis

(A) COD income can be offset if bankrupt or insolvent (§108)
(B) Taxable only in the year lender releases liability
(C) Sales price at sheriff's sale or fair market value

PLANNING TIP: If the fair market value is low enough, this can create a deductible capital "loss," with the accompanying increase of COD income being completely excluded by the bankrupt or insolvent investor!

Nonrecourse debt. As discussed previously, the rules generally are the same as for foreclosures, that is, the transaction is treated as a sale.

There is no ordinary COD income until the liability is released. What happens if the lending institution exercises its right to recover, via a deficiency judgment, for the unrecovered portion (e.g., Sharon's $15,000 in the previous example)? In this situation the lender does *not* release the owner from liability and decides to collect the deficiency. This results in the borrower's not having COD income unless, and until, the debt is discharged.

Losses are possible. If the adjusted basis of the property exceeds the amount realized at time of transfer, there is a loss [Rev. Rul. 73-36, 1973-1 CB 372; *E. Harris,* 34 TCM 597, TC Memo, 1975-125].

> *Example:* **A loss on foreclosure.** Linda purchased property for $135,000 with an $80,000, 30-year mortgage (recourse debt). After eight years she has accumulated depreciation of $35,000 (15-year life), leaving her an adjusted basis of $100,000, but she has paid down the mortgage to only $75,000. Linda stops making payments, the lending institution forecloses, the property is sold at a sheriff's sale for $60,000 and *the lending institution forgives the remaining amount due.*

$75,000
———————
Recourse debt

           $15,000 Ordinary income   Step 2
           Income from discharge of debt

$60,000   (A)
———————
Sales proceeds

                $40,000 loss   Step 1
           Gain (or loss) from foreclosure

$100,000
———————
Adjusted basis
(A) COD income can be offset if bankrupt or insolvent (§108)

Repossession

Repossession is the act of taking back property from a buyer who has failed to make payments when due.

Is it a forced taking? If repossession amounts to an involuntary transfer of the property by the secured creditor, which is most often the case, the tax consequences to the borrower are the same as those outlined in the "foreclosure" section.

Or is it a voluntary transfer? If, on the other hand, repossession amounts to a voluntary surrender of property by a borrower to the secured creditor, the tax consequences parallel those for the deed in lieu of foreclosure.

Abandonment—A Voluntary Surrender of Property by the Borrower

Abandonment occurs when an investor voluntarily surrenders possession of real estate without vesting this interest in any other person. Is an abandonment treated like a sale or exchange? Early case law indicated that certain abandonments were not sales and might result in an ordinary loss [*W. W. Hoffman*, CA-2, 41-1 ¶9280, 117 F2d 987].

An abandonment is treated like a sale. Recent Tax Court cases find that a sale occurs when property is abandoned and that a capital loss, rather than an ordinary loss, results for the borrower [*E. L. Freeland*, 74 TX 970, CCH Dec. 37127; *M. L. Middleton*, 77 TC 310, CCH Dec. 38,124, *aff'd* CA-11, 693 F2d 124, 82-2 USTC ¶9713; *L. J. Arkin*, 76 TC 1048, CCH Dec. 38,017; *J. W. Yarbo*, CA-5, 84-2 USTC ¶9691, *aff'g* 45 TCM 170, CCH Dec. 39513(M), TC Memo 1982-675].

> **Example:** A taxpayer abandoned a residence when the fair market value of the residence was substantially less than the amount of the first and second mortgages encumbering the house. The IRS states that an abandonment is like a voluntary sale (per §1001). The IRS also suggested (but did not rule) that the §1034 rollover provision may be available [PLR 9120010].

Other courts have ruled that abandonment does not create a taxable loss, as there has been no sale or exchange since the taxpayer has not committed to the foreclosure action.

Short Pay or Short Sales—How Are They Taxed?

One California phenomenon in the residential mortgage market is dubbed a "short pay" or a "short sale." Typically, the lender agrees to the sale of mortgaged property by the debtor for an amount less than the outstanding nonrecourse debt. In addition, the debtor usually is required to pay some cash to the lender.

The problem. If the loan being extinguished is nonrecourse, is the sales price the loan (reduced by the cash the debtor pays to the lender) or is it the amount that the new buyer actually pays for the property?

COMMENT: It seems the debtor is merely selling the property on the lender's behalf (the lender must agree to the sale) and that the amount realized by the debtor is the amount of the debt pursuant to §1.1001-2(a)(1) as would be the case if the lender took back the property.

Example:

Basis	$130,000
Outstanding loan	105,000
Sales price	85,000

Does the transaction result only in loss on sale as follows?

Basis	$130,000
Debt	− 103,000
Loss on sale	$ 27,000*

Or, does the transaction unfairly result in cancellation of debt (COD) income and loss on sale as follows?

Basis	$130,000
Sales price	− 85,000
Loss on sale*	$ 45,000*
Debt	$105,000
Sales price	− 85,000
COD income	$ 20,000†

---

* Loss would not be deductible if this were the debtor's personal residence.
† Yet the same taxpayer would have $20,000 of "phantom" income. Under the first scenario, there is no "phantom" income.

TAX PLANNING: The IRS has unofficially told this author that it will respond to the above scenario soon! Make sure you check with your tax practitioner for current status.

REPOSSESSION OF SELLER-FINANCED PROPERTY

When the seller forecloses on property sold to another on the installment plan, what are the tax results for the seller? Nothing, you say, as the seller is just getting back what he or she originally owned? Wrong!

A gain is recognized when property is reacquired. Even though the foreclosure has the seller (lender) in effect reacquiring property he or she previously owned, the seller now has all the payments previously made by the exbuyer *and* the entire property back! Therefore, the government has devised a system that basically converts all the previous payments into taxable gain, limited only by the original gain itself. This can be very troublesome, as usually there is no cash to pay this "phantom" gain. As a matter of fact, the repossessor/seller normally has to pay repossession expenses to his or her attorney—and then, in addition, owes taxes to the IRS [§1038].

Requirements of the repossession rules. *Section 1038 is mandatory.* Therefore, if a seller forecloses on an installment contract, the gain must be calculated as described in this section [§1.1038-1(a)(1)].

What is the purpose of the reacquisition? The reason for the reacquisition must be to secure the rights of the seller under the purchase-money mortgage and not simply to reacquire the property for income or appreciation purposes. The note and the mortgage must give the seller the right to take title to, or possession of, the property. The note may be recourse or nonrecourse [§1.1038-1(a)(3); §1.1038-1(a)(2)(ii)].

Default is not necessary—but the reacquisition must be based on a default (or default is imminent) under the original sales contract. In other words, §1038 is not available if the seller simply repurchases the property [§1.1038-1(a)(3)(i)].

The manner of reacquisition is generally immaterial (e.g., voluntary, involuntary, sheriff's sale, strict foreclosure, abandonment, etc.) [§1.1038-(1)(a)(3)(ii)].

The property can be repossessed from anyone. The person from whom the property is repossessed need not be the original purchaser so long as the debt can be traced back to the original sale and is secured by the property, but the repossessor *probably* has to be the original seller [§1.1038-1(a)(4); §1038(a)].

Determining the amount of gain upon foreclosure. The gain upon reacquisition of property is equal to the cash and fair market value of other property (other than the purchaser's, i.e., buyer's, obligations) received by the seller (i.e., lender) prior to the acquisition, less the gain previously reported [§1.1038-1(b)(1)(i)].

Limitation on reacquisition gain. The gain reported cannot exceed the total gain less the gain previously reported and any reacquisition costs paid by the seller because of the foreclosure [§1.1038-1(c)(1)]. What does this mean?

Formula for calculating gain on repossession.

Gain from foreclosure (before limitation)

1.	Cash received prior to reacquisition	$ _____
2.	Less: Gain previously reported	− _____ (A)
3.	Equals: Gain before limitation	= _____

(A) _____ × _____ ÷ _____
    Total prior cash received ×   Gain   ÷   Contract price
                                             (Gross profit ratio)

Limit on gain from foreclosure

4.	Sales price	$ _____
Less:		
5.	Basis at time of sale	+ _____
6.	Gain previously reported (line 2)	+ _____
7.	Reacquisition costs	+ _____
8.	What seller paid to reacquire	+ _____
9.	Subtotal	− _____
10.	Equals: Limit on gain	= _____
11.	**Gain resulting from acquisition**	_____ *

_____

*[smaller of (3) or (10)]

What is included in "cash received prior to reacquisition"? The amount of the cash received prior to reacquisition includes all payments and other property transferred by the buyer to the seller *and* all payments made for the seller's benefit (including underlying mortgage payments) unless the debt was placed on the property after the sale [§1.1038-1(b)(2)(i)].

Payments by buyer to seller at reacquisition. "Cash received prior to acquisition" also includes any payments made by the buyer at the time of repossession to settle the contract. Of course, any interest payments received are taxed as interest, not principal payments [§1.1038-1(b)(2)(ii)].

What is "sales price"? Sales price is the gross sales price reduced by the selling commissions, legal fees and other expenses incident to the sale [§1.1038-1(c)(3)].

What are "reacquisition costs"? These are amounts paid by the seller to reacquire the property, including court costs, attorney fees, auctioneer costs, title costs, advertising, and recording fees [§1.1038-1(c)(4)(i)].

What is included in "what seller paid to reacquire"? The assumption of (or subject to) indebtedness that is not an indebtedness of the buyer to the seller shall be considered an amount paid by the seller in connection with the reacquisition. For example, if the buyer placed another mortgage on the property after purchase, which the seller now is subject to, this new mortgage (be it a first, second or otherwise) is considered "what seller paid to reacquire" [§1.1038-1(c)(4)(ii)].

> **Example:**   Shirley purchases real property for $20,000 and sells it to Paula for $100,000. Under the contract Paula pays $10,000 down and gives a $90,000 installment note, with a properly stated interest rate, to be paid at $10,000 a year over the next nine years. Shirley properly reports the gain on the installment method. After making two installment payments, Paula defaults and Shirley accepts a voluntary reconveyance of the property in complete satisfaction of the indebtedness. Shirley pays $5,000 in connection with the reacquisition of the property. The gain Shirley must report on reacquisition is show below [§1.1038-1(h), (Example 1)].

Gain from foreclosure (before limitation)

1. Cash received prior to reacquisition	$30,000
2. Less: Gain previously reported	− 24,000(A)
3. Equals: Gain before limitation	= $ 6,000

(A) $\dfrac{\$10,000 + \$20,000}{\text{Total prior cash received}} \times \dfrac{\$80,000}{\text{Gain}} \div \dfrac{\$100,000}{\substack{\text{Contract price} \\ \text{(Gross profit ratio)}}}$

Limit on gain from foreclosure

4. Sales price		$100,000
Less:		
5. Basis at time of sale	+ $20,000	
6. Gain previously reported (line 2)	+ 24,000	
7. Reacquisition costs	+ 5,000	
8. What seller paid to reacquire	+ _____	
9. Subtotal		− 49,000
10. Equals: Limit on gain		= 51,000
11. Gain resulting from acquisition		**$ 6,000***

---

*[smaller of (3) or (10)]

Basis of reacquired property. The basis of the reacquired property is the adjusted basis of the seller in all indebtedness of the purchaser on the date of reacquisition, increased by the amount of the reacquisition gain recognized by the seller and by the amount paid by the seller in connection with the reacquisition. A formula makes it easy to compute the basis for the previous example [§1.1038-1(g)(1)].

Basis of reacquired property

12. Remaining debt to be received	+ $70,000	
13. Debt adjustment	− $56,000 (B)	
14. Adjusted basis of debt		+ $14,000
15. Plus: Gain on reacquisition (line 11)		+ $ 6,000
16. Plus: Seller's reacquisition costs (line 7)		+ $ 5,000
17. Equals: New basis		= $25,000

(A) $\dfrac{\$100{,}000 - \$30{,}000 = \$70{,}000}{\text{Remaining debt to be received}} \quad \times \quad \dfrac{\$80{,}000}{\text{Gain}} \quad \div \quad \dfrac{\$100{,}000}{\substack{\text{Contract price} \\ \text{(Gross profit ratio)}}}$

No bad debt deduction. No bad debt deduction is allowed upon reacquisition, and if the seller deducted a bad debt deduction in a year prior to the reacquisition, this bad debt deduction must be included in income in the year of reacquisition [§1.1038-1(f)(1); §1.1038-1(f)(2)(i)].

Repossession of personal residence—sell it within one year. If a homeowner is forced to repossess a principal residence that was previously sold on an installment contract and he or she had excluded all or part of the gain because of the $250,000/$500,000 MFJ exclusion rule, this repossession gain method is not applicable *provided* that the property is resold within one year from the date of reacquisition. The reacquisition is disregarded and the subsequent resale of the home is treated as a sale occurring on the date of the original sale of the home. If the home is not sold within one year, these repossession rules apply, even to the sale of a personal residence [§1.1038-2(a)(2); §1038(a)].

Character of the gain. If the gain on the original sale was reported on the installment method, the reacquisition gain maintains its character (e.g., if the property was a capital asset, the reacquisition gain would be a capital gain; if the property was a §1231 business asset, the gain would be a §1231 gain) [§1.1038-1(d); §1.453-9(a)].

Holding period of reacquired property. Because the reacquisition of the property acts as a revocation of the original sale of the property, the holding period of the property after its reacquisition includes the period the seller held the property before the original sale. Therefore, the holding period does not include the period between the original sale date and the reacquisition date [§1.1038-1(g)(3)].

CONCLUSION

Settlement of a mortgage debt at a discount may create cancellation of debt, which is ordinary income, for the borrower. On the other hand, foreclosure generally creates a taxable sale. A deed in lieu of foreclosure is also considered a taxable sale. Bankruptcy and insolvency provisions soften the income tax created. When property is financed by the seller, known as a purchase-money mortgage, the reduction is simply a reduction of the purchase price and not a taxable event.

Index